LOST?

LIVERPOOL FC AND ENGLISH FOOTBALL AT THE CROSSROADS

ANTHONY CARRAGHER

Matador
9 Priory Business Park,
Wistow Road, Kibworth Beauchamp,
Leicestershire. LE8 0RX
Tel: (+44) 116 279 2299
Fax: (+44) 116 279 2277
Email: books@troubador.co.uk
Web: www.troubador.co.uk/matador

PB ISBN 978 1788035 637
HB ISBN 978 1788036 016

British Library Cataloguing in Publication Data.
A catalogue record for this book is available from the British Library.

Matador is an imprint of Troubador Publishing Ltd

Printed and bound by CPI Group (UK) Ltd, Croydon, CR0 4YY
Typeset in 11pt Aldine by Troubador Publishing Ltd, Leicester, UK

For Gavin and Melissa. Love always.
To all of my family, the same.

To Siobhán, love and thanks for your endurance
and invaluable and innumerable contributions.

ACKNOWLEDGEMENTS

Thank you to my mother for always encouraging any creative spark or influence. For telling me stories of the poet Patrick Kavanagh. For providing every opportunity one could need. For allowing me to find a voice. To my departed father and brother, thank you for kindling within me a love for Liverpool FC. Despite the enduring wait, the good times have been too many to mention. To the rest of my family thank you for the love, support and advice. To Louise, you always encouraged, that is not forgotten. To Siobhán, without your incredible love and assistance I would still be toiling today. A big thank you also to Brendan Rodgers, Roy Evans, David Fairclough, Terry McDermott, Guillem Balague, Ossie Ardiles and Christopher Shankly-Carline for their contributions. To the Liverpool family worldwide, YNWA.

CONTENTS

PROLOGUE

His father would have been proud. He had loved to watch Pele. What a player, 'the greatest of them all' he would say. For Pele to praise his son, to say that he had made Suarez a better player, and, maybe more importantly, a better man, well, that would have made his day. Brendan missed his father. When he arrived at Anfield he thought of him. Taking the reins at one of the biggest clubs in the world, he hoped that somehow, somewhere, his father was looking down on him, happy, proud. He'd see, too, that his son had his work cut out. Liverpool finished a lowly eighth the previous year after an awful campaign. Yet, he'd know his son's resolve, his determination. For he'd taught him to be a fighter, never to quit.

He was back at his desk at Melwood, late Sunday afternoon. He could rest later, now he needed to analyse that performance. He wouldn't stop until his team were back where he believed they should be. They weren't far from the top four now. A few more wins, let the new players bed in further and take that momentum into the winter schedule. Today's game proved to him that the players still wanted it, they'd been great. But for a defensive slip-up, it would have been a derby day victory at neighbours Everton, always a morale booster. A draw was okay though, another hard away fixture marked off the calendar. They should have won at the Emirates too. In truth, the table lied a little, they deserved to be higher. With those extra four points in the bag they'd be in the Champion's League shake-up. The luck would even out by season end he hoped. It was still early days with this new team, that should not be forgotten.

Things weren't as bad as some were making out. He'd taken a lot of flak recently, from all angles. He felt like a human shield. He'd been blamed for the sale of Sterling in the summer, why? He had no idea. He developed the kid, helped make him into the player he was. Forty-nine million wasn't bad business, but he hadn't wanted to sell him. Suarez neither. He had helped develop him too, shown him how to hone his predatory skills. Seventy-five million for Luis. When he had these players, when Daniel was fit and before Stevie left, he showed everybody. The fans knew it, the banners said it. 'Make us Dream'. He had. They'd gone so close. Won twelve from their last fourteen. Then the slip.

He'd been voted League Manager of the Year. Had everybody forgotten? Now he had another batch of players that the club had bought for him. Give him some time and he'd make it work. But please, give him players with character. He'd wanted control of the football decisions from day one. He'd heard about the crazy rules with Comolli and all that baseball stuff. Should he have come here, compromised himself? Yes, this was Liverpool. He knew how to play the Liverpool way. He'd watched the short triangular passes of their great teams when he was just a boy. Give the fans football that was exciting and dynamic, he believed in that. But the players, he needed the players. The club paid for fifth, so wasn't fifth par? Many had been scarred by the semi-final defeat to Villa. Then came the lack of fight at Stoke. He wasn't on the pitch. He'd put out eleven players who had done it before for this club. How was their capitulation all his fault? Yet it was he who apologised to the fans. Human shield again. Give him some time and he'd work out who could bring the club forward and who couldn't. God, he'd gone the whole of last season with no recognised striker and still nearly qualified for the Champions League. So, eight games gone, early days. Tough away trips to Stoke, Arsenal, United and Everton off the schedule. Time to kick on. The bright October sun shone through the office window, from here things could only get better. Then the phone rang.

PART I

THE RISE AND FALL

THE WAITING GAME

'All I know is that the hours are long… and constrain us to beguile them with proceedings which… may at first sight seem reasonable, until they become a habit.' — Samuel Beckett, *Waiting for Godot*

Existence is a peculiar thing. We have a finite period of time to spend on this earth and then we are gone. From where we came and to where we go, nobody knows for sure, but we all, or most of us, have our own ideas, or have been fed somebody else's. As the clock ticks, second by second, minute by minute, one would imagine that we might endeavour to slow this withering creep towards the inevitable. Yet, the reverse is often true. We spend time packing our days to the brim with activity, entertainment and distraction. If it's a short stay, well then let it be a great stay. We strive to live to the maximum, to suck the very essence from life's marrow, before it all disintegrates and fades away. We align ourselves to people, to causes. These are the kindred folk with whom we will share the voyage. We attach ourselves to structures and groups, which we hope will define us to others. 'Look, this is who I am.' And above all, we hope. We hope for good, for more, for enlightenment, for meaning.

Samuel Beckett, an Irish Nobel Laureate, wrote *Waiting for Godot* in 1949. Beckett's masterpiece is a minimalist, stripped-back play, centred around two vagabonds, Vladimir and Estragon, who wait day by day for what seems a futile eternity, hoping an unspecified person named Godot arrives. Their lives are filled with despair and drudgery, but nothing changes and still they wait, on and on. Who or what Godot represents we do not know, Beckett remained vague, both within the text and after its publication, that being the whole point one imagines. For some, he is God, for others, meaning. For many, Godot is hope.

Many of us have chosen sport to be one of our amusements, a daily or weekly habit to kill hours, to entertain us, before slipping the mortal coil. In Beckett's work we find a mirror to some stark truths. Our obsession, for those of us who are obsessed, knows no end. We can't seem to loosen the grip, always looking to the next game or season, as Vladimir and Estragon look to their next day. Their hope is to meet Godot, for something to change, and in a way, so is ours. We endlessly wait and hope for something to happen. To lift that elusive trophy, win that big game, or even just to steal a glimpse of a fleeting moment of brilliance. For we know that, in sport, anything can happen, but maybe just not what we wanted. The funny thing is that even if our Godot did arrive, we mightn't realise it, for often the fulfilment of one dream quickly leads to new yearnings.

Liverpool Football Club wait too. A club that has stood at the very summit of European football wanders lost in the wilderness, seeking the path home. The path that leads to glory. The Reds of Merseyside have won the European Cup five times and its less illustrious cousin the UEFA Cup three times. Only three clubs, the two giants of Spanish football, Real Madrid and Barcelona, and AC Milan of Italy can boast of having lifted more major European silverware. Yet, even though Liverpool's most recent European triumph arrived in 2005, with the help of a miracle in Istanbul, the more perplexing truth is that the Reds of Merseyside have only played in the tournament eight times in the last twenty-seven years. Liverpool FC are undeniably European Royalty, but more often than not these days, they are not even invited to the ball. The fault lies at home. The domestic title has not been lifted since 1990.

Since then, Liverpool's average league finishing position has been 4.5. The first of the billionaire owners started to arrive and take control of English football in 2003, when Roman Abramovich bought Chelsea. Then in 2005, the Glazer family acquired Man United. Three years later, Sheikh Mansour took power at Man City. Today, all three clubs sit firmly above the Reds, as do Arsenal. In the last five years Spurs too have leapfrogged Liverpool as the Reds' average finishing position slipped to sixth. So, what next? A further slide or can the Reds reclaim their former lofty perches? Will the wait for a league crown go on? Past thirty years? Forty years? Half a century?

Liverpool are owned by Americans, they have been since 2007.

Today's variety are an investment group named FSG, before that it was two cowboys named Hicks and Gillett. It is hard to discern the motivations of new custodians. When the club was founded and led by local families, local men, sporting and community ambition was always the goal. Now, we are not so sure. The objectives of overseers who live across the Atlantic, and who only wash up on Liverpool's shores two or three times a year, are much harder to gauge. One could fall into the trap of believing that they are only here to make money, for that is what their day jobs entail.

FSG announced they 'came to win'. Did they? Can they deliver? They've done it before, back in their own homeland, with that great old American pastime baseball. Yet at Liverpool FC they are no closer to achieving success now than when they arrived in 2010. Our club's Godfather Bill Shankly proclaimed that, "Liverpool Football Club exists to win trophies." Is this still the case? The league title has not been lifted for over a quarter of a century. For myself, my son and all those of our Red persuasion the wait goes on. Hope sparks and ebbs, but somehow it still burns. We are many. Millions and millions of people all over the globe wait – men, women, boys, girls, young and old. We have a common bond. We are Liverpool FC. My son and I embark on a journey with our beloved team, to see how we arrived at these barren crossroads and to vision where we might be headed. To test Shankly's maxim, and ascertain does it still hold true? This is the story of our journey into that void. This is a story of a lost football club trying to find its way out of the wilderness.

HOPE

'Learn from yesterday, live for today, hope for tomorrow. The important thing is not to stop questioning' —Albert Einstein

Liverpool are far from alone in the world of sport. Many others also wait. Some have waited longer. At last, recently, for some of the long-suffering, breakthroughs have been achieved. Historic defining days, that it seemed might never arrive, were suddenly and delightfully occurring. These stories gave Reds fans hope. They gave all sports fans hope.

The Cleveland Cavaliers Basketball team had waited since their foundation in 1970 for glory to arrive and at times it nearly did. Divisional and Conference titles were collected, but never the elusive National Championship. In 2003 a rising star named LeBron James would be selected by the 'Cavs', with the first overall pick of the NBA draft. Eighteen-year-old LeBron had grown up some forty miles away in Akron, the only child of a sixteen-year-old single mother, Gloria. As a kid, he would shuffle from school to school as his mother was forced to move in search of work and shelter. Life wasn't easy. On the basketball court, 6ft 8in James would rise to national prominence, becoming one of the biggest names in the sport. But his contract with the Cavs had run down, and, come 2010, he was a free agent. James had reached the conclusion that his home state team could not fulfil his dream of winning the NBA title and in a special TV programme called *The Decision*, he announced, before a watching audience of 13 million people, that he would be joining the Miami Heat franchise in his pursuit of glory. Cleveland Cavaliers owner Dan Gilbert immediately wrote an open letter to fans on the Cavs website, denouncing James' decision as 'selfish', 'heartless', 'callous', and a 'cowardly betrayal'. Gilbert guaranteed that the Cavs would win an NBA title before the 'self-declared former King'. Hatred and vilification jammed the airwaves in Cleveland, and the Ohio air reeked with the smoke of burning LeBron jerseys.

The Cavs couldn't follow through on their owner's promise. The next season would deliver a paltry nineteen wins from eighty-two games, this including a record twenty-six-game losing streak. In the Miami sunshine King James was making hay and, for some, justifying his move, as he lifted two NBA crowns during a four year spell. Incredibly though, this story wasn't over. In 2014 James would re-sign with the Cavaliers prophesising that he would lift the title for his home state team. Two seasons later the King delivered on his vow. The Cavs came back from a 3–1 deficit to beat reigning champions, the Golden State Warriors, 4–3 in the NBA final, with James winning the Most Valuable Player award. The Cleveland Cavalier's forty-six year wait for a title had ended with the help of one of the best players of all time. "I understand what everyone in north eastern Ohio has been through these last fifty-plus years and I am happy to be a part of history," said James in tears as he wrapped his arms around the Larry O'Brien Championship Trophy. Godot had arrived.

Fourteen years earlier, in the world of baseball, FSG, an investment consortium consisting of commodities trader John Henry, TV producer Tom Werner, businessman Les Otten and the New York Times Company, became the successful bidders in the auction of the storied franchise, the Boston Red Sox. Despite being one of the most revered organisations in the sport, the Red Sox had not won the World Series since 1918. They were jinxed, or so some people believed. When star player, and maybe the greatest baseball player of all time, Babe Ruth, was transferred to rivals New York Yankees on December 26th, 1919, so began the 'Curse of the Bambino'. Boston's winning days were over, and with Ruth to the fore, it was the Yankees instead who grew from strength to strength, with Babe lifting four more World Series crowns to add to the three he had won with the Red Sox.

By 2002, the Curse had plagued Boston for over eighty years. But FSG were clever guys, businessmen first, sports lovers second. They were inspired by a new statistical approach to the game espoused by amateur scribe Bill James called 'Sabermetrics' and most notably effected in practice by Oakland Athletics' coach Billy Beane. Beane's efforts at

Oakland would be immortalised in the book and movie of the same name *Moneyball*. John Henry, head of FSG, made his money spotting trends early, jumping on board and riding them all the way to the bank. He saw what was happening with James and Beane before most people were paying attention and he loved it. So much so, that he tried to bring Beane to the Red Sox on a 12.5 million dollar five-year deal. Initially, Beane accepted, but then changed his mind and stayed with Oakland, to be near his young daughter. FSG did however manage to convince the Oracle Bill James to come on board, but he would need help.

James could work the numbers and statistics but FSG needed somebody to manage the outputs, put them to work in a structure. They needed a disciple of this new analytical evidence-based approach to management. If Beane had proven that James's academic methodology worked better than the old-fashioned gut-feeling, hunch-following, tobacco-chewing, ex-player-turned-talent-scout approach, well then wouldn't it be wiser to search in academia for an academic? So, FSG bucked the trend, and found their man in the shape of Yale educated Theo Epstein. Epstein was no baseball man, but he had smarts. He was Ivy League and well connected. His grandfather was an Oscar winner, having written the screenplay for *Casablanca*. Yet he was only twenty-eight years old, a rookie kid entering into the grizzled world of American baseball. What Epstein lacked in experience, he made up for in spades with confidence, charisma and character. Soon he would put this cocktail of traits to excellent use, signing Kevin Millar, Bill Mueller and David Ortiz, all either cast-offs or forgotten veterans. It was classic Moneyball – find value where others can't see it. Epstein had worked the player roster to find inefficiencies in the trading market where other franchises couldn't and had assembled an eclectic player roster that would eventually lead the Red Sox to the promised land.

With an ageing, but highly motivated team, the Red Sox would finally break the Curse in 2004 after an eighty-six year wait. Further championship success would follow for the team built by Epstein in 2007 and 2013. In addition to identifying inefficiencies in the market, Epstein had developed an uncanny knack for helping mould youthful prospects into proven and respected talent. For owners this formula was gold dust. The 2004 winning version had one home-grown player, the

2007 version had eight. By the time Epstein would leave the Red Sox in 2011, twenty-six of the thirty Major League Baseball teams had hired new coaches. Only seven had the former prerequisite attribute of having actually played professional baseball, the remainder carrying the Epstein DNA template of having a private school or an Ivy League education. All, bar three of the twenty-six, were under the age of fifty, again a break with tradition. James, Beane, FSG and Epstein had changed the face of baseball forever.

On the shores of Lake Michigan, along the windswept streets of Chicago, and under the bright lights of historic Wrigley Field Baseball Park, a new journey awaited Epstein. It could never be said that he didn't have courage. This time the challenge was even bigger. The Chicago Cubs had not won the World Series since 1908. Just like the Red Sox, the Cubs had also been blighted by a dreaded hex – 'the Billy Goat Curse'. In October, 1945, a local tavern owner named Billy Sianis was turned away from the Cubs versus Detroit Tigers World Series game when he attempted to bring his pet goat into the stadium. The story goes that Sianis was so mad that he set the dreaded curse. Oddly, this doesn't explain the barren thirty-seven years before 1945, but hey it's a good story. So when cursed, who you gonna call? A curse-buster of course. When Epstein was summoned in 2012, to say no was impossible. The famous stadium, the storied brand, the opportunity, it was all too appealing. But lightning couldn't strike twice, or could it? The Cubs were in a worse state than the Red Sox ever were. "Play it again Theo," his grandfather Philip G Epstein would have urged.

Four years later, on the night of November 2nd, 2016, the Cubs faced destiny in Cleveland. The World Series was tied at three games to the Cubs, three games to the Cleveland Indians. Having trailed the series 3–1, the Cubs had already gone to the well, more than once, somehow clawing themselves back into contention and forcing a seventh game. The last and final 'winner takes all' tie would decide whether the 108 year wait and the curse of the Billy Goat would be exorcised, or whether the Indians would end their own lengthy drought, which extended back to 1948.

Baseball games are played over nine innings, with both teams batting and pitching alternately in each. For two and a half hours the Cubs dominated the game, but as the winning line drew near and the midnight hour approached, the jitters took hold and bit by bit the Cubs started to crumble. A place in history seemed too heavy a millstone. Chicago's fans held their heads in their hands and watched on through trembling fingers. Not again, surely not again. How could this be happening, after leading 5–1 entering the bottom of the fifth inning? No team had blown such a Game 7 lead, not since 1924, but the Cubs were doing their level best to create new records. In the eighth inning, the Indians tied the game and now the momentum had shifted to the home team. By the end of the ninth and final innings, the teams were tied at 6–6. And so, for only the fifth time in history, an extra innings would be required to settle the game. The Cubs were reeling, they were on the ropes, punch-drunk. The Indians circled ready to finish the game off. But then a funny thing happened, a miracle even, a moment of fate. It started to rain.

For seventeen minutes it rained. Both teams retired to the locker rooms. A temporary reprieve had been granted to the Cubs, a stay of execution. Could they regroup? Could they focus their minds, believe that their destiny wasn't predetermined? It didn't have to be the age-old failure that had become oh so familiar for the Cubs, that which had become their calling card. Instead they could rise to glory, end the curse now, once and for all.

It was after midnight when play resumed and suddenly the Cubs were firing again on all cylinders. To fold would have been easy, but not this time. The Cubs were choosing the harder path, the braver path and on this historic nail-biting night they were going all the way. And so, on November 3rd, at 12.47 a.m., the longest drought in American sport ended after ten exhausting innings and four hours and forty-five exhilarating minutes. The Cubs had won the World Series by 8–7, in one of the greatest final games of all time. The city of Chicago erupted.

"We're normal people," said the World Series Most Valuable Player, Ben Zobrist, as the clubhouse clock ticked past 2 a.m. "We get nerve-wracked and anxious, just like everybody else." Cub's general manager Jed Hoyer spoke of the rain delay being "divine intervention". Zobrist would have the final word, "You know what? I think we just shit-canned those curses."

Having sealed the deal, the Cubs and the city of Chicago could celebrate winning the most astounding series, and the most incredible Game 7, in baseball history. And so they did, with an estimated five million people lining the streets to greet the return of their heroes. Only seven times in history had more people congregated in one place for one reason. Chicago had turned blue in honour of the victorious Cubs.

So, when a prodigal son returns and lifts his city and his team to glory, when a college kid who never played baseball breaks two curses that lasted a combined 194 years and, when five million people take to the streets of Chicago, how can anybody say that 'Sport doesn't matter'?

How many things in life can generate the feelings of elation, belonging and love that these events did? On days and late, late nights like these, life can take on a wonderful ethereal beauty. For the Cavaliers, the Red Sox and the Cubs, Godot had arrived. Finally, all the waiting seemed worthwhile. These stories serve as a beacon of hope to all who still wait, as we do.

Our story begins across the Atlantic, in Northern England, eighteen months before the Cubs found salvation.

TWIST OF FATE

'And when something awful happens, the goodness stands out even more...'
—Banana Yoshimoto, *The Lake*

"We had no excuses. It was just a disaster. A catastrophe. Everything that could go wrong, did go wrong. There was no fight, no balls, no character, no passion. I couldn't believe I was in a Liverpool team. We were 5–0 down at half-time." Steven Gerrard relives the memory of his last ever game for Liverpool, his swansong. "It should have been a day to remember, instead it proved to be a horror show."

Liverpool were enduring a woeful end to the season. Heads had dropped and form had dipped alarmingly after a Champions League place drifted from reach. Yet nobody could have foreseen just how bad things would get. Sunday 24th May 2015 and it is half-time at the Britannia Stadium in Stoke. The scoreboard doesn't lie but even for those present this was hard to believe. Stoke 5 Liverpool 0. Mighty Liverpool, my Liverpool of nearly forty years devotion, five nil down to mid-table Stoke at half-time. It must be a mistake. But no. Not only has the season ended in a slow and agonising whimper, but on the final day, the wheels have come off royally. At full-time the game finishes 6-1, and the result consigns Liverpool to their biggest defeat since 1963, seven years before I was born.

Thankfully, I'm not at the game, I'm at home with my son who turns to me with a bemused look on his face, and asks, "Can we ever win the League again?" For once I have no positive reply to offer him, no vestige of hope. All I can do is watch on as the Liverpool team, kitted in all-black, fitting for this funereal end to a terrible season, trudge dejectedly from the pitch.

Great actors and singers get an encore, a red velvet curtain framing their departure. Gerrard could only sink to his knees and wonder what he had done to deserve this. He hadn't folded though, he never did. "I scored a goal, in the seventieth minute. I didn't give up". When Gerrard scored this, his last ever goal for Liverpool, in his final game, a touching moment occurred. Not just the Liverpool fans cheered, but the whole ground rose, stood and applauded. It was a fitting tribute for a great player. But it couldn't relieve the anguish Gerrard would feel from such a horrible send-off. "I didn't want anything so humiliating to happen to me in my last game for Liverpool. But I have to live with it now."

However, Stoke was not the worst day Gerrard had experienced in the red shirt of his hometown team, not by a long shot.

***

Thirteen months earlier, April 2014. Scrunched together we stand, my son and I, outside the Shankly Gates on Anfield Road. There are still ninety or so minutes till the 2:05 p.m. kick-off, yet thousands of Liverpool fans fill every available space, blocking the road outside the stadium. Song by song we work our way through the club's famous anthems and slowly but surely the atmosphere cranks up.

'...All around the fields of Anfield Road, where once we watched the King Kenny play, Stevie Heighway on the wing, we had dreams and songs to sing, of the glory around the fields of Anfield Road...'

Normally the streets are not this mobbed hours before a home game, but today is no ordinary day. This is no ordinary game. This is a shot at redemption, the chance to climb back into paradise, to reclaim a throne lost a long time ago, and to fulfil the wish of every Liverpool fan of this generation. It's the chance to win the English League for the first time since 1990. Technically it can't be won today, but a win or a draw would leave the Reds needing only four points from their remaining two games to secure the title. Flags catch the wind, rise and fall, as smoke from red flares conceals the bright midday sun. Electricity surges in the air.

'...Poetry in motion, tra la la la la, poetry in motion, tra la la la la la, poetry in motion, tra la la la la, we're the best football team in the land, yes we are...'

So far the 2013/14 season has proven an incredible roller-coaster ride. Manager Brendan Rodgers and his unfancied young team have shocked the critics. Against all the odds, Liverpool now stand on the cusp of their first title in twenty-four years. The football has been flamboyant, swashbuckling even. A carefree attacking philosophy, a 'we can score more goals than you' approach endearing the team to the football world. The media declare that 'the neutrals' hope Liverpool make it over the line and break up the financially doped duopoly of Chelsea and Man City.

'...When you walk through a storm, hold your head up high and don't be afraid of the dark...'

The sight of the flags and the singing of our famous song brings tears of pride and love, which I wipe away quickly before my son can see them, to escape any ribbing for being an emotional sop. Football itself doesn't make me cry, but the sound of our glorious anthem, sung with emotion and pride, well that's another thing altogether. We are identified worldwide by this song and no matter how many times I've heard it, it never fails to send shivers down my spine. Again the tears well up as I look to my boy. He hasn't noticed, entranced as he is by the sea of red before him. I tap him on the shoulder, gesturing around me as I do, and say, "We. Us. These Liverpool fans. We are the chosen ones. Few clubs in the world can match this – the passion, the carnival, the flags, the songs. Don't forget this son, this is special."

'...At the end of the storm, there's a golden sky and the sweet silver song of the lark. Walk on through the wind, walk on through the rain and you'll never walk alone...'

I'm still terrified by the games that remain, particularly this one and hand on heart, I think we'll fall short. It might just be self-protection, for we've been let down so many times before, but these niggling doubts, I can't shake them. For the style and panache we've shown, for the dignity displayed by our manager and for the sheer audacity of it all, to fail will be an enormous shame. A travesty even.

"This team, this amazing, youthful, attack, attack team. Can you believe this is *our* team?" I ask my son.

He wears a huge grin on his face. He absorbs the scene around him by osmosis, every chorus strengthening his bond. Until now, I've thought that, possibly, he just followed for my sake, but here, now, I can see that he has become a fan in his own right. Today it's Chelsea who are in town, led by José Mourinho, one of the game's most successful managers. If nothing else, the Portuguese, self-proclaimed 'Special One', loves to spoil a party. Nobody said ending a drought would be easy.

Chelsea park the bus and don't come out to play. Few, if any, are better at shutting down a game than Mourinho. Liverpool dominate the first half, do nothing wrong, miss a few half chances and then, tragedy strikes. With forty-four minutes on the clock, the ball is passed towards Gerrard. He moves to collect it, but incredibly Liverpool's captain, their mercurial talisman, does something he's hasn't done in his seventeen years at the club, in over half his life. He slips…he falls. Shocked reverberations ripple silently through the stadium as the earth quakes beneath his weight. Gerrard lies prone on the ground, just inside his own half. He's the last man, the only outfield Liverpool player left between the halfway line and the goal. The ball runs invitingly free. Gerrard tries to rise, to stretch and reach it, but it's too far, it's too late. We can all see with crystal clarity what will happen next. Demba Ba, Chelsea's Senegalese striker pounces gleefully on the offering and in a flash, is gone, advancing on Liverpool's goal at the Kop end. Mignolet, the Red's goalkeeper comes to meet him, but within seconds the ball nestles in the net as 43,000 Reds fans watch on in horror and silence. The travelling Chelsea fans go crazy, this is beyond their wildest dreams. This match means little to Chelsea, bar the wicked enjoyment of scuppering Liverpool's chances. The two clubs have developed an unsavoury rivalry in the last ten years. Liverpool fans deride Chelsea for their lack of history and heritage, for being a plaything of a rich Russian billionaire. Chelsea claim Liverpool live on past glory. So for the Londoners, to be the hammer that drives home the nail, ably assisted by their enemies' most revered son, well life couldn't get any better. The second half brings wave after wave of Liverpool attacks but few real chances are created. Schwarzer, the Chelsea keeper, saves well, down low to his left from a Joe Allen shot. A Luis Suarez effort is blocked in the box and then in the last minute Chelsea break forward from a botched Liverpool corner kick and Fernando Torres, once a hero of Liverpool red, scores to secure a 0–2 win. It feels like all the air has been sucked out of Anfield. But Reds fans leave no soldier on the battlefield. A homage to Liverpool's most revered son rings around the old historic coliseum:

'...Steve Gerrard, Gerrard, he passes the ball 40 yards, he's big and he's fucking hard, Steve Gerrard, Gerrard...'

Resilient to the last, the Liverpool anthem quickly follows:

'...Walk on, walk on, with hope in your hearts and you'll never walk alone...'

Walking back to town, we plot the possible title run-in scenarios. Our destiny no longer resides in our own hands. If Manchester City win their last three games, they are Champions, simple as that. My son is incredulous. "I can't believe he slipped, not Gerrard, not after all he's done." He does not reproach, more despairs at the sad bitter irony of it all.

***

For it to be Gerrard to fall and effectively cost Liverpool their first title in twenty-four years (City would go on to lift the trophy with Liverpool finishing second) was beyond ironic, it was cruel. If any Premier League player of his era deserved a winner's medal, then it was Gerrard. For nearly twenty years he propped up average Liverpool teams, at times single-handedly. He refused a move to Chelsea that would have guaranteed success, instead choosing to be loyal to his home team, to the team that his ten-year-old cousin Jon Paul Gilhooley travelled to watch at Hillsborough in 1989, a game that he never returned home from. For Gerrard it's personal, always has been.

Gerrard will be remembered for seventeen years of near unblemished service, not just for one moment, in one game. In a 2013 poll of fans he was voted the club's greatest player of all time. Since his debut as an eighteen-year-old in 1998, it seems that he has played in every position bar goalkeeper. He represented the Reds as Captain for fourteen years, the longest serving in club history. He became Mr. Liverpool – the benchmark, the pillar. An icon whom each fan could look to and believe in. A player that gave you hope. So, for Gerrard, in the autumn of his career, to be within touching distance of his dream, only to slip, it is hard to find the words. Shakespeare would lick his lips and dip his quill.

Gerrard's great moments in red are too numerous to mention

and many will never be forgotten. The late goal against the Greeks of Olympiakos that helped send Liverpool towards Istanbul and the 2005 European Cup Final. The Final itself where he would inspire his team to the most unlikely comeback in footballing history. Three nil down at half-time to the mighty AC Milan, Liverpool were out on their feet, dead and buried. But somehow the Reds picked themselves up. A neck-snapping sixteen-yard header from Gerrard woke Liverpool from their self-pitying slumber on fifty-three minutes. Six incredible minutes later the scores stood level at 3–3. Liverpool had somehow done a Lazarus and had risen from the dead. Tied at 3–3 after normal and extra time, the game went to penalties, with Liverpool triumphing 3–2 on spot kicks long after midnight. FIFA would describe the game as the greatest in club football history. For Reds fans, it became known simply as 'The Miracle of Istanbul'. One year later in Cardiff, a virtuoso solo performance saw Gerrard score two goals, including a last-minute equaliser, to lead the Reds to FA Cup Final glory against West Ham, in a game now known as 'The Gerrard Final'. When games are named after you, little else needs to be said.

When people talk of Gerrard the same phrases keep repeating. 'single-handedly', 'virtuoso', 'solo performance', 'carrying the team'. In no way should these words infer that he was a selfish player, nothing was further from the truth. On countless occasions Gerrard sacrificed his own game for that of the team, playing out of position to plug a hole. Jamie Carragher summarised his captain's contribution, "Stevie was inspirational, playing in the middle but popping up on the left and right for our cause in a desperate bid to compensate for our overall inadequacies". Gerrard was able to do it. With his natural talent he could play anywhere.

In many ways the fact that Gerrard stood so tall amongst his peers, betrays the problem with his era. The great Liverpool teams had been built as a collective. Shankly had started it that way, deliberately. Other teams at that time had bigger names – stars such as Best, Moore, Bremner, but it was Liverpool's team ethic that saw them through. Shankly demanded a socialist structure where no man was bigger or more important than another, except for him of course. He would declare in his growling Scottish brogue, "The socialism I believe in is everybody working for the same goal and everybody having a share in the rewards. That's how I see football, that's how I see life. Liverpool was always a family club where no man was bigger than the next. It believed in a humbleness and dignity, a way that was uniquely about being Liverpool". Former Chairman John Smith recalled how the club recruited from within to maintain that ethos, "we wanted to keep the promotions and changes within the club, to maintain our family atmosphere".

It's not that Gerrard wanted to overshadow those around him, he just did. Inferior players wilted in his presence, afraid to express their own talents. When we think of his era, we don't think of the managers first, like we do with Shankly, Paisley, Fagan and Dalglish. The first name that comes to mind is his own, Gerrard. It was his presence that loomed largest. The exception to this of course was Rafa Benitez. Under Benitez, Gerrard played his best football and Liverpool reached the top again, winning the European Cup in Istanbul. Only in this relationship was it clear who the boss was. Gerrard would say, "Our working relationship was ultra-professional and his frostiness drove me to become a better player. I had a hunger to earn a compliment from him, but also a hunger to let him know he really needed me as a player. We were like fire and ice. Passion surged inside me, while Rafa was the strategic thinker."

The great Liverpool teams were never dependent on one or two individuals. They were machines, with eleven working parts, all necessary, all important. Of course, as Orwell might say, some parts were more equal than others and with players such as Keegan, Dalglish, Hansen and Souness, that was inevitable. Shankly declared, "A football team is like a piano. You need eight men to carry it and three who can play the damn thing".

Each Liverpool manager of this barren period bemoaned the player or players that got away, the signings that could have made the difference. Souness missed out on Alan Shearer, Roy Evans wanted Teddy Sheringham. Houllier was too slow to grab Ronaldo, United nipping in ahead. With a quarrelling board, Benitez missed many targets, such as Dani Alves and Simao, that could have made the difference. Spurs star player Dele Alli had agreed a deal with Brendan Rodgers but the board felt his wage demands were too high for a fledgling nineteen-year-old.

The lesson seems clear, if Liverpool can't gild their dressing room with big money signings, then a return to the Shankly 'collective' principle must be the way forward.

Gerrard's slip only highlights how difficult it is to achieve the great moments, how many things can go wrong. After the slip, Liverpool slid. Rather than challenge again, the Reds reverted to recent type and shifted into reverse gear. Later that summer Luis Suarez would be sold to Barcelona for seventy-five million pounds. For most of the following season, his goal scoring partner in crime, Daniel Sturridge, would be injured. Gerrard's legs were slowing as he approached his thirty-fifth birthday and with an absence of quality around him, even his game suffered. Liverpool went from scoring 101 goals in the 2013–14 season to notching only half that amount in 2014–15. You can't lose nearly fifty goals and still contend for the title. They didn't, slumping from second to sixth. A year and a month after the infamous slip, Steve Gerrard would play his final game for Liverpool in that humiliating 6–1 defeat at Stoke. If any player in Liverpool's illustrious history had deserved to win a league medal, it was Gerrard, but alas, fate doesn't always reward the deserving.

The wait would go on.

THE DARKEST HOURS

"In Memoria e Amicizia (in memory and friendship)" – Heysel memorial plaque at Anfield

Five days after the Stoke debacle, harrowing memories are revisited. On the thirtieth anniversary of the Heysel disaster, members of the Liverpool team that played on that fateful night in Brussels congregate at Anfield to pay thier respects. Phil Neal, who captained the Reds in a game that UEFA and Belgian police urged both clubs to play, whilst corpses lay motionless on the ground, places a wreath at the Heysel memorial in the Centenary Stand. Flags at the stadium fly at half-mast as they do all around the city of Liverpool.

May 29th, 1985 brought the darkest hours in Liverpool FC's then ninety-three years of existence. An ugly shameful stain that can never be cleansed. It should have been a joyous, carnival occasion. Two of the greatest clubs in the game, Liverpool and Juventus, meeting in the European Cup Final. Instead tragedy unfolded when trouble broke out between rival supporters before kick-off. The previous year in Rome it was Reds fans who were attacked by knives, slashed and beaten up. That had left a mark. At Heysel, it is believed by most that Liverpool's fans were the aggressors, although the precise facts have never been fully determined. What is clear is that Liverpool fans at one end of the ground rushed an adjacent 'neutral' zone where Juventus supporters had congregated. The Italian fans retreated, causing a wall to collapse. In the chaos that followed thirty-nine people, mostly Italians, were either crushed to death or died from asphyxiation. Fourteen Liverpool fans would later be convicted of involuntary manslaughter.

The disaster unfolded in the aftermath of years of hooliganism and violence on the terraces of European football. It also unfolded in the decrepit old Heysel Stadium that was not fit-for-purpose. But ultimately it unfolded due to mindless thuggery.

Football is the beautiful game. A simple yet artistic game, followed by most who inhabit our planet. All should not be tarred by the same brush. Some people have sense. Some don't. Those that do should act in every way possible to prevent those who don't from damaging that which is precious and which brings joy to so many. We may not be our brother's keeper but we are guides for our sons and daughters. Never again can such darkness fall on light.

May they never walk alone.

PREY

'Summer was a book of hope. That's why I loved and hated summers. Because they made me want to believe.' —Benjamin Alire Sáenz

Summer is a desert for football fans. Days and weeks pass slowly, devoid of the media circus that follows the game during the regular season. Gone are the pre-match build-ups, the games themselves, the post-match interviews, analysis and reviews. Gone too are the countless pundits and analysts that offer their daily opinions only to contradict them completely within a matter of weeks if the prevailing wind changes direction. In the throes of the season, managers, players and fans live day to day. The next result can change the complexion of matters entirely. Summer helps calm the nerves and encourage the long view. One can look to the future when the present isn't blowing up all around you. Summer has a further upside. There is no disappointment in the desert, no defeats, no injuries, and no mistakes. The memories of former debacles eventually fade into the sands of time. Players leave, but few who have worn the red of Liverpool go on to better things. After playing for one of the best, the common trajectory is downwards. Only the very, very best shine elsewhere. Players arrive, and help instil hope that finally, the missing cogs have been found and the machine will now work again. Then, at last, with the magical sunshine days of August the new season brings the river flooding and football, like life, renews afresh and starts again.

The summer of 2015 however, brings little to lift the mood. The abject memories of the 2014/15 season still rot and fester, where in their last nine games Liverpool earned a miserable eight points from an available twenty-seven, culminating eventually in the 6–1 Stoke disaster. The vultures still circle. Such poor form, were it to be extrapolated over an entire season, would have seen the Reds relegated having collected only four points more than last place Queens Park Rangers. However, this alarming dip in form is not the only open wound Liverpool fans have to deal with in the slow summer months. Another ugly drama unfolds, one that pierces right to the heart of the most important issue of all.

Raheem Sterling is a wonder kid, a bright young thing. Born in Jamaica, Sterling began kicking a ball from the age of three in the violent Kingston neighbourhood of Maverley. Sterling would follow his mother to London aged five. At nine he would learn of the brutal murder of his young father, not yet thirty years old, slain outside his home. Sterling never speaks of the tragedy, but the loss of a loving father seems to define his ambition in many ways. He would sign as an apprentice with Queens Park Rangers at fourteen. Whilst a host of big clubs watched his burgeoning talent grow, it would be Liverpool and Rafa Benitez who secured his signature in 2010. At the tender young age of fifteen he commanded a transfer fee of a million pounds, no small sum for a youthful rookie that still required plenty of nurturing and development.

Bit by bit Sterling's career blossomed and eventually, in 2012, under the managerial guidance of Kenny Dalglish, he made his first team breakthrough. The following season, 2013/14, saw Sterling come to full blossom when a convergence of elements catapulted him firmly into the spotlight. One of these elements was Luis Suarez, the volatile Uruguayan that Dalglish had signed from Ajax two seasons earlier. In 2012/13, Suarez had been unluckily pipped to Player of the Year by Spurs' Gareth Bale, mostly due to his poor disciplinary record, which included a lengthy ban for biting Ivanovic of Chelsea. Prior to this momentary loss of sanity, he had looked nailed on for the accolade as he stormed Premiership defences up and down the land. Come the 13/14 campaign he was on a redemption mission. Suarez shone from the start and his brilliance inspired and elevated all around him. Beside him another force was awakening in Daniel Sturridge. Sturridge had left Chelsea to sign for Liverpool in January 2013. At Chelsea, he had been overlooked and loaned to various clubs. Sturridge was determined to prove he had what it took to be a big club and big time player. Alongside the peaking talents of Suarez and Sturridge, Sterling would soon become the third element of a much-feared strike force.

Despite being blessed with blistering pace and a strength of body that belied his tender frame and height, Sterling's touch and positional sense needed work. New manager Brendan Rodgers made sure he got this help, carefully teaching the raw young talent how and when to make the right runs, perfecting his timing to get in behind opposing defences. Sterling was a quick study and alongside Suarez and Sturridge, the fearsome trio terrorized whoever came before them. During that 2013/14 campaign, the SSS combo as they became known, notched sixty-two goals from an incredible team tally of 101, a record top flight total for the Reds. Add Gerrard to the mix and the goal count rose to seventy-five from four players. On the attack, Rodgers' team were a match for any in the club's proud history.

Sterling had made it as a big time footballer at the tender age of twenty. By December 2014, the entire football world knew of his mercurial talents when he was awarded the European Golden Boy award, only the second Englishman to receive the honour, after Wayne Rooney in 2004. The award was created in 2003 by Italian newspaper *Tuttosport*. Thirty footballing publications around Europe were invited to nominate five players. Sterling would be picked from a shortlist of forty and his name now nestles alongside former winners such as Sergio Aguero, Paul Pogba, Cesc Fabregas and Lionel Messi. The kid from Kingston had come good, bigtime.

For a club like Liverpool this story should have been gold dust, a new hero was born. As before, with players such as Robbie Fowler, Michael Owen, Steve McManaman and Steven Gerrard, a young raw talent had been developed and was coming through the ranks to take the mantle as talisman and help lead Liverpool into a new footballing era. However, after the near miss of 2013/14 when Gerrard's slip cruelly put paid to a shot at glory, Liverpool again drifted backwards as if grieving, unable to deal with the loss. It wasn't just any title loss, many had been lost before and by definition you will invariably lose more than you win in professional sport. But this time a win would have seen the curse lifted, the curse of twenty-four years. The grieving deepened when the SSS was dismantled. Suarez moved to Barcelona for £75 million, Sturridge took a permanent berth on the medical table and Sterling was left to toil manfully alone upfront.

In February with a few short months left of the 2014/15 season the first soundings of discontent became apparent. Sterling was refusing to sign a contract extension. His agent began waging an ugly media war with the club and Sterling himself engaged in some ill-advised interviews. The mood of the fans was turning poisonous, with the popular refrain being that the young kid from Jamaica was greedy and spoilt. All he wanted was an enormous payday, either from Liverpool or via a move to another club. Liverpool had offered £100k a week in wages and the view from the 'man in the street' was that if a twenty-year-old kid was not willing to accept such an offer from a football institution such as Liverpool, then in some way he was morally corrupt. Liverpool fans are renowned for open-mindedness, patience and the willingness to give players and managers the benefit of the doubt. Recent evidence of this could be found in the forgiveness shown to Luis Suarez after his various spats with officials, opposition and even after his first failed attempt to force the club to sell him to Barcelona in the summer of 2013. But now Sterling, a young twenty-year-old buck, was taking on the club itself, its manager and its owners. Many disgruntled Reds fans looked on with disgust. How dare he?

But when Sterling spoke, he pleaded that money wasn't the issue, not the sole issue anyway. For fans, the common denominator when assessing a player's motives always seems to be money, it is the lazy stock barb. Yet, money doesn't make a player put his face in where studs are showing. Most elite sportsmen reach the top because they are hardwired to compete, driven to win. For their troubles they get paid top dollar. Nobody seems to question some half-a-voice reality star or wooden actor getting paid a king's ransom. If one listened, Sterling's comments suggested that Liverpool lacked ambition, that the team lacked world class talent to augment his own and that Liverpool, the proud owners of five European Cups, eighteen league titles, with more silverware glimmering in its trophy room than any other English club, couldn't match *his* ambition. Liverpool couldn't guarantee the trophies and the success *he* yearned for. It seemed preposterous, but deep down in the hearts of many Liverpool fans a raw nerve had been touched, this was the elephant lurking in the corner. "Will we ever win the league again?" The question echoed over and over.

The Sterling saga rumbled on as the season wound down in depressing fashion. Now it looked like it wasn't just Gerrard who was leaving, Sterling was heading for the door too. These two opposing tales were casting large shadows over the entire club. Before Gerrard's final game at Stoke, Sterling's agent claimed publically that his client would never sign a new contract for Liverpool, not for all the money in the world. This hardened the fans' view even further, Sterling was fast becoming a hate figure and, fortunately for him, Rodgers took him out of the fray for the ill-fated trip to the Britannia. The result would hardly have persuaded Sterling to change his plans. Liverpool FC were in free fall.

Sterling wouldn't be seen again in the famous red. Liverpool's owners demanded £50 million from any club who wanted to sign the rising star. Big teams hate to sell to a domestic rival, a transfer into Europe always being preferable, but sometimes you just have to take the money. Eventually, Manchester City stumped up £49 million and finally, in July 2015, the Sterling saga reached its conclusion. What worried most Liverpool fans was whether a new precedent had just been set. Were the once mighty Liverpool now a 'selling club'? Liverpool along with every other club sells players but the bigger clubs try to control their own destinies, conduct business on their terms. They prefer to sell when players have passed their peak, this being the conclusion reached when Liverpool sold a slowing Fernando Torres to Chelsea for £50 million. Liverpool prefer to move unsettled players to the continent, to where they can't hurt you. Keegan went to Hamburg in 1977, Souness went to Sampdoria in 1984, Suarez to Barcelona in 2014. But the sale of a young player, with maybe ten great years ahead of him, to a team that would be fighting it out against you at every step, and for every honour available, this smelt wrong.

Sterling's desire to jump ship on Liverpool so early in his career was making a statement, loud and clear. For him, Manchester City were now 'bigger' than Liverpool. In recent times this couldn't be doubted. Backed by the mega-wealthy Sheikh Mansour of oil-rich Abu Dhabi, City have more resources than any club in the world, and during the Sheikh's reign they've not been afraid to splash this cash, with over one billion lavished on players and stadium development in less than a decade. Another £49 million on Sterling was a small outlay in their relentless march forward, a march which in the last four years had brought two Premiership League crowns.

Modern footballers have little affinity to any one jersey. Whereas Steven Gerrard played for one club only, his home-town Reds, Sterling, a boy from Jamaica, was now on his third by the age of twenty. But even Gerrard had toyed with the thought of leaving his beloved club to fulfil his ambitions. The fact that he seriously considered a move to hated foe Chelsea, a club despised by Reds fans, who see it as representing the mirror opposite in values to their own, tells its own story. Players want money for sure, but more than that, they want to win. Just ask LeBron James. For Gerrard, a Liverpool lad, a move to Chelsea would have proven unforgiveable in the eyes of Reds fans. Jamie Carragher told him so – "If you go, don't go to Chelsea, if you go there, it won't matter how many League titles you win, you'll never be able to come home and have the respect of the Liverpool fans. You've got to consider the implications for the rest of your life." Sterling has no such devotion to Liverpool, it is not home, he is a professional athlete and he can decide where best to showcase his talent. If the clubs, owners, managers and fans can be ruthless, then why not the players?

Football has its ecosystem like all other walks of life. Smaller, less illustrious clubs develop young talent, relying on their academies instead of their bank balances to find and nurture bright young prospects. These clubs sell to bigger and richer mid-size clubs and eventually those clubs, if they have polished a gem, sell it on to the biggest and most powerful clubs of all. After such a move the player is normally delighted to stay, he has reached the top. After this, any eventual split is commonly instigated by the club itself, if they have grown unhappy with performance, or become smitten with a brighter, younger or better talent. The decisions can be ruthless, cold and unerring. If the player doesn't play ball, more often than not he will be banished to the youths. However, when a football club decides a player's days are numbered, fans don't fall out of love with them. Clubs can in essence execute a range of callous cut-throat decisions that may affect both players and fans but still retain love and adoration. But woe betide a player who decides to act on what he believes is best for his own future, for the future of his family, for the achievement of his ambitions, as hell hath no fury like that of a righteous multitude. The weight of the world will crash down with a two-faced thud on his presumptuous dreams.

I couldn't begrudge Sterling his move and, unlike the vitriol of popular opinion condemning him as a money grabber, to me it always looked like a footballing decision, a career decision. This was the most alarming thing. Now that he had departed I wasn't worried about Sterling at all, he was never my true concern. More importantly, where did the whole saga leave Liverpool FC? Rodgers had now been stripped of two of his front three attackers and, in Suarez and Sterling, two of the brightest players in Europe. Liverpool's remaining forward Sturridge's constant ailments literally added injury to the insult. It was clear that the Reds were now prey.

PART II

THE KING IS DEAD

BACK TO THE FUTURE

'Usually, there is nothing more pleasing than returning to a place where you have endured hardship.' —Tahir Shah

It's the opening weekend of the new football season, August 9th, 2015. The big kick-off is usually accompanied by balmy sunshine and today proves no different. The fixture list was released on June 17th and some mischievous soul decided that sending Liverpool straight back to Stoke, the scene of the crime, where the Reds suffered crushing and abject humiliation in the 6–1 defeat, would make for good opening day drama. They were right. It is to be the first time in Premier League history that the exact same fixture is played back to back. The talk of Liverpool players and fans has been of little else in the weeks preceding the game. The nightmare is to be revisited. Battle cries have sounded as to how the rematch offers a chance to exorcise the ghosts. On the flip side, if the Reds fail again, it would be a hugely demoralising start to a make-or-break season.

My son and I walk along Matthew Street on our way to Lime Street train station, Liverpool. We pass wreaths and floral bouquets laid outside the famous Cavern Club, the birthplace of the Beatles – tributes to the late Cilla Black, one of Liverpool's favourite daughters. Cilla's character, possessed of the quintessential Liverpool traits of warmth, devilment and a sharp sense of humour, had endeared her to so many far and wide. The flowers remind me of how close the community of Liverpool feels, despite being one of England's larger cities. In its heyday described as the New York of Europe, it is now a place unlike any other, with its immigrant history, its global perspective and its militant soul. There is a clarity of identity in Liverpool which defines it as a nation of its own, gazing out to the world and not back over its shoulder. Yet all the while it feels like a village, as if everybody knows everybody else.

The Liverpool-to-London train edges away from the station and snakes its path south-east, until eventually the impressive wrought-iron Britannia Bridge, spanning the Mersey River in a large arc at Runcorn, looms into sight. There are two bridges really, one is the old railway bridge built in 1868 and just upriver is the arched Silver Jubilee Bridge which carries road and foot traffic. Below us the Mersey glistens and laps up to golden sandbanks along its shores. As my son listens to music on his headphones, I drift into a restful snooze.

On arrival in Stoke-on-Trent we take a short walk around the town. It's small, and today, incredibly quiet. A lazy Sunday afternoon in Staffordshire. The pubs are busy though, filling with home fans, wearing their vertical red and white striped tops. At old Stoke Minster, also known as 'the Church of St. Peter ad Vincula' (Peter in Chains), we stroll through lush green gardens set back from the road. The term 'Stoke' means 'holy place' or 'meeting place' and the Minster acts as a focal point for the city which was formed from a conurbation of six separate towns. This holy site dates back to the sixth century and is an idyllic green oasis in a bland urban setting. Wandering through the church graveyard we peer at the names and dates, speculating as to the lives of those that went before us. We notice the gravestone of Josiah Wedgwood, 1730–1795, founder of the famous Wedgwood ceramics business and also a zealous anti-slavery campaigner. This region formed the heart of ceramic production in the UK in the eighteenth century and became known as 'the Potteries'. Stoke-on-Trent's skyline was once dominated by thousands of bottle kilns, their smoke-spouting chimneys towering over the nearby buildings, as they fired the clay within. Where Manhattan had skyscrapers, Stoke had its kilns, the effect of both on the skyline, sights to behold. Just as pottery in Staffordshire and Stoke-on-Trent goes back a long way, so too does football. Stoke City FC, founded in 1863, were one of the founding members of English football, the club being the second oldest in the country and the world (after Notts County founded in 1862). Fittingly the team are also known as 'The Potters'.

Rodgers and his players are not the first Liverpool team to visit Staffordshire with the nightmarish memory of a 6–1 drubbing festering in their minds. One hundred and fifteen years earlier, thirty-seven-year-old Liverpool manager Tom Watson must have been feeling similar trepidation travelling to Stoke for his side's second game of the 1900/01 season. Liverpool FC, founded in 1892, had not managed a victory at the Victoria Ground in six attempts. Indeed on Watson's first trip to Stoke on 6th February 1897, he could only look on aghast as his team were thrashed 6–1 by a rampant Potters side.

After founding in 1892, Liverpool endured a yo-yo existence between the First and Second Divisions. An ambitious board decided a different approach was required. They needed the best. Across the country, on the north-eastern coast, a precocious thirty-five-year-old manager named Tom Watson had led Sunderland to three Division One titles in four years. Doubling his wages, Liverpool managed to secure Watson's services for the start of the 1896/97 season. The pressure was on. Could he repeat his success with a club yet to establish itself as a top tier team? Watson immediately set about change. The team needed to be fitter and new additions were required. Out went the blue and white quartered jerseys inherited from the formation days with Everton, and in came the now famous red. The 'Reds' were born. The 1898/99 season would go to a final-day decider between Liverpool and Aston Villa, but Villa would triumph 5–0 at Villa Park. By the turn of the new century Watson's glory days at Sunderland must have seemed a distant memory, as he struggled to achieve success with the Reds.

So, when Liverpool arrived at the Victoria Ground on 8th September 1900 they had yet to record an away victory at Stoke. On twenty minutes, Maxwell put the home side 1–0 ahead. But on forty-four minutes, Tommy Robertson would equalise to make the score 1–1. A late eighty-sixth-minute goal by Liverpool's new star predator Sam Raybould, would see the Reds secure the win. Raybould would go on to become the first player to score 100 League goals for Liverpool (from 162 appearances). Liverpool would build on their promising early start and as they had two years previously, they travelled to the Midlands on the final day of the season needing to win their last game to secure glory. This time the setting was the Hawthorns and the opponents were West Bromwich Albion. A 0–1 win would see Liverpool become the first champions of the new century and see the Reds lift their first League title. It had taken Watson five years to do it, but his class had finally shone through.

The *Daily Telegraph* would report – '*Liverpool at last – After nearly a decade of ups and downs between the divisions, Liverpool have finally won the league title'*. And so began the gloried history of Liverpool FC.

***

August 9th, 2015. Match time is 4 p.m. at the blustery but sunbathed 28,000 seat Britannia Stadium. After all the hype and the pre-match billing it's no surprise that the game itself is a dour affair. Rodgers approaches the match cautiously, keen not to relive the horror show. His two new full backs Clyne and rookie Gomez rarely cross the half-way line. At half-time the score is 0–0. The second half is a brighter affair but again openings are scarce. The game drifts towards a nil-all stalemate when at last a moment of magic breaks the deadlock. Liverpool's five foot seven inch Brazilian, Philippe Coutinho, summons up the courage and the wizardry that has eluded his fellow combatants. Receiving the ball from debutant Gomez, he spins on a sixpence leaving marker Sidwell in his wake. Within a few strides he has moved ten yards infield, surging towards the Stoke defence and goal, behind which three thousand travelling Liverpool fans are congregated. A sense of expectation ripples through us. We know what this exceptional player is capable of. Before his pursuers can catch him, Coutinho lets rip from all of thirty yards. It's a curling thunderbolt that the lunging Stoke goalkeeper Butland can only fingertip into the roof of the net. From our vantage point behind the goal we can see it all happen as if in slow motion and before the net even ripples we are leaping in celebration. Eighty-six minutes gone and Liverpool lead 1–0.

The clock ticks down and after three minutes of extra time, at long last the final whistle blows. Unbridled joy erupts amongst the Liverpool players, fans and coaching staff. This was a dangerous mission and defeat would have left the club mired in a negative limbo, open to ridicule from all corners. Instead victory consigns the 6–1 debacle to rest, not to be dredged up until the next time the Reds suffer collective inertia. For Brendan Rodgers and his team the past is history, the future is now the story.

THE INNOVATORS

'There's a way to do it better – find it.'— Thomas Edison

You may never have heard of St Totteringham's Day, not everyone has. In fact, it doesn't necessarily fall every year, but has done for the last twenty. It's also not a religious feast, well not exactly. For one, St Totteringham never actually existed, and secondly, he or she never performed the two miracles required by the Pope to be declared a Saint in the Catholic Church. That said, St Totteringham's Day is a 'holy' day of sorts, created and celebrated by fans of Arsenal Football Club. It arises annually on the day, if it arrives, when Arsenal have mathematically finished higher in the League than their nearby north London rivals, Tottenham Hotspur, hence the 'tottering'. Arsenal fans believe this day can fall as early as March and certainly by the end of April. At the very, very latest it might arrive in early May. The fact that it has fallen for each of the last twenty years says much about who rules the north London neighbourhood. But when Arsenal started out, this north London rivalry didn't exist, for the simple reason that, at that time, Arsenal hailed from south of the Thames, from Woolwich to be precise.

The Royal Arsenal munitions plant manufactured armaments, ammunition and explosives for the British armed forces, south of the river at Woolwich. At its peak, during the First World War, the Royal Arsenal site was three miles long, one mile wide and sprawled over some 1,300 acres with around 80,000 employees. For all intents and purposes it was a city within a city. The early origins of the Royal Arsenal lie with the creation of a dockyard in Woolwich by Henry VIII. The yard was originally founded for the construction of the 'Great Harry', an English carrack or 'great ship' of the King's Fleet in the sixteenth century. Contemporary with the 'Mary Rose', the 'Great Harry', King Henry

VIII's flagship, was even larger, having a complement of 700–1,000 men. Eventually the Royal Arsenal would become the largest military-industrial complex in Europe to service the world's largest empire.

In 1886 a group of workers from the armaments factory grouped together to form a football team. It is not hard to guess the origin of the club's nickname 'The Gunners' and of its crest, consisting of a cannon. The club's first name was 'Dial Square', a square located within the Arsenal complex. Before long that name would change to 'Royal Arsenal' and this in turn to 'Woolwich Arsenal', the name that the club would enter the League with. Arsenal became London's first representatives in Division One when they gained entry in 1904. It would not be until 1913, that Woolwich Arsenal would make the move to Highbury, just four miles from Tottenham's White Hart Lane and today's rivalry would take root. On September 6th 1913, Arsenal played their first game in the Islington Borough at home to Leicester Fosse, winning 2–1. That match day programme proudly stated that Highbury was *'the most accessible ground in London'*. Arsenal's principles were also pinned firmly to their collars – whilst having a *'keen appreciation for a good solid shoulder charge'* the directors informed their patrons that *'intentional hacking, bashing or smashing do not coincide with their ideas of sportsmanship'*. After a couple of seasons in their new home the club's name would change again to 'Arsenal Football Club' and then 'The Arsenal', until finally we were left simply with 'Arsenal'.

The League at that time, was dominated by clubs from the footballing heartlands of the Midlands, the North East and the North West. Making progress wasn't easy and in their first twenty years the Gunner's highest finish would be 6th place. But if you want to be the best in football, two simple prerogatives are mostly true. Get the best man to manage off the field and get the best players to play on it. In 1925, Arsenal turned their eyes to manager Herbert Chapman. Chapman had inspired Huddersfield to an FA Cup Final win in 1922, followed by two consecutive League title wins in 1924 and 1925. Upon arrival in Islington, Chapman immediately set about making changes.

With gates booming and the London crowds crying out for a successful team to support, Chapman recognised the scale of the opportunity. His tenure would see Arsenal spend lavishly on exciting new players, so much so that they would earn the moniker – 'The Bank of England Club'. In came stars such as Cliff Bastin, David Jack, Alex James and Eddie Hapgood to bolster an already strong squad. Chapman would become known as a great innovator, implementing new tactics and formations and also changing the club's image. He was maybe the first football manager in the modern sense of the word, taking complete control of the team rather than letting board members pick the side. Along with tactical innovations, he was a strong believer in physical fitness, introducing a strict training regime and advocating the use of physiotherapists and masseurs. The famous red shirt would be changed to include white sleeves. Numbers would be added to the backs, white hoops to the stockings. The club's crest and logo would be modified. Floodlights would be introduced to the stadium and although not permitted by the FA until twenty years later, they would assist Chapman's team with training through the winter. Chapman would lobby and succeed in having the local Gillespie Road tube station change its name to simply 'Arsenal', still the only tube station in London to be named after a football team. With change, came success.

In 1930, Chapman's Arsenal would defeat his former employers Huddersfield in the FA Cup Final 2–0. A year later Arsenal would lift their first ever League title and the first for any side from the country's capital. A then record points tally of sixty-six from forty-two games was achieved in the process. Another League title would follow in 1933 but then disaster would strike. Chapman would catch a cold watching a football game on a freezing New Year's Day in 1934 and his condition would rapidly worsen. Pneumonia set in and the great man would be dead only five days later. The Gunners and the game of football had lost one of its greatest innovators and icons.

But Chapman had laid solid foundations. New managers Joe Shaw and George Allison would win the League again in both 1934 and 1935, completing an incredible three-in-a-row hat-trick. A further FA Cup trophy would be added in 1936 with Arsenal beating Sheffield United 1–0, along with a fifth League crown in 1938. If London had lagged behind in the first thirty years of League Football, Arsenal had changed that landscape completely entering into the 1940s, and had become the dominant force in the game. Then came the Second World War, a war in which Arsenal lost more of its playing staff than any other club.

After the war the Gunners would win further league titles in 1948 and 1953. Then a drought set in, until physiotherapist Bertie Mee was given a shot at the manager's job in 1966. Arsenal lost two League Cup Finals in succession before winning their first European trophy in the 1970 Fairs Cup Final (replaced by the UEFA Cup), defeating Anderlecht 4–3 over two legs, with future Liverpool star Ray Kennedy scoring their only goal away from home. One year later and the sun shone even brighter over Islington when League and Cup double success arrived.

The celebrations must have been wild, for the hangover would last eighteen long years until Arsenal managed another crack at the title. Scotsman George Graham, a stalwart of the 1971 Arsenal double winning side, was now manager and he was building a tough and resolute defensive side that won games by the narrowest of margins coining the terrace songs, ironically sung by Arsenal's own fans, of '*boring, boring Arsenal*', and '*1–0 to the Arsenal*' – so common a winning scoreline had that become. Adams, Dixon, Bould and Winterburn, formed a more than formidable back four with David Seaman guarding goal behind them. Thomas and Merson provided attacking flair in midfield with Alan Smith the target man upfront. But if the songs proclaimed boredom, there was to be nothing boring about the night that Arsenal's drought would end.

After a ding-dong battle in the League title chase between Arsenal and Liverpool, the title came down to a last day decider between the two top sides, in a fixture rearranged in the aftermath of the Hillsborough tragedy and the delayed FA Cup Final between Liverpool and Everton that ensued. Arsenal travelled to Anfield, needing to win by two clear goals, to play a tired and emotional Liverpool team. The Gunners led by 1–0 but with the clock ticking down in injury time, their fate seemed sealed. What happened next will never be forgotten. Michael Thomas would somehow be allowed to break the Liverpool defensive line and close in on goal. A sweet little lob over Liverpool's keeper Grobbelaar and Arsenal had snatched glory from defeat with virtually the last kick of the season.

Arsenal's Perry Groves would talk wistfully about that famous night. "It was a cup final where we were the unbelievable underdogs. There are not many cup finals where you go in two goals down basically. But having to win by two clear goals took the pressure off completely because nobody gave us a chance. And to be honest, not many of the players believed we could go and win. The only one who really 100 per cent believed we could was George Graham. He gave us our team-talk when we went in on the Wednesday, and said: 'I really fancy our chances'. The players looked at each other and thought, 'Is he going mad?' He said, 'I've thought about the game, and we're going to play a sweeper', and a lot of people forget, we always played 4-4-2, that was our system, that was the way we trained. David O'Leary was brought in to play as the spare man at the back, and we all thought: 'He has gone mad, because we've got to go and win by two clear goals, but he's playing an extra defender'. At the time it didn't make sense, but it was tactical genius because his plan was to get in at half-time 0–0. 'If we concede the first goal we're finished,' he said. 'You ain't going to score three. It just doesn't happen at Anfield. But if we get in at half-time 0–0 we've won half the battle, and then we'll have a chat at half-time and I fancy us to nick a goal in the second half, and if we do then it's all about momentum, pressure gets to people. If we can score, the momentum will change and all the pressure then goes on Liverpool.' George said: 'If we go one goal up I can make some changes, take a defender off and we'll go 4-4-2 and put Martin Hayes on and then we'll put Perry Groves on and then we'll really go for it, the gloves are off then, we've got a great chance and I think we'll win it.' And Smudger scored in the fifty-fourth minute with his header, and I was on the bench watching it and you could actually see the tension in the game change completely. As soon as that goal went in the atmosphere in the stadium altered. Their fans thought 'hold on a minute, we could actually lose this'. They had top international players like Steve McMahon, John Barnes, Peter Beardsley, Ray Houghton, Alan Hansen; even *they* started to feel the tension and the pressure, and you could tell it in their faces."

With the title won, Groves also remembered the incredible reaction from the home fans. "We got a standing ovation from the Kop, who had stayed there [after the final whistle] because I think they appreciated the way we'd gone about the game. We didn't go there and try and boot them off the park, and they're a very respectful crowd. They know good football."

Arsenal would lift the crown again in 1991 and cup wins would follow in the FA Cup, the League Cup and the European Cup Winners

Cup in the years that followed. However the Gunner's League form would dip as the empire of Manchester United began to rise.

Then a renaissance man named Arsene Wenger would arrive to shake up the English game forever.

THE IMPRESSIONIST

'To my mind, a picture should be something pleasant, cheerful, and pretty, yes pretty! There are too many unpleasant things in life as it is without creating still more of them.' —Pierre-Auguste Renoir

In 1860s Paris, a revolution of sorts was taking place in the art world. A new form of painting, later described as Impressionism, was being born. The name was derived from a painting by Monet titled 'Impression: Soleil Levant' (Sunrise). This new style captured the feeling of movement and light, it was fluid and dreamlike, with its style in stark contrast to the traditional values of clean lines and near photographic replicas of real life scenarios. Instead, the free brushstrokes of the new Impressionist vanguard gave you a sensitivity, a vision, an impression indeed, rather than an exact. The conventional art world greeted the new form with derision and scepticism. But there are always risk-takers and instigators. Paul Durand-Ruel, an exiled French art dealer living in London, was one of these. A meeting with Monet and fellow Impressionist painter Pissarro in London in 1871, was to transform the futures of all three. Durand-Ruel fell in love with the new movement and without delay he started to buy as many works as he could of the relatively unknown Monet, Pissarro and other artists of the new style. Only three years earlier, Monet had tried to commit suicide by flinging himself into the Seine, bereft by his abject poverty, yet now a benefactor had come and maybe even more importantly, a believer, a disciple. Durand-Ruel became the original champion of Impressionist art. Today the movement is revered worldwide with Monet, Pissarro, Cezanne, Renoir and Van Gogh viewed as masters of the form. To paint as if photographing a view is today often frowned upon. How things change. In February 2015, Sotheby's art dealers in

London sold five Monets for a combined value of $86 million. That is how to take a risk and call it right.

In 1996, David Dein, then Chairman of Arsenal Football Club, a former sugar trader, took a risk on an unknown football manager who was plying his trade in the football backwaters of Japan. The manager's name was Arsene Wenger. The *London Evening Standard* ran with the headline 'Arsene Who?' But Dein had 20/20 vision and clarity of thought. He could see that English football was still mired in the bad old days of blood and thunder football, poor discipline, awful dietary practices and very often non-existent technical analysis. In Wenger he saw a game-changer, a philosopher and student of the game. Still, to this day, many clubs can't look further than ex-players or TV pundits for their next managerial choice. With Wenger, Dein was getting a man who spoke five languages and held a Master's degree in Economics and Sociology from Strasbourg University. Just like Durand-Ruel before him, Dein had changed the face of art, the art of English football.

Wenger was born in Strasbourg in 1949. His father managed the local village team. After a modest playing career he obtained a manager's diploma in 1981. Following an unsuccessful period at Nancy, which saw him depart in 1987, Wenger took charge of AS Monaco. With the Principality, Wenger won Ligue 1 in 1988 and guided the Red and Whites to victory in the Coupe de France in 1991. However, failure to recapture the league title in later seasons led to his exit from the club in 1994 by mutual consent. He briefly coached Japanese J-League side Nagoya Grampus Eight, who won the Emperor's Cup and Japanese Super Cup and it was from Japan that Dein plucked his man and offered him a shot at the big time. Glenn Hoddle who played under Wenger at Monaco recalled, "He introduced so many new things to me; warm-ups, warm-downs, vitamin injections. He was a miracle worker. When David Dein asked about Arsene, I just said 'Go out and get him'."

David Dein once explained, "My mantra always was, and I always used to say this, when I'd wake up in the morning and I'm shaving in the mirror, I'd say – 'Get a winning team, everything flows from there'." Straight away this was what the Dein and Wenger combo set about doing. Wenger put his faith in his countrymen and signed three relatively unknown Frenchmen, Patrick Viera, Emmanuel Petit and

Nicolas Anelka for combined fees of £6 million. Their names didn't set the British media alight but within two years all three would be World Cup winners with France. To complement these French musketeers, Wenger signed the brilliant Dutchman Marc Overmars for £7 million.

Wenger didn't just focus on signings though. He introduced a flamboyant, fast-flowing style of play. 'Boring, boring Arsenal' was being consigned to the history books. Out too was the British footballer's diet of bangers and beans, washed down by beer. Nutritional programmes and personalised exercise regimes were to become the norm under the new manager. Before his first game in charge, Wenger banned the team from eating chocolate, provoking outrage. He recalled, "We were travelling to Blackburn and the players were at the back of the bus chanting 'we want our Mars bars!'" These ideas took time to gel with wily old dogs such as club captain Tony Adams and others. Adams would say, "At first, I thought, what does this Frenchman know about football? He wears glasses and looks more like a schoolteacher. He's not going to be as good as George Graham. Does he even speak English properly?"

Wenger himself admitted that Arsenal were 'a little bit crazy' to give him the job: "They were crazy in the sense that I had no name, I was foreign, there was no history. They needed to be, maybe not crazy, but brave."

However, Wenger listened to his players too and slowly won the respect of the senior British contingent. Arsenal would win the double in Wenger's first full season, an incredible feat, particularly given that Man United were in their prime. Three second place finishes would follow, plus a 2001 FA Cup Final defeat to Liverpool, but Wenger kept developing young talent whilst investing cleverly in the transfer market. Freddie Ljungberg and Thierry Henry would arrive for £3 million and £10.5 million respectively. Both would prove to be fantastic signings, with Henry developing into Arsenal's and possibly even the Premier League's best ever striker.

Arsenal would do the double again in 2001/02, lift the FA Cup in 2003, win the League again in 2004 and once again lift the FA Cup in 2005. The 2004 side would win the title without losing a single game, the first time this had been achieved since Preston North End in 1889, who went unbeaten over twenty-two games in the inaugural Football league competition. For Arsenal to manage the feat, over thirty-eight games in the modern era of football, they would rightfully earn the nickname 'The Invincibles' and be awarded with a golden replica of the Premier League trophy.

Less positively, however, Wenger's Arsenal had made negligible impact in European competition. Then, at last, in 2006 came the chance for the Frenchman, the great modern innovator of the English game, to achieve global immortality. Every great manager needs a European Cup in the cabinet, it is the currency that separates the all-time best from the mere elite. It was Arsenal versus Barcelona in the Champions League Final in Paris. I have never cheered for any club team bar Liverpool, but that day in 2006, I cheered for Arsenal, more so I cheered for Wenger, for this professor of the beautiful game, this man who loved football for what it could be. Paris was to be Wenger's defining masterpiece. But Jens Lehman, his trustworthy German goal minder, would be sent off early and Arsenal would lose 2–1, leaving the Barcelona of Deco, Ronaldinho and Eto'o (with two subs on the bench named Xavi and Iniesta) to secure their first European Cup for fourteen years.

Paris would not be the ending to Wenger's first ten years that any football loving fan would have wished for, but yet what a ten years he had given us. What brushstrokes, what artistry, what grace. In that decade from 1996/97 to 2005/06 Arsenal finished in an average League position of second place. In a study of League performance for the whole of the twentieth century, Arsenal came out on top, achieving a long run average League position of 8.5, just pipping Liverpool at 8.7. So, to say that Arsene's first ten years were revolutionary would be an understatement. However, the English game was growing familiar with this new movement, and with Wenger the Impressionist. Clubs the length and breadth of the land were either mimicking Arsenal's style or adapting their play to nullify it. For the north Londoners, success was becoming harder to achieve.

Paris had left a scar but it had also exposed a flaw, one that to this day Wenger's side have not solved. A midfield consisting of a youthful Cesc Fabregas and Gilberto of Brazil never dominated. In fairness, being short a man didn't help, but no Arsenal midfield has managed to replicate the sheer drive, skill and efficiency of Wenger's first vintage of Petit and

Viera. In his second decade in charge, Wenger's sides metamorphosed into more stylish but rather lightweight structures. They would remain a top-four team, always qualifying for the European Cup, but never strong enough, physically or mentally, to endure the gruelling English season and emerge as winners. FA Cup wins in 2014 and 2015 have temporarily kept the wolves at bay, but they still circle, growling. In Europe another crack at glory seems as far away as ever, Arsenal falling at the feet of the superpowers of Munich and Barcelona, whenever they meet. As England's third best team of recent years, the north Londoners have proven a let-down on the continent, but hopefully someday, with the bespectacled French professor at the helm, they can crack it. Now, with his own fans calling for his head, Wenger needs to build a new, tougher and more resilient team if he is to see out a third decade.

In defence of his second decade, if he needs any, the building of the Emirates, the Gunners' fantastic new home, cost nearly £400 million and put the club into massive debt. This saw Wenger exercise prudency in the transfer market when others were breaking the bank. The guaranteed Champions League football that Wenger supplied, along with the certain £20–£30 million per year riches that it brought, has paid down the Emirates debt to very manageable amounts. In many ways when Arsenal fans arrive at their new Islington stadium every week, they are visiting the home that Wenger built. This should never be forgotten. Thierry Henry is effusive in his praise of the Frenchman, "It's a no-brainer that Arsene has changed Arsenal. Were they successful before? Yes, but in a different way. Now they're known for the football they play. That's all down to him." Steve Gerrard agrees and praises both the club and the man, "Arsenal are very classy. They have a class manager in Arsene Wenger, with class players, and they play the game the right way. I have great respect for Arsenal because they do things properly."

And just like Liverpool, Wenger also had to compete with the newly minted riches of Chelsea and Man City. Their extravagance would see the Economics student complain of 'financial doping'. Wenger's preference had always been to develop players. He refuses to mimic the open chequebook policies of others, taking instead the long view. Mostly he manages to produce very competitive teams doing this, but as long as the sugar daddies are allowed to financially inflate their clubs as needed,

Wenger and Arsenal face as tough a ride as the Reds of Liverpool and the rest of the also-rans. The grumblings persist among Arsenal's fans that even after the debt has fallen, Wenger remains too parsimonious in the transfer market, unwilling to move from his rigid principles. One could applaud such nobility. During Wenger's Arsenal years his sides have averaged League finishing positions of 2.7 to Liverpool's 4.5. Both clubs have work to do.

Arsenal's club motto is *Victoria Concordia Crescit* or 'victory through harmony'. Yet it seems that harmony is in short supply around this patch of North London. Many Arsenal fans believe that it is time for Wenger to go. The argument is that his last ten years have been unsuccessful and that he has lost his way strategically as the game has veered towards younger, more energetic and tactically driven managers. In the Arsenal fanzine *Gooner* a poll shows the divide in opinion amongst Gunners fans with 13 per cent voting that Wenger should leave immediately, 46 per cent saying he should leave at the end of his contract in 2017 and 41 per cent wanting him to stay longer. Even David Dein (now no longer an Arsenal board member or shareholder), the man who signed Wenger, who saw his artistry before any other, would say – "You can't tell a ten-year-old son that our club is financially stable, we believe in financial fair play, we're looking after our finances well, we've got money in the bank. The child says, 'Where's the trophies?'"

***

Only three games into the 2015/16 season and Arsenal fans were already grumbling. A first day defeat at home to West Ham was one of the reasons. A growing disquiet towards their manager was another. Up next was an early litmus test for the Gunners and for their visitors, Liverpool. Rodgers and his team would be in no frame of mind to help the prevailing mood. The uplifting opening day win at Stoke had been followed by a solid, if uninspiring, 1–0 midweek home win against new boys Bournemouth. Now it was time to rubber-stamp the recovery at Arsenal. Five months earlier at the Emirates, Arsenal stuffed Liverpool 4–1 as the Red's 2014/15 season stuttered to an ignominious conclusion. So now, on a damp and drizzly August Monday night, Rodgers was hoping that his team could again wash clean the memory of another insipid display. They would, with flying colours. The Reds, dressed in black, would play the home team off the pitch with some breathtakingly fluent football and, but for the repeated heroics of Arsenal's goalie Cech, a comprehensive victory would have been achieved . Despite only one point being collected after a 0–0 draw, it was the performance, if not the result, that promised much. Seven points from nine and it was starting to feel like Rodgers was righting his listing ship.

WAR AND PEACE

'The Bible tells us to love our neighbours, and also to love our enemies; probably because generally they are the same people.' —G.K. Chesterton

It's Saturday lunchtime, September 12th 2015 and rain falls incessantly on the grey streets of Manchester. The gloomy clouds overhead show no sign of breaking and we duck into a small coffee shop to grab a bite. This morning, not for the first time you will find, I woke with a brooding feeling, an ill portent about what was to come. Now, as I stare out at the bleak wetness, this sense of foreboding and anxiety only worsens. This dread is not new though, it has been building bit by bit over the last two weeks, from the morning of the disastrous West Ham game. A defensively inept, error-strewn performance resulting in a 0–3 home defeat saw all the goodwill, which Rodgers had been eagerly restoring, vaporize in an instant, leaving behind only a fuming and doubting vacuum for Liverpool fans to fester in. It seemed that the failings of the previous season had not left the pitch nor the minds of the fans in the stands.

Today Liverpool play arch-rivals and bitter nemesis Manchester United. Since the 1800s, an era when Liverpool was the largest industrial port in the world and Manchester the textile hub of the British Empire, these cities have clashed. Back then, the Mancunian response to high charges for transporting and holding goods at the Liverpool docks, was to build the Manchester Canal all the way to the Irish Sea and, in doing so, eliminate reliance on their neighbours. Since then it has been tit for tat in industry, culture, entertainment and in more recent times, football. The two cities are home to four Premiership teams. Liverpool and Everton in one, United and City in the other. In recent years Manchester has taken the mantle from Liverpool as the current 'home' of English football. The city of Liverpool has notched up twenty-seven titles (Liverpool eighteen and Everton nine) compared to Manchester's twenty-four (United twenty and City four). London trails both on twenty (Arsenal thirteen, Chelsea five and Spurs two).

Today's clash is still the biggest in English, and maybe even in world, football. Spain's *El Clasico* of Real Madrid versus Barcelona may have more glamour and certainly, these days, more quality, given the presence on the pitch of two of the greatest players of all time in Lionel Messi and Cristiano Ronaldo, but as far as global viewing audiences count, the clash of the Red adversaries from England's North West wins hands down. With an estimated 700 million worldwide viewers, it nearly doubles the figures of the Madrid/Barcelona tie and it also dwarfs viewer numbers for many other mega sporting events from the Champion's League Final (estimated 176 million) to American Football's Super Bowl (estimated 160 million). While neither Liverpool nor Manchester United currently reside at the top of the League table, they are still the main attraction for football fans far and wide.

The reasons are self-evident. English football has always been the most watched and talked about league in the world, despite its often inferior quality compared to others, be that Italy's Serie A in the late eighties or Spain's La Liga since 2011. Liverpool and Manchester United stand without rivals as England's two greatest teams. Liverpool have won forty-one major trophies to Manchester's thirty-nine, Arsenal trailing in third at twenty-nine. Crucially both Liverpool and United have a European prestige that has eluded their peers, and it is this which cements their global recognition and status.

United were the first English team to enter the fledgling European Cup in 1956, Chelsea having been dissuaded by the English FA the year before. The cup had been the brainchild of the French football magazine *L'Equipe*, which had canvassed for a European tournament, competed for by the domestic champions of the various nations. The FA saw the new continental tournament as unnecessary competition to an already congested home fixture list. In May 1956, the visionary United manager Sir Matt Busby decided that the Red Devils would defy the FA and enter.

Backed by his chairman Harold Hardman, Busby led United and

England onto the continent for the first time and marched all the way to the semi-final, where they eventually succumbed, losing 5–3 on aggregate to Real Madrid over two legs. A year later 'the Busby Babes' attempted once more to conquer Europe, however, terrible tragedy befell them in what became known as the Munich Air Disaster. On February 6th, 1958, the charter plane carrying the United team and officials returning from their away tie at Belgrade, had stopped to refuel at Munich-Riem airport. Heavy snow was falling and the pilots had already abandoned take-off twice due to a technical hitch. On their third attempt, slowed down by slush on the runway, the plane failed to gain enough speed to achieve take-off and crashed through the end of the runway, breaking apart as it did so. Of the forty-four on board twenty-three would die, including eight team players. United would rally, re-group and play on. That May, AC Milan would defeat them 5-2 in the semi-final. Incredibly, only ten years later, after many years of recovery and rebuilding, Busby led a reconstructed team, which included George Best, Bobby Charlton and Denis Law, to European glory. At Wembley, United would defeat Benfica 4–1 after extra time to win the 1968 European Cup, the first such triumph for any English side.

In Liverpool, Bill Shankly had been busy too. He had transformed Liverpool FC from an average second division outfit into one that was capable of matching and beating the great Busby team. Before an encounter with United, Shankly explained tactics to his team. A model pitch with miniature players was set out on the dressing room table. Walking to the board he lifted the figurines of United's three attacking players, three of the best players in the world at the time – Charlton, Law and Best – and he put them into his breast pocket. Turning around he scoffed, "Don't worry about them, they can't play at all."

The sixties saw the two north-western cities compete as cultural hubs. Manchester was booming economically and was a hotbed of fashion. Liverpool had a swagger like no other city, with the emergence of swinging dance clubs, the Merseybeat sound and a new band called the Beatles. Of equal importance was the developing battle for football supremacy. Shankly's Reds lifted the title in 1963/64. Busby's United won it in 1964/65. Liverpool came back as victors in 1965/66 and then United were crowned again in 1966/67. A fierce rivalry was brewing.

United legend Denis Law recalled, "We believed that if we finished above Liverpool then we would win the League. They felt exactly the same about us and for that marvellous period of the 'Swinging Sixties' we were both right. I was a great friend of Bill Shankly, having played under him at my first club, Huddersfield Town, but that didn't prevent us from being overwhelmingly keen to beat each other. The same was true of Matt and Bill, who were very close, but it didn't stop them doing everything humanely possible to come out on top."

As Busby had done with United, so Shankly too would lead Liverpool into Europe, winning the UEFA Cup (today's Europa League) in 1972/73. His successor Bob Paisley would then lead Liverpool to a further UEFA Cup success in 1976. One year later Paisley's Reds would match United's feat and become the second English team to lift the hallowed European Cup in 1977. Further wins would follow in 1978, 1981, 1984 and 2005. With a total of five Red successes, only Real Madrid and AC Milan have won more.

From the late seventies and through the eighties, Liverpool were also building a dynasty in England, lifting ten League titles in comparison to United's zero. Liverpool had left Manchester in the shade. Yet it wasn't all good news. Liverpool would experience darkness and tragedy at Heysel and Hillsborough. The rivalry had become fiercely hostile with no love lost between cities and fan bases. On the pitch studs and flailing arms abounded. In the stands the fans engaged in cruel chants mocking the dead of the opposing clubs. Matches would be scarred by crowd violence and hooliganism. The ugly side of tribalism had come to the fore.

Then along came Alex Ferguson who swore, with a distinct deficit of charm, that he would "knock Liverpool right off their fucking perch". It takes one type of man to say it, another beast altogether to go and do it. All the while, Liverpool helped him ably as they consistently shot themselves in the foot. 2005 European Cup winner Jamie Carragher remarked, "Much as I respect Ferguson as a manager, I must disagree with him. He didn't knock Liverpool off their perch. Liverpool fell off it. He didn't have to lift a finger against us, let alone give us a shove. Every wound Liverpool has suffered has been self-inflicted." By the time Ferguson had retired in 2013, United led Liverpool domestically with twenty titles to eighteen. Liverpool still led the way in Europe, now by five European

Cups to United's three, Ferguson having lifted two European crowns to cement his place in the all-time list of great managers.

If Liverpool's dominance over United in the seventies and eighties had fuelled hatred and envy in United's fans, then Ferguson's turnaround in the nineties and noughties only mirrored such feelings in the hearts of the Kop. Layer by envious layer, battle by fiery battle, so mushroomed the greatest rivalry in world football. The last time a player has been transferred between the two famous clubs was in April 1964 when Phil Chisnall moved from United to Liverpool. This statistic alone tells you everything you need to know about the clash. Every other major rivalry such as Madrid and Barcelona, Milan and Internazionale, Celtic and Rangers, Munich and Dortmund, have all seen multiple player transfers between clubs. In the great north west of England this just could not be countenanced.

Manchester-born Chisnall reminisced about the move; "When I was growing up, there wasn't the often-bitter rivalry which exists today in football. As somebody growing up in Manchester in the mid-fifties, I was by no means alone in going to watch United one week and City the next. When I was transferred to Liverpool it was not the big deal it would be were it to happen today when it would be made big to sell newspapers. The move to Liverpool came as a surprise. I was called in by Busby to be told he had received a bid from Liverpool. I didn't have to go but they were top of the league and they must have thought I could do something for them. I was only twenty-one years of age and in those days you didn't have all the advisers like they have today. You simply made up your own mind yourself. Money wasn't an issue as I was on £35 when I went to Liverpool which was an increase from what I was earning at United. It was a good wage, probably twice the average wage at that time, but nothing like today. When I made my debut at Old Trafford I was earning £12.50 and after ten games I was given a rise to £17.50 with £2 for a draw and £4 for a win. When I joined Liverpool there was competition from the likes of Roger Hunt, Ian St John, Peter Thompson and Ian Callaghan so it wasn't any easier getting a game. It was an amazing time to be in Liverpool in the mid-sixties."

***

By midday the rain has stopped and we are having an early lunch in a small Italian café near Deansgate. Peculiarly, we can hear beating drums and then gradually through the café window I see the source, an Orange Order marching band approaches, stomping through the city in full pomp and glory – orange sashes, black suits and white-gloved flagpole bearers. I'm not very religious, so I find this pageantry and ceremony somewhat baffling, as I would with parading groups of any religious belief. My son asks me what is it all about and I start to explain, but halfway through he's bored and isn't listening anymore. I can't blame him, to be honest. It's interesting to observe how absurd many children find the ritual and ceremony of religion when they haven't been raised to bow their heads or to fear, revere or respect it. Mine have been raised not to disrespect, which is a whole different matter.

Then the thought crosses my mind, this is what hordes of football fans must look like, decked out with hats, scarves and flags in their team colours on their way to or from a stadium, without the white gloves that is. Thousands of fans, mostly men, on the march, must be an intimidating sight for the uninitiated and an exhilarating one for those who are part of the army. In an interview on Granada TV in 1981 featuring the former Prime Minister Howard Wilson and Liverpool's Bill Shankly, Wilson asked Shankly about his passion for football. "It's a religion, too, isn't it… a way of life?"

"That's a good expression, Sir Harold," replied Shankly, "it is a way of life. And it's so serious that it's unbelievable. And I wonder what all the rest of the world does."

Today's game will be the first time since the formation of the Premier League in 1992, that neither Man United nor Liverpool will field a local player. This is an unfortunate by-product of the modern game. Fans love to see one of their own in the team, it heightens their feeling of involvement, of association. Former Liverpool player Steve McManaman comments on BT Sport TV, "We haven't got the Nevilles, the Carraghers anymore, that type of player who fights and knows what the occasion means. It's nostalgic, but I find that quite sad."

The managers, players and ex-players have been building today's game up all week. Both teams have started slowly and their performances have been roundly viewed as average, lacking fluidity and not living up to the high standards that both sets of supporters crave. It is imperative for clubs like United and Liverpool to not only win, but also to entertain. Neither have achieved that so far this season, and they sit side by side in the table with seven points apiece, both already five points adrift of pace-setters Manchester City.

Liverpool manager Brendan Rodgers, in an attempt to prime his players for the battle ahead, tells reporters, "United is a huge club and will always be under scrutiny, the intensity of this fixture is still there. The players will feel it. This is the biggest derby game in the history of this League. Winning a game like this can give you a psychological boost."

I wonder though, morbid football clouds still darkening my thoughts, if the opposite is also true. Defeat could set us a long way back. It was a 1–2 defeat at home to United the previous March, at a time when Champion's League qualification was still possible, that put a season-ending downward spiral in motion. A draw today will do fine, I tell myself.

I love the rivalry of Liverpool and United. I love the intensity, the passion and the colour. I love the history and the high stakes. Without a foe or an arch-enemy, your hero or favoured protagonist lacks meaning. Sherlock is defined by Moriarty, Batman by the Joker. We want a rival to beat so that, as winner, we can compare our success, measure it. As humans we strive for success, it's hardwired. Beating Man United is glorious, that cannot be denied, but for me, that is where it stops. Hatred doesn't come into the discussion, not in any real sense, not given the tragedies that both clubs have witnessed, not given that we are all the same beneath the scarves and the flags. All fathers, sons, mothers, daughters, brothers, sisters. I try never to use the word 'hate' in my life, it's possibly the ugliest word in the English language.

Less heralded have been the tales of goodwill and humour between the two clubs, who are more similar than they would care to admit.

After the Munich Air Disaster in 1958 many felt that Manchester United as a club would struggle to continue. Twenty-three people died in the crash, eight of these being United players and three club officials. Manager Sir Matt Busby lay in a German hospital recovering. Busby's friend, Bill Shankly, offered five first team Liverpool players to

Manchester United to help in the crisis, with the Reds also offering to pay their wages.

Kenny Dalglish, in his capacity as manager, was receiving condolences from many in the game after the Hillsborough tragedy in 1989. He recalled a phone call from Sir Alex Ferguson. "'Anything you need, Kenny, I'm here for you,' said Alex Ferguson. Then he made an inspired suggestion. 'I'll send some fans over to pay tribute.' The rivalry between followers of Manchester United and Liverpool runs very deep, and is often very bitter, so it was a marvellous idea of Fergie's to get some of his fans to come across and stand shoulder to shoulder with Liverpool fans in their hour of need. As long as I live, I'll never forget Fergie's exceptional gesture. It didn't surprise me, though, because Fergie is absolutely magnificent in any crisis. He's famous in football for being straight on the phone, offering assistance or advice." There have been compliments too from Ferguson. Rafael Benitez recollected, "I remember Sir Alex sent me a letter of congratulations when we won the Champions League, praising the tactical changes we made at half-time."

On September 23rd, 2012, United travelled to Anfield. It was Liverpool's first home game since the Hillsborough Independent Panel announced its findings. The Panel had found that there had been avoidable catastrophic failures before, during and after the disaster. The Prime Minister apologized to the families of the dead and to the survivors on behalf of the government. After twenty-three long years Liverpool Fans had been exonerated of any blame whatsoever. The fact that United were the opponents on a day when there would be such an outpouring of grief was worrying, given the unfriendly rivalry. But, once again, United and their manager stepped up. Ferguson wrote in a letter addressed to United fans before the game:

> *'...Our rivalry with Liverpool... It cannot and should never be based on personal hatred. Just ten days ago, we heard the terrible, damning truth about the deaths of ninety-six fans who went to watch their team try and reach the FA Cup final and never came back. What happened to them should wake the conscience of everyone connected with the game. Our great club stands with our great neighbours Liverpool today to remember that loss and pay*

tribute to their campaign for justice. I know I can count on you to remember that loss and pay tribute to their campaign, I know I can count on you to stand with us in the best traditions of the best fans in the game.'

My son and I stood on the Kop that day and held aloft part of a red and white mosaic that covered three quarters of Anfield. On the pitch the teams lined up and to their great respect, the United players wore white tracksuit tops with 96 emblazoned in red on the back. Sir Bobby Charlton and Ian Rush together released 96 red and white balloons into the afternoon sky. I explained to my then eight-year-old son as best I could the significance of the gestures.

Of the many tales of friendship which exist between the clubs, there is one which appeared a little misguided. By the time the 1914/15 football season had kicked off, Britain had already declared hostilities against Germany. The sense of hollowness and detachment that war must bring, along with the financial hardship and rationing imposed, may help to explain the peculiar circumstances of what came to be known as the 'Good Friday Scandal'. When Liverpool travelled to Manchester to play United on the Good Friday of 1915, United's top League status looked precarious. One hundred years ago, no great animosity existed between the clubs, this point being proven when, prior to the game, a group of United and Liverpool players met in a Manchester pub. However, this meeting went beyond normal camaraderie or professional respect. What was being hatched was a plan to 'fix' the game and the score line. The gang agreed that United would be allowed to win 2–0 and that the players or their accomplices would wager on this result. Liverpool players stuck to their bargain, they were awful and United cruised to a 2–0 victory. An inquiry found eight guilty, four from each side and all were banned from the game indefinitely. With the benefit of the win, United only just avoided the drop.

Today, the vitriol is so intense that it's hard to imagine the players and managers of the two great clubs being cordial, never mind the fans. Another spot of match fixing seems quite unlikely. The bitterness fuels great drama and atmosphere, yet for me, any hostilities need to remain verbal and stay inside the ground. I cheer my team on, that's it, end of story. What the opposition fans do or say is irrelevant to me. I don't teach my son hatred and never will, not against anybody. I don't hate another football fan just because he supports a different club, the thought of that is ludicrous to me. In football, we are just mirrored souls wearing different colours, each seeking to be part of something wonderful and glorious. Liverpool need Manchester United and Manchester United need Liverpool, this to me seems clear, a symbiotic relationship if ever there was one. Nietzsche said, "Whoever lives for the sake of combating an enemy has an interest in the enemy's staying alive." Lunch is over, the marching band have gone, it's time for the main event.

THE REVELATION

'You have persevered and have endured hardships for my name, and have not grown weary.' – Book of Revelations 2:3

Old Trafford, Manchester United's football stadium, looms high in the chilly evening sky. We cross the iron Trafford Swing Bridge which spans the historic Bridgewater Canal below. Ahead of us are two old red-brick warehouse buildings, both with the signage 'Liverpool Warehousing Company Limited' emblazoned on their walls. To see the name 'Liverpool' so clearly and so close to United's revered home, brings a silly smile to my face. These warehouses offer a glimpse of a past when Manchester and Liverpool competed as industrial cities for trade and commerce, and of how the Bridgewater Canal and its successor, the Manchester Ship Canal, would shape the history of the two cities. Today the warehouses are derelict and unused and the trade battle has become a sporting one at the arena next door.

We walk up the Trafford Wharf Road past Sam Platts public house outside of which a gathering of United fans are in full voice singing their George Best song to the tune of Norman Greenbaum's 1969 hit 'Spirit in the Sky':

'Going on up to the spirit in the sky
It's where I'm gonna go when I die
When I die and they lay me to rest
I'm gonna go on the piss with Georgie Best.'

I am always impressed by how witty and inventive football fans' songs can be. This is another example, albeit of questionable taste, given that George Best died in 2005 aged fifty-nine, after a long battle with alcoholism. That said, families can always indulge in black humour at their own expense and Best was one of the most revered sons of United, if not its prodigal son. The *Manchester Evening News* reported on 22 May 2015, that Best's son Calum had endorsed the song, describing it as brilliant. I tend to agree, though I don't share any of this with my own son.

The sun has broken through as we reach the ground and the electric buzz that possesses football stadia and their environs pre-game starts to course through my veins. The ominous mood that has held me since early morning at last starts to lift. We take in the statues of Busby and Ferguson. Then the bronze of the United trinity, Best, Law and Charlton. What players, I think, icons of the game. Under the Stadium, in the 'Munich Tunnel' we read the various glass and copper plaques displayed in memory of the 'Flowers of Manchester', the name adopted for those who perished in the disaster. This is all new for my son and I see thoughts whirring in his young mind. These events must seem so dated to him, stories from another age.

Kick-off is at 5.30 p.m., the first evening kick-off between Liverpool and United in over a decade. Police prefer lunchtime kick-offs for this game, they help minimise the chances of trouble between rival fans. The earlier the kick-off, then the less alcohol consumed, plus the game will start and end in daylight.

We reach the away-end turnstiles and join the queuing Liverpool fans. We are separated from the home fans by mounted police. A small number of idiots in both groups hurl abuse at each other while the police and match stewards bark orders. I get a push from a burly orange-clad steward to enter the line for a body search and I am tempted to push back but I don't. I can see from his eyes that the lights are on, set to dim that is, but the house is empty. I don't expect to be touched, except during the body search and from an official it is way too aggressive. I understand these guys are under pressure but if that is how a father with his son is treated, then lord help us. Thankfully, it's the first time I've been even slightly 'manhandled' at a football game. My son looks for my reaction, and I smile back to him, whilst arching my eyebrow towards the steward with a look that I hope conveys a number of things, most of all contempt. The tension and simmering aggression in the air is not nice for children, nor adults come to think of it, and I wonder should I have brought him? Inside the ground, my worries ease as everything is calm. Now it's only about the football.

Liverpool's players are doing short shuttle sprints at the corner flag nearest to where we are stood. They get a huge ovation. I can discern a sheepish look on one or two of their faces, a look that says they don't deserve this support from 3,000 travelling fans after their display at home to West Ham. They need not worry though, hope and allegiance spring eternal in supporters' hearts. Today is a new day with new opportunities. I'm now starting to feel optimistic. "We can beat these," I declare. My son smiles in response, but the look in his eye is not so sure. The records give good cause for his uncertainty. Over eighty-three previous encounters at Old Trafford, United have won forty-two, Liverpool sixteen and the remaining twenty-five have been drawn.

He is right. United are poor, but Liverpool are awful. United win 3–1 and again Rodgers is left deflated by his meek and brittle defence. Many Reds fans have left long before the finish. I never leave a game before it's over, even if hope is lost, you must stand your ground, anything can happen. Liverpool fans proved this in Istanbul. Yet I can understand the disillusionment. It must have been hard to endure the lacklustre home defeat to West Ham, I only watched it on TV. To have it followed up by this display is a punch to the stomach. But it's more than that, Liverpool fans rarely boo their own team or leave a ground early. These are clear indications of deep-rooted disenchantment taking hold. We can all feel it and it is cancerous in its virility and acceleration. I feel for Rodgers. Once more his players have let him down.

We leave a few minutes after the final whistle and enter the river of exiting United fans. Both supporters mix freely, without trouble or fuss and soon it's just a sea of heads bobbing up and down on their way back to cars, trains and buses. We walk for thirty minutes or so, all the way to Manchester city centre. Initially United fans are singing and buoyant but as the crowd thins out, we are left to our own thoughts. I'm a little astonished when my son tells me that he loved it. He loved the stadium, the atmosphere, seeing the great players on both sides and witnessing two superb individual goals from Liverpool's Benteke and United's Martial. I smile and ruffle his hair. I'm proud of him. That's the spirit!

That's what football should be about. Excitement, great players and great goals, regardless of who wins or loses. At last my mood starts to lift and I am filled momentarily with the joy of a thought, a revelation even. This is the course that the rest of my football life needs to take. I need to just enjoy it. Enjoy the grace, the dexterity, the touch and the skill that makes this game an art form and makes it the most played and loved in the world. The beautiful game.

KAAMOS

'A man must dream a long time in order to act with grandeur, and dreaming is nursed in darkness.'—Jean Genet

The Polar Night arrives in November for those living above the Arctic Circle. As the month advances, days become shorter and shorter until daylight is lost completely with the region plunged into a sunless gloom lasting up to three months. Kaamos is the word that the Finnish use to describe this prolonged period of darkness, this elongated Polar Night. Liverpool toured Finland in early August, when the sun shone and when the footballing buds of hope were forming in pre-season. Now it must seem to Brendan Rodgers and his team that they have returned to Finland and that their own personal Kaamos has arrived. It's only nearing the end of September but it feels like winter around the fields of Anfield Road. Dark brooding clouds are engulfing the club and all who associate with it. Disenchantment becomes viral, poisoning like a stealthy contagion. Rumours swirl in the chilly winds that owners, the FSG group, are looking to sell out, they too frustrated by the lack of progress. Manager Brendan Rodgers says that the team have lost their 'identity' and that the players look 'nervous'. The more vociferous, but still possibly the minority of Liverpool fans, are calling for blood, starting with the manager.

In the Arctic, during these dark periods, deep depression, often accompanied by bouts of heavy drinking, can become a way of life for some. Depression is setting in amongst Liverpool fans and one could forgive them if they too bunkered in and found some solace in their local watering holes.

A 1–1 result at home to lowly Norwich, coming after the lame defeat at Old Trafford, is not the tonic needed to lift what is becoming a deep-rooted malaise. Eight points from the first six League games sees Liverpool sit 13th in the League table. Combine this form with the last nine games of the 2014/15 season, these also producing a return of eight points, and it is clear that the team is stuck in a horrible slump which has yielded a paltry sixteen points from fifteen games. That level of form is not remotely good enough to even contemplate the lofty ground occupied by the top four and, if anything, it's a guaranteed road to relegation. It also betrays an underlying weakness of Rodgers' tenure, streakiness. Only in 2013/14 and before 'the Slip', did it all hang together long enough for a sustained assault at glory.

Before Norwich, Rodgers spoke of finding what had gone missing, "I think it is good I have an identity as a coach and a way of working that is clear. I am confident we can get back to playing that way. When you look at the first five games we haven't been at that level of intensity." This is a plea to a fan base on the precipice. 'Stand by me' it implores, Rodgers knowing full well that without the fans' support, his days are numbered. When the crowd turn on a manager, no matter what long-term plan the owners or manager may have, you can start sharpening the axe. A baying crowd will always get their way, every manager knows this, every fan knows this and in many ways, so it should be. It is the last vestige of control that can be exerted from the terraces to counteract the power of the billionaire owners and the mega wealthy players. 'If we walk, you are nothing,' is the clear refrain, sometimes voiced, sometimes muted, but always simmering below the surface. And it is true. Football is nothing without the fans. Billion-pound TV deals would drastically diminish if armchair viewers were asked to watch games played out in front of empty seats. Where's the theatre in that? Thankfully, football still needs its match day supporters, the die-hards who sacrifice one or two days a week to feed their addiction. The game must be careful not to alienate too many, for to do so, would be to kill the golden goose.

It seems that matters can't get any worse but they do. Following Norwich, fourth tier Carlisle arrive for a midweek League Cup tie. On a cold and dark Wednesday night it takes Liverpool ninety minutes plus extra time and then penalties to seal a narrow victory. The embarrassment is excruciating. Some of the Liverpool players run to their keeper Adam Bogdan and leap in jubilation to greet him. Most of the 42,000 crowd look on in disbelief as do the remainder of the less jubilant players. This is not a victory to be celebrated, this was a mortifyingly awkward humiliation. The 6,000 travelling Carlisle fans celebrate as if they had won the cup and rightfully so, they have silenced a giant of the game at their own fortress. They are no less ruthless than any travelling set of supporters when weakness is meekly displayed before them, and they sing the usual refrain to Rodgers – *'You're getting sacked in the morning'*.

Even though the League Cup ranks below both the League and the FA Cup in prestige, this was a new low, a watershed. The fans had turned out in mass to support their team for what appeared to be a golden opportunity to inject some turbo, score some goals, put weak opposition to the sword and build much needed confidence. None of that had been achieved. Audible boos rang around parts of the famous old ground. John Aldridge, a former Liverpool great, was surprised. "I've been going to Liverpool for fifty years now, since I was a kid, and you very rarely hear boos round the place… there was a very small section but it is something we are not used to at Anfield."

Wednesday night and all day Thursday sees the scavengers converge on Anfield, smelling the decay. The Internet buzzes with calls for the head of Rodgers and the media tear shreds from his black designer suit.

The widespread derision isn't reserved to the English media alone. *Marca*, the Madrid-based Spanish newspaper, run with a full-page story under the banner 'Liverbluff'. In Madrid, they remember John Toshack, a former Liverpool great and also a one-time manager of Real Madrid. He always said of his former team, "Liverpool fix the roof leaks before they happen," but *Marca* laments how this is no longer the case. It seems Rodgers has no friends and that his departure may be imminent. The press announce that it is a matter of when and not if, and a local Liverpool reporter, James Beecroft, runs a story that claims to have an inside track to the Boston owners and to the fact that a decision has already been made to look for a new manager.

Thursday comes and goes amid a media frenzy assessing what has gone wrong and why the project has failed. Poor transfer dealings are blamed, bad tactics, too many changes and a loss of any core philosophy. It seems in the midst of all of this negativity, that Rodgers is already gone, yet no official announcement has been forthcoming. A few solitary voices call for a stay of execution. Roy Evans, the former boot room stalwart and ex-Liverpool manager, pleads for calm, "Once everybody gets into this stigma that the manager is to blame for everything, people tend to run away with that. They've got to give him maybe just a little more time, it's still very early in the season, things can turn around in two or three games."

Danny Murphy, a former Liverpool midfielder, who had the honorable distinction of scoring the winning goal for the Reds away to Manchester United, three times in four seasons, claims, "Two seasons ago, when Liverpool were close to winning the league, Brendan showed a lot of intelligence in terms of tactics and changes in formation. He's shown a lot of bravery at times, maybe too much with changing the systems and personnel. But it is now at a point when, come Christmas, if things haven't picked up, there is a time for everyone."

And still silence pervades Anfield's inner sanctum and equally across the Atlantic in Boston. But many others are not silent and a noisy storm swells and rises in Liverpool and across the globe amongst Reds fans. Bad times bring the loudest voices. What seems clear from this multitude of social media sources, interviews, phone-ins and so on, is that the trust of many if not most of Liverpool's supporters has gone. A vociferous contingent wanted Rodgers gone in the summer, after the disgrace of how the team had finished the season before. The 1–3 home loss to Palace, the 6–1 away defeat to Stoke. The horrible 0–3 mauling at home to Real Madrid in the Champions League. The lame FA Cup semi-final exit at Wembley to a poor Aston Villa side, whom Arsenal would go on to demolish in the Final. So many bad performances. Yet many too wanted to give the erstwhile Irishman another go. Give him time to bed down the new signings. He had done so well in such a short time.

At his Friday press conference, Rodgers has the look and body language of a beaten man. He seems resigned to his fate and in some way ready for it. Yet with his rhetoric he fights on – "I hope to be a manager for twenty years, I know it won't be twenty years at Liverpool, but while I am here I want to fight for the club and the players. I know we need to get results and I embrace that challenge. I'm a much better manager than three years ago. The message is to stay with the team. It only takes a couple of results. One win and you are back in the top four."

The humbling draw and penalty win over Carlisle has echoes of the recent past, though. Exactly five years and one day previously, Roy Hodgson, the then Liverpool manager, welcomed Northampton town to Anfield for a League cup third round game. Northampton were also a lowly fourth tier team, but incredibly they went one step better than Carlisle and they knocked the Reds out on penalties. Carlisle was a shocker but these things happen in English football, to all teams, Liverpool fans know that. Yet, when Northampton turned up in September 2010, only 22,500 fans turned out to watch. In spite of the lack of trust and confidence that is clearly now evident amongst the Liverpool faithful, 42,000 turned out to welcome Carlisle. That says something, it talks of a last vestige of hope for this team and for Rodgers.

Liverpool's fans are renowned for their patience, more so than most, but every manager has a tipping point and once the Rubicon has been crossed there is no way back. Rodgers seems acutely aware of this and also of the rules of being prey. Show weakness and you are dead. He talks of things not being any different than before, "It [the pressure] is the same as it ever has been. It's part and parcel of being the manager at such a great club."

For his resilience, Rodgers deserves respect, he carries a heavy burden with great poise and dignity and he is constantly in search of the solution, whether that be the team formation, tactics or motivation. But these seem to be the darkest of days for him and his team, rarely has the clear sky and bright sunrise seemed so far away.

Still, these are early days, it is only late September and even in the polar Arctic the sun eventually rises.

ON THE EDGE

'If you are at the edge of a precipice, your every step is vital!'
—Mehmet Murat ildan

In England's North West, football's heartland, a young manager still in his forties looks up to the stands. A banner reads, "Three years of excuses and it's still crap – ta ra." The message is clear and reflects the feelings of many in the stadium, it's time to go. On the pitch the team in red shirts are losing 1–2 at home to Crystal Palace. The stadium is only two-thirds full. Thirty-three thousand have turned up, fourteeen thousand less than the opening game of the season. Times are bleak, as bleak as they've ever been. It's been over two decades since the club's last League title win and the fans have grown restless with another stilted campaign. The manager would confess that this was 'the darkest period he ever suffered in the game'.

However, this is not Brendan Rodgers in the dugout, neither is it Anfield nor Liverpool FC. Instead the banner is unfurled at that other home of north-western footballing power, Man United's Old Trafford, and the manager whose head is being called for is Alex Ferguson. It is December 1989, and despite the protestations, the United board hold firm in their knowledge that slow, yet effectual, change is taking place, even if not evident to all. The season would end with an inglorious thirteenth place League finish but green shoots were sprouting. New players were slowly starting to gel and Cup success arrived with an FA Cup final win against the same opponents, Crystal Palace. The following season United would rise to sixth and in 1991/92 the improvement would continue with the Red Devils finishing in second place, losing the title to a late surge from Howard Wilkinson's Leeds United. Then in 1992/93, in the inaugural Premier League season, United would break their twenty-five-year duck and be crowned champions in Ferguson's sixth season as manager.

Rodgers could only dream of being afforded such patience, yet time was exactly what was needed. With the loss of key personnel and the major turnover of players that had to happen in both of the previous summer transfer windows, he needed to let the team bed down, to gel, to learn how to play in the formations and style that he demanded from them. It took time for players to settle at Liverpool, commonly more than a year. This wasn't new, it happened in the old days too, when new signings were gradually introduced to the starting line-up over time. Yet Rodgers knew he was on the clock, success was demanded, the glorious run to second place now all but forgotten. In many ways the early form had become the noose around his own neck. He had promised too much, too soon, with too little. Next up at Anfield were Aston Villa. Starting the season, Villa's manager Tim Sherwood was one of the bookie's favourites at 8/1 to be the first Premier League manager to be axed. If bookies are to be believed, and from all accounts they do get it right more often than not, then Liverpool's Brendan Rodgers' fate seemed even more perilous, with his price being lowest of all at 5/1. Nigel Pearson of Leicester City had already pipped both of them to the dubious award, after a collapse in his relationship with the club's Thai owners. Five weeks after guiding the Midlands club to a remarkable escape from Premier League relegation, Pearson surprisingly departed the day before the transfer window officially opened.

Come Saturday 26th September it's still red alert for both Rodgers and Sherwood, their bookies odds having shrivelled to be the next neck on the block. Villa sit seventeenth after one win in six games. Liverpool lie four places higher in thirteenth. Both managers are under severe pressure and with the average tenure of a Premier League manager being under two years it is not hard to understand why.

Prior to kick-off there seems a scarcity of true believers around Anfield, but neither is there defeatism. Yes, Rodgers' stock is low and trust levels are perilously near, if not on, the floor, but these fans are footballing people, they know it is early days. A few good results, a bit of momentum and then 'who knows what might happen?' is the feeling. More than most, they just need something to cheer. Today they get it as Liverpool run out 3–2 winners helped by two superb goals from the returning

Sturridge. A solid attacking performance in a match dominated by Liverpool brings three valuable points and a lifeline for the embattled Rodgers. For Villa another season fighting the drop looks likely. A dreary thought for such a proud and historic club.

Imbued by the victory Rodgers comes out fighting in the media. He talks of the silly hysteria that pre-empted the game and of a conspiracy to remove him amongst certain people unnamed. The comments are understood to reference ex-players. Rodgers has played his 'the whole world is against us' psychology card. Yet one swallow doesn't make a summer and Liverpool have not emerged from their dark night just yet, not with away trips awaiting in October to Everton, Tottenham Hotspur and Chelsea. By Halloween it will either be time to come out from under the covers or to roll over and hide. Trick or treat?

BLOOD BROTHERS

'So did y'hear the story of the Johnstone twins? As like each other as two new pins, of one womb born, on the self-same day, how one was kept and one given away?' — Blood Brothers, Willy Russell

Everton FC had already won the recently inaugurated English League in 1891 before Liverpool FC had even been born. The Blues had been founder members of the League, along with eleven other clubs in 1888. Then in 1892, a moment of fate occurred. The club's owners and administrators had a quarrel and Everton left their home on Anfield Road and moved half a mile away across Stanley Park to their new base, Goodison Park. What they left behind was soon to become Liverpool FC.

Everton FC had originally been formed by a local Methodist church, St Domingo's, with the club starting life as 'St Domingo's FC'. Not long after, the name was changed to reflect the broader catchment area. As one walks from Liverpool City towards Anfield or Goodison one passes along the Everton Road and through the borough of Everton. It was an obvious name to choose. Back then the club president was a man named John Houlding, who had been the Lord Mayor of Liverpool. He arranged with some local land owners, the Orrell brothers, to lease land at Anfield Road that would become Everton's new home ground and upon which they could cater for the mushrooming crowds that were eager to see the games. Houlding himself lived on Anfield Road and owned a local public house, the Sandon House Hotel. Before matches the team would get changed in the Sandon and then trot 100 metres to the ground to play the game. With the development of the stadium in mind, Houlding bought Anfield from the Orrells and when the lease came up for review with Everton FC, he looked to increase the rent. In today's business world this would be described as a 'conflict of interest'. Everton's board saw things no differently. They took umbrage and in March 1892, Everton FC decided to leave Anfield Road and make the short move across the Park. Everton's crest depicts the Everton Lock-Up, a small round tower with a coned roof, built in 1787 and located on Everton Brow, close to Anfield. These Georgian lock-ups were used by local Justices of the Peace to house drunkards and criminals overnight. No doubt the departing Everton board contemplated the lock-up as being a suitable home for John Houlding and his cohorts.

Houlding was miffed. He had done no wrong. It was obvious to any businessman that the rental levels should increase. The facilities had improved and time had passed. What remained were three players, a discarded blue and white football kit and a football pitch complete with newly built stands. What to do now? There was only one thing for it, start again. Do it better. And so Liverpool FC was born in March 1892, taking Anfield as its home. One child had left the womb and now it was time for the other to emerge. Liverpool and Everton are twins of sorts, closer than even the one mile distance between their two stadiums would have you believe and with their separation in 1892, so began one of the fiercest and yet friendliest sibling rivalries in world football.

Siblings never grow up the same, nature and nurture conspires to always shape them uniquely. Football clubs are no different. It was the younger brother in this scenario that travelled more, achieved more, grew richer and received broader acclaim for his successes. It was he who became a sore, a blight in the eyes of the brother who stayed home. Liverpool conquered Europe and developed a global fan base. Everton refer to themselves as 'the People's Club', an insinuation that their brother had grown too flash, too cosmopolitan to be local. "This is the People's Club on Merseyside. The people on the streets support Everton," extolled David Moyes after becoming Everton manager in 2002.

Nil satis nisi optimum is Everton's club motto, 'Only the best is good enough', and Everton, as a club, have certainly striven to live by that creed. They have won nine League titles (as many as Chelsea and Manchester City combined) and five FA Cups. Under the management of Howard Kendall, Everton finished first, second, and then first again in the years from 1985 to 1987. They also appeared in four FA Cup Finals in that decade, losing two to Liverpool in 1986 and 1989. But Everton did defeat Watford 2–0 at Wembley in the Cup Final in 1984 and that allowed them a crack at Europe the year after. They would grab the chance with both hands, beating Rapid Vienna 3–1 in the European Cup Winner's Cup Final in Rotterdam, after knocking out Bayern Munich in the semis. Everton's European record would have been more illustrious had they not suffered from the five-year ban imposed on all English clubs following the Heysel stadium tragedy, involving their brother Liverpool.

Yet when tragedy came calling once more at Hillsborough in 1989, Everton Football Club and its supporters offered more support and help to Liverpool than anybody could have imagined, proving that blood, family and friendship, are always more important than a mere game of football. Roberto Martinez, the current Everton manager, spoke at the twenty-fifth Hillsborough memorial service held at Anfield in April 2014. "How can you die watching the game you love? That is not right. That is not fair. What happened afterwards was not fair or right either. To have to fight for the good name of those you lost is appalling. I know I don't have to tell you, Everton are with you. You know that." Stephen Gerrard recalled Martinez's words, "Applause resounded around Anfield. We clapped hard for Everton, in debt and gratitude." Yet make no mistake, this confrontation can be visceral. On the pitch Everton's rivalry with Liverpool is fierce and this fixture has proven the ugliest in English football with more red cards brandished and players sent off than in any other tie. Off the pitch it's a family affair, a civil war. Brother against brother, wife against husband, grandson against grandfather. Some of Liverpool's most revered players have even straddled both sides of the divide. One of them, Carragher explains, "I was Everton-mad growing up. I was a regular at all away games, but there are things about the club I can't stand now." Robbie Fowler's story was no different, "I was a proper Everton fan, I went to the games with me auld fella and me Uncle John from as young as I can remember." Both are Red till dead now. Mostly relations are civilized in the city, Blues and Reds living and working side by side. In the week before the game, hardly anything else is discussed and after the game fans of the losing team hide away, unwilling to be derided and mocked by their conquerors.

Bill Shankly understood the rivalry and wasn't shy about aiming a psychological dig in the direction of the Blues. "In my time at Anfield we always said we had the best two teams on Merseyside – Liverpool and Liverpool Reserves." Shankly went as far as to banish the colour blue from Liverpool's stadium, training ground and anywhere else he could find it, even incredibly from some of his players' houses. Liverpool's then Vice Chairman Peter Robinson, after continuous harassment from Shankly, went home to his wife and instructed, "Let's get rid of that blue carpet in the living room".

Rafa Benitez, the former Liverpool manager and a man that many would love to see take on the mantle again someday, in one of his less inspired moments, and in sheer frustration after drawing 0–0 to a defensive minded Everton team, once described the Blues as a small club. Benitez was frustrated that they had played like of one the smaller teams by shutting up shop. He was mistaken. Everton are a big club, their history and success demands that recognition. Size and stature should not be measured by wealth or financial backing alone. Yet they have lost their way in recent times, not unlike their younger brother. Like Liverpool, Everton failed to adequately grasp the commercial opportunities that the new modern era of Premiership football brought and gradually they lost competitiveness. Through a lack of investment and possibly ambition, they have stood still in time, and since those halcyon days of the eighties the trophy cabinet has only opened once more for an FA Cup triumph in 1995.

At Everton's away game to Southampton in August 2015 a plane circled overhead with a banner trailing from its tail fin that read, 'Kenwright and Co, it's time to go.' Bill Kenwright is Everton's owner and Chairman. His stewardship has seen Everton operating stably and within their means, yet the period has also seen the famous club fall behind its peers. In the same time frame, Manchester United floated on the stock market to incredible success and were then bought by the billionaire Glazer family from the United States. Liverpool are on their second set of American owners and Arsenal have had Russian and US billionaire investors. Chelsea have been bought by the Russian billionaire Abramovich and Manchester City are now bankrolled by the endless riches of Abu Dhabi's Sheikh Mansour along with a Chinese minority investment. While Liverpool have just about clung on to the coat tails of those ahead, Everton have been left behind. Their fans long for a new stadium to replace the crumbling Goodison Park but Kenwright has been unable to get the right backing or deal. From this perspective, it is all too easy to understand the ire of the Everton fans who hired the bi-plane for its south coast fly by. Kenwright, a local lad made good and now a CBE, made his money as a West End theatre producer and has an array of long running hits to his name, including *Joseph and his Amazing Technicolor Dreamcoat*, *Guys and Dolls* and *Cabaret*. His best known, longest running and probably most successful production, has been that of Willy Russell's *Blood Brothers*. A story set in Liverpool, of two fraternal twin boys, separated at birth, whose life paths take them in different directions until eventually they entwine again in bitter rivalry. I've yet to see the production but I do wonder if, on stage, one brother wears blue and the other red?

THE TRIAL OF BRENDAN RODGERS

Juror #6: "You think he's not guilty, huh?"
Juror #8: "I don't know. It's possible."
Twelve Angry Men – Sidney Lumet

It's the morning of the Merseyside derby, Sunday 4th October. Cold, crisp and sunny. In weather like this I prefer to walk from town to the stadium. A nice forty-five-minute uphill stretch of the legs to shake off the cobwebs. My son moans, "Can we not get a bus or a taxi?" I keep walking. I like to share this time with him, talk with him, about him. I try to listen, allow space for his thoughts to develop. Today though, it's all football talk. Reports have been swirling in the gossipy air; if the Reds lose the derby then Rodgers will be fired.

If victory at home to Villa restored a glimmer of hope to Reds fans, then it quickly evaporated a few days later after another disappointing display, this time in the Europa League at home to Swiss minnows FC Sion, the game ending 1–1. Any recovery had been porcelain-fragile.

Everton away is a tough fixture at any time, but coming now, well it's taken on monumental importance. "If we lose today it could be the end of Rodgers," I say. "Good," replies my son quickly and then he follows up with, "Well I don't want to lose, but if it means the end of Rodgers, well then that's good."

I know already that my son wants a change, he's been clear on that for a while, probably since the end of last season, since Stoke. Me, I'm caught in the middle somewhere, I like Rodgers and I can't quite work out whether he can pull himself out of the mire or not. I'm sure he has managerial quality, he's proven that, yet in the back of my mind I've always sensed that when Gerrard slipped, so too did Rodger's golden opportunity to become a Liverpool legend.

The very same year, in 2014, the same opportunity presented itself to Diego Simeone and his Atletico Madrid team in Spain. They somehow got over the line, beating Barcelona and Real Madrid to the title, after waiting 18 years to do so. All across Europe and around the world fans had cheered on both Atletico and Liverpool in their pursuit of glory. Both had represented romantic, nostalgic football, days of yore. Where Atletico pushed on and built on success, Liverpool once again blew it and retreated backwards. Now with Suarez, Gerrard and Sterling gone and Sturridge always injured, it was hard to see how Rodgers could get back to those highs, get as golden an opportunity again. He had scaled too high too soon. The next climb would be slow and gradual yet it felt that some magical aura had evaporated. Did anyone have the patience and will to go again, together?

Yet Rodgers and his team had made us dream in those breathtaking days. "Do you not remember the Chelsea game, when we nearly did it? Do you not remember how we felt about Rodgers then? He was Shanklyesque," I say to my son. He looks at me with a smile.

"I do Dad, but that's gone and so are Suarez and Stevie. Remember Stoke. Remember West Ham this year, Norwich too. Sion. Carlisle." I marvel at the clarity of youth, sentiment absent from clinical assessment.

"Yes, I remember all of those miserable games, who wouldn't," and the truth is I remember more besides. The Villa semi-final, Real Madrid at Anfield, Crystal Palace at Anfield. Such a lengthy list tells its own tale, as do the statistics. Percentage possession of the ball in games has fallen from 60 per cent down to 50 per cent. The goals have dried up, the defending is shambolic. We have no width and our number of crosses into the box is the second lowest in the League. No wonder Rodgers admits that we have lost our identity.

"And what about the signings?" he asks. "What a waste of money!"

Rodgers has overseen the spending of nearly £300 million on new signings in his time and recovered roughly £200 million in sales. That's £100 million net spend over three and half seasons. Less than £30 million net spend a year is not going to threaten the big boys, so on this issue I'm very sympathetic. He's been governed by a Transfer Committee so it's hard to know who is at fault, if anyone. With a smaller budget, Liverpool can't afford any mistakes. Buying players is an imperfect science. Some will fail, it's inevitable. The bigger boys can hide their failures, they just loan them out and buy somebody else. For Liverpool, a hole is left. Additionally, without year in and year out Champions League football to offer, Liverpool's buys have been from the second tier of talent, or from the younger unproven ranks where the hope is that a rough diamond can be unearthed and polished up shiny.

"They are not as bad as the media would have us believe," I respond, "for them a player is either great or terrible, no middle ground, I don't buy that. Most of them are very young and new to English football. In the old days, a player would get two to three years to prove themselves. Look at Henderson, he started very slowly for a year or two and now he's our captain, first name on the team sheet. Liverpool are afforded no slip-ups, because we are chasing the pack and our budget is limited. The big boys, they can spend freely, make mistakes and they don't seem to matter, because with the law of averages, if they spend enough money they'll find some good players."

"Which mistakes?" he asks, unconvinced.

"Well Chelsea bought big on DeBruyne, Van Ginkel, Schurrle, Salah, Cuadrado – all good players, but all gone now or on loan. That's not to mention Torres for £50 million and Shevchenko for £30 million, both relative failures."

"Okay," he replies, "and City?"

I think for a bit and reply, "Jo, Sinclair, Robinho, Boateng, Rodwell, Mangala, Savic, Jovetic."

"United?"

"Di Maria for £65 million – for twelve months football? Ferguson bought well except for maybe Anderson, Zaha, Kagawa and you may never have heard of the *amazing* £8 million Bebe." He smiles and confirms that no, he hadn't heard of Bebe, not till now and my point is proven.

"Okay, so who has been good for us?" he asks.

"Well let's start at the back," I reply. "For all the criticism that Mignolet [£9m] gets, he is still very high in the clean sheets table and also he is one of the best shot stoppers in the League. I like him even if I'm nearly alone in that department."

"Yeah, me too," my son replies, "but he's no Courtois [Chelsea's keeper]" he continues.

"At the back I like Sakho [£17m]. I really like Clyne [£10m] and I think Moreno [£10m] can get better. What a signing young Joe Gomez [£3.5m] looks like, he's only a baby, only six or seven years older than you for God's sake. Lovren [£20m] has failed but I'm still convinced there is a quality centre half hiding in there somewhere, waiting to burst out, if he could stop tripping over himself. By the way few were better than Ferguson at buying centre halves – Ferdinand, Pallister, Bruce – but they all took time to settle, years even. It's a very tough position in the modern attack-focused game."

"Yes," he replies, "I agree with most of those, except there is no way that Lovren will ever make it, he's awful."

"Midfield, I like Lallana [£26m] but he's been blighted with injury and it's never really got going for him. Coutinho, well we know that he's the signing of the decade, bought for £8 million, probably worth £50 million and more now, you can't argue with that. Emre Can [£10m], only twenty and already a German International, he's a quality buy too."

"Can and Coutinho – yes," he agrees, "Lallana – no, not consistent enough."

"What about Joe Allen [£15m] though? What a waste of money that was," he continues with disdain. I can't disagree on this one, he's been average at best. One of Rodgers' earliest signings, having played for him at Swansea, Allen was unwisely given the moniker 'the Welsh Xavi' (Xavi being one of the greatest Spanish and Barcelona players of all time and the master of controlling midfield and the tempo of a game) by Rodgers and like a colossal weight it hung. Many Liverpool fans have grown to dislike Rodgers for what they see as his excessive hyperbole and Allen was a prime example. He could never be compared to such a master of the game. That said, and to be fair, he is another player whose time at Liverpool has been blighted by injury.

"And what about the new guys, they are hardly doing the business either, are they?"

"It's probably too early to judge them," I respond, "let's see at the end of the year who has done what. Benteke [£32m] looks good to me and it's too early to write off a young foreign player like Firmino [£29m], I'd only judge him next year to be honest."

"I'd score more than Origi [£10m]" he says laughing and here I agree, I can't see it in this player, he has a 'Bambi-on-ice' feel to him, yet he is only twenty years old and it's a new environment.

What is clear though is that Rodgers is right about one thing, this team needs time. It is full of players glued together over the last two years, full of youth trying to find their feet in a red-hot cauldron.

"And what's happened to Markovic [£20m]? If he was here, I'd have him starting in the team," my son continues.

"Yes, I can't work that one out really, all very odd," I reply. The purchase of twenty-one-year-old Serbian Lazar Markovic was a peculiar case indeed. Bought from Benfica in the summer of 2014, he fitted perfectly with FSG's desired policy of buying young players and developing them into better, more rounded and ultimately more valuable players. This was their way of 'boxing clever' against the muscled financial clout of the big four. If an inspiring coach/manager could get more than the sum of the parts, then success could follow. Markovic had performed extremely well as a young twenty-year-old winger, helping Benfica to the Europa League Final in his final days in Portugal. Liverpool had managed to pry him away from other very interested suitors and his future looked bright. With the extremely congested fixture list that six guaranteed games in the Europa League would bring, it had seemed logical that Markovic would become a valuable squad member in 2015/16 and that he would only blossom further. But no, instead of that logical plan, it was decided to loan the young prospect to Besiktas of Turkey, only twelve months after being signed for the sizeable chunk of £20 million. It seemed that a chasm existed between whoever was in charge of signing the players and Rodgers, whose job it was to select the team. Twenty million pounds was a lot of money to send to Turkey on a crusade, when performances were needed here and now in England. Hard logic to fathom, from either a footballing or financial perspective.

Even though I like Rodgers, I do worry about his erratic track record with identifying talent. He wanted to sell Henderson in his first year at the club and now he's his captain. He wanted to sign an ageing Clint Dempsey (who eventually moved to Seattle in the North American Major League) instead of Daniel Sturridge. On the pro side though, Rodgers helped develop Suarez into a penalty box predator and also nourished Raheem Sterling's talent to the point where he was sold for £49 million.

He reinvented Steve Gerrard as a defensive midfielder in the near-title-winning campaign. These are but a few examples of his man management and coaching ability and it seems that the current squad still speak well of him and play for him. Rodgers commented following his time at Reading and Swansea about having to make decisions on players more quickly, maybe he had accelerated this process just a little too much I wondered.

"When the old owners were threatening to sack Rafa Benitez, there were fan marches in protest," I tell my son. "Hundreds and hundreds would march before the games, holding aloft a large framed photograph of Rafa, in the style of the Ayatollah icons held aloft in Iran. He was a god at that time. When you think about it, Rafa led us to wins against all the great clubs of Europe. We won in Barcelona, in Madrid, in Milan against both of the Milanese giants. We beat Chelsea in two European Cup semifinals – even with all of their riches." When I think of what Rafa did, I do wonder whether we can or should endure any longer with Rodgers. There are no fan marches today.

"You didn't see a lot of those games, or you were too young to understand, but Rafa made us great again. No team in Europe wanted to play us. We are so far from that now. In the end it's all down to players," I tell my son. "It's all on the pitch, you need star quality to be better than the opposition. And a manager requires the stature, and the presence to be able to attract them. Rafa signs Torres, Rodgers signs Borini. Rafa signs Alonso, Rodgers signs Allen. Rafa brings us to two European Cup Finals, Rodgers guides us to fifty-fifth in the UEFA rankings."

With this fact I manage to defeat most of my earlier arguments and I see with crystal clarity that we've been buying squad players, not stars, not players who could travel around Europe and strike fear into any opposition.

"If they change him, they must have somebody lined up. Who would you like?" I ask.

"Klopp," comes the immediate reply.

My son loves the players of Klopp's successful Borussia Dortmund era and they populate a lot of his PlayStation teams – Lewandowski, Reus, Gundogan and Hummels – all unknown players turned into superstars under the German's guidance.

"Who would you pick?" he turns the question on me. Even in spite of what seems to me to be the damning evidence that compels a change, I find it hard to say I want anybody. I would love Klopp, yet I hate to see Liverpool managers fired, it's always better if they retire gracefully and successfully, just like the old days. You want every Liverpool manager to say goodbye as the cloth is falling from a statue newly erected in their honour. But these are new days and that hasn't happened for a while. Shankly spoke about upgrading his players in his diary, serialised during the summer of 1962 in the Liverpool Echo, and if this is part of the manager's playbook, then it must be an option for the owners too. Would Klopp or Ancelotti be an upgrade on Rodgers? Both are proven winners and winning is proven to inspire even more winning, it's a scientific fact. Rodgers was an unproven gamble, one that now appears to have failed.

"I hope we win today, win at Spurs, then at Chelsea and that Rodgers guides us back into the Champions League. Win one of the cups along the way, preferably the Europa League, then the rest of Europe will take some notice of us again. But if all that doesn't work, give me Klopp," I eventually reply.

"Yeah, right, keep dreaming."

As we approach the ground our jury is being called for judgement. The evidence seems clear and just as in the Henry Fonda movie *Twelve Angry Men*, I think I've been won over by the weight of proof proffered by my son's clear perspective. But we weren't two angry men, not even an angry man and a boy. We were worse than that, we were two apathetic fans and this was the most damning indictment of all. The hope had been drained from us, game by game, limp performance by limp performance and that could only result in one outcome, and deliver one verdict.

The gathering blue and red fans close all around us and we are reminded, if we needed reminding, that the plight of Liverpool's manager can be forgotten for the next few hours, a stay of execution has been granted. Right now, there is a Merseyside derby to be battled for, civil war is in the offing.

THE KING IS DEAD

'Every new beginning comes from some other beginning's end.' – *Seneca*

Sunshine bathes most of Goodison Park and the home crowd is in full voice. The atmosphere is as loud and frenetic as I've witnessed for a Merseyside derby at Everton. The home fans can smell blood and hope is high that their boys in blue can take advantage of any Liverpool vulnerability. Talk before the game is of how well the Toffees are playing and of how poor Liverpool have become, yet the teams are separated in the table by only one point in Everton's favour.

Liverpool's team and 3-5-2 formation is unchanged from that which beat Villa at home the week before. Mignolet in goal, three center backs in Skrtel, Sakho and Can. Two wing backs, Moreno and Clyne. Milner and Lucas in midfield, with Coutinho in front of the two strikers, Ings and Sturridge. Henderson, Benteke and Firmino are still injured. It's the first time in thirty years that Liverpool enter a derby with no Scouser in their team.

Rodgers' Liverpool are up for the scrap and despite dominating early proceedings, just can't break the deadlock. As the half drifts onwards Everton lift their game with the help of a vociferous home crowd and now it's the Blues who start to take control. Barkley turns neatly and Lucas takes him down midway inside the Liverpool half. Barkley takes the free kick himself and puts a vicious curling zip on the ball as it travels North to South, head-high into the Liverpool box. Naismith rises unchallenged near the penalty spot and whips a point-blank header goal-bound. It must be the opening goal but no, incredibly Mignolet flings a strong left hand to meet the bullet header and somehow manages to flip the ball up and over his crossbar for an Everton corner. It's a superb save. Shortly after, Everton's McCarthy meets a deflected Deulofeu cross with a stinging shot from inside the Liverpool box and again Mignolet makes a stunning save to keep the game level.

Liverpool, who have been on top for much of the first half, are now suddenly on the rack. But they gather themselves and after a sweeping counter-attack they win a corner. An in swinger from Milner is met by Danny Ings, unmarked inside the Everton box, and from two yards out he heads the ball down and into the back of the net. The Liverpool fans erupt with joy. A solid fighting first-half display has been rewarded and maybe, just maybe, this is the start of something. A win away in the derby can be season defining. The impetus provided can prove inspirational. But as a Liverpool fan I should know not to count my chickens, I should know not to count on anything at all. Only a few minutes later and on the stroke of half-time, Liverpool's defence implodes again. Can makes a mess of a Deulofeu cross and whacks it straight into the path of Everton's big striker Lukaku, who in the blink of an eye, controls the ricocheting ball and dispatches it gleefully into the back of the Liverpool net. 1–1 .The half-time whistle blows.

The second half passes with a lot of huff and puff, a little squabbling, some fighting and a few half-chances. The last fifteen minutes see Everton finish on top but never really threaten to win the game. And so the 225th Merseyside derby finishes all square at 1–1. A point at Goodison Park is never a bad outcome, but leaving the ground, we can't help but feel that with a little more composure and ambition, all three points could have been collected. What is clear though, is that the players are still fighting for Rodgers. Nobody has given up. He retains his unbeaten record in this most local of all local fixtures.

Back in the city we head for some afternoon lunch and listen to the post-match interviews. Rodgers is defiant in his call for more time; "If we are to replicate what we did two years ago, we will have to build something. That will take time, whether it is me or somebody else. That is frustrating for the supporters, but there are new players. For me, when you are at such a huge club, you are always going to get other managers linked with your club. It is where you are, the level. I have never felt anything other than secure and that is not being complacent. I was brought here to do a job, I signed a new deal and I think the owners, as much as anyone, know the rebuilding that needs to be taken and they know that takes time unfortunately."

Earlier in the week Rodgers was on the front foot, highlighting his proven abilities. "I know how to manage top players. If you give me the tools, I'll do the work. There are very short memories in football, the team was in eighth place when I got here. We built a team to excite people throughout European football that should have won the League. All the good work gets forgotten. That's how it works."

It's not true though, no Liverpool fan has forgotten the good work, but it's the subsequent season of relegation form that is harder to forget. Directions, trends, momentum are key tools of analysis in any boardroom and the current trajectory won't have been lost on owners FSG. Nobody can say for sure if the knife has reached the bottom.

Still, it's hard to find anything wrong with what Rodgers says after the game and I find myself nodding in agreement at the TV. Yet our manager's body language appears jaded, he looks tired and even though he has repeated on many occasions that he is not under pressure, he looks it. It's hard to know how secure he is, the fans are on the brink and need more to cheer about than one win in the last nine games. The last two League games have been more encouraging and if only we could get some of our key players back fit, well, who knows? The owners till now have been remarkably quiet, as is their style, it's hard to know how much credit Rodgers has left in reserve with them.

At six thirty p.m., three hours after the game, we find out. Arsenal have been playing in the late afternoon fixture, beating Man United 3–0 at the Emirates, and that has cheered us up no end. We'll take Arsenal over United any day of the century. During the post-match analysis SKY TV's Ed Chamberlain interrupts the broadcast with breaking news. "Brendan Rodgers has left Liverpool; Brendan Rodgers is no longer the Liverpool manager."

A statement from Liverpool's owners is read out by Chamberlain;

'We would like to place on record our sincere thanks to Brendan Rodgers for the significant contribution made to the club and express our gratitude for the hard work and commitment. Although this has been a difficult decision, we believe it provides us with the best opportunity for success on

the pitch. Ambition and winning are at the heart of what we want to bring to Liverpool and we believe this change gives us the best opportunity to deliver it. The search for a new manager is underway and we hope to make an appointment in a decisive and timely manner.'

The studio pundits, who include two former Liverpool greats, Graeme Souness and Jamie Carragher as well as the former Arsenal star Thierry Henry, all show visible shock. Gathering their thoughts they respond to the news. Carragher appears angry. "The owners' track record of making decisions over the last two or three years has not been good enough, it's been miles off. He was maybe fortunate by staying on at the end of last season. His staff moved on, new staff came in, he's spent £80 million and then seven games later Liverpool are changing a manager – that's what I don't like about it. Just do it in the summer, if that's the situation. It finished poorly if you look at the semi-final against Aston Villa, games against Hull, Palace and then that finish at Stoke. So he was lucky to keep his job. I'd prefer them to have done it in the summer, but he's been there three years, he hasn't won a trophy and they've played Champions League football once. That's not good enough for Liverpool."

Then maybe tellingly, Souness wonders why FSG appointed the man from Northern Ireland at all, implying that Rodgers was too inexperienced and lacked a winning track record. He had been a big gamble. "With all due respect to Brendan Rodgers, I just don't see how they gave him the job in the first place, they are replacing Kenny, he wins the League Cup and if it hadn't been for Petr Cech, they might have won the FA Cup against Chelsea." Souness continues questioning FSG's motives, "They take big bets on young players, hoping they will develop them into good or top players and sell them at a profit, it hurts me to say this, I think Liverpool have become a selling club."

Carragher continues: "Liverpool have won one Carling Cup in ten years, Liverpool are becoming Tottenham, they think they are a big club, but the real big clubs are not worried about them or who they buy, or what they're going to do. I'm not just blaming Brendan Rodgers and this set of players. What are these owners of the club going to do to get Liverpool back where they need to be?"

Thierry Henry chimes in and claims that FSG are only 'using the

Liverpool brand' for commercial purposes and Liverpool are 'not a big team anymore'.

So after three years and one hundred and twenty-five days in charge, Brendan Rodgers is gone and five years into the FSG reign it seems that the club is regressing again. I feel numb, saddened, this feels like a bereavement in some odd way. My son, whilst not expressing happiness, believes it is the right thing. I'm not quite there yet, I'm in shock, a period of grieving will follow before I can resolve whether it is the correct decision or not. What FSG do next will also be critical, they have used the word 'opportunity' twice in their statement and that tells me that they already have a new man in mind, one whom they believe to be an upgrade. Whoever is appointed to succeed Rodgers will shine a light on the true level of their ambition, I hope it is sky-high, as high as ours.

Liverpool played well in the derby and that made the timing of the decision taken later that evening somewhat surprising. I've always liked Rodgers and what he stood for, I think most Reds fans did. He wanted our football to be played the proper way, the Liverpool Way, and he possessed lots of, what Steven Gerrard described simply as, 'class and dignity'. I loved the roller-coaster ride he took us on in 2014. When Brendan arrived, we had just witnessed one of the most abject seasons ever from a Reds team, when Liverpool collected the lowest percentage of points available since 1953/54, fifty-eight years before. Only fifty-two points were amassed from the hundred and fourteen available (46%), with the Reds losing fourteen of thirty-eight games. Forty-seven goals scored and forty conceded may have been the worst statistic of all. Most tellingly, the team had no style or identity. An ill-conceived idea about playing wingers with a tall centre forward had failed miserably. That wasn't Liverpool. This was a team, let us not forget, that included Gerrard and Suarez.

It could be argued, with maybe a grain of truth, that Suarez made the Rodgers reign look better than it was but, that said, every great manager has had great players. There is more truth in the fact that Rodgers made Suarez a better player than he had been before. Suarez acknowledged this when the South American superstar striker said: "He is one of the best coaches in Europe. If it was not for Brendan, then I know I would not be the same player that you see at Barcelona today. Such a big part of my education is down to him and his management. Of course, he works to make the team stronger but he really works on a one-to-one level with the players. He will sit down with each player at the club, and work on where you can improve, where you can exploit opposition, he leaves nothing to chance. He is a very intelligent man. If the players at his next club listen to his words, they will become better players for sure." Suarez was constantly urged by Rodgers to spend more time in the danger zones, and less outside the box. The golden results of his advice shone for all to see.

It was also Rodgers who transformed Gerrard into a deep-lying midfielder, in doing so, extending his playing career. Maybe he should have gone the whole hog and converted him into a centre half, who knows? It was Rodgers who taught Sterling how to 'break the line', how to time his runs beyond the defence. Sterling would say, "He's one that I definitely learnt a lot off, in terms of playing me in different positions, making me understand the roles and maturing in certain systems. He gave me a lot of confidence as well." It was Rodgers who built a team that scored 101 league goals (fifty-four more than the year before he joined), and went so close, closer than any Liverpool manager over those long twenty-six years. For that he was voted Manager of the Year in 2014 by his peers, the League Managers Association. For sure, the League was lost in defence but hopefully as Rodgers matures as a manager he can create teams capable of winning at both ends of the pitch. Given time, he may have ended the long wait and in hindsight it's clear he left behind a healthy collection of both youthful and experienced players. In the cold shadows of the departed it was always going to take time for him to rebuild a team without Gerrard, Suarez, Carragher and Sterling. Maybe with more of that priceless commodity he could have pulled it off? Now, we will never know.

When the initial shock subsides, we both agree, that despite all that had been positive, it has been coming. The fizz has gone, he has been a dead man walking for some time now and only a big start to the campaign could have saved him. That wasn't achieved by the players. FSG are not afraid to make hard decisions. As owners of the Boston Red Sox baseball team, they have fired five general managers and also five coaches in the last ten years. They have now replaced three Liverpool managers in Hodgson, Dalglish and Rodgers (the latter two having been FSG appointments) in five years of ownership. Making the right decisions is more important. It seems clear that their next appointment needs to prove successful if Liverpool are ever to play catch-up on their rivals. The Reds can't waste any more time.

As the story unfolds, former Liverpool players, too, have their say.

Jamie Redknapp is supportive, "The football Liverpool played at times was fantastic. You could say that was because he had Luis Suarez, but he certainly gave him the right role. He handled every situation. He's had to deal with Raheem Sterling leaving the club, he has lost Steven Gerrard this season, so he's had a lot to deal with, to a certain extent. But as soon as things start to go wrong, and there was a clamour for a change at the club with the fans, it becomes very difficult for you." John Aldridge is surprised at how rapidly events unfolded, "I thought Brendan was going to be given more time to turn it around, but you move on, that's what football is all about. It's a result business and Liverpool has a massive stand to fill with nearly 10,000 more seats and they have to get the feel-good factor back, maybe that might have tipped the balance."

Later that week we hear from Brendan Rodgers himself, as he issues his own statement via the League Managers Association.

'I am, of course, incredibly disappointed to be leaving Liverpool Football Club. It has been both an honour and a privilege to manage one of the game's great clubs for the last three years. I have worked every day to represent the club to the best of my ability, to develop both individual players and a team that the club's magnificent fans can be proud of. There have been some very memorable moments during my time at Liverpool and I would like to thank all of the players for their hard work and commitment. The current squad is one in transition, but they have some real talent and are showing a strong sense of togetherness. I expect to see them continue to grow and develop over the coming weeks and I wish them and my successor well for the rest of the season. Liverpool has a magnificent football heritage and I have nothing but respect and admiration for the history, tradition and values that make the city and the club so exceptional. As well as my players, I would like to thank everyone connected with the club; Fenway Sports Group, the Liverpool directors, in particular Ian Ayre, my

coaching staff, the staff throughout the club, the volunteers, the Academy staff and its young players and of course the amazing Liverpool fans for their unwavering support, passion and dedication which has made my time at the club so special. Finally, I would like to give a special mention to John W. Henry, Tom Werner and Mike Gordon. They gave me this great opportunity and even though we will no longer be working together I am sure our relationship and friendship will continue into the future.'

Good man Brendan, honourable to the last. Still, all I can think of is how unfortunate it is. In football, it is always the manager who is pushed out in front of the firing line. Just as with sacrifices of old, the baying crowd satisfied only when blood is finally let, for blood must flow. I can't help thinking the problems lie deeper than Rodgers and that the people we should really be focusing on are sitting behind him, obscured from view. Rodgers made us dream, he came closer than the six managers before him and for that he will be remembered fondly.

AT THE END OF THE STORM

'The greatest accomplishment is not in never falling, but in rising again after you fall.' — Vince Lombardi

It was well over a year since he departed Anfield when I caught up with Brendan Rodgers. For the first few months Brendan kept a dignified silence. He didn't fill the airwaves with venom or 'woe is me'. He stayed out of the limelight, got on with his life, and left Liverpool FC to get on with theirs.

In May 2016, eight months after leaving Anfield, Rodgers walked into another storied home, Celtic Park. The man from Carnlough, Co Antrim was fulfilling a boyhood wish as he donned the mantle of manager of Celtic Football Club. By the end of August, after six play-off games, Rodgers and his new team had secured their berth in the group stages of the Champions League and Celtic were back in the big time. As the season progressed his team would take on, and beat, all-comers. By February 2017 a place in history beckoned. With the league title already secure, bar the mathematics, an even bigger achievement seemed plausible. The opportunity to go the entire season undefeated. Twenty-six games played, twenty-five wins, one draw, no defeats – it was still possible. No team in Scottish history had ever managed the task. Few anywhere had. Since World War II less than ten teams in Europe had pulled it off, these of course including Arsenal's Invincibles.

Further records were up for grabs. Having already lifted the Scottish League Cup, Rodgers' team could also become only the fourth Celtic side ever to win the domestic treble. They were on target to surpass: most goals scored in a season (116), most points collected (103) and most wins (thirty-three). So, it seems there is life after Liverpool after all. I hope Rodgers bags the lot, he deserves it.

Rodgers tells me of his ambitions. "Obviously to be the very best that I can be. I enjoy new experiences. Liverpool was the first time in my life where I was in a position for more than three years. I've always felt the need to maybe move and look to a new challenge you know. I entered into my fourth season at Liverpool and that was the longest I have been in a position. That was how much I enjoyed the challenge of Liverpool. For me, now, I love my life here, my experiences at Liverpool have made me a better manger at Celtic. It's an incredible historic club Glasgow Celtic, it's a huge club, it's rich in its history, and its fan base. It's not rich in financial terms, in terms of where clubs in the Premier League are. I'm really enjoying coaching again. I'm developing players, seeing an improvement in players. I've been given the responsibility to be the architect of a club again. I work best when I am at a club where the ownership and the board put total trust in my work, and here I was able to come in and impose my way of working on it straight away. What the future holds? I never think so much about that now. I think my ambition is to be the best that I can possibly be, whichever club I am at. To leave a legacy with each club in terms of making enjoyment for supporters."

Brendan had touched on the shorter tenures of modern football managers, all eggs in the here and now, the future being a dirty word. I enquired as to how he thought it affected the job, the task at hand. "I have had a huge admiration for the work of Bill Shankly, Bob Paisley and those really successful managers. Coming here you felt a bit more of what Jock Stein was like in his period but the years that those guys lasted in clubs, that's long gone. It doesn't happen anymore. Everything about modern football is very short-termism. What you have to try and do is make that impact as quick as you can, be the best that you can be, knowing that sometime the supporters will get tired of you and maybe players get tired of you, so as long as you do your best, and go to each challenge and be as positive as you can."

When Rodgers took over at Liverpool he inherited a can of worms. The short tenures of both Hodgson and Dalglish meant that the club had no real plan for the future. 'Moneyball' had failed and the Director of Football Strategy Damien Comolli's head had rolled for it. The team had no discernible style of play and had finished eighth the season before. It had been a woeful season. Liverpool had only managed six home wins all year. A meagre 46 per cent of available points had been won following fourteen defeats, this the worst return since 1954. The team included Suarez, Gerrard, Carroll, Downing and Henderson, all big names, yet performances were awful. Something wasn't working.

Within two years he was chasing the title, leading Liverpool to their fourth best ever points achieved/available percentage (in the top tier), his team scoring over one hundred goals, yet conceding fifty at the back. Rodgers recounted to me how the story had unfolded. "The first six months of my time there we were creating something that took a little bit of time to get going. The second part of the season, our first season, we started to show that potential, and then the second season we were on this magic carpet ride of performances and attacking football that was lauded throughout Europe."

Then came Chelsea at home. "We played very, very well in the game. We obviously had a disappointment just right before half time, and then in the second half what happens is we chase the game. It becomes too emotional for us. We try to make up for what happened in the first half. And Chelsea defended really well. They were deep in the game, and we just couldn't make the breakthrough. It was a huge disappointment, and that was the game that changed it for us no doubt. But that season was so emotional, I'll always carry that with me, and to go to a club like Liverpool, to impose the style which we created, to make the supporters dream. I felt then, it was just about the time factor in terms of looking to roll that out again. What I take away from that is that at least my team, we made the supporters happy, we made them believe and we made them dream, that we could do it. Everyone talks about the pressure of the last ten games, and how it works, but in our last fourteen games of that season, we won twelve games, and we only drew one and lost one. Obviously the loss was the killer one, and everyone looks at that. Would I have done anything differently? I wouldn't. We played really well in that game."

"How hard will it be for Liverpool to break through, you've been there, seen the obstacles that get bigger every year?" I ask him.

"It's extremely difficult, because like you say, the finances now in the game allows not just the top teams but the teams below that to compete. That season that we finished runners-up, we obviously had no European football. That gave us a chance to coach the players the best we possibly could. We spent a lot of time on the training ground working on ways of how to win games, and then if we got stuck we would change systems and it took a lot of coaching time and players improved."

"And the players have to be the right ones, they have to want to develop, to learn," I suggest.

"If you are not in sole charge of bringing players in, there are players coming in maybe without the profile you want. I like players that are coachable. Players that want to improve, players that want to be better," Brendan continues, "normally those types of players, they are good people, they want to improve, they want to be better, they recognise their failures and where they can learn and improve, and those are the types of players that I work best with. Maybe Suarez was very spirited but he wasn't temperamental, he was spirited. He loved football, he wanted to improve, he wanted to be better, and what we created at Liverpool in terms of a team made him and some of the other players better and he obviously recognised that. But unfortunately, I'm not so good with the maverick type player because my teams are very much based around the team, they are not reliant on one player. Of course, certain players will flourish in the style I impose on the teams, and sometimes it's more the attacking type players, and in my time at Liverpool, I would like to think that Luis progressed. When I first came in people pointed the finger that he didn't score so many goals and needed too many chances, but in the couple of years with me he got fifty-plus goals, we asked him to get into certain areas on the field, you know, in order to bring his talents through. So, like Sturridge, Coutinho, Sterling, these players all were able to develop within the structure with which we played, and for that you need a certain type of mentality. Then when you get into the Champions League element you are playing a lot of games, there's less coaching time, and there's maybe a little less time for the players to improve, so you are looking at more ready-made players."

"So it's getting tougher and tougher?"

"Listen, there's no doubt I think Liverpool will win the league at some point but of course, year on year, it gets more difficult you know. Going back to the years when they were successful, Liverpool spent money, bought quality players. In the seventies and eighties, if there was a big transfer fee, then that was just as likely to be Liverpool as anybody else. At the beginning of the Premier League the money just spewed out, so other teams have become stronger. It's such an incredible club Liverpool. The joy of working there and to manage there was incredible, to travel the world to see the effect that it has all around the world, was truly incredible, but I also think there needs to be a realism, which is very difficult for supporters. Any supporter wants to see the team win and win trophies – it is, it is very, very tough. What I found in my time was that we raised the expectations to such a level that when we actually dropped down a little, it was deemed a dramatic failure. The reality was that when we went in to Liverpool the team was eighth and that was where it finished, and within two years we created a team that had gone from forty-nine goals a season to one hundred and one goals a season, and in doing so we gave the supporters that entertainment, that creativity and that hope that we could win. So, it is tough but it's a fantastic challenge and that's the great prospect when you manage Liverpool. It's an extremely difficult challenge but it's a great challenge."

Throughout our chat Rodgers is warm, gentlemanly and effusive in his respect and admiration for his former club. There are things he can't talk about and won't, as is his dignified and honourable style. He should always be respected for that. Pele said that Rodgers made Suarez a better player, but more importantly, also a better man. Rodgers smiled when reminded. "The first thing I thought of was my father. Pele was a hero for my father and to receive a compliment like that from, in my father's eyes, the greatest player ever, of course it was very humbling."

Rodgers had lost both his parents before he joined the Reds, and during his reign difficult hurdles faced him and his family in their private lives. But he never showed it, never gave less than 100 per cent to the job. "I think that no matter what is going on in your life, it's very, very difficult, especially when something as emotional as that can be in terms of parents, and things not going so well for you. Yet I've always tried to really focus on my job and when I was at Liverpool there were a number of things that were going on in the background, but I never let that background noise affect my job. I like to think that's how I've always been. You know, that whatever is happening outside, in your football life you always try to have stability, and keep as calm as you can. If you can install in players that, you always try to help them be the best person they can be, you know, and it's not just about the football, when you represent a great club like Liverpool, you are really an ambassador for the club. You have to think of others in terms of your behaviour, so yeah, it's something that always carries with me in relation to dealing with people."

They say never go back, yet I can't help thinking that Rodgers will only improve as a manager. He has an intelligence and a dignity about him that will take him a long way. So, I ask him the thorny question. "Would you go back?"

Rodgers doesn't hesitate and replies assuredly,

"Yeah. 100 per cent. I loved my time at Liverpool. I know if I went back ten years from now, I would be a better coach, a better manager for all my experience, but in particular the experiences at Liverpool. It is a club that I have a lot of affinity for. It's an absolutely remarkable club. It's a great club. Obviously it was sad how it ended, that was obviously tough, but it's life and it happens."

It's a funny old game as they say, someday… who knows?

PART III

LONG LIVE THE KING

PARADISE LOST

'O sun, to tell thee how I hate thy beams, that bring to my remembrance from what state I fell, how glorious once above thy sphere...Long is the way and hard, that out of Hell leads up to light.' —John Milton, *Paradise Lost*

With Rodgers gone, two names are whispered over and over. Klopp and Ancelotti. The majority of Reds fans hope that Klopp will be crowned, yet Ancelotti is a favoured contender too. Klopp exudes youthful drive, passion and dynamism while Ancelotti epitomises poise, class and grey-haired wisdom. Both are proven winners.

My son prefers Klopp, as do I, but he can't believe that he's even in the running. "Why would he come to Liverpool?" he asks. "We're crap." Kids are a little like the media, it's all or nothing.

"That's probably why," I respond. "It's the challenge of rebuilding an empire."

"Empire?" he asks. "That's gone."

"True," I reply, "but that doesn't mean it can't be restored. Empires rise and fall. Imagine being the man that brings back the golden years. Instant God status." My son considers this thoughtfully but says nothing.

In the history of European football, we have seen the rise and fall of a number of great footballing empires, clubs that bossed their peers at home and further afield. Real Madrid won the first European Cup in 1956 and would go on to lift the next four trophies and complete an unmatched five in a row sequence. Their second dynasty would begin at the turn of this century when they would lift three European Cups in the space of five years. Madrid hold the record for European Cup wins with ten successes by 2015. In Spain, they have led the way also, winning La Liga a record thirty-two times with Barcelona next best with twenty-three. They are, by some distance, the most successful club side in the history of European and World football.

Next best in Europe are Milan with seven European Cup wins. The Rossoneri ruled the continent from 1989 to 1994, lifting the cup three times in six years. Milan also hold eighteen Italian Scudetti, second only to, but still a long way adrift of, the Old Lady of Juventus, she cosseting a whopping thirty-three.

Three sides sit in third place with five European Cup wins: Liverpool, Barcelona and Bayern Munich.

Nobody touches Bayern Munich in Germany with their twenty-five Bundesliga wins dwarfing the next best FC Nurnberg with nine. Munich's reign in Europe came in the mid-seventies with wins in 1974, 1975 and 1976. This dominance arrived hot on the heels of the golden period of Ajax of Amsterdam, who also managed a three-in-a-row from 1971–73.

Following Munich's dominance, another red force would rise in the shape of Liverpool FC. With two UEFA Cups already collected in 1973 and 1976, Liverpool would go on to win four European Cups between 1977 and 1984. Back at home, Liverpool bolted into the distance collecting eighteen domestic league titles by the end of 1989/90, leaving Arsenal (nine) and Manchester United (seven), both trailing far behind. By any measure the Reds were imperious and dominant right across the length and breadth of their European Empire. When Bill Shankly, Liverpool's spiritual father, arrived at Liverpool FC, the club was literally in decay and lay stranded in Division Two. Yet he dreamed big. "My idea was to build Liverpool into a bastion of invincibility. Had Napoleon had that idea he would have conquered the bloody world. I wanted Liverpool to be untouchable. My idea was to build Liverpool up and up until eventually everyone would have to submit and give in." How his wishes had come to pass. Yet as Empires rise, so too do they fall.

***

Once more we watch the documentary of the Istanbul final. Gerrard rises and scores an impossible header. Running back to the centre circle he waves his arms twice, in a lifting motion, like an eagle rising from the ground. Maybe even a mythical Liver bird. My son was born one year before Istanbul but still he can relate to it, it seems tangible to him. The images still appear modern; 2005 is really not that long ago.

He can connect too with some of the team from that game, a few of them are still playing. Xabi Alonso with Bayern Munich and John Arne Riise, until recently, with Fulham. Jamie Carragher is a permanent fixture on TV in his punditry role. Steven Gerrard is the most tangible link of all. My son has watched him play in the flesh, many times. Seeing Gerrard lift the European Cup makes that success real and relevant to him. It links him to past glory and provides hope for the future. I remind him that Liverpool own that European Cup now. You get to keep it when you've won it five times. The victories before that don't mean so much to him.

It is hard for him to understand exactly how dominant Liverpool were. I can see the doubt in his eyes when I tell him that we are a 'big' club. He hasn't seen the evidence, not with his own eyes, not on the pitch anyhow. In the stands, few can match the Reds' fans; their altar, the Kop, their cathedral, Anfield. Yet, on the green turf, the crop has been thinning. It's not all doom and gloom mind you. Since their last League win in 1990, Liverpool have won nine major trophies consisting of a European Cup (2005), a UEFA Cup (2001), three FA Cups (1992, 2001 and 2006) and four League Cups (1995, 2001, 2003 and 2012). This haul alone exceeds that of most clubs over their entire history, but of course the elephant in the room is the empty space in the trophy cabinet awaiting the return of the one that Bob Paisley called 'our bread and butter', the domestic crown. Twenty-five years and counting. Waiting, still waiting.

Yet if Liverpool are a 'big' club and a footballing Empire, and of course they are, on both counts, they are also a club enduring an equally big slide. The club's average League finishing position over the last fifty years has been third, however, since 2010, that has fallen to sixth. The following table illustrates the long run form of the current seven best Premier League teams and also charts their most recent form since both 2000 and 2010.

Average Final League Position since year	1966	2000	2010
Number of years	50	16	6
Liverpool	3.3	4.4	6.0
Manchester United	5.0	2.1	2.8
Arsenal	5.2	2.8	3.5
Spurs	8.9	7.6	4.8
Everton	9.0	8.9	7.3
Chelsea	10.9	3.0	2.7
Manchester City	14.8	9.6	2.3

The ten most successful clubs in European history have been racking up League titles since Liverpool's last win in 1990. The table below makes it clear, that of all the giants, it is Liverpool who have been snoring longest.

Club	No of League Wins (since 1990)
Barcelona	13
Bayern Munich	13
Man United	13
Ajax	10
Juventus	9
Real Madrid	7
AC Milan	7
Benfica	7
Inter Milan	3
Liverpool	0

These findings are stark and the warning bells must be sounding loud and clear around Anfield. While Liverpool FC continue to decline, the competition grows even stronger, even fiercer. Ahead of the Reds sit not one good team, nor two, but four modern day behemoths. Chelsea, the two Manchester clubs, United and City, and Arsenal. On the form of the last six years, Spurs have also passed Liverpool and they are not for stopping either. How did such a lofty Empire crumble and fall so far, from European Royalty to Premier League also-rans? The answer was simple. Timing, very bad timing.

THE PERFECT STORM

'An especially bad and rare situation caused by a combination of adverse and unfavourable circumstances' – Defn: Perfect Storm – Oxford Dictionary

Two things happened in 1992 that would change the face of football forever. The English League Division One, the top tier of the domestic game, was rebranded as the Premier League, and the European Cup, the premier trophy in Europe became the Champions League. The principal motivation behind the changes was one thing, and one thing only, money.

In England, the Premier League television rights were being acquired by the new pay-per-view satellite TV company, BSkyB. Their commitment to show more live games, provide an enhanced viewing experience, and offer increased analysis and debate, were all very welcome to the average football fan, but now they were going to have to pay for the privilege. The marketing slogan was 'it's a whole new ball game' and never were truer words said. The success of the rebrand proved spectacular, with the global TV popularity of the Premier League exploding, along with the value of its TV rights, which commanded more than any other sporting tournament on the planet. In 1992, BSkyB paid £161 million for the right to show sixty live games at an average cost of £2.7 million per game. The pumps had been turned on and the money kept flowing. By 2015, the Premiership TV rights were being sold to BT Sport and BSkyB for a total combined value of £898 million, nearly £11 million per game. Most of this money has gone to the clubs and from there straight into inflated transfer fees and players' wages. It has also resulted in an influx of global talent. Today 66 per cent of the players in the Premier League are non-English born, versus just 27 per cent in 1992.

On the continent, the European Cup had become the Champions League. The rebrand was driven by the desire of members of G14, an organisation of fourteen of Europe's leading footballing superpowers (including Liverpool, Man United and Arsenal), to have a more certain exposure to European football, and the glamour and riches it brought. Previously only the winners from each domestic league secured entry to the European Cup the following year. However, with the superpower countries of England, Italy, Spain and Germany each having up to three, four or even five elite clubs, the sums didn't add up. One from four or five wasn't going to work. Football was becoming boom-time in a hi-tech media age that needed content, and the big boys sought to build global franchises to take advantage of the burgeoning financial opportunities. One appearance every couple of years on the main stage wasn't going to gild the lily. Yet the changes weren't all about money. The game needed a facelift to rid itself of the ugly tarnish of hooliganism that had tainted the seventies and eighties. In addition, the paying audience were more excited about watching Bayern Munich v AC Milan, than they were Verona v AC Milan. One you could sell, one you couldn't. So group stages were added and available qualification spaces were extended. Now in the larger expanded format, more than one team could qualify from each country. This resulted in an improved chance for the big clubs to firstly gain entry on a more consistent basis, and secondly, having qualified, to play more games, with at least six matches guaranteed. The rewards were lucrative with minimum group stage qualification payments reaching £20 million. It wasn't long before an annual ticket to the grand European ball was more sought after than FA Cup or League Cup silverware.

What all this meant was that any club who managed to be domestically successful from the start of the 1990s, effectively had a licence to print money. Enormous wealth was being derived from the improved TV deals at home and in Europe, as well as from the enhanced commercial opportunities such as shirt advertising, that the clubs could negotiate due to the increased exposure. Gate receipts improved too, from larger match day attendances. If you could peak in these times, you had it made.

Having ended their long drought, it was Ferguson and United who were in the ascendancy. For Liverpool, the opposite was true, they weren't peaking, they were plummeting. The Reds found themselves in a perfect storm. Everything was going wrong. Off the field, the disasters at Heysel and Hillsborough had laid the club and its supporters low. On the field, the team drifted, rudderless. A long and slow decline had begun.

The timing was awful. This was the moneyed era, the time to make hay. A successful team that generated major cash flows could create a virtuous cycle of continued glory, money feeding the glory, glory spewing money, and so on and so forth. However, Liverpool's continued domestic mediocrity, judged by its own extremely high standards, resulted only in stop-start progress. With each new manager came a new squad, the old plan shredded. All consistency was lost, and time and time again, the Reds would find themselves restarting from base camp in their attempts to make it back to the summit. Worse still, just thirty minutes down the Lancashire M62 Motorway, their arch-enemies had firmly grasped the opportunity, and had become the dominant force in English football.

Manchester United's timing was better than good, it was magnificent. A London Stock Exchange flotation in 1991 bolstered their coffers allowing funds for a stadium expansion and team rebuilding. Under Alex Ferguson's guidance, United won their first League title in twenty-six years, and in the process the inaugural Premier League trophy, in 1992/93. It was their eighth crown. Today, twenty-three years later, they have amassed a further twelve Premier League trophies which, cruelly for Liverpool, both coincided with and contributed to their downfall.

With the wealth that top football clubs could create, combined with the glamour and publicity that the game now attracted, a new phenomenon would appear in the early 2000s – the era of the billionaire owners, the money dopers. First came Roman Abramovich taking ownership of Chelsea in 2003. Within two years Chelsea had won the title, their first in fifty years. In the ten years from 2005 to 2015, Chelsea would spend a net £373 million in the transfer market and would lift three further titles. In 2008 Manchester City would be taken over by the Abu Dhabi billionaire Sheikh Mansour. Four years later, Manchester City would lift the title, their first in forty-four years. In the ten years to 2015, City would outdo Chelsea and spend £678 million net in the transfer market and would lift the title again in 2014 after Liverpool's late collapse.

Money alone doesn't guarantee success, but eventually enough of it will see you through. Along with the bags of dosh, it also helps to have the right manager at the helm. Chelsea could spend less of their billionaire's hoard, given they had one of the best in the business, Jose Mourinho. Manchester United were led by Sir Alex Ferguson for seventeen years, who many argue was the greatest of all time. City spent considerably more, probably for the reason that they chopped and changed managers, never fully satisfied with any of them. From 2005-2015, Manchester United would spend a net transfer sum of £286 million with Liverpool spending £280m. On the face of it those sums should have made Liverpool somewhat competitive, but they didn't. It's harder to chase success than to build upon it. United's spend added an additional layer of quality to what was an already successful squad, one that had won it all. As the best, they would attract the best, building seams of talent upon talent, success upon success. Liverpool could only look on as the gap widened.

Now, United lead the all-time table with twenty title wins, Liverpool have fallen to second with eighteen and Arsenal have thirteen. In Liverpool's frantic attempts to return to the top, new foundations were never allowed time to settle, to strengthen, and, after each false dawn, the club would again experience that horrible sinking feeling. From 2006 to 2015, two from the new big three, of United, Chelsea and City, would nearly always occupy the first and second place positions at the end of the season. The Premier League had become an exclusive VIP lounge. The only non-member to crack the top two in those ten years would be Liverpool – twice, with two second-place finishes. If the bouncers were feeling generous and allowed third place to mix with the elite, then Arsenal would find themselves sipping champagne with the VIPs. Spurs could only look on forlornly, kicking their heels in the queue having amassed just one meagre fourth place Premiership finish.

Today with Liverpool lacking the financial clout of those now firmly entrenched above them, the Reds will somehow have to act brighter, smarter and better than the rest. This will prove an enormous task. Can American owners Fenway Sports Group conjure a magic formula that works? Since their tenure began in 2010, Liverpool have slid backwards with the glorious exception of Rodgers' gatecrashed party in 2014. If my son felt Klopp was out of our league, it wasn't hard to see why. Did FSG? Did they still have the ambition to win? Did they still have the will? We only had a few rolls of the dice left to find out.

THE OUTSIDER

'It seemed funny to me that the sunset she saw from her patio and the one I saw from the back steps was the same one. Maybe the two different worlds we lived in weren't so different.' — S.E. Hinton, *The Outsiders*

It's late in the season, play-offs time. John Henry of FSG watches from the owner's seat as his team, the Boston Red Sox, go down in the final stretch to one of their dreaded foes, the Yankees. Another year of waiting has come to pass. History suggests they are cursed. Yet Henry has only owned the franchise for two years and he doesn't believe in curses, he believes in hard work and results. He believes in watching trends and following momentum. He believes in making the system work to your benefit through endless analysis and research. Find anomalies and quirks that can be utilised and taken advantage of. Knowledge is king. He knew when he acquired the Red Sox that change was needed so he backed a hunch, and hired from leftfield. In came Sabermetrics pioneer Bill James. In too came Theo Epstein, a young Yale University graduate, to become the youngest general manager in Major League Baseball history. Here now, with the taste of defeat in his mouth, he keeps calm in the knowledge that it's early days. Still, it will be hard to lift everyone's spirits after going so close, only to fall short yet again. The most galling part is that defeat could have been avoided. If only his coach had stuck to the game plan. For they have a plan, a detailed plan. It is October 2003, long before Henry ever knew who Liverpool FC were.

Henry, a college dropout but mathematical genius, is a self-made billionaire having amassed a fortune working his system of identifying trends, assessing their causes and acting on the findings by buying or selling the opportunity. This is the world of high finance, Hedge Funds. Buy low or early and then ride the wave. Buy contrarian and wait for the tide to turn. So when Henry and business partner Tom Werner bought sporting franchise the Boston Red Sox for a whopping $700 million in 2002, the financial community raised an eyebrow and wondered. Why was Henry buying a baseball club for a record price, it more than double the amount ever paid for a Major League Baseball franchise? The team were poor, the stadium old. The Red Sox were the perennial hard luck story, not having won the title pennant since 1918, the franchise supposedly haunted by a curse which had festered ever since the Red Sox sold legendary batter Babe Ruth to their biggest foe, the New York Yankees. On the face of it, the buyout didn't make sense, nor did it fit with his modus operandi.

In 1881, Al Spalding, owner of the Chicago White Sox remarked, "Professional baseball is on the wane. Salaries must come down or the interest of the public must be increased in some way." Spalding couldn't have been more wrong and over 120 years later he was still wrong. Henry knew it. The reason why was in the trends. Overall revenue generated by baseball in the US was on the rise from $1.4 billion in 1995 to $8.0 billion in 2013. In 2014 new TV deals would see TV income rise from $744 million to $1.5 billion annually, a twofold increase. It was the foresight of this revenue accretion that had Henry and FSG excited.

The initial reception for the new owners in Boston was frosty. Who were these 'out of towners' taking possession of their beloved Red Sox? Only rivals, the New York Yankees, could claim to possess more prestige or heritage. Yet, as the Yankees behemoth campaigned victoriously, the Red Sox giant slumbered and snoozed. Slowly and methodically, FSG began to prove themselves to the doubters. The key partners moved home to Boston and set about establishing allies in the local business and political community. They were seen about the club more, their presence noticeable compared to the more withdrawn approach of the previous custodians, the Yawkey family. FSG understood that success on the pitch was driven by success off the pitch. Henry's team quickly set about rectifying the area that came easiest to them, the maximisation of commercial revenues which had been stagnant before their arrival. New sponsorship deals were signed, TV contracts enhanced and merchandising opportunities expanded.

On the pitch they had become devoted to Sabermetrics. This was the philosophy originated by amateur baseball scribe and statistician Bill James. An aspiring writer and obsessive fan, James began writing self-published baseball articles after leaving the United States Army in his mid-twenties. Many of his first baseball articles came whilst double jobbing on night shifts as a security guard at a pork and beans cannery in Kansas. Instead of flowery match reportage, a typical James bulletin posed a question e.g., 'Which pitchers and catchers allow runners to steal the most bases?' and then presented data and analysis that offered an answer. James coined the term 'Sabermetrics' for his work, named after the Society for American Baseball Research (SABR).

James believed that if a baseball franchise applied his findings and utilised his new logic to how they constructed their playing roster, they would have a chance to succeed against the odds. If more attention was focused on the statistical performance of players and how games were won and lost, then teams could adapt their playing style, player selection and payment processes to give them the best chance of winning. The baseball season spans over 150 games and with such a large number of ties, individual quirks and occurrences get evened out and statistics and trends become more pertinent. James's philosophy was famously adopted to great success by Billy Beane at the Oakland Athletics's in California and this achievement was immortalised in the book and then movie of the same name, *Moneyball*. In its simplest form the philosophy involved building an eclectic playing roster. Instead of paying for top-dollar established stars, Sabermetrics espoused the development of youth talent and the signing of cheaper players who had otherwise been overlooked, due to perceived defects, lack of form, or for being too old. It also involved signing players that were needed to fill voids that existed within the squad instead of stockpiling in positions that were already well catered for. In a nutshell, a franchise could build a team of functioning components, devoid of big name stars, but none the less competitive statistically. In the 2006 MLB season, the Athletics ranked twenty-fourth of thirty major league teams in player salaries but had the fifth-best regular-season record. They reached the play-offs in the four consecutive years from 2000 through 2003. In 2002, they became the first team in the hundred plus years of American League baseball to win twenty consecutive games.

So enamoured were FSG with this ground-breaking approach to the game, that they gave Bill James a call in 2002 and asked if he wanted to join up with them in Boston. James jumped at the chance. The dream team of FSG, Epstein and James was born.

And so when the dust had settled on season 2003, the fans of the Boston Red Sox got to learn what owners FSG were made of. Although performance had improved significantly on and off the park, and despite the value of their investment having at least doubled, FSG were still not happy. They had vowed to not just break the curse, but to become multiple winners of the World Series Pennant. Coach Grady Little was fired and back to the drawing board went Epstein and James to see what talent could be added to the roster. They needed a coach that would stick to the plan. A coach who was willing to buy in and believe, parking his ego at the door. Proven winners need not apply. Up and coming, making your way? Willing to buy in and wear the T-shirt? If yes, then come on in. Up stepped Terry Francona.

2004 brought a winning campaign and another place in the end of year play-offs. If a team could win four of these ties in succession, then they would be World Champions. If Boston could do it, then they would break the now eighty-six-year-old curse. First up, yet again, were the New York Yankees. The Red Sox team, self-coined 'the Idiots', due to their off-pitch partying antics and the eclectic nature of their personalities, seemed to be living up to their moniker. Three games in and they trailed 3–0 in the series. Then something astounding happened. The Idiots started to adopt a devil-may-care attitude. Things couldn't get any worse, so they started to play and more importantly they started to win. Incredibly, the Yankees were vanquished 4–3 and the Red Sox were on the path to glory. They would not lose another game till the end of the season and on October 27th the Red Sox were crowned World Series winners and the curse was lifted. The eighty-six-year wait had ended and Boston partied like never before.

FSG had triumphed, their game plan had worked, but they weren't finished. They would win the World Series again in 2007 and 2013 and by 2015 the value of the Red Sox franchise had escalated from $700 million to over $2 billion. Not everybody was completely enamoured though. Francona, who had led the Red Sox to their 2004 and 2007 victories, would remark of his former bosses, "Our owners in Boston, they've been bosses for ten years. They come in with all these ideas about baseball, but I don't think they love baseball. I think they like baseball. It's revenue, and I know that's their right and their interest because they're owners and they're good owners but they don't love the game. It's still more of a toy or a hobby for them. It's not their blood. They're going to come in and out of baseball. It's different for me. Baseball is my life." What seems clear is that owners don't need to love, they need to manage. They need to have a plan to win. If they execute that well, then the lovers can make things happen.

In a fitting accolade to a man that broke the mould, Bill James was named in *The Time 100* in 2006, *Time* magazine's list of the 100 most influential people in the world. Red Sox owner John Henry penned the following tribute in his honour. "*The Red Sox raised a few eyebrows by hiring maverick statistician Bill James in 2002. That was before the team won its first World Series in eighty-six years. What we now know as Moneyball and Sabermetrics came from James. He taught us, among other things, that individual ballparks have a profound effect on a ballplayer's production, that the largest variable determining how many runs a team will score is how many times the leadoff hitter gets on base, that much of what we perceive as pitching is actually defence. What I call Jamesian principles infuse our thinking with a perspective that is objective rather than subjective. What James demands is that we take the time to listen to what the game is telling us over and above what we are predisposed to believe.*"

Theo Epstein, too, would heap praise on James. "*The thing that stands out for me is Bill's humility. He was an outsider, self-publishing invisible truths about baseball while the Establishment ignored him. Now, twenty-five years later, his ideas have become part of the foundation of baseball strategy. But where's Bill? Where's the gloating? Where's the publicist? He's like somebody outlining the Internet in the eighties and watching silently as it comes to pass.*"

Nightshift at the cannery had changed the face of baseball forever.

ARBITRAGE

'I will tell you the secret to getting rich on Wall Street. You try to be greedy when others are fearful. And you try to be fearful when others are greedy.'
—Warren Buffett

With the Red Sox running to plan, another fascinating opportunity was to fall Henry and FSG's way, one that looked faintly familiar. When Henry attended a meeting to learn about an English football club named Liverpool FC, hosted by New York-based merchant bankers Inner Circle Sports, he expected to depart offering a polite 'thanks, but no thanks', but the more he listened, the more intrigued he became. Henry would remark, "A number of parallels emerged with the situation that existed in Boston when we arrived. The Red Sox and Liverpool were both historically successful clubs which had lost their dominance, and both had beloved old grounds not up to modern money-making standards." This was a story he had heard before; a sleeping giant. A long, long period of waiting for success. If not a curse, then the next worst thing. A secondary regional city formed by immigrants. A fabled sporting franchise, now floundering from underperformance on and off the pitch. An ageing stadium which would require a stay or leave decision. But of more importance than all of that heritage stuff, a huge new TV deal that would result in booming revenue generation over the long term. Henry put his phone away, sat up and listened. This was his ballpark and it was game time.

The story just got better and better: Liverpool had an incredible global fan base, despite enduring a lengthy fallow period. English clubs were allowed to keep any and all earnings garnered for themselves, unlike US franchises who adopt a socialist sharing structure that helps keep all boats afloat. And last, but not least, the price. English sporting franchises traded at a discount to their American counterparts. Apart from maybe Man

United the clubs hadn't developed and maximised their marketing and commercial opportunities. They hadn't learned how to convert a fan's love into a client's purchase, not fully anyway. A clear arbitrage existed. With the price that Liverpool was being offered at, all it needed was a quick lick of paint and it could be sold the next day for a profit. It was worth more in the US than it was in its homeland. Yet a quick sale wasn't FSG's plan. They liked the Long Arbitrage or the Time Arbitrage beloved of Private Equity investors. Buy low. Add value. Sell high. The longer they held, the more profit they would make. Henry was in deal mode.

Back in his office Henry would tell his partners of the deal, he was growing more convinced by the day. "If we could acquire this for the debt, I really feel like we would be stealing this franchise. In some ways they really are in the dark ages – especially competitively. The best and brightest are not presently working on English soccer. But the English Premier League is bigger than the NFL, NASCAR, MLB and the NBA internationally. Only Formula One can begin to compare in viewership. This could be a steal. Every buyer believes what potential Red Sox buyers believed, you have to build a new stadium. And they believe the stadium will cost more than £350 million! That's why there are no bidders. We would probably take the same approach we took to Fenway Park. But we'd be looking to limit investment in the facility to eight figures. Then how much is this worth if we recruit the best and the brightest to run the soccer operation?" FSG had made up their minds.

On October 15th 2010, John Henry and his FSG partners bought Liverpool FC for the knock-down consideration of £300 million. The purchase price was used to repay the crippling debt that the club had been saddled with from the previous owners, debts that had taken it to the cusp of financial ruin. FSG had stood up as white knights, but this wasn't a nostalgic sporting dream or a fit of hubris. This wasn't a goodwill gesture for the betterment of Liverpool FC and the many individuals and businesses of that city that depended on the club's welfare. Instead it was a cold and calculated business decision that one day was expected to return a profit, a substantial profit. Yet again, the process of rebuilding a club with limitless potential began, one that needed steady, clever and ambitious hands on the tiller.

***

Five years later, October 2015, and Liverpool fans were worried. FSG's approach to the transfer market wasn't working, nor was their infamous Transfer Committee. Roughly £100 million in net-spend over five years wasn't going to bridge the gap to those above. If anything, it was widening by the year. A squad full of journeymen wasn't going to work either. Where had all the stars gone? One solitary trophy, the League Cup under Dalglish. Failed managers racking up – Hodgson, Dalglish, Rodgers. Moneyball had worked with the Red Sox but the concept didn't translate to football. What had happened to the promises of building a winning team? And where exactly were the owners, the seldom seen financial hotshots who rarely attended a game that didn't involve a bat? Had FSG lost interest after five years of ownership? Rumours circulated that they were keen to sell the club, the collapse of FIFA's Financial Fair Play rules scaring them away. Chinese bidders were banging down the door, or so the media claimed. When the news of how Rodgers was fired by phone emerged it didn't help. They couldn't even fly in for that? That wasn't the Liverpool way.

All this, while FSG's investment had risen in value from $300 million to $1 billion. Would all this profit be stripped away, never to be seen on the Red side of the Atlantic? It showed at best a lack of respect and, at worst, possible apathy. FSG's mettle was being tested again. Did they really want to win, or was a rising investment valuation enough to balm the wounds of continuous failure?

Despite all, it seemed the majority of fans still supported FSG. A list of strong credits stood to their name. They had, in many people's eyes, rescued the club from the brink of financial disaster. They had solved the stadium conundrum that had meandered for nearly twenty years. FSG's financial nous was delivering big improvements in corporate and commercial revenue. As it did in Boston, improving off-field earnings would help to deliver on field success. Having cleared the club's debt, FSG had built a profitable base again and any surpluses were being made available to the manager for squad strengthening.

Credit can run out. In financial markets, when the mood shifts, the momentum change can wreak havoc. How FSG acted next suddenly seemed of vital importance. A vacuum had been left by Suarez, Carragher, Gerrard and now Rodgers. All the time the team spiralled downwards in a whirl of poor form. Liverpool fans were worried. Had five years been wasted with FSG and their bastardised footballing version of Moneyball? They had been accused formerly of not being baseball fanatics, so it was obvious they were certainly no football experts. Did they know what they were doing?

Moneyball hadn't worked for Rodgers, who from day one protested against having a Footballing Director role above him and having to deal with a transfer committee. Yet these were the roles that FSG needed to manage their Moneyball plan. These roles would help develop a system of statistically driven, value for money player recruitments. These roles would stay constant as managers came and went. As in Boston, FSG had picked a developing coach to execute the blueprint. They didn't want established winners loaded down with their own ideas and philosophies on how to run a football team, or egos that would demand financial profligacy in the transfer market that Liverpool couldn't afford. Although Rodgers lacked a successful winning track-record he had performed admirably at Swansea, he had a football philosophy that was transportable and most importantly for FSG, he loved to develop young players.

However, football is not baseball and behind the success of the best teams, usually there sits an inspirational manager. Alas it had not been Rodgers. Now, the big question on every Liverpool fan's mind was, who would their owners hire next? This would be the litmus test of their true ambition for the Reds. Another 'up and coming' manager who would manage the 'philosophy' would be met with derision and rebellion. In the history of football, when great clubs achieved a resurrection, it was rarely on the back of an unproven manager. More often than not it required an established winner, a manager who would inspire confidence and command respect, somebody who had been there before and who could stand tall amidst the adversity and pressure that managing the biggest clubs brought. It needed a manager who could unite and inspire the fans, improve the players and who would challenge the owners. Had FSG the balls to recruit such a man?

Reports surfaced that New England Patriots owner Robert Kraft turned down the chance to buy Liverpool because he thought it would be too hard to compete amidst the Premier League mega-money clubs.

"We had a chance to buy it before Hicks and Gillett and I came very close to doing it. I want to win at everything I do and I think the way that people can spend money there without any limits or do things outside of the UK, it just would be hard to compete. I personally believe you don't go into sport to make money. You go into sport to win. There is nothing else that bonds things together like teams. People like myself that have the privilege of owning a franchise that is important to the community, we are stewards of trusteeship and we have to take it very seriously." If Kraft didn't think he could win with Liverpool why then did FSG think it was possible, while spending less money, from a lower starting position than the direct competition? What was becoming clear was that someday they would realise a fortune, regardless of whether Liverpool won or lost and so it seemed the Reds might be caught in a bind.

A tipping point had arrived in the history of the club. With the new financial bounties that lay ahead and with the gap widening to the deep-pocketed clubs at the top, it looked like Liverpool had arrived at the crossroads of destiny. With bated breath Reds fans awaited their owners' next move.

HEIR TO THE THRONE

'A leader is a dealer in hope.' — Napoléon Bonaparte

May, 2008 and Dortmund have finished the season in a lowly thirteenth place. CEO Hans-Joachim Watzke is keen to arrest the slide. Watzke's reign started with a bang, overseeing a successful flotation of the club on the German Stock Exchange at the turn of the millennium, as Dortmund harnessed the feel-good factor earned from its first and only Champion's League success in 1997. Further success would follow with a sixth Bundesliga title win in 2002. That same year the Black and Yellows would narrowly lose the UEFA Cup Final to Feyenord, 3–2. However, it doesn't take long for things to go pear-shaped. By 2005, after years of overspending and poor management, Dortmund sat on the brink of bankruptcy, with 80 per cent having been wiped from the value of its shares. The club drifted.

So, come the summer of 2008, Watzke was determined not to repeat the financial profligacy of earlier years. Dortmund needed a new vision. It was time to focus on developing youth and playing exciting football again. Together with Footballing Director Michael Zorc they isolated one target to be their new head coach, an up-and-coming, charismatic young manager. A man possessed of unbridled energy and a unique coaching vision. A man named Jürgen Klopp.

***

Seven years earlier, in February 2001, with twelve games to go in the German second Division, small-town Mainz stare down the barrel at relegation. In a bold move the directors appoint one of the players to be the new manager. For some, it smacks of desperation and a shallow pool of interested candidates. In the press room, reporters look to each other and ask, "How will this guy with no experience in management rescue a sinking ship?" But the hierarchy at Mainz had detected leadership qualities in their centre half, Klopp. They knew well his character, having watched him play over eleven years, firstly as a striker and then as a defender, as he notched up 337 appearances and fifty-two goals. For much of that time, inside the tall frame of a committed never-say-die footballer, the heart of a want-to-be manager was beating. When offered the job, Klopp accepted immediately, but only on the proviso that he wouldn't play again. Klopp would comment later that he would have quit playing earlier if the management opportunity had come sooner. For most players, managing is a chance to stay in the game, but it never matches their playing days. Klopp was different. This was what he had always wanted, to be a manager. He had led the players on the pitch, now he would lead the club from the line. General manager Christian Heidel described Klopp's initial talk with the players: "He was an incredible motivator, I remember his first meeting. If I'd been given a pair of boots, I would have played too." Six wins in his first seven games would set the foundation for a remarkable escape from relegation.

The following season Klopp set his and the club's hopes a little higher, this time promotion to the top tier was the coveted prize. Klopp had already experienced agony as a player with Mainz when a first ever promotion to the Bundesliga was lost on the last day, Mainz losing 5–3 at Wolfsburg, after a Gerrardesque slip from Klopp himself had allowed Wolfsburg to lead. What stayed with Klopp was that if they had got that close before, then they could pick themselves up and do it again, and maybe more. And they did, nearly.

Thirty-three games into Klopp's first full season as Mainz manager, things couldn't have been going better for the small town team from the banks of the Rhine. Mainz held a six-point lead on the promotion-chasing pack. Just three points were needed from their last three games to secure promotion. Then the wheels came off. Draw, draw and a defeat in the final game saw Mainz lose out on the very last day once more. Klopp and his team were crestfallen, Klopp remembered that they had felt as if it had been 'the only chance in their lives'. However, on returning to Mainz, ten thousand people gathered in the carnival city to welcome their vanquished heroes home. It was then that Klopp realised they had found something special. "They trust in us," he would say. The following season would again bring last-day misery and for the third time in six years, Mainz had fallen at the final hurdle on the final day. Yet again, in the beautiful Cathedral Square, in a small city rebuilt after World War II, a community would come out to greet the team that meant so much to them. This time it was Klopp's turn to lift the 20,000 that had gathered. "We will try again," he vowed "you have to believe." And try they did, and succeed they did, at Klopp's third time of asking as manager. And so, in the autumn of 2004 Mainz played its first ever game in the top flight of German football after 100 years of waiting. After three successful years at the top, Mainz would be relegated back to the second division and a year later Klopp would call time on his eighteen-year stay. Once more Cathedral Square filled to say a teary goodbye to a man who had put Mainz back on the map.

Klopp had made his mark for all to see and the list of clubs interested in securing his signature grew lengthy. However, he had eyes for only one, a sleeping giant. When that giant, in the shape of Dortmund BVB, came calling in 2008, Klopp and his close, trusted team of Buvac and Kraiwetz embarked on a new adventure. Dortmund's Watzke would remark, "With Jürgen Klopp, Dortmund have been able to acquire their dream candidate." In Dortmund, Klopp had found a club that could possibly match his own boundless ambition. Dortmund were bigger and bolder than Mainz ever could be. Forty-year-old Klopp was effusive, "I am delighted to be here, now I want to help this team compete again." And compete they did. Few who were swept along would ever forget the ride. Once more it took three years for success to arrive. Bayern Munich's dominance in German football is all-conquering and overpowering. The Bavarians have nearly three times as many titles as any other team and when a competitor arises to threaten their dominancy, Munich commonly resort to enticing away their manager or their players and sometimes even both. Yet within three years Klopp's breathless high tempo footballing team had vanquished Bayern and it was Dortmund who sat at the pinnacle of German football.

There are many similarities between Klopp and the departed Brendan Rodgers. Both managers made their way with small unfancied clubs in

Mainz and Swansea, both gaining promotion to the big Leagues. Both propagated an exciting and energetic brand of football. Both built teams with clear footballing identities, teams that were instantly recognisable by their tactics and energy. However, while Rodgers' more demure personality was often overshadowed by his star players such as Suarez, Gerrard, Sturridge and Sterling, at Dortmund, Klopp's messianic zeal was leading a collection of newcomers to become the youngest ever team to lift the German crown, and in doing so moulding future world stars in Lewandoski, Gotze, Gundogan and Reus. Dortmund's general manager would call the feat 'the greatest achievement in our history'. It's not surprising therefore that Klopp was always the biggest and brightest attraction. This he regretted. "My players know that I don't stand above them," he would say, "I'm behind them, supporting them in everything they do. When Bayern do well, they aren't dubbed the Jupp Heynckes' team; just Bayern. In Dortmund everything is linked to my name. I don't need it and it really annoys me."

Both Rodgers and Klopp would take on what seemed like insurmountable foes and both would overcome and make their name as winners, as new managerial kings. Well that's nearly how it happened, had Rodgers not fallen at the very last hurdle. The gap between failure and success can be miniscule.

For Klopp's team a second successive title would be theirs the following year. On the 12th May 2012, Dortmund had the chance to win their first League and Cup double but in their way, once more, stood Munich. Klopp's Dortmund proved unstoppable and the mighty Munich were dismantled 5–2 with Lewandowski grabbing a hat-trick. By now Klopp even had his own song, 'Kloppo du Popstar', by Baron Von Borsig. He was already a bona fide Dortmund legend. With the homeland conquered, Klopp set his sights on Europe for the next campaign. The yellow and black machine went on a relentless winning march through the continent. Real Madrid would be conquered on the way to a final showdown at Wembley Stadium, with none other than Bayern Munich yet again. In the first ever all-German final, Bayern would seal victory and secure their fifth European Cup success. Although Dortmund had lost the final by the narrowest of margins, worldwide, they had gained the support of countless fans with their breathtaking style, the colour and verve of their supporters and the vigour and energy of their maverick young manager. During Klopp's Dortmund era he and his team encountered as good a Munich side as there has ever been, Bayern reaching the Champions League Final in 2010, 2012 and 2013 and winning ten Bundesliga titles from the turn of the millennium. Somewhat chastened by the experience of battling the monster, Klopp would say of them – "Bayern go about football in the same way that the Chinese go about industry, they look at what others do and then they copy it, with more resources and more money." This quote alone encapsulates how incredible his and his team's feats had been. By the end of the 2015 season, Klopp decided that his stay at Dortmund was reaching its expiry date, his task not helped by Munich, who would buy or steal, depending on your point of view, some of his best players in Lewandowski and Gotze. Klopp called time on his rule and commenced a self-enforced football sabbatical. Once more an entire city went into mourning.

***

A few days pass and slowly the rumour gains momentum. Reds fans dare to dream. It seems that Jürgen Klopp is being lined up to be the next Liverpool boss. Just maybe, FSG share the vision that Watzke and Zorc of Dortmund had before them. They believe they have found the man to transform the club, from top to bottom. Some commentators suggest his stature is too big for Liverpool, that his position in world football is now loftier than that of the five-time European Champions. The sad truth is that this might just be true. He's certainly had no shortage of suitors. Ramon Calderon at Real Madrid confirms that Klopp rejected Real Madrid in the past. Klopp reveals that Man United wanted him after Ferguson retired but that the timing was wrong. For Klopp to be linked with the Reds is big. Big time excitement, big time news and a big time opportunity. Wednesday comes and rumours circulate that Klopp will be unveiled as the next Liverpool manager by the end of the week. The frenzy reaches fever pitch on Merseyside, and worldwide. Social media sites are clogged by chattering Reds disciples awaiting their new King. A plethora of words are used to describe Klopp – mad, mercurial, box office, popstar, genius, leader, saviour. All are positive and it seems impossible to find a negative comment or story. In a world awash with bitter comment, this is a phenomenon. A man with no enemies, no skeletons.

Renowned stars from across the soccer world line up to offer their thoughts on the possible appointment. Few names are bigger than Franz Beckenbauer, a player who still holds claim to be one of the best ten footballers to have ever played the game, anywhere, at any time. A winner of the World Cup as a player and as a manager and also the President of Bayern Munich, Dortmund's long-time tormentors. Beckenbauer is sure of Klopp's abilities, "He is fantastic. He is one of the best coaches I know in the whole world, and he was really a milestone for Borussia Dortmund. He took over the club and made them into a world-class team. If Liverpool has the chance to sign Jürgen Klopp, then they should do it."

Watzke, Klopp's former boss at Dortmund, has witnessed his abilities first-hand. "He can do every job, he can make every club (better) and Liverpool is very similar to Borussia Dortmund, it has the same structure and the same fans. It is a marvellous club. He makes every player he has better. For the club, it's wonderful to work with him because he has a very big understanding for the problems of the club. He gives a warm feeling to the whole club and the seven years at Dortmund was wonderful."

By Thursday evening the coronation is confirmed, Jürgen Klopp will become the twentieth man to manage Liverpool Football Club and all across the world Reds fans celebrate ecstatically. The consensus is that Liverpool and Klopp are a perfect match.

Liverpool legends are excited too. Steven Gerrard confirms what we are all feeling – "It is an exciting time to be a Red." Even old adversaries are complimentary. "Strong personality, very strong, very stubborn and determined. His career at Dortmund was a stellar rise to the top and I think he'll do very well. I don't like saying that, it being Liverpool, because I'm worried about it, but, no, he'll do well," says Sir Alex Ferguson.

A news conference is announced for the following morning and my son asks if he can have the day off school. I compliment him on his audacity, but still say no. A clip on the ear sends him to bed and I promise to record everything and watch it again with him when he gets home. A huge day awaits in the history of Liverpool Football Club and I too climb into bed filled with the eager and excited anticipation of a young child at Christmas. When sleep eventually comes, one thing dominates both our dreams. The arrival of the new King of the Reds.

THE PASSION OF KLOPP

'I would rather die of passion than of boredom.' — Émile Zola

Klopp stands out, he is noticeable. Born in Stuttgart, 'Kloppo' as the Germans call him, is married to Ulla and has two sons. He looks younger than his forty-eight years. Over six foot tall, he carries a permanent toothy smile on his stubbly unshaven face. Warm eyes sparkle behind cool designer glasses and a quiff of golden hair sweeps from one side of his forehead to the other. On the sideline he is a flurry of constant motion and ebullient energy. For the TV cameras, he is a producer's dream – eloquent, effusive, witty, if not occasionally a little angry. Never dull. A sparkling, quotable, charismatic charmer. His comments are intelligent, thoughtful, passionate and plentiful. A confident man never afraid to speak his mind. If he calls it wrong he apologises. He's a cool cat in a dressed-down, unkempt hipster kind of way. Klopp's arrival will certainly provide Anfield with a much needed injection of charisma and personality.

His achievements at Dortmund surpassed all expectations. Although a great club, Dortmund hadn't expected to be challenging for the title every year, never mind winning it. The Reds are undeniably more ambitious and success will be demanded. Winning the League was a surprise at Dortmund, it will be a prerequisite at Liverpool if Klopp's reign is to be seen as successful. That is why the vacancy is available. Is success easier to achieve when expectations are lower? I'm not sure. Was that why Klopp succeeded and Rodgers didn't? This will be the toughest assignment yet of Klopp's career. The task of ending Liverpool's drought is the single hardest mission in world sport. It is hard to find an established sporting empire that currently waits longer for success. The San Francisco 49ers, now twenty years since their fifth Super bowl win in 1995, seem the closest comparable.

Paul Lambert, the ex-Norwich City and Aston Villa manager, played for Dortmund in their European Cup winning side in 1997. A tough tackling midfielder, possessed of a skilful touch too. After hanging up his boots, Lambert studied for his coaching badges, taking the Pro-Licence course in Germany in 2004. Alongside him sat one Jürgen Klopp. Lambert remembers him well – "You don't forget Jürgen Klopp! He was a humble guy but good fun to be around. A top guy." Lambert speaks about a subsequent coaching trip to Dortmund to study Klopp's ways. "I went over for nine days and it was fantastic. I took loads of things away from it in terms of the way they work. It was excellent. He's got a great back-room staff," says Lambert of Buvac and Krawietz, concluding "the three of them work really well together."

Klopp is known for the identity of his teams, for their intensity and work rate. He remarks, "We want to enjoy our own game. Okay we like to win, but if we lose our way, it's okay. If it is the way of someone else, you cannot work with this. So that's it, it's very emotional, very fast, very strong, not boring, no chess. Of course, tactical, but tactical with a big heart. Tactical things are so important, you cannot win without tactics, but the emotion makes the difference. Life in our game, that's important." Klopp wants passionate football. He talks of how he believes football should be played and celebrated. "I show them photographs of how Barcelona celebrate, I don't use videos because I don't copy Barca's style. But you see them celebrate goal number 5,868 like they've never scored before. This is what you should always feel until you die."

So it seems Liverpool will become a team shaped in the image of Klopp himself – emotional, tactical, strong. Full of life, never boring. At Dortmund he said, "The fans should not only recognise us by our black and yellow jerseys. Even if we play in red, everyone in the stadium should think, that can only be BVB. When you sit in this stadium with your eyes closed, you should sense there is a passionate team on the field below."

Klopp achieved his Dortmund successes by blooding young players and transforming them into stars. FSG must have been licking their lips at the thought of a similar masterplan being effected at Liverpool. Alongside Spurs, the Reds have the youngest squad in the League, with an average age of 25.4. It is the stated FSG plan to buy young players, then mould them into better ones, who can either fulfil Liverpool's ambitions or be sold at a profit to continue a spend, sell and reinvest cycle. This is the new Moneyball bible, one designed to compete with the mega riches of City and Chelsea and less so United and Arsenal. It's not rocket science, but as with everything in life, the key will be in the execution, in the 'making it happen'.

At Dortmund, the now household names of Lewandowski, Reus, Gundogan and Gotze all started as unknowns under Klopp. Can he work the same magic with players like Origi, Firmino, Can, Ojo and Grujic? To succeed, he will have to.

LONG LIVE THE KING

'It's so dark right now, I can't see any light around me. That's because the light is coming from you' — Lang Leav, *Poet*

It's December 1959. Liverpool FC are mired in the Second Division and have been for some time. Memories of their last League title triumph in 1947 are a faded blur. The stadium is a mess and the training ground is hardly fit for purpose, its buildings unloved, its pitches bare and patchy. The playing squad is patchy too, at best. Upon closer inspection it's simply not good enough. Liverpool are searching for a new manager. Key skill set required – miracle worker. Title – Messiah. Who would be brave enough to risk their reputation on such a bleak test? This was the hard way, failure seemed inevitable. Step forward Bill Shankly. Years later he would remember the dilemma he faced – "I was at the time leading as peaceful a life as any football manager can lead in the sheltered calm of Huddersfield. Was I to step out of this into the cauldron atmosphere of Anfield to undertake a task which, however much I put into it, could end in failure? I decided that even if the risk I was taking was great, it was one which I had to take, because I am an ambitious man and I knew that Liverpool club and its supporters were ambitious too." And so arrived the Saviour.

October 9th, 2015 and Liverpool FC are at as low an ebb as they were all those years ago, before a fiery Scotsman arrived with his magic wand. Okay, the stadium and training facilities are, or will soon be, top class, but as before, the playing squad looks average. Only once in the previous five years have the Reds finished higher than sixth place. New talent is required, but Liverpool must manage with a financial budget that is a fraction of the competition. Worse still, the competition have already bolted and are nearly out of sight. Liverpool can only cling on, with an argument of heritage and history, to their belief that they are a big club, a force to be reckoned with. To this backdrop, the managerial announcement is made. Jürgen Klopp is the new manager of Liverpool FC. The club's TV channel have the honour of the first interview. Millions look on, and listen, transfixed, in silence, awaiting the new gospel.

***

Claire Rourke LFC TV Presenter to Jürgen Klopp:
Welcome to Liverpool Football Club

Jürgen: Thank you so much.

Q. *How do you feel?*
A. *Great, I have no other word for this, today was a crazy day, with all that happened in Germany, and what happened here, when we landed, but it's an absolutely great feeling for me, it's a big honour for me, yes it's absolutely for me one of the biggest moments of my life. I am here together with my family, not my whole family, one son is at home, but we are here together and it still feels like a dream.*

Q. *What attracted you to Liverpool Football Club?*
A. *Everything. All I heard about, all I read about, all I felt when I saw, not too many matches in my life, but some very important games I could see and yes, I love football, yes and all the intensity of football in Liverpool, that is very good for me, I always thought about working in England, and because of the type of football, and because of the intensity of football, and Liverpool was first choice, and now I've got the opportunity to work here, it is the best thing I can imagine.*

Q. *What did you need to consider or would you say it was an easy decision?*
A. *(Loud laugh/Big grin) It was not the most difficult decision but of course I end my contract in Dortmund four months ago and I had to think about what I would do in the future, I have to develop myself and think about all the things that have happened in the last fifteen years. But now I have had a holiday for*

four months, and of course it's enough, it was really cool, it was great. Fifteen years in a row I worked as a manager, always until the last day of the season I had to work, because when you look at my little history in football, it was always until the end. I seem to be a guy for thirty-four or thirty-eight match days and so, that was really hard and then I try to relax and feel that I am not the football-only guy and I get interested in many different things and I have a few perfect meetings, with very clever and smart people, to talk about football, to talk about nutrition, to talk about so many different things, then I felt if somebody tempting will call me, then I am prepared and that's what I did, but most of all now I'm really relaxed. I had six very cool years in Dortmund, one hard one, the last year, but of course as a package it was perfect, eh. I want to do something new and now I'm here.

Q. *Let's talk about Anfield.*

A *Yeah.*

Q. *How much are you looking forward to that becoming your home and being the manager for those fans?*

A. *Yeah. My English is not good enough for this, to express this, not at the moment, you will have to speak to me about this in a few months again, but of course I am pretty excited, I want to see it, I want to feel it, I want to smell it, I want to do everything, when I came here with Dortmund one year ago, I was really excited, for me it was historical of course and then I came in, yes it's a great place. There are some places in football but this is the most special place, of course, OK, Borussia Dortmund stadium Westfallenstad is a great stadium really, I had another perfect little, little, stadium with Mainz, but this is the most historical place and yes I am looking forward to it, and in this moment I don't know what I feel, but it will be good.*

Q. *How important is it, to you, to have or create that special connection with the supporters?*

A. *I understand football. Look if people are not interested in football, we can put some sticks in a park and play football, it's still a perfect game, but it's only this game, because of the fans, that's what I know, what I think, what I feel and we have to… it's a song… we have to entertain them, we have to make their lives better, that is what we do, because football is not so important, of course not, we don't save lives or things like this, we are not some medicine people or doctors, how you say it? It is our job, yeah, that they can forget their problems for ninety minutes and then they can talk about the game for three days after the last game and for two days about the next game, and that is how I want to live, if I am not a manager, it is the way I would live, because I love this game so much, and it is why I am really trying to be as close as possible to the fans, but of course it is not always possible to be so close to the fans, because it is my job, I have to work, I need time for this and so it is not always like the fans want, but it's as often as possible.*

Q. *Do you feel like you understand what it is to be a fan?*

A. *I was on the stand, of course in Stuttgart as a child and I enjoy it really, it is perfect, it is the perfect place and now I will be here, and I can go in all the places in the stadium and everyone will tell me, here happened this, here happened this, he shoot here, Stevie G, Robbie Fowler or whoever and that's pretty cool.*

Q. *Do you think you'll need to adapt to English football or how do you think you will adapt?*

A. *Of course I will adapt but maybe I have to, I don't know, but this moment I don't think about this, because it's football and I know English football, I watch so many games, and we played against English teams and some things are different but that's not so important at this moment, because it only is football... Don't forget, it is a game and we all have the same rules and the pitches are similar in size, so it's not so difficult. My experience is listen, see, feel and then see about what you change, and now I have to do these three things and I have to think about what I change or adapt because we play football for a long time, I was a player, I am now a manager, I don't want to make it too complicated. It's very important that the players can understand easily what you want because it's a game. You have to play from here (puts hand to his stomach) and not from here (points to his head) and so that's the cool thing, that's the reason why I could play too. (Laughter)*

Q *What similarities do you think you will face here at Liverpool to what you faced at Dortmund, in challenges perhaps?*

A. *Maybe this is the biggest challenge in this moment in world football but I'm never, I was never a guy for the easy way, I'm not interested in this and this is, in this moment, the most interesting job in world football, because it is not so bad, because twelve points, I read the newspapers, aaargh, it was a disaster, only twelve points, but only four or so to other positions in the table, it's interesting, nobody is patient anymore, so we have to think about what we can change, and that is, yeah, that is my job now, but I need help of course, and I have to start to work and we will see, but I know what I want. First I will have to talk to the players of course, and we will have to find a common way, and who wants to do, what I sometimes propose, what I want? Yeah...they can be a good friend of mine [loud laugh]... that is not such a bad thing to be a good friend of mine, because I'm really loyal.*

Q. *How do you assess the squad that you are inheriting here at Liverpool then?*

A. *I'm here because I believe in the potential of the team, that's why. If Liverpool ask me and I see the team and I go – 'my god' – and shaking my head, then no, no. Everything is good of course in this moment, we are not the best team in the world, who cares? Who wants to be the best team in the world today? We want to be the best team in the world tomorrow or one other day, that's all, but what I saw from outside was absolutely okay. I saw some good matches, I saw some not so good, that's normal in football, you have some problems, you have to solve them, so it's not important. The important thing is we have speed, we have technical skills, we have technical good defenders, we have good strikers, good midfielders, some wingers, so we now we have to see who is fit for first game against Tottenham and then we have to make a team for this game, and then we can start, it's not so... I'm not a dreamer, I don't want to have Cristiano [Ronaldo], Lionel [Messi] and all these players, no, no, I want these guys. It was a decision for these guys and now we start working.*

Q. *Can you tell us what style of play we can expect?*

A. *A wild one. [Loud laugh]*
In this case, in football, all the world-class teams play possession football, that's cool. I don't watch this really, I like to watch this, Bayern Munich, great team, great club, Barcelona, yes, Real Madrid; maybe on some days, I don't know, Man City? Nobody starts as a ball possession team, you cannot start and say 'okay, now we have the ball and the other players have to wait', so the first thing always, maybe in life, you need to have a stable defence, that's the

first thing always, because you only can stay confident in a game, when you know that not each offensive move of the other team is a goal, so that is the first thing and always when you start a development, nobody starts from the top of the table… only a few teams, you always have a lower position, our position is absolutely okay, so we can start our development, today, tomorrow. If it's possible, can we be the hardest team in the world to beat, let's try to be this, if you are this, you cannot be such a far way to be a team who can win games, but first of all we have to talk to all LFC fans, to talk about what are expectations, because expectations can be a real big problem, like a back pack with twenty kilos more. It's not so cool to run with this, we have to talk about this, we have to think about this, and then we can start.

Q. *Do you think you need a lot of time to implement your style, your philosophy?*

A. *Of course it needs a lot of time until the end, but not to start. I'm not here to promise you, that we will see against Tottenham the absolute new LFC, but some of the new LFC would be cool, if somebody could see it, that is what we will try to do, but everything in life takes time… but the only thing nobody gives time to is development, but because now if somebody feels they have waited enough for success then… (Slams fist into his palm)… Re-Start! (Laughs aloud)… and then anything can happen!*

Q. *There's been a lot of media talk about the transfer structure within the football club, so what is your take on it, there has been a lot of talk about how players have been acquired and what conversations have you had, if any, with the owners about that?*

A. *It's a really funny thing, because it was absolutely no problem between FSG and myself, we talked about this, it's nothing, if two smart or intelligent or clever guys sit together at the table, you both want the same thing, so where can be the problem, we all want to be successful. The only thing for me is that I have the first and the last word but I don't want to spend money that the club doesn't have, I'm not interested in that, I don't want to hold a player if he doesn't want to stay, if he wants to leave, I have to go and I say no, no – you have to stay, I have to work all day with these guys, nobody will sell a player I want to work with, even if it's a good deal, and nobody want to buy a player, without my 'yes', so everybody is okay, I don't need more.*

Q. Will you be bringing any of your backroom staff?

A. Yes, of course, my two brothers in mind, Zeljko and Pete. Great guys, you will see it, you will feel it when you see them, they are cool, are absolutely football maniacs, they work pretty hard and they are my perfect partners in this job, because as a manager you always have to make decisions, you always have to think about so many different things and in my opinion, it's very important that you have somebody that can talk to you, can talk about everything. I make the decisions of course, but I need very good people around me, not only these two guys, I'm really looking forward to the rest of the staff of LFC and want to learn from them, want to use their power, but of course this will take time and when I know what they are all able to do, but at this moment we start with these three guys. We have Pep and John in our training team, two Dutch guys, my first time to work with Dutch guys, it's not too far away from Germany, so maybe we can talk in German, it would be good, so I'm looking forward to it.

Q. You mentioned that success won't happen necessarily overnight, but what are you hoping to achieve here at Liverpool Football Club, short-term and long-term?

A. Success.

Q. What is that success?

A. Yes, that is relative, that's right, always, that is what we have to talk about, there are Man City, Man Utd, Chelsea, Arsenal, Tottenham, I hope I don't miss any other team, they want to be successful in the table, and why should they reach and we don't or why we reach it and they don't, so it's not important what I think at this moment, it's important what we can do together to change. In this moment, all the LFC family is a little bit too nervous, a little bit too pessimistic, a little bit too in doubt. They all celebrate the game, it's a great atmosphere in the stadium, but it's not… they don't believe in this moment. They only want to see a great five years ago, ten years ago, twenty years ago, history is great, but it's only to remember. Now we have a possibility to write a new story, if we want, but for this we have to clear a few things, and maybe we can do this in the next few weeks. I'm not the guy to say this year will be the best year in history of LFC, if it happens we can celebrate it, but if not, we have to work further.

Q. *Okay, finally what is your message to those Liverpool supporters?*

A. *The message to those Liverpool supporters… (Klopp pauses, looks away, thinks, then looks back to the camera, to face the fans worldwide)*
We have to change… from doubters to believers… (points at camera)… Now!

***

I turn to my son and he turns to me and in unison we pronounce, "We believe". With a man like Klopp at the helm, how could we not?

PART IV

STATE OF THE NATION

SURVIVAL OF THE FITTEST

'Isn't it nice to think that tomorrow is a new day with no mistakes in it yet?' — L.M. Montgomery

And so Jürgen Klopp's English adventure begins. Some teams and stadiums he knows from his Dortmund days, Arsenal, Man City, but mostly this will be a maiden journey. In many ways today's English game is new to us all. The last big change came with the advent of the Premier League. Now with huge TV deals and with each of the twenty Premier League teams ranking in the global top thirty rich list, a new age has dawned, the moneyed age. Many teams have been taken over or have received injections of cash from new investors. Those that haven't, have the 'For Sale' signs up. Billionaire owners abound as do sniffing private equity funds. No longer will having £50 million in the bank allow you to play in the Premier League casino. Transfer spend records are broken every time the window opens as more and more international stars arrive on English shores. Stadiums rise to greet these new icons. Liverpool, Spurs, Chelsea, West Ham, Crystal Palace, Stoke and Everton all plan or are in the process of building new or refurbished facilities. How high the balloon will fly nobody knows, but what is clear is that all has changed. For the better? Only time will tell.

First up for Klopp is a trip to Tottenham Hotspur and White Hart Lane. Spurs legend Danny Blanchflower was captain of the Spurs team that won the League and Cup double in 1961. His words have become the maxim for the club and are repeated on displays throughout their stadium – 'The Game is about Glory'. Blanchflower argued, "the great fallacy is that the game is first and last about winning. It's nothing of the kind. The game is about glory. It's about doing things in style, with a flourish, about going out and beating the other lot, not waiting for them to die of boredom." DNA and genome advances suggest that we all descend from a tribe of East African herdsmen. When you listen to the great voices of football, similar genetic threads exist, a line running through the sinews and the fabric of these men and their philosophies. When our new manager Klopp enthuses over "full-throttle football" and proclaims "we want to ooze vitality" we can hear clearly the echoes of Blanchflower and maybe too some ghostly murmurings of approval. Klopp argues that his teams "would rather hit the bar five times than not shoot on goal four times. For the fans it's like a drug. I don't just want to win, I also want to feel!" Glory indeed.

As a teenager, I read the seminal football book *The Glory Game*, wherein author Hunter Davies chronicled a year following the Tottenham team of 1971/72 on their travels around England and Europe. It was one of the first books to afford the everyday man a view inside the workings of a football club, with Davies mingling with manager Bill Nicholson and his players in a way that might prove impossible these days. That team included such greats as Mullery, Jennings, Knowles, Chivers, Peters and a very young Perryman and the book's finale saw Tottenham lift the 1972 UEFA Cup, beating Wolverhampton Wanderers 3–2 over two legs in the final. The 1972 victory was the second of Tottenham's European triumphs, the first a European Cup Winners Cup win against Atletico Madrid in 1963, secured by a score of 5–1, when Tottenham notably became the first British team to lift a European trophy. Following Davies' journey sparked in me a fondness for the Spurs and in an odd way planted the seed for this book.

Tottenham sought to defend their UEFA Cup trophy the following season and it would be Shankly's Liverpool who would arrive on April 25th, 1973, to meet Spurs in the semi-final. Liverpool legend Phil Thompson spoke of that encounter.

"That was a huge match to be involved in. I didn't play in the first leg when we won 1–0 at Anfield, with Alec Lindsay scoring, but I started in the second leg at the Lane and I was only nineteen years of age at the time. I can remember a Steve Heighway shot hitting the back of the net just after the half-time break. We knew we'd got a crucial away goal and so it proved as it was the strike that saw us through to the final." Liverpool went on to lift their first European trophy, defeating Borussia

Monchengladbach of Germany in the final. Spurs would attempt an English three in a row in the UEFA Cup in 1974, but would lose the final to Feyenord. The seventies were indeed glorious for both Spurs and Liverpool.

I've been a Liverpool fan since the age of six, so no team can compete with the Reds, ever, but as a lover of the game itself, there are certain clubs that I prefer over others. As I mentioned, Spurs are one. When I think of Spurs I think of stylish, glamourous football. Attacking football. I think of a certain swagger. I picture waves of crisp white shirts, dark navy shorts and still clean white stockings surging forward, devil may care. On the downside, I think of underachievement, of a lack of mental and physical strength, of coming up empty-handed. A term common in football parlance that I've only recently become familiar with is – 'to do a Spursy'; to fall short, to fail to live up to expectations. The Spurs I grew up watching in the late seventies and eighties were a team full of guile and skill with players such as Hoddle, Hazard, Archibald and captain Steve Perryman. They matched the swagger of Davies' Spurs team and they too would win the UEFA Cup in 1984, along with consecutive FA Cup victories in 1981 and 1982. Spurs alumni is awash with players known for their flair and panache – Hoddle, Gascoigne, Waddle, Greaves, Lineker, Ardiles, Ginola, Keane and most recently Bale. We meet one of these greats, Argentinian Osvaldo 'Ossie' Ardiles and he talks about the Spurs of today and of his fellow countryman, manager Mauricio Pochettino. "Mauricio is a determined coach, a quiet, hard-working man who gives everything to the club. He is first in and last to leave." I ask whether he believes that Spurs have changed, and whether today's team are any closer to making the breakthrough and becoming a top team again. The answer comes quickly. "It is all there now. The infrastructure is right. The owners, the manager, the new stadium. Yes, Spurs can do it." When Ardiles leaves, I tell my son, who has no idea who I was talking to, "that man won the World Cup in 1978 when Argentina beat Holland 3–1 in Buenos Aires". He nods his head with respect and looks behind to catch another glance.

It is now close to match time, which today is the early Saturday morning 12.45 kick-off, and we head for the stadium. In his book, Davies describes approaching White Hart Lane on the very first page. "*The home of Tottenham Hotspur Football Club is at 748 High Road, N17. You could easily miss it, if you were rushing along the High Road, with your head down. It's set slightly back from the road with the main entrance down a little lane beside a pub, the White Hart. But once you've stepped back and taken it all in, it's hard to believe that anyone could miss it. The stadium lurks behind the High Road like a vast battleship with its floodlights towering over the rooftops for miles around."*

I stand outside the White Hart pub and try to imagine what Davies saw all those years ago. Today, the length along the Tottenham High Road is vertically exposed from ground to sky, the buildings all gone, only a construction hoarding to conceal the ongoing development works behind. The plywood fencing proudly displays design plans for Spurs' new 61,000-seater stadium, due for completion by August 2018. An increase in capacity of 25,000 (69%) tells the story of Spurs' ambition. When Davies watched Tottenham beat Wolves to the UEFA trophy in 1972, 54,303 were in attendance. Being a London-based team, in a globally watched League, is in some ways a licence to print money. The stadium design is remarkable and shows the advantages of a new build project over a refurbishment. It will house the largest single tier seated stand in Europe holding 17,000 fans, surpassing Liverpool's Kop end which holds 12,500. Spurs' new stadium will also house two retractable pitches, one grass, for Spurs' games, and the other artificial, which will accommodate other sports, these to include American Football. Spurs' directors have signed a ten-year tie-up with the American National Football League (NFL), whereby White Hart Lane will play host to two NFL games each year. Under the chairmanship of Daniel Levy, Spurs are positioning themselves to be one of the winners in these boom times. It seems clear that the most financially astute clubs, both on and off the pitch, will succeed most in the next fifty years.

That is what drives Liverpool's owners FSG too, the need to make sure that Liverpool are positioned at that top table. Only through financial security can the Reds attempt to crack the top four dominated by Chelsea, Man City, Man United and Arsenal. Liverpool's history and global fan base keeps them ahead of Tottenham in this quest, but not by much. London holds great appeal to new players and fans alike and Spurs are catching up on the Reds and threatening to pass. Liverpool's fall from grace has seen Tottenham finish ahead of them in six of the last seven seasons. These two teams are the next best after the top four, but which one of them, if either, can go on and crack the cartel?

When Jamie Carragher said Liverpool were in danger of 'becoming a Tottenham' after Rodgers' dismissal, his comments would have riled both sets of fans. Liverpool's, with their team being compared to a club who has only ever won two League titles and has never managed to get further than a European Cup quarter-final. Tottenham's, who now feel that their club has passed Liverpool, both on and off the pitch. For me, the statement was misguided. Yes, for sure Spurs have, for most of their history, flattered to deceive, and yes, the phrase 'to do a Spursy' was coined by their own fans for good reason, but Tottenham are still a proper football club and always will be. The game cannot be only about clubs with the most money. That product is untenable. What Carragher's words do achieve is to provide an extra edge to today's game, if it was needed. The clash of the modern-day wannabees.

Spurs sit two places and just one point ahead of Liverpool in eighth position. Brendan Rodgers might break a wry smile at how odd that seems, given that the mood in North London is positive. Manager Pochettino has been in charge now for roughly a year and slowly but surely Spurs athletic style has taken shape. They pride themselves on running farther and being fitter than the opposition. Klopp likes his own charges to run forever too, so today we can expect no let-up. Last team standing wins.

We enter the South stand via Park Lane and we spot some new flags in the away end, made for the occasion. 'We Believe' says one, above five gold stars which denote Liverpool's European Cup successes. Here is an immediate and direct response from the faithful to Klopp's interview request. 'Jürgen Meister' reads another. Klopp himself, track-suited in black, is on the pitch putting his new team through their pre-match paces. Eventually Klopp and his team leave the pitch and head down the tunnel to make final preparations in the dressing room. It's a chilly grey, overcast morning. The rain has held off, so the lush green pitch gets watered by the sprinklers. These days most Premier League teams prefer to play on the slicker and more even surface that a wet pitch offers. A little give in the ground also helps to protect expensive limbs. Maybe the insurance policies demand it moist.

The teams emerge followed by the managers. Klopp stands by the dugout where fifty or more photographers have gathered, eager to capture the first images of the German's English odyssey. Klopp looks through them as if they don't exist, fully focused on his charges as they prepare for the launch of yet another new Liverpool era. Our new manager has opted for a 4-2-3-1 formation with Mignolet, Clyne, Skrtel, Sakho and Moreno at the back. In front of them sit Can and Lucas. Ahead of those are Milner, Coutinho and Lallana with Origi up top.

Straight from the kick-off we see the first signs of Klopp's influence. The German task-master wants his men to run and run and that is what they do. When Spurs have the ball, their players are hunted down by packs of Red and hurriedly they have to release it or lose possession. Liverpool are harrying relentlessly in Klopp's 'Gegenpressing' style, which effectively translates from German as 'pressing against'. The early exchanges are dominated by the Reds, as Spurs fail to cope with Liverpool's ferocious energy. Klopp applauds every sprint and tackle from his standing position on the line. However, in possession, Liverpool forget to switch to calm mode and time after time, control of the ball is lost too quickly. Spurs slowly take control and, but for Mignolet, the Reds would be trailing at half-time.

The second half sees more of the same. Two sides run and tackle aggressively, but the game lacks guile and quality, with zero time or space on the ball to think or act. This is an athletic fight-out. Kane forces Mignolet into another good stop and Can shoots wide from distance late on. Come ninety minutes, nobody has managed to break the deadlock and for the second game running, Liverpool can thank their oft-maligned keeper for a hard-earned point. All in all, from a tough away assignment against an in-form team, Klopp must be happy with the draw. Later the statistics show the change already effected by Klopp after only one week in the job. Liverpool have run more kilometres in the game than any other team that season. Jamie Carragher remarks, "That's like having an extra player on the pitch." The truth of that observation remains to be seen.

Leaving the stadium, my son and I agree that athleticism won out over skill. The playmakers on the pitch such as Coutinho, and Eriksen of Spurs, were nullified. This was not the Glory Game, possessing none of the vision or grace of a Hoddle, Ardiles, Barnes or Dalglish. Moreover, it was the poster child for a modern game styled on physical power. Yet it is early days in the kingdom of Klopp and it feels that, on today's evidence, things can only get better. He vowed to build a team that could defend and compete first. In time, they can earn the right to play and express themselves.

Our trip to White Hart Lane has cemented firmly in my mind one truism for the future. In this new Premier League only the fittest both on and off the pitch will survive.

GREEN SHOOTS

'The secret to getting ahead is getting started.' — Mark Twain

As with every new manager that comes through the Anfield door, Liverpool fans burrow in for the long haul. We are a patient bunch on the whole. If we believe that the new incumbent has sufficient character and ability for the job, and that his ambition is a match for the club's and our aspirations, then we buy in. Owners FSG talk about winning but run a club that operates to tight budgets, our net transfer and wage spend but a fraction of those ahead of us. The crux will be how to magically bridge the expectation gap. Fans want to win titles and European Cups. With outspending the opposition not an available option, Liverpool will need to outwit them instead. It will take a manager and team of some ability to pull it off. Klopp has a winning track record, he's done it before. Can he do it again? If he does he will place himself firmly amongst the best managers in the history of football.

Klopp informs the media that no targets have been set by the owners. No top four mandate, no trophy lifting requirement. What they do want is to see a playing personality, a shape and style that is identifiable and within which young players can grow and become better. All of this seems eminently sensible to me, Klopp is a renowned developer of fledgling talent and with so many of these players being both youthful and new to the club, a little time will be needed by all parties. If by year-end we can see a team playing consistently, if not necessarily at 'full-throttle', then with at least more throttle than before, that will do nicely.

The performance at Spurs certainly had more energy and it was a good result for Klopp in his first outing against a talented, confident and well-structured team. Five days after the trip to White Hart Lane, Liverpool welcome Rubin Kazan of Tatarstan to Anfield for the Reds' third Europa League group game. Liverpool's European campaign has started slowly with two successive draws against Bordeaux and FC Sion, so a win against Kazan might be imperative. Yet Liverpool has an Achilles heel, well two to be precise. The left heel is the weight of pressure and expectancy the players feel when they take to their home field. Klopp did his homework and he nailed it on the head. Liverpool fans don't believe. They want to, but it's hard after so many setbacks. Few were truly surprised when Gerrard slipped. It seemed that after twenty-four years of waiting, bad things would happen and they did.

I've witnessed it so many times at Anfield, the Reds enter the last ten minutes one-nil up and suddenly silence envelops the great stadium. Every missed pass is met with an anguished gasp. Confidence seeps from timid players. The nervousness is palpable, the fans want it too much and this transmits to the pitch below, suffocating the boys in Red. Klopp has asked for one thing from us, to be believers, not doubters, knowing that if that sense of belief can wash down from the 45,000 fans in the stands onto the pitch and engulf the players in positivity and confidence, then once again Anfield can become a stronghold, a bastion.

Liverpool's dodgy right heel is shoddy defending. Klopp has diagnosed the problem, vowing to build a team from the back. Both of the Reds' Achilles are exposed against Kazan. Prior to kick-off, the team and Klopp are given a rapturous reception by everybody in the old ground and the Kop end is blanketed with flags and scarves to greet their new leader. The match programme depicts a graphic poster of Klopp, in the same style as the iconic 'Hope' posters that accompanied Barack Obama's first presidential campaign. Everything about the occasion seems momentous. Millions of Reds fans worldwide greet this new dawn of hope. Owners FSG are in the crowd to witness Klopp's first home game. Alas, new beginnings are often built on old foundations, regardless of how fissured they might be. The Reds limp to a 1–1 draw and the feel-good mood that greeted the night is more subdued as we leave.

The fixtures come thick and fast for new King Klopp. With little time to train, let alone plan, it's hard to know what to expect when the Reds take to the pitch. Three days after Kazan, Southampton come to town. They are a strong and bright outfit, full of dangerous players, a team that loves to surprise the big boys. Liverpool play very well but can't add to their single goal lead. A late Southampton equaliser sees the game finish 1–1 and once more, Liverpool manufacture a draw from a win. Still, the signs have been good, some players are looking brighter than before, Lallana and Leiva in particular. The full-backs are showing considerably more in attack and confidence levels seem higher. It is very early days but clear shoots of optimism take root.

Wednesday 28th October and Liverpool play their fourth game in eleven days, hardly time for the first pages of Klopp's manifesto to be read, never mind learned. It's in at the deep end for the new boss. Bournemouth are back on Merseyside for a League Cup tie, fielding a strong side. Klopp fields a team which includes a number of youth players, untested at this level. Still, the kids have obviously heard that with Klopp a path to the first team exists, not just notionally, but for real. They rise to the occasion and dominate throughout. Liverpool go through to the Quarter Final with a 1–0 victory. Progress in the cup competitions, even the lesser ones, is never to be sniffed at.

More green shoots.

HISTORY REPEATING

'If men could learn from history, what lessons it might teach us! But passion and party blind our eyes, and the light which experience gives us is a lantern on the stern, which shines only on the waves behind.'
Samuel Taylor Coleridge

Prosperity brings change and a tide on which most boats should rise. It also makes lawlessness unattractive to the average person who prefers to get ahead by peaceful means. From 1881–1913 the Gilded Age arrived in America and the gun-slinging days of Billy the Kid, Butch Cassidy and Jesse James were consigned to history. After the bitter conflict of the Civil War and the turmoil of reconstruction, the nation had the chance to stabilise and settle. There was a surge in industry and population as immigrant masses came to America to start a new life. Before them lay a land of opportunity with vast natural resources. A group of industrialists were coming to the fore, identifying and grasping the potential that this burgeoning state provided. Andrew Carnegie would accumulate a treasure-trove from steel and ironworks. JB Duke would make his fortune from tobacco. Cornelius Vanderbilt would dominate the shipping and railroad businesses. JP Morgan would excel at mergers, bringing Edison General Electric and Thomson-Houston Electric together to form General Electric. Andrew W Mellon and John D Rockefeller would build empires in aluminium and oil. Yet, for every one tycoon, there existed hundreds of thousands of poor, dishevelled souls. As in the old world of monarch states and religious empires, the new world showed little ability or desire to alleviate mass inequality. The most powerful businessmen of this era would become known as the 'Robber Barons'. As the stench of corruption saturated the air, the downtrodden started to revolt at the exploitive power held by those Barons. The masses had reached breaking point. Antitrust laws would be passed and monopolistic companies would be broken up. An example of this was Rockefeller's Standard Oil Company being divided into nearly ninety smaller entities such as Chevron and Exxon. To this day, inequality and the fair distribution of wealth remains a divisive and unresolved issue in the world's richest country.

If inequality is still rife in the United States, it bears no comparison to that being experienced in modern-day Russia, sometimes referred to as 'the Wild East'. In a 2014 report on inequality, Credit Suisse bank concluded that due to the gulf between the rich and poor, Russia 'deserves to be placed in a different category'. The report found that 111 people owned 19 per cent of the wealth and that the wealthiest 10 per cent controlled 85 per cent of all wealth in Russia. Around the world there is roughly one billionaire for every $170 billion in household wealth, in Russia that is one for every $11 billion. These statistics are staggering. One wonders why anarchy and revolution don't grab hold, but in a paternal, respect-driven society, where the ruler and his military exercise extreme power and control, the conclusion must be that opposition is futile. Fatalism takes over.

Upon his election in 2012, Vladimir Putin vowed to bridge the gap, but under his reign the divide only worsened. It is alleged by some that Putin himself has amassed a fortune of over $30 billion and that he is the richest man in Europe. In Putin's defence he inherited many of the problems that Russia endures. When in June 1991, Boris Yeltsin became the first directly elected President in Russian history, following the disintegration of the former Soviet Union (which had included countries such as Armenia, Azerbaijan, Belarus, Estonia, Georgia, Kazakhstan, Latvia, Lithuania and Ukraine), wide-ranging reforms including privatization and market and trade liberalization were undertaken. Yeltsin destroyed any Soviet legal and political institutions that did not harmonize with his counter-revolution. His government dismantled all significant social and economic rights that workers retained from the conquests of the 1917 revolution. What resulted was a major economic crisis, characterized by a 50 per cent decline in both GDP and industrial output between 1990 and 1995 and a fall into social unrest. Criminality escalated as violent underworld gangs proliferated. Life soon became a cheap commodity in the Wild East. Marilyn Berger, in an obituary to Yeltsin in the New York Times, wrote, *"In the chaos that accompanied the transition from the centralized economy inherited from the old Soviet Union, most people saw their circumstances deteriorate. Inflation became rampant, the poor became poorer, profiteers grew rich, the military and many state employees went unpaid and criminality flourished."*

Between 1990 and 1994, the country's death rate increased by an astounding 40 percent. Male life expectancy fell from 63.8 years to 57.7, and for women, from 74.3 years to 71.3, a phenomenon unprecedented during peacetime in modern history. Years later, these figures remain at 59.1 and 73, far below their former Soviet levels. After cardiovascular disease, the leading causes of death were accidents, suicides and homicides. Alcohol-related deaths tripled in the first four years of the counter-revolution. Crime became an enduring feature of Russian life. Capitalism was playing its dark hand once more. Privatization shifted control of enterprises from state agencies to individuals with inside connections to the government. Many of the newly rich moved billions in cash and assets outside of the country in an enormous and unprecedented capital flight. The depression of the economy led to the collapse of social services. The birth rate plummeted while the death rate skyrocketed. Millions plunged into poverty, it rising from a level of 1.5 per cent in the late Soviet era to 39–49 per cent by mid-1993.

One orphaned child named Roman Abramovich would make a startling rise to prominence during the Yeltsin years. Having dropped out of college, he would then make his fortune in a series of controversial oil export deals in the early 1990s. Abramovich formed an alliance with billionaire Boris Berezovsky, a key protagonist within Yeltsin's inner circle, to take over Sibneft, an enormous oil producer and refiner, during the cheap privatization sell-offs. Abramovich also came, reluctantly, he claimed, to buy the giant Krasnoyarsk aluminium smelter in early 2000. He would sell the aluminium business in 2003 to Oleg Deripaska, a man even richer and more publicity-shy than he, who came to the attention of the British public when politicians George Osborne and Peter Mandelson were spotted on his yacht off Corfu in 2008.

Not long after selling his aluminium business and weighed down with cash, Abramovich, while attending a Man United vs Real Madrid match, would be bitten by the football bug. His close friend, and future manager at Chelsea, Avram Grant, would explain. "He went there, watched the game start and within ten minutes said 'I want to buy a team.' He was almost in shock at the atmosphere, the theatre. He then needed to find the team he wanted." In July 2003, only months after attending his first game, Abramovich's eyes and wallet would finally settle on Chelsea FC of the leafy Fulham Road in West London. In a meeting lasting less than thirty minutes, a deal would be executed, all due diligence being deferred till afterwards. The BBC would report on the takeover at that time, *"Chelsea football club is to be bought by Russian billionaire Roman Abramovich in a deal worth £140 million ($233m). The surprise takeover – the biggest in British football history – was finalised late on Tuesday after talks with long-time chairman Ken Bates. Bates bought the club in 1982 for just £1, while taking on debts of £1.5 million. Although the club has prospered, debts have grown and it is estimated the new owner will stump up £80 million to cover them. On top of that, Mr Abramovich is buying just over half the shares of Chelsea Village, which owns the football club, for thirty-five pence each – putting the total value of the club's shares at £59.3 million. The Russian businessman pledged to plough even more resources into the club while Mr Bates said the deal would move Chelsea onto the 'next level'. 'We are delighted to agree this deal to acquire what is already one of the top clubs in Europe,' Mr Abramovich said. 'We have the resources and ambition to achieve even more given the huge potential of this great club.'" Bates added, "Football has been in terrible trouble in this country recently – it's clocked up huge debts and the transfer market has collapsed. I think what this could signal is the arrival of overseas sugar-daddies. If this is the start of the super-rich invaders it'll be very, very interesting to see how the fans react to it." Former sports minister Tony Banks said he wanted more information on Mr Abramovich's business background. "I want to know whether this individual is a fit and proper person to be taking over a club like Chelsea. Until that question is answered, then I'm afraid the jury is out," he told the BBC. "A sale has been arranged to an individual we know nothing about."*

For Abramovich, his new-found love of football and Chelsea FC gave him all the reasons he needed to take cash out of a changing Russia. In 2005, he would sell his 73 per cent stake in Sibneft to gas titan Gazprom for $13 billion. In a world where money seems to always end up back in the same hands, Gazprom are now a major sponsor of the Champions League, from which Chelsea earn millions of pounds year on year.

In the eight years prior to Abramovich taking over at Chelsea, Man United had won six league titles and Arsenal had won two. Within two years Abramovich's Chelsea would spend over £200 million in the transfer market, (during the same period United, Arsenal and Liverpool would average yearly spend of £33 million) and in 2005 under new manager Jose Mourinho, the title would be won for the first time in fifty years. Prior to Abramovich's arrival, Chelsea had lifted eight major trophies in nearly 100 years of existence. Twelve short years and £2 billion of investment later that tally had risen to twenty-one, and now included five League crowns and one European Cup. All had changed for Chelsea and for anyone who loved English football.

Life in London for Abramovich and his Chelsea Blues was rosy. But away from the pitch, his Russian legacy had followed him to English shores and when his old ally Boris Berezovsky took a legal case against him in London's Commercial Court for fraud concerning shares in Sibneft, the same shares Abramovich had sold for $13 billion, the normally media-shy and rarely quoted Abramovich had to open up, in the full glare of public scrutiny.

Berezovsky would mention Abramovich too in connection with a murdered spy named Alexander Litvinenko. In 2006, the former Russian spy Litvinenko, who had changed allegiances to work for MI6, would be poisoned with polonium after meeting two Russians in a Mayfair London hotel. It is believed the radioactive polonium was added to his tea. He died slowly in hospital twenty-three days later. It seemed like a plot straight from a James Bond movie. Berezovsky would release statements to the court claiming that Alexander Litvinenko, in the year before his murder, had been investigating the laundering of a huge amount of money belonging to Putin and Abramovich. Abramovich's testimony was stark concerning the brutality of the notorious Russian aluminium wars of the 1990s. "Every three days, someone was being murdered," he would recall.

Finally, amidst a barrage of claims and counterclaims and a web of financial dealings that smelt fouler than an overflowing cesspit, Berezovsky would be deemed an unreliable witness and the case would be dismissed. Within a year Berezovsky would be found dead, in a locked bathroom, at his ex-wife's Surrey home. No third party has ever been linked to the death. With the ghosts of the past sleeping once more, Abramovich could return to his beloved Chelsea and his bullion hoards.

Abramovich is not the only Russian oligarch to have spent his lavish riches on high profile sporting franchises. In January 2015, Forbes declared Alishar Usmanov as Russia's richest man, with a fortune estimated at $14.7 billion, and the world's fifty-eighth richest person. Usmanov owns roughly 30 per cent of Arsenal FC and from all accounts he seems determined to own it all one day. Mikhail Dmitrievitch Prokhorov was another young Russian to avail of Yeltsin's bargain-basement sell-off of precious Russian state assets. Prokhorov, worth an estimated $10.9 billion, now owns the Brooklyn Nets basketball team. It is said that one day he wishes to challenge for the Russian Presidency. One hopes that the Russian people somehow feel part of, and gain satisfaction from, their selfless offerings to the betterment of these sporting empires and that they don't need to fork out too many roubles for replica Chelsea, Arsenal or Nets kits. However, not everybody was happy with the syphoning of money abroad to be spent on playthings for the rich and famous. Yury Luzhkov, the mayor of Moscow, didn't mince his words or sit on the fence when accusing Abramovich of 'spitting on Russia'. He would also remark at a gathering of young Muscovites, "When Abramovich buys Chelsea it is not the kind of good deed that is essential for our spiritual atmosphere. It is self-interested patronage for one's own profit and that kind of good deed is alien to us." Patriarch Kirill, the head of the Russian Orthodox Church and a powerful moral arbiter in Russian society, said Mr Luzhkov's outburst was "very correct and necessary." He then appeared to castigate Russia's wealthy oligarchs himself, declaring, "The names of people with colossal fortunes were mentioned today, but I do not know whether they feed ten people each day."

If you browse Chelsea FC's official website you will find this description of the club's formative years from 1905–1910.

"In just a few short years the personality of Chelsea FC was being established; wealthy, ambitious, fashionable and with immense drawing power."

It seems history repeats, over and over.

NORTH AND SOUTH

'I know you despise me; allow me to say, it is because you don't understand me.' —Elizabeth Gaskell, *Author, North and South*

Liverpool fans sing a song about Chelsea that simply goes *'Fuck off Chelsea FC, you ain't got no history, five European Cups and eighteen Leagues, that's what we call history'*. Given the nouveau financially juiced-up entity that we know as Chelsea FC today, with its twelve recent years of blazing glory reducing the previous hundred years to shadowy dimness, it is tempting to believe that they don't. Although tempting, it would be totally untrue. Chelsea have history and plenty of it.

In 1896, an English businessman Augustus Mears and his brother Joseph purchased the Stamford Bridge Athletics Ground and later the nearby market garden with the intention of developing one of the country's finest football stadiums. The game's popularity was flourishing and a letting to an improving team could prove a lucrative financial investment. Mears hoped local side Fulham FC might be enticed to his new stadium, but they spurned his advances. For nine years he would sit on his investment and then, whilst negotiating the sale of the land to the Great Western Railway Company for use as a coal yard, a funny thing happened. While out walking with a close friend, Fred Parker, Mear's Aberdeen terrier would inexplicably bite Parker's ankle and draw blood. Parker's reaction surprised Mears. He brushed the incident off and playfully scolded the sheepish dog. Parker had been trying to convince Mears to form his own football team to make use of the Stamford Bridge site, and now with Mears somehow enamoured by the man's character, legend says that he decided there and then to follow Parker's advice.

And so, on the evening of 10th March 1905, in an upstairs room at the Rising Sun pub, Chelsea FC was formed. Mears' stadium finally debuted with a friendly against none other than Liverpool FC on Monday 4th, September 1905. The programme that day would ask its patrons, *"Well now, what do you think of our ground, and the stand and the terracing? Good enough for Second Division football, is it not? And it is only a baby as yet. Wait until it is fully grown, and then, well, we shall see what is Chelsea. We don't expect to stroll into the First Division, but we shall get there in time. Hearty congratulations to our friendly opponents today upon their elevation to the Upper House. And may we follow in their footsteps."* Chelsea would beat Tom Watson's Liverpool 4–0.

Chelsea lived up to the promise of their first programme with promotion to the First Division being achieved in 1907. Chelsea's nickname 'the Pensioners' was adopted in homage to the pensioners from the nearby Royal Hospital Chelsea, a retirement and nursing home for former members of the British Army, where pension entitlements are exchanged for board and lodging. To this day, the football club provides eight free tickets to the retirement home for use at every home game.

Despite growing crowds, success would prove elusive for the Pensioners. So much so, that when Alfred Hitchcock made *The Thirty-Nine Steps* in 1935, the fact that Chelsea rarely lifted silverware was joked upon. In this classic film, a music hall entertainer, Mr Memory, takes to the stage to field questions from the audience, always finding the correct answers in some corner of his vast mind.

In the crowd a heckler shouts a question about the FA Cup, "When did Chelsea win it?"

"63 BC in the presence of the Emperor Nero!" Mr Memory replies.

When the Pensioners lifted the League trophy for the first time in 1955 it would prove an emotional day for chairman Joe Mears, son of co-founder Joseph Mears and nephew of the father of Chelsea, Joe Mears. At last, after half a century of toil, sweat and no little ambition, Chelsea had lifted the title. It seems that for those who wait long enough, reward will come.

Chelsea's biggest rivalry involved near neighbours Fulham, and in more recent times the London elite of Arsenal and Spurs. Animosity between London clubs and their northern cousins also made for spicy sporting duels, no doubt fuelled by a long social history of capital elitism and northern militancy. Down through the ages we can find plentiful examples of this clear sense of divide, between the haves and the have-nots. In 1571, the people of Liverpool sent a petition to Queen Elizabeth, praying relief from subsidies, signing off as *"Her Majesty's poor decayed town of Liverpool."* In 1883 the *Pall Mall Gazette* described Blackburn Olympic fans arriving for the FA Cup Final at the Kensington Oval as *"a northern horde of uncouth garb and strange oaths"*. So, when northern teams arrived to play in London, it was no surprise that they felt they needed to leave a mark on their soft southern brethren. A feisty rivalry developed between Chelsea and Leeds United in the sixties and seventies after a series of fiercely contested and controversial matches. These culminated in the 1970 FA Cup Final battle between the two clubs. Chelsea would win 2–1 at Old Trafford in the first FA Cup Final replay since 1912, after the initial game at Wembley ended 2–2. These games are widely remembered as two of the most aggressive matches in English footballing history.

Fifty years on from their only League title win in 1955, the self-proclaimed 'Special One', Jose Mourinho, having just lifted the European Cup with Porto, arrived at Stamford Bridge to take the helm of Abramovich's turbo-charged club. His star-studded team would include new signings Cech, Carvalho, Makelele, Drogba, Robben, Duff, Crespo, Bridge and Geremi amongst many others. Added to these was the English backbone of Terry and Lampard. Chelsea were becoming a colossus. The title would be lifted in 2005 at the first time of asking. In Europe, Rafa Benitez's Liverpool would beat Chelsea in the semi-final of the Champions League. Another fiery north-south rivalry had begun, one which grew fiercer with each passing year and still burns hot to this day. Again, it is fuelled by a perceived contrast in the ethos, style and fabric between the two clubs. Flash cockney bravado meets militant socialism. New money versus established history. All the clichés were there and most rang true. Jamie Carragher explained how Liverpool fans felt. "Chelsea, as a football club, characterised everything they despised. After Abramovich arrived Chelsea behaved like they had a divine right to be instantly considered one of Europe's greatest clubs, just because they were wealthy. Their approach seemed as much about belittling everyone else, as promoting themselves. They represented the opposite of all I believed in. Unlike Liverpool they didn't have the emotional bonds to go with their economic might. They had plenty of what we needed –

money, but The Kop possessed something they couldn't buy, and which can only be bred over the generations – passion."

Whatever the reasons, when Blue meets Red, sparks fly. They did again in 2007 when, once more, Liverpool stopped Chelsea at the semi-final stage of the European Cup. Mourinho couldn't deliver for Abramovich that which he desired most – the European crown, and it was Liverpool who always seemed to be in the way.

But if Mourinho couldn't deliver in Europe, he had no problems at home as Chelsea hoovered up two League titles, one FA Cup and two League Cups over three years in an incredible haul of silverware. Yet managers don't survive long around ruthless owner Abramovich. The media somewhat unjustifiably portrayed Mourinho's team and their style of football as dour and unattractive and Abramovich evidently agreed. He decided on change. Mourinho would join Inter Milan where he would lift the European Cup for a second time and after his time in Italy he would lead Real Madrid to the La Liga title in Spain. Back in London, Roberto Di Matteo would at last lead the Russian's lavishly assembled team to European Cup success (the first London club to do so and only the sixth side from a capital city to lift the trophy). Apart, Abramovich and Mourinho had both succeeded at what they couldn't achieve together, conquering Europe. In 2013, Abramovich would turn again to Mourinho and the feuding couple were back together. In 2014 Chelsea would finish third behind Rodgers' Liverpool and Champions Man City, and in 2015 Mourinho's Blues would lift the title once more, with the help of expensive new recruits Oscar, Costa and Fabregas.

So when Klopp's Reds made the journey south to Stamford Bridge on a sunny bright October morning they were arriving at the home of the Champions. Yet you would hardly have known it. In-fighting had blighted Chelsea's start to the League, most of it caused and led by an increasingly dour and bitter Mourinho. A scowl was never far away and the newly dubbed 'irritable one' even managed to have a full-blown fight, played out in public, with one of his club's medical physicians, Eva Carneiro. Chelsea were adrift in the table in 15th place with eleven points from ten games. Liverpool, albeit in ninth place, had only three points more. Neither team could be happy with their predicament. The media claimed, in classic football parlance, that Mourinho had 'lost the dressing room'. He scoffed at the idea – "Ask the players. If they tell you they don't trust me, it is the only thing that can make me resign – the only thing. Ask the players and don't go with fake sources."

If hopeful green shoots had been the story of Klopp's early reign then Saturday 31st October, Halloween no less, would bring the first full blooming vision of what a Klopp masterclass could look like. Klopp and Mourinho had met six times before, with Klopp holding sway impressively with five wins. Previously it was Dortmund versus either Real Madrid, Chelsea or Inter, today it was the snarling foes Liverpool vs Chelsea. Two stunning goals from Coutinho and one from Benteke would seal a richly deserved 3–1 victory as Liverpool outclassed Chelsea in a way not seen for quite some time by the Red faithful.

Leaving the ground, Chelsea fans grumbled more about their players than their manager. The Special One is revered in these parts, and for those of the Blue persuasion, rightly so. Yet, I can't help thinking that we are watching one of the great managers in decline. It must get tiring to have to wage a new war every single week. Although siege mentality worked for Ferguson at United, and also during Mourinho's first reign at Chelsea, I'm wondering how many times one can go to the same noxious well.

The stroll back along the Fulham Road into Knightsbridge is a walk past some of the most expensive land and property on the planet. A disproportionate sprinkling of ridiculously expensive high-performance cars line the kerbs along with some old-school Bentleys and Rolls Royces. Around here it seems important to show what you are worth. London has become a haven for the world's wealthiest, offering all the rewards of a cosmopolitan western metropolis. If you have money, great, you are welcome. How you sourced it, nobody seems to care. How long this cosy relationship lasts is anybody's guess as the rich get richer and the poor get poorer. Yet for now, it works. Just.

WHEN THE COCK CROWS

'Sometimes it is necessary to be lonely in order to prove that you are right.'
— Vladimir Putin

There is little time to celebrate Liverpool's sacking of Chelsea at the Bridge. The games continue to come thick and fast and a long trek to Kazan awaits. The 5,000 mile round trip to Russia sees Liverpool win for the first time in Europe this season, a Jordan Ibe strike securing a 1–0 victory. Next up are a Liverpool bogey team, Crystal Palace, who beat the Reds home and away the season before. Leading up to the game Palace manager Pardew boasts that his team can beat Liverpool at Anfield and that they will attack. This will be a test for Klopp's resurgent team, and for the faithful in the stands to see if they can expunge the lingering doubts concerning Liverpool's consistency.

In an end-to-end game, mostly dominated by Liverpool, incredibly it is Palace who take the lead 2–1 late on. Yet there is time for an equaliser, up to twelve minutes remain. Standing on the touchline Klopp looks exasperated. He looks behind him, to where a small minority of Liverpool fans are leaving the ground early. On the pitch the team continue to battle but create little. The final whistle blows and Klopp has experienced defeat for the first time as Liverpool manager. Later, in his press conference, he plays a chess move. Klopp talks about feeling alone as he watched fans leave. "After the goal on eighty-two minutes, with twelve minutes to go, I saw many people leaving the stadium. I felt pretty alone at this moment." Ignoring the vast majority of fans who stayed to the death, he has chosen to isolate the deserters. He evokes thoughts of the Liverpool anthem which glories in the fact that no Red ever walks alone. Yet here, within a month of arrival, Klopp claims that he, our leader, our would-be messiah, has felt isolated. We have forsaken him. Checkmate.

It is a message to everybody at the club after his first defeat. It is time to up the ante, to stop wallowing in defeatism. He declares boldly that the team is not beaten until they decide to be beaten. With twelve minutes left, eight goals could have been scored he argues, mathematically anyhow. It is a call to arms. He beseeches his players too, to give the fans more to believe in, more to cheer for, a reason to stay to the bitter end. It is a call from a winner imploring all of a Red persuasion to get behind him.

***

Next up is a trip to Manchester City. The media attempt to stir a pseudo war over the pre-season Raheem Sterling transfer saga. Various City players are quoted as saying that Sterling would be able to stand up the to Liverpool boo-boys. Jürgen Klopp deals with the affair best and puts the transfer in due context.

"I don't know anything about Sterling's story but I know about similar stories and it is normal. This is Mario Götze's story with Dortmund. You cannot hold the player when he doesn't want to be there. It doesn't work. So, you have to take the money and do something smart with it. Always, the will of the players is very important. First of all we have to try to become a club in the future that nobody wants to leave."

During the summer of 2015 Liverpool spent £80 million but this seemed miniscule compared to City's £144 million spree which saw the Sky-Blues dish out £49 million for Sterling, £6 million for Fabian Delph, £36 million for Nicolas Otamendi and £54 million for Kevin de Bruyne. Klopp's largest ever purchase with Dortmund was that of Henrikh Mkhitaryan from Shakhtar Donetsk in 2013 for £21 million. No wonder he talks about having the time and patience to develop a team and its players. "That's the truth: I like to build up teams – it's what I really like in football," he says, "but I have no problem with a different way. I'm not here because we cannot buy expensive players! No, no, no, different reasons." When asked if he could ever see himself spending £50 million on one player, he jokes in reply, "£15 million or £50 million?", before continuing, "there is no reason not to buy for so much. If you are a football romantic, I don't want to buy, but if we want a player and that's the price, we have to think about it. Yes, it is better you have players in your own squad that are worth £100 million but don't want to leave, that's the best thing. This is what we try to do for the future. But it's okay when other clubs do this, I have no problem. It's only a big, big, thing to talk about here. I'm six weeks here, but compared to Germany, where only two clubs sometimes talk about money, all the rest don't talk about money and that's because there is a big difference between Bayern and the rest, because they don't have that much. So, they try to do their best. If you talk about money, you don't speak about development. Why should you develop when you can buy? That's the truth."

"There is nothing negative with your mentality," he continues, "it's different, of course. But I am not here to always talk about money. I am here to give the team some help to develop and that's what we'll do. Money is only one part of success. The rest is work. That is what we are doing. We don't think about Man City. I don't know what kind of story you want to write, money against no money or whatever. But there is no decision about the result on Saturday, so we can fight for it. That's all I need."

I have wondered for some time whether I've been falling out of love with football and its inflated egos and riches, its inequalities and its predictability. I'll never leave though, it is a passion for life, but some of the innocence has been lost. The honesty too. Before, earnest toil earned its rewards. Today, it's more a case of spend a fortune, win a trophy. Klopp is helping me to love again, his words hold truth. Hard work, smarts, drive and ambition, they still count. They did for Mourinho in his early days at Porto and more recently for Simeone at Atletico Madrid and of course for Klopp at Dortmund. As each day passes the believer in me awakens and slowly but surely, I start to fall back in love.

RISE OF THE MACHINES

'What I'd really like to control is not machines, but people'
— Stephen Hawking

An away trip to league leaders Manchester City is an opportunity for the massed press ranks to pen their Klopp progress reports. The season before, under Rodgers, Liverpool managed only one miserly point away to the top four teams. These games can define a club's campaign, if you can hold your own in these battles, then you can play anywhere against anybody. With only one month gone in our new manager's tenure, it's a big ask to expect too much from the short trip to Manchester.

With a two week break for international duties, for the first time Klopp has been afforded time to work with his players in training. He towers on the practice pitches, teaching the way of the high-press and the intense passion play. Over and over, again and again, feeding them as much as they can digest. They need to be able to work as a pack, know when to wait, when to track, and then when to pounce, each man following the last into the hunt, into the relentless chasing down of the opposition. Liverpool's attacking players need to become hungry hunters, constantly stalking and hassling the opposition, knocking them off their stride, preventing them from building possession from the back and controlling the tempo of the game. It's a plan that worked a treat at Chelsea with Firmino playing as a roaming striker. That had been a perfect exposition of the false number nine as the Brazilian led the line but also drifted backwards at times, diverting defensive traffic away from the danger zone, creating space for his teammates to accelerate into. Fluidity, flexibility. Poetry in motion.

***

We arrive at the stadium. Not the Etihad, but its smaller sister arena, built next door by City for their underage teams. When you have so much money, then why not have an Under 21's stadium on your forecourt, one that many lower league teams would be proud of. City and their owners are thinking big, their sights firmly set on domestic and European domination. Opposing fans hold lingering hopes that the oil rich Sheikhs will eventually get bored and that a more even playing pitch returns, but as we gaze now at the seated spaceship that is the superb Etihad Stadium, this seems unlikely. City's home ground has been expanded in the off season by nearly ten thousand seats and today 55,000 will be in attendance. Next season this will rise to 61,000. Premier League stadiums keep getting bigger and bigger and the game's allure shows little sign of waning at home or abroad. It's my son's first time and he declares the Etihad as his favourite ground, after Anfield of course. Kids love all that is bright, shiny and new, whilst older dogs like me cling to the last vestiges of tradition and history, before everything becomes too glossy, immediate and disposable. Some people tell me Anfield is antiquated, but I still love every last brick of the coliseum. But heh, in truth, this place ain't that bad either. Funnily I'm not sure whether City need the larger arena or not and I wonder is the building programme an ego play, an attempt to prove that they can be as big as their cross-town rivals? Empty sky-blue backed seats can be seen regularly at City's home games, even on big European nights. Recently acquired fans can prove hard to please if their sole aspiration is glory. I wonder, if the oil money happened to dry up and City struggled to challenge for the top honours, would the newly found fans start to drift away leaving even more vacant seats?

Browsing through a City fanzine called *King of the Kippaz*, my eyes fall upon a piece penned by one of the regular contributors that explores the financial commitment of the major sides. It opines that, *'the USA based owners [i.e. Man Utd and Liverpool] simply don't want to spend the amount of money required to advance to the latter stages of the Champion's League or even to win the domestic league. For them, third or fourth is good enough. There was only really us [City] and Chelsea who seemed to have the desire to win both trophies, but with Abramovich having already invested £1 billion, you now have to wonder whether you can even include them in that group. The danger could be that the Premier League becomes a singularly boring competition in the future. This might be good for an ambitious club like us but the danger is that it becomes as uncompetitive as La Liga or the Bundesliga.*' I glance through the article again, a second check for irony or self-deprecation, or evidence of some subtle lambaste from the author against financial doping, this betraying his romantic yearning for footballing days of yore, but I can't find it, not a trace. Incredibly this was written on the straight-up. It seems in today's football world, injections of oil money equates to ambition and desire. For the author of this deluded piece, it seems that even Chelsea are not 'ambitious' anymore because their spending has slightly waned. In that case Liverpool must be flatlining. Oh for the days of Shankly, Busby, Clough and Revie, when it wasn't only the dosh that mattered, when football smarts counted too, and oh too for the days when football supporters had the grey cells to understand the difference.

Inside the Etihad, the City fans sing their anthem, 'Blue Moon', and then, in honour of the 129 people who lost their lives in the ISIS terrorist attacks in Paris a week previous, La Marseillaise is sung throughout the stadium. A mark of respect from the football community. It is a touching show of solidarity and fitting given that seventy-two French players ply their trade in the Premiership. This has proven a tough fixture for the Reds since the oil dollars started pumping into the Blue half of Manchester, with City winning four of the last five at the Etihad. Prior to that Liverpool had won eighteen from twenty-two against City, home and away. And who said it's not about the money? The Reds will need to be at it from the off. They are.

Liverpool start at a blistering pace and are at City's heels relentlessly. Firmino gets the nod up top, just as he did at Chelsea. Pressing endlessly behind him are Coutinho, Lallana and Milner. From the back Clyne and Moreno prowl the wings to offer wider support. Behind the front men Can and Lucas are snapping and biting at the City midfielders. Six minutes in and Sagna, City's right back, stumbles over the ball thirty yards from his goal. Like a lithe cheetah Coutinho is upon him in a blink and before Sagna can lift himself from the ground, hunter and ball are gone, both now closing in on the City penalty box. Coutinho slides a ball forward to Firmino and continues his run looking for a return pass. Firmino obliges. The City defence are at sixes and sevens and in the panic that ensues, the ball strikes centre half Mangala's left foot and bounces into the back of his own net, 0–1 to Liverpool. That's how to get out of the blocks. The City faithful who had begun the game with songs abusing Steven Gerrard and mocking Liverpool's loss of Raheem Sterling are now silenced. All around us Liverpool fans are delirious, this is the start we had hoped for.

From the re-start, City rally and take the game to Liverpool. Skrtel is immense as the first line of defence, blocking cross after cross. City attack again and inside the box Skrtel slides to the ground to stop City's goal king, Aguero. The ball appears to strike his hand, but to our relief, the referee waves play on, no penalty. The Sky Blues hardly have time to breathe as Liverpool hunt them down in an aggressive pressing masterclass. Firmino plays his roaming role to perfection, holding the ball up for oncoming teammates, distributing play with supreme accuracy and closing down the City defence at every opportunity. Halfway inside the City half he chases what seems a lost cause against two City defenders Mangala and Demichelis. Somehow it is the Brazilian who escapes with the ball and sets off on a diagonal run for the corner of the City box. He catches a glimpse of Coutinho who has darted into his wake and without skipping a beat, Firmino curls a pass forward along the slick turf. The delivery is inch perfect and as Coutinho arrives in the box, the ball meets his run. With one touch he side-foots it home under the legs of despairing City keeper Joe Hart. It's delirium again all around us. 0–2 to Liverpool, twenty-three minutes gone.

And then, a goal to be watched over and over. On thirty-two minutes, Moreno picks up a loose ball and passes to Coutinho. Coutinho swivels and plays the ball to Can. Can is forced to retreat out of the City area, directed back towards his own half. He looks up to play the ball the way he faces, but then, catching everybody by surprise, instead he back-heels it, returning it into the City box from whence he came, leaving three defenders frozen in limbo in the process. Not everybody is surprised, the quick mind of Coutinho sees things before they happen and he is onto the loose ball in a flash. He heads towards goal, drawing towards him the attentions of the remaining City defenders and those of keeper Joe Hart. But before anybody can reach him, he side-foots the ball to Firmino, who in turn passes the ball from three yards into the empty net, 0–3 and now it is party time on the terraces. Liverpool are at their exhilarating and swashbuckling best and this thirty-two minutes has been as good as anything from the Reds in a long, long time.

'Poetry in motion, la la la la la, Poetry in motion, la la la la la, Poetry in motion, la la la la… We're the best football team in the land, yes we are. We are Liverpool, tra la la la la…'

City are shell-shocked. Liverpool are jubilant. My son is goggle eyed. Liverpool continue to pour forward at every opportunity and, but for Hart, it could be a cricket score. Just as I'm telling my son that we need to take this lead to half-time, Liverpool gift City a soft goal. From a defensive mix up, Aguero pounces, runs at the Reds' defence and curls an unstoppable shot low to Mignolet's bottom left corner. In the blink of an eye, its 1–3. Half-time arrives with no more goals. It's been pulsating, end-to-end entertainment and as good a half of football as one could hope to see.

The second half can't match the relentless drive of the first but still it's high-quality fare. On eighty minutes Liverpool win a corner kick and Lallana sends a high ball across the danger zone. Substitute Benteke challenges in the air and the ball breaks loose to Skrtel who sends a high velocity right foot rocket flashing past Hart into the back of the City net. The Liverpool players race after Skrtel who has sprinted to celebrate with the travelling supporters. Klopp gives his assistant Buvac a huge bear hug on the side-line as Pellegrini, the City manager, can only look on and grimace. Game over, 1–4 to Liverpool and the sky-blue seat backs become visible all around the ground. It's been twelve years since Manchester City have conceded four goals at home. Liverpool's boys from Brazil have delivered a little slice of the Copacabana to west Manchester. A lusty rendition of *'You'll never walk alone'* rises from the away end and carries across the otherwise empty stadium. It is then followed by the new Jürgen Klopp song, sung to the tune of *'Live is Life'* by Opus.

'Jürgen Klopp, na na na na, Jürgen Klopp, na na na na.'

Successive away wins at Chelsea and City have firmly cemented a place for the German in the hearts of the Reds' faithful.

PIRATES OF THE SOUTHERN SEAS

'So throw off the bowlines. Sail away from the safe harbour. Catch the trade winds in your sails. Explore! Dream! Discover!' — Unknown

Southampton, a port city on England's southern coastline, shows traces of human population all the way back to the Stone Age and has been conquered and settled by the Romans, the Anglo Saxons and the Normans. Here on the shore, one can imagine days long past. Cold and exhausted sailors showered by sea spray gather on deck, hearts filled with cheer at the sight of safe harbour. Ahead on land, medieval fortress walls stand proud, windows aglow with the fire and warmth that burns within, comforts beckoning tired souls home. This is a town built to be reached by water, built for the water. Seaports are special places. On their stone docks and their slippery ramparts we can envision the lives of our fore fathers as they set forth on journeys of discovery or necessity. We can imagine the excitement and difficulty of their expeditions and picture their return. Canvases billowing, hulls cutting through choppy waves, arms raised aloft in salute to those on shore. We made it, we are home.

The story of Southampton's marriage with the sea has filled many volumes. Not far from where I stand, some four hundred years earlier, a determined group of individuals would leave comfort and friends behind and embark on a hazardous journey across the Atlantic Ocean. Some 100 people, many of them seeking religious freedom, voyaged west from Southampton on the Mayflower in September 1620, in search of a new world. In late December, the group landed at Plymouth Harbor, Massachusetts, where they would form the first permanent settlement of Europeans in America. These original settlers became known as the Pilgrim Fathers, or simply as the Pilgrims.

On these same stones, many walked to take their berth on the historic liner RMS Titanic. Five hundred Southampton homes lost fathers, sons and daughters who had proudly taken employment on the finest transport vessel of its day. How glamourous that adventure must have seemed in 1912, and how tragically it ended. The dead are commemorated all around this picturesque town, from the Engineers Officers Memorial opposite the World War I Cenotaph, to the Titanic memorial at Holy Rood, where ornate seagulls fly in the wrought-iron gates. Inside rests the Crew Memorial and outside in the courtyard a large iron anchor prods us to remember. Now over a century later, seagulls screech and squawk as a blustery gust lifts my scarf and I walk up Bugle Street, passing the Duke of Wellington and then the Titanic pub. Here I stop for a coffee and some contemplation, a small token of respect.

For the second day of December, it's unusually mild and my multiple layers are keeping me snug. Stone lions holding spears guard the Bargate Monument in the centre of town but thankfully my progress through goes unhindered. Southampton is a lovely mix of new and old. A bustling city lies inside old fortress town walls. The streets are abuzz with young people doing what young people do, having fun. It's not a pre-football crowd, more an exuberant festive gathering spilling out from the City's University. Ahead is a Christmas market, complete with wooden stalls and seasonal decorations. The smell of mulled wine and hot food draws me closer. Soon Christmas music fills the air and parents and young children look upwards. Santa and his reindeer have arrived at Above Bar Street. It's an impressive sight as the large sleigh complete with human Santa hovers fifty feet above the market below. With forty-five minutes to kick-off, I decide that I've had enough mulled wine, it's game time.

Liverpool come to Southampton on a wave of momentum and confidence. The victory at Manchester City has been followed by two home wins, the Reds defeating Bordeaux 2–1 in the Europa League and Swansea 1–0 in the League. This run of three consecutive wins has secured progression in Europe, with qualification to the last thirty-two assured, and has also lifted the team to the lofty heights of sixth in the league table. Cause for optimism indeed. Winning is what matters most in football and after three victories in a row some pundits are talking about Liverpool as title contenders. When put to Klopp, he laughs and rightly so.

To add to the good news some of the injured are on the mend. Sturridge is a prolific finisher, the type of player who makes goal-scoring look simple and who finds space in a crowd. For him time slows under pressure. Conversely his thoughts and instincts sharpen. He is a predator of the highest quality. An artist, but a delicate one and quite often a broken one. Henderson is the complete modern player, possessed of an engine to get from box to box He can tackle, pass, dribble, create and score goals. The type of footballing machine to make Klopp drool. No wonder he is the captain. Both players made their long-awaited returns coming on as substitutes in the home win over Swansea. Both finished the game uninjured. With games coming every three to four days and with the stockpiled Christmas fixture list awaiting, quality additions to the playing roster are early seasonal gifts.

I follow the scarfed and kitted hordes along the dimly lit streets. You don't need a map to find a football ground, just follow the colours. I make my way past Houndwell and Hoglands Parks, heading east of the town's hub. Around a corner the source appears, St Mary's Church, its tall spire serenely illuminated by soft beams. Here 130 years ago, twenty-four years before the building of the Titanic had even commenced, the leaders of St Mary's Church decided to found a football team. That team, originally named Southampton St Mary's, would eventually become simply Southampton FC. From here, the swelling crowd takes a left into what seems to be an industrial warehousing estate. Around another turn and the newer, bigger and much larger cathedral of St Mary's 32,000 seater football stadium fills the vista, its bright lights making it seem like day, not night, as it beckons us forward to tonight's service.

Southampton have, for most of their existence, managed to survive in the top echelons of English football, however in 2009, when Swiss businessman Markus Liebherr's takeover rescued the club, the Saints had fallen to the third tier. Liebherr's investment in the team, the stadium and crucially the management structure, helped to restore Southampton to the top flight. Astute ownership decisions have seen Southampton safely established in the top ten since. The south-coasters have shown that a 'Moneyball' type approach can be adapted to football if your expectations are tempered. Buy young talent from Europe's lesser leagues. Give this talent its legs and an opportunity on the big stage. Hire young bright and energetic coaches to manage those legs and then sell the refined package to the bigger clubs for substantial profits. For examples, one only need look to Liverpool's team to see the presence of former Saints Dejan Lovren, Adam Lallana and Nathanial Clyne, the trio collectively sold to the Reds for the tidy sum of £58 million. Aligned to this 'buy low and sell high' philosophy, Southampton FC is also home to one of the League's brightest academies, with many of its graduates, such as Gareth Bale and Luke Shaw, coming through the club's youth ranks before being blooded and then sold. This 'feeder club' existence seems to be a fact of life for Southampton, their best talent realising that the club is a stepping stone, not a destination. Enter a very keen multi-billionaire and this might change, but that does not seem to be the business plan of Katharina Liebherr who inherited the ownership reins after her father's death in 2010. It remains steady as she goes on the coast and why not? It's worked a treat so far. Managers seem to cut their teeth here too. Pochettino built on the successful job done by Nigel Adkins before being offered a prized move to Tottenham. European Cup winner and former Dutch great Ronald Koeman now fills the hotspot. I doubt it will be long before a 'larger' club comes knocking at his door.

The match day programme includes a nice little bonus, a reproduction of the programme produced for the semi-final of the 1987 League Cup, played between these same two clubs. Then, Chris Nicholl was Saints manager and Kenny Dalglish was at the Liverpool helm. Liverpool's team included Hansen, Whelan, Lawrenson, Rush and Molby, amongst others. Peter Shilton, the great England goalkeeper, played for Southampton along with Liverpool's very own 1977 European Cup hero Jimmy Case, having since moved to the south coast. Mark Wright played at centre half. He would go on to sign for Liverpool in 1991 for £2.5 million, a national record fee for a defender at that time. Back then, Liverpool triumphed 3–0 over two legs, but would lose the final 2–1 to Arsenal.

Tonight's game kicks off at 7.45 p.m. and by 7.46 p.m. Liverpool are 1–0 down. Klopp has chosen to play youth team player Conor Randall at right-back and he gets exposed a little by the tricky Tadic. Emre Can comes to offer help and only manages to compound the problem. A cross into the box floats over the heads of the Reds' defenders and is met powerfully by Sadio Mane to give second choice Liverpool goalkeeper Adam Bogdan no chance. In all, Liverpool have made six changes from the Swansea victory and early on they look vulnerable. Another ball swings in from the left wing and it's nearly 2-0, but for a solid save from Bogdan. The worrying thought runs through my mind that maybe Klopp, new to English football and its proud cup traditions, has underestimated Southampton's desire to lift their first silverware since winning the FA Cup in 1976, when defeating Man United 1–0, their only major trophy win. The south-coasters are at pretty much full strength and are up for this game from the start. That said, I can't see any other option but to rotate and rest players who have been playing relentlessly game after game. Tonight was never going to be easy, Southampton hold a grudge against Liverpool, the Reds having plundered three of their star players in the last two years in Adam Lallana, Dejan Lovren and Nathaniel Clyne. We must be viewed as pirates, pirates who pay top dollar mind you. Despite the bounty that has been deposited into the Southampton coffers, and which was accepted in their boardroom with wide eyes and grinning mouths, vicious abuse rains down from the home support in the direction of Lovren and Lallana. I feel it will be a long night. There is no let-up on the pitch, Southampton are mauling Liverpool and the Reds cling on for dear life.

On twenty-five minutes the momentum changes. Thankfully one of the changes made by Klopp was to play Daniel Sturridge from the off. Sturridge latches onto a wonderful cross-field pass from Allen, slips to the left of his marker and then fires home a low left-footed equaliser into the bottom of the net. 1-1 in the Cup Quarter Final. It's Liverpool's first real attack but that's all Sturridge needs. One chance, one goal. Four minutes later and Liverpool are ahead. Emre Can fools his marker with a clever flick inside and then, with the outside of his right boot, he lofts a curling ball diagonally over the heads of the Southampton defenders and into the danger area. Sturridge runs on to it and meeting the ball first time he drives it into the back of the net. Five short minutes has seen Liverpool turn the game on its head, 1–2 to the pirates. Southampton's players look shell-shocked and I can understand why, they don't deserve to be behind, yet they are.

Liverpool's tails are up and they take control of the game, laying siege to Southampton's defence. On forty-five minutes it's 1–3. Moreno fires back a clearance from a corner and the young Belgian, Divock Origi, given a rare outing by Klopp, manages the slightest of touches and guides the ball home. The Reds fans are delirious in the Northam Stand and the chant goes up *'he's winning 3–1, he's winning 3–1, Adam Lallana, he's winning 3–1'* to the tune of the Beach Boys' *'Sloop John B'*.

The second half starts as did the first, with Southampton banging away at Liverpool's door in search of a way back into the game. They go close and really should notch a second goal, but don't. And for this profligacy they pay heavily. On sixty-eight minutes, Liverpool's substitute Jordan Ibe beats his man and feeds a ball through to Origi. The striker runs on to the pass and from the edge of the Southampton penalty area fires a rifled, unstoppable bullet into the roof of the net, 1–4 to Liverpool. That fantastic feeling arrives, one seldom enjoyed by football fans of any persuasion. The ability to relax, stress-free and simply enjoy the game in the full knowledge of certain victory. No nervous fretting, no pulling out hair, no nauseous feelings. This lead is surely unsurmountable, it's time to celebrate and unwind. Within five minutes the victory is in zero doubt. Jordan Ibe traps a perfect Moreno cross on his chest and on the half-volley he fires the ball home.

'He's winning 5–1, he's winning 5–1, Adam Lallana, he's winning 5–1.'

This wakes the Southampton fans from their shock and to their credit they out-sing the away end for the remainder of the game. Over and over we listen to their *'Oh when the Saints go marching in'* anthem. It's hard to sing when you've been hung, drawn and quartered, but they do. The rout is not over though as Origi bags his hat-trick in the eighty-sixth minute, getting on the end of an exquisite cross from Liverpool's Australian youth player Brad Smith. Soon the chant goes up again, another goal added to the total:

'He's winning 6–1, he's winning 6–1, Adam Lallana, he's winning 6–1.'

The game ends and as the Southampton fans shuffle away, they are clapped by the Liverpool's fans, a show of admiration for having stuck with it to the dour end. For us, it's time to *'hoist up the John B's sail, see how the mainsail sets, call for the captain ashore, it's time to go home, we better go home'*.

THE PITS

'There are no wastelands in our landscape quite like those we've created ourselves.' — Tim Winton

Sipping our warm drinks, we gaze out of the cafe's large clear window to the Christmas market outside, which huddles under Grey's Monument in Newcastle upon Tyne. The forty-metre-tall pillar stands proudly in a small square at the junction of Grey Street and Grainger Street. Atop the column sits a statue of Charles Grey, the second Earl Grey and a native of Northumberland, England's most northerly county. Grey served as Prime Minister from 1830–1834 and was instrumental in passing the Reform Act, abolishing slavery and empowering the rights of Catholics. Today he is best remembered for a subtle tea flavour named in his honour. Under Grey's gaze, Christmas shoppers and weekend tourists mill around the stalls and go busily on their way. South of the monument, Grey Street sweeps in a curve downhill towards Dean Street and the River Tyne. The buildings stand uniform with their neo-classical and Georgian architecture and proud sandstone edifices, lined in a delicately falling arc along the path of a hidden underground burn. Sir John Betjeman, a UK Poet Laureate, said of Grey Street, "As for the curve, I shall never forget seeing it to perfection, traffic-less on a misty Sunday morning. Not even old Regent Street London, can compare with that descending subtle curve." In 2010 Grey Street was voted 'Best Street in the UK' by BBC radio listeners. It forms part of the area known as Grainger Town, an historic city quarter, designed and constructed by a local developer Richard Grainger and built in the period from 1824 to 1841. The majesty of this area, consisting of a collection of interweaving streets, with over 400 listed buildings, is superbly captured in the masterful Louis H. Grimshaw oil painting simply titled, 'Grainger

Street, Newcastle Upon Tyne' which hangs in the nearby Laing Gallery.

It's my first visit and I am quite taken by how historic, diverse and genuinely beautiful Newcastle is. My son agrees and nods his approval. Earlier that morning we visited the old castle ruins that are Newcastle Castle and after which the city was named. The Old Keep was built in 1080 by Robert Curthose, son of Norman king, William the Conqueror, who defeated King Harold Godwinson at the Battle of Hastings in 1066. Before being named Newcastle the area was known as Pons Aelius, named after the family of the Roman Emperor Hadrian, and consisted of a Roman Fort settlement with a bridge spanning the Tyne. Newcastle had always been a strategic location, sitting as it did on a key travel artery, 247 miles north from London and 88 miles south of Edinburgh. Today parts of Hadrian's Wall can still be found in the area. Built in the period from 122 to 128 AD, the great divider ran from the banks of the River Tyne and spanned all the way west across the North of England to Solway Firth on the Irish Sea. It is believed to have been designed as a protective structure to keep the Barbarians out of civilised, settled Roman territory.

In more recent times the Newcastle upon Tyne and neighbouring Wearside regions gained relevance nationwide and their identity locally, for being hotbeds of industrialism. Family after family, generation after generation, earned their living from working in the blackened mining pits or on the shipbuilding docks. Coal was the main source of energy produced in the UK in the sixties but gradually it slipped into decline, as government sought the closure of inefficient collieries and regulators sought the use of cleaner fuels. A low point was reached in 1984 when Prime Minister Margaret Thatcher ordered the closure of over twenty mines, which led to the year long miners' strike. The so-called 'Iron Lady' stood firm and the death knell for the coal mining industry was sounded. In January 2005, Ellington Colliery, the last deep coal mine in the North East, shut down, bringing centuries of local history and culture to an abrupt end. Paul McMillan in the *Evening Chronicle* reported on January 27th, 2005,

> *"Just five weasel words were needed to end centuries of our industrial heritage. 'Gentlemen the pit is closed' were the words from Ellington axeman Gerry Spindler. What it meant was that the last super-pit, in a*

once proud industry battered by unrest, was closing. Opened in 1909 as part of the Ashington Coal Company, its workforce soared from less than 800 at the outbreak of the First World War to 1,200 in 1921 and to an all-time high of 2,179 at the time of the 1984 strike. In 1983 the pit set a record, producing one million tonnes of coal in twenty-nine weeks. From employing more than 2,100 men in the 1980s, the announcement has left the region's 340 remaining miners out of work and the surrounding community stunned. Once there were 200 pits across the Northumberland and Durham Coalfields and at the end of the Second World War, there were 148,000 men employed in the mines. It was North East coal which fuelled the industrial revolution and the heavy industries that sprang up across the region."

Two paintings hang side by side back in the City's Laing Gallery. The first titled 'Going Home' 1888 by Ralph Hedley shows two miners returning home from Blaydon's main Colliery, near Gateshead. The men carry safety lamps, one of which is the Geordie Lamp, this lamp invented by Robert Stephenson, himself a Northumbrian, who would find further fame in the development of the steam engine and the steam train, many of which would traffic the black stuff away from the pits towards city and industry. Some believe this is where the use of the term 'Geordie' to describe people from Newcastle upon Tyne derived, given the intrinsic link between local families and the mines. Beside this hangs another painting, this one by Norman Cornish titled 'Pit Road'. This canvas depicts a brooding grey sky and a sombre mood as a miner heads home from the pit. Stooped low and with back bent over, the man seems broken and the image somehow captures a lost industry and in many ways a lost identity. Cornish, renowned for his pictures of mining community life, spent more than three decades working as a coal miner himself before making a successful career as an artist. He was the last painter from the so-called Pitman's Academy, a pioneering arts community established in north-east England in the 1930s. Whilst 'Pit Road' is moody and melancholic, most of Cornish's work exudes a nostalgic warmth for his lost community. Cornish would say, "This special world of mine is constantly changing and many of the people who inhabited it are no longer with us. Many of the places that once helped to make up that world have also passed into time. The local collieries have gone, together with the pit road. Many of the old streets, chapels and pubs are no longer more. Many of the ordinary but fascinating people who frequented these places are gone. However, in my memory and I hope in my drawings, they live on." Cornish died in 2014 aged ninety-four.

These days, ironically and with an unsurprising show of what is known as 'Northern Spirit', Newcastle has reinvented itself as a clean industry, green town. What art Cornish could conjure from that, one can only wonder. Cornish also painted many bar scenes of the pit men supping their glass of ale after work. Now the bars throng with youthful life. Hen and Stag parties abound, as Newcastle transforms by night into a thriving destination for those in search of hedonistic fun.

Newcastle is also known for something else, something that has provided slightly less enjoyment of recent times. Football. In a region that has lost large chunks of its social identity with the transition from Industrial Revolution to the modern Internet-driven financial banking age, local people have sought a sense of meaning and identity, now more than ever before, from the institutions that remain. Prevalent amongst these are the football clubs. Not that this region was not football crazy in the past, of that there can be no doubt. Newcastle, Sunderland and Middlesbrough were all amongst the biggest and most prestigious clubs in English football in the early twentieth century. The region served as a hotbed, a footballing incubator for young, talented players and managers. Bob Paisley's and Kevin Keegan's families grew up but a few yards apart in the small mining village of Hetton-le-Hole. A roll call of local greats includes Brian Clough, Don Revie, Bobby Robson, Jackie Milburn, Bobby and Jack Charlton, Howard Kendall, Paul Gascoigne, Alan Shearer, Alan Kennedy and the aforementioned Keegan and Paisley. Michael Walker's book *Up There* asks us to wonder how glorious it could have been, if most, or even some of that talent pool could have been harnessed locally. For many and various reasons, it wasn't and most of these greats left and found fame and glory elsewhere. League titles and European Cups were collected, but none in the name of the North East. Eventually some would return such as Keegan, Shearer and Robson, all weighed down with the bulk of their travelled successes, as if explorers returning home with riches from afar. In Spain, Atletico Bilbao build their team to consist only of local Basque players, all encouraged to stay at home, to play for Basque pride. If this had been achieved in the North East we would be now talking about Newcastle and Sunderland in the same breath as Liverpool and United.

Newcastle have won the League four times, the last time nearly a century ago, in 1927. Sunderland have bettered this with six crowns, their last title coming in 1936. All of a sudden Liverpool's twenty-five year wait doesn't seem so bad. Newcastle United started out in red but at a club meeting in 1894 it was resolved, "that the Club's colours be changed from red shirts and white knickers to black and white shirts (two inch stripe) and dark knickers." The club's devotees have followed these famous colours ever since and one can only admire a fan base that keeps turning up week in, week out, always in the face of repeated failure. Newcastle fans are particularly worthy in this regard. The Toon Army, as they are known, (Toon being local dialect for Town, Newcastle being a one-club town), can be counted on come hell or high water. Liverpool great John Barnes recalled his time at the Magpies. "The passion of the Geordies is unbelievable. These Newcastle supporters had no success to savour, simply false dawns and shattered expectations, but they waited and hoped, and dreamed. They are special fans."

On the road to winning their last major trophy, the Fairs Cup in 1969, crowds of 75,000 people flocked to Newcastle's home stadium, St James' Park, to see their beloved Magpies. Sir Matt Busby once said, "If you put eleven black and white dogs on the field at Newcastle, you'd get 30,000 coming to watch".

Today, Newcastle's home ground is an all-seater stadium with a capacity of 51,250 and week after week there is rarely an empty seat to be seen. Unless, that is, there has been a militant action planned by the supporters and a 'stay away' or a 'walk out' campaign has been activated. Newcastle supporters have seldom had custodians who matched their own passion and loyalty. In 1998 the UK's *News of the World* Sunday newspaper alleged that then directors, Douglas Hall and Freddie Shepherd had described the team's star player Alan Shearer as Mary Poppins, laughed at fans for paying large sums for the club's replica shirts and labelled the city's women 'dogs'. All in the course of frequenting a Spanish brothel. Hall and Shepherd applied for an injunction but Justice

Lindsay ruled, "If someone wants to keep something confidential, talking about it in a Spanish brothel is not the way to do it."

However, Hall and Shepherd did hold office when Keegan's Newcastle team, dubbed 'the Entertainers', led the title race for most of the campaign in 1995/96. Unfortunately, a late dip in form, combined with a surge from Manchester United, would see the Magpies pipped at the last. The long wait since 1927 would go on. Managers came and went, including more Liverpool old boys in Dalglish and Souness. Terry McDermott would act as caretaker. Yet none could crack the enigma and bring success to the North East. Alex Ferguson would say, "Newcastle are the most difficult club to manage in the game, gobbling up managers and spitting them out again, with hardly a pause. If they regarded their managers as something more than ships that pass in the night they might achieve the stability and consistency that is the basis of success at any club."

In 2007, Mike Ashley, billionaire founder of Sports apparel company Sports Direct took ownership. Regrettably, Ashley did not heed Alex Ferguson's advice and since his arrival Newcastle have seen eleven managerial changes in eight short years. His tenure has been ill-fated and the Toon army have called for his departure more than once. The club remains in what seems a state of constant flux.

★★★

It's cold now, but nice and wintery, great weather to walk in. Thankfully the gales and incessant rainfall of storm Desmond, which has left much of England in flood, have now passed through. Darkness has descended and ahead, looming large in the late afternoon sky, sits St James' Park. If one were to build a castle today, this would be the site, its lofty promontory affording unobstructed views on all sides of any approaching enemy. Today, the would-be pillagers are Liverpool FC. Upwards we climb with the thousands of others that now converge upon the stadium. We reach the back of the Gallowgate end, named for its proximity to Newcastle's old Gaol and Gallows. The *Newcastle Chronicle* explores its grizzly history – *'The Gallows Hole was a place of public execution in the vicinity of the current St James' Park. There were some very grim spectacles. In 1650, twenty-two people, including fifteen witches, were hanged in one day. Capital punishment was not confined to those who had taken another person's life. In 1783, William Alexander was hanged for forging a bank note, and in 1786 Henry Jennings was executed for stealing horses. The last hanging took place in 1844, only three decades before the first ball was kicked at the site. For those of us who've spent many a grim afternoon standing and sitting at the Gallowgate End, spare a thought for Mark Sherwood of Blandford Street who had murdered his wife. The condemned man was taken by cart to the gallows, in front of the elegant Leazes Terrace, sitting on his coffin!'*

Inside the stadium, we climb the endless steps that take you to Level 7 at the top of the Leazes Street Stand, where up in the clouds one eventually finds the seats designated for the away fans. Puffing for breath, we locate ours. Behind us is the wall and a metre or so above our heads is the roof. You can't get a loftier or more remote view in this stadium or maybe the whole of Newcastle. We look down to the pitch and can just make out which Reds players are lining up for kick-off. All around are views out and over the bright lights of the city. All around too are expectant and ebullient Liverpool fans still warm from the glow of the flogging dished out at Southampton. Now to build on recent momentum.

Klopp has urged his players to start fast and they do, but the play is scrappy and some early pressure tails off. Eventually the game settles down into a turgid and damp affair. Newcastle have no ambition to get out of their own half but Liverpool aren't much better. The half drifts by without great incident and the sides go in at 0–0. My toes are numb from the cold up on Everest and the break brings an opportunity to move and get a hot cup of tea. My son doesn't complain, he doesn't seem to feel the cold like I do.

I've felt an apprehensive foreboding about today, but heh, that's hardly new. The build-up to the game has been littered with pundits saying that the Reds are back in the title race. Even some of the players have caught the bug. As any Red fan who has lived through the last twenty-five years will know, as soon as the players and media start saying we are back, then certain doom awaits just around the corner. The first-half display has left me feeling edgy. Newcastle are poor and it is easy to see why they are near the bottom of the table. Even a draw here today will be a bad result. Away from home, Klopp's pressing style works best against teams that come forward, who attack and leave space behind. Chelsea, City and Southampton fitted this bill, Newcastle don't. Whether by design or ineptitude, they have hardly ventured out of their own half and have left no space for Liverpool to advance into. If this is manager McClaren's strategy, it is a good one.

Liverpool start the second half as badly as they finished the first and Newcastle grow into the game, their confidence flowering. On sixty-two minutes Klopp has seen enough. Sturridge replaces Benteke and Lallana replaces Firmino. Immediately Liverpool improve but still the overall quality is poor, with sloppy passing and zero intensity. Klopp's full throttle football is on whimper mode. With sixty-nine minutes on the clock Newcastle score. What looks like an innocuous attack causes panic in the Liverpool box and a Wijnaldum shot deflects into the net off a flailing Skrtel. The Newcastle fans can hardly believe it, their first shot on goal and they lead 1–0. Liverpool react and at last pour forward. Milner crosses to Moreno and the Spaniard scores with a looping lob over the head of goalkeeper Krul. But no, no goal, the linesman flags for offside. It's a shocking decision. Engaged in futile late attacking forages, Liverpool leave the back gate wide open and in steal Newcastle in the ninety-third minute for a second. This time Wijnaldum gets a goal that he can call his own with no assistance from Skrtel. Newcastle have had two shots on goal and they score with both; 2–0, game over.

It's been one of the worst games of football that I've ever witnessed. Not even my son can muster any enthusiasm after this performance and together we walk back into town feeling the pits.

THE SHOW MUST GO ON

'The show must go on, I'll face it with a grin, I'm never giving in'
— 'The Show Must Go On' — Queen

After the Newcastle frightener, Liverpool travelled to Sion in Switzerland, where a dour 0–0 draw on a frozen pitch saw the Reds claim top spot in their Europa League group. Three days later, West Bromwich Albion visited Anfield and once more Liverpool floundered. Leading through a goal from captain Henderson, it looked like the Reds would push on. Instead, heading into the last ten minutes Liverpool trailed 1–2. Both West Bromwich goals had come from corners, basic set pieces which Liverpool had failed spectacularly to defend. Only a late, late, late ninety-eight minute equaliser from the ever improving Divock Origi saw Liverpool rescue a 2–2 draw and what might prove to be a valuable point. However, a point of a different sort had been proven by Klopp. If the fans stay to the very last, if they believed, then good things could happen. His lament after the home defeat to Palace now bore fruit. No trophies had been won and, in fact, Liverpool had slipped up in a game that they had desperately wanted to win, but most importantly, a Klopp philosophy had been born. It was a mantra of old, making a welcome return. Never say die. Shankly, too, understood the importance of late goals, of never quitting. He remarked, "One season we scored goals in the last five minutes of about nine matches and this gave us anther psychological lever. I told my players, as time wears on they are becoming more afraid of you. When their trainer says there are only ten minutes to go, that makes them all jittery. 'Christ, they are due one now' they think. We got to the point where we knew we would win."

To stamp the new agreement, Klopp marched his troops to form a line in front of the Kop at the game's finale. Arm in arm, all raised together, they saluted the cheering fans. We all knew what it meant. The bond had been sealed. We would go to the bitter end together. Later the media would deride what they believed was a misplaced show of celebration from a club of Liverpool's stature, for what was only a scrappy home draw to lowly West Brom. Yet they missed the point entirely, by a million miles. It was this bond between fans and team that Klopp had developed so successfully, first at Mainz 05 and then at Dortmund. It was this unity that led to the incredible success he achieved with both of those teams. It was this belief in playing to the very last that saw his Dortmund team score two goals in injury time in the European Cup quarter final at home to Malaga in 2013, when all hope had been lost.

This was the bond that had started to fracture at Anfield at the end of the Rodgers reign, and which Klopp rightly identified as needing repair. His defiant words after the Palace defeat at home, when he said he felt alone after some fans left early, resonated with every Reds fan. "It is not over, until we decide it is over."

***

Left along Main Street and then a right turn and before long, Vicarage Road, Watford is in sight. A vision comes and goes; Rush, donned head to toe in white, three red stripes on the sleeves, belting one in from the corner of the box. Those were the days.

"What do you expect today?" I ask my son.

"I think we'll win two or three nil," he replies full of confidence, the memory of Newcastle obviously expunged from his mind.

"You are not worried about how lacklustre we were against West Brom at home?" I ask.

"No, that was at home and they parked the bus, this is different, we are away and we'll cut them open," he responds. I remind my son that Liverpool actually lie two places below Watford in the table, eighth versus sixth.

A win today at Watford and the West Brom point would practically take on a positive glow. Three minutes in and nothing is glowing except possibly our goalkeeper's embarrassed cheeks. An innocuous cross drifts towards the front post from a Watford corner kick. Bogdan, in between the sticks, in place of the injured Mignolet, reaches out to catch the ball at chest height, but only manages to drop it at the feet of Watford defender Ake, who gleefully pokes it into the net from one yard. He wheels away in delight, not fully believing his luck. We look at each other in bewildered bemusement, Liverpool have again gifted a goal to the opposition. Once more it comes from a corner. "Shocking," is all my son can muster. I'm speechless.

It's a windy wet day and Watford are hoofing every ball high into the sky, for their two strong forwards, Deeney and Ighalo, to chase. The pair have been a revelation in the League this year bagging fifteen goals between them (Ighalo ten, Deeney five). In contrast, Liverpool's entire team have managed only twenty goals. The deadly duo are winning every aerial battle, with their scavenging teammates leaping on every breaking ball. Liverpool resemble a herd of frightened antelope. It's not pretty or purist and at times it seems more akin to rugby, but it is oh so effective. Running onto an enormous welly upfield, Ighalo out-muscles Skrtel with ease and bounces an angled shot past the poorly positioned Bogdan and into the Liverpool net off the right-hand post. 2-0 to Watford and only fifteen minutes gone. The 17,000 home fans inside the 20,000 capacity stadium are bouncing as they sing Nigerian Ighalo's name over and over to the tune of Spandau Ballet's hit song 'Gold'. For Ighalo, a kid from the slums of Lagos, it's another chance to earn some real gold to send home to his family in Nigeria and to the orphanage he plans to open. Football is full of motivations, some nobler than others.

Liverpool are no better in the second half. As at Newcastle, the Reds leave the back door open as they search in vain for a way back. On eighty-five minutes, Watford's golden boy Ighalo seals all three points, putting the yellow and black hornets up 3–0. To the onlooking Klopp, Watford must resemble his old marauding Dortmund team. We stay to the end, because we have been told to never give up, but today it was the team that surrendered early. A 3–0 disaster. Klopp is starting to get the hang of this record setting business. Today has seen Watford's biggest ever victory over Liverpool.

As the dumbstruck Reds fans shuffle silently out of the ground, still bewildered by what they just witnessed, the stadium announcer bellows the news that Watford have risen to fifth place in the League and are only one point off the top four and the Champion's League places. Real Madrid versus Watford, wouldn't that be a story.

***

On the same day that Liverpool are being beaten up by Watford, in a footballing galaxy far, far away, Yokohama, Japan to be precise, Barcelona, the Champions of Europe are playing Argentinean team River Plate, Champions of South America. The scoreline is the same as that at Vicarage Road, but it is there where all comparisons end. The gap in quality is truly interstellar.

In Yokohama, Luis Suarez bags two goals as Barcelona triumph 3–0 to become World Club Champions. Speaking to FIFA reporters later he says, "It's nice to play in these tournaments. The Intercontinental Cup is now the Club World Cup, and it's something that's excited me since I was a boy when I used to wake up at six in the morning to watch these games. It's one of the dreams I had yet to fulfil." It is that passion and desire for the game that has seen so many South American kids transformed from street scrappers to global superstars. It is that hunger that drove Suarez to Liverpool's lucky door for three wonderful seasons. But it was also that drive which saw him leave, in the knowledge that his dreams would be better fulfilled elsewhere. And so they have been. Suarez is a star in a team of stars, the brightest of which is Lionel Messi. The triumvirate attackers of Messi, Suarez and Neymar may just be the finest three-card-trick that football has ever seen. In winning the Japanese final, Barcelona added the World Club title to their earlier 2015 triumphs of the Spanish league, the Spanish Cup, the European Champions League and the European Super Cup.

These imperious heights seem fantastical now to Reds fans. My son has only seen TV pictures of when Liverpool played in these games. Following the drudgery witnessed at Watford, he can't quite conceive that only ten short years previously, it was Rafa Benitez's Liverpool who were amongst the last two in the world and who were playing in Japan, losing unluckily 1–0 to Sao Paulo of Brazil. Sometimes you don't know how good you have it until it's long past and gone.

***

That night Klopp insists that Liverpool's pre-planned Christmas Party goes ahead and that every player stays till 1 a.m. and joins the sing-along. After the 3–0 debacle, many managers would have cancelled the party, particularly English ones, running scared of a potential media storm, where the same old tired story of footballers partying and not caring would be rolled out. Not Klopp, he does the right thing and not one fan complains, 3–0 or no 3–0. A team that wins together, loses together. The show must go on. Merry Christmas boys.

MAD DOGS AND ENGLISHMEN

'Tell me baby do you recognize me? Well it's been a year, it doesn't surprise me' – 'Last Christmas', Wham

Liverpool have the rare luxury of one full week to recover from the Watford debacle and any Christmas party hangovers before Leicester, incredibly the League leaders on Christmas Day, arrive at Anfield for the traditional Boxing Day fixture. One year earlier Leicester lay rooted to the bottom of the table and were certainties for the drop. Then began an escape that Houdini would be proud of, led by manager Nigel Pearson. Carving out result after result, somehow by May 2015, the Foxes had cheated relegation. It was widely viewed as a footballing miracle, but little did we know that it was only the start of an even more incredible story. This Christmas's Leicester are unrecognizable to those Foxes that came before.

Pearson was replaced by the Italian and former Chelsea boss, Claudio Ranieri and many commentators remarked that Leicester would struggle to maintain their exuberant and unexpected form. Several even predicted they would suffer the drop, their execution having only been temporarily stayed. However, to everyone's amazement, the Foxes only improved further and with the outstanding performances of striker Jamie Vardy and midfield creator Riyad Mahrez, Leicester have continued their march. And so, amazingly on December 26th, in the richest League in the world, the minnows of Leicester sit in first place.

Liverpool, still smarting from their defeat to Watford, make three changes, with Klopp opting for a 4-2-3-1 formation instead of the ineffectual 4-3-3. Origi starts at centre forward and Mignolet and Lovren return from injury to replace the dropped Bogdan and the newly injured Skrtel. Lucas is rested.

The game proves a pulsating affair with Liverpool the better team throughout, their play slick and exciting. Come the final whistle a 1–0 win is fully merited.

Yet despite the victory, Klopp worries that his team may be running on empty. The congested winter schedule has proven somewhat to his chagrin, as he complained to the media all week of how negative it is for players' peak performance. He says that in Europe they look at English football and they know this, they know that they are tired. Too much football, too many trophies, no winter break, players always susceptible to injury. But football at Christmas and the New Year is a tradition in England and whilst the rest of Europe takes two weeks off for recuperation and players head to the Dubai and Florida sunshine, the hardy English soldiers battle on. Liverpool are finishing the year with a divided squad, one half fit, the other injured. The wounded now include Flanagan, Gomez, Rossiter, Milner, Allen, Ibe, Ings, Sturridge, Skrtel and Origi. With the hectic schedule, managers need to rotate, but Klopp has few choices, so on his weary troops must hobble. Only mad dogs and Englishmen play football at this time of the year.

IN THE STORM

'There are some things you learn best in calm, and some in storm' — Willa Cather

It's blustery in Sunderland, well to be precise it's downright stormy. Frank has been blowing for a number of days now and strong gusts push us towards the stadium and the approaching evening kick-off. Frank is the sixth in the series of storms to be allocated a name under the new Met Office programme designed to assist the public with safety warnings and blizzard defences. He follows in the wind trails of Abigail, Barney, Clodagh, Desmond and Eva, each of which have raged on and off on our travels since mid-November. Earlier in the day, from the Seaburn promenade, we watched the breathtaking ferocity of tumultuous swollen waves on the North Sea. Nature can be a frightening thing as witnessed by the havoc wreaked across the country in the build-up to Christmas, but storms don't stop football, not in England. Nothing does. In a country decimated by unprecedented flooding and gale-force winds, the football show still goes on. It's the English way.

Storm or no storm, the Liverpool fans have again turned out in their thousands and tonight we take our place behind the North goal, in the Carling Stand Upper. Forty-five thousand have gathered to see the final Premier League game of 2015. Standing proud on the banks of the River Wear, this stadium reflects local heritage, having been constructed on the vacant site of an old coal mine, the former Monkwearmouth Colliery. Built into the hole in the ground that the pit vacated, the playing surface and part of the stands sit several metres below ground level. It's an impressive arena, and in 2001 it was voted by *Total Football* magazine as one of the ten best stadiums in the World. The design pays homage to both the region's industrial history and to Sunderland's proud shipbuilding heritage, with the entire structure bedding into the land, as if a ship in water. Outside, stands a statue of the Davy lamp used by miners in the pits, many of these miners now forming the club's fan base. From this source derives the name – the 'Stadium of Light'.

Growing up, I subconsciously viewed Newcastle as a bigger club, not fully aware of Sunderland's history, but any Sunderland fan will remind you that they hold six league titles compared to the Magpie's four. Sunderland don red and white vertical stripes but their nickname is the 'Black Cats'. The black cat origin stems from 1805 and a gun battery located on the River Wear, which was renamed the Black Cat battery, after the night watchmen kept hearing a mysterious miaow from a wailing black cat. Sunderland are also known as the Mackems, this a colloquial name for people from Sunderland and also for their accent, not to be mistaken with Geordie.

If Newcastle were in trouble before Liverpool arrived bearing early Christmas gifts, then Sunderland's plight looks much worse. They sit second from bottom having amassed a paltry twelve points from eighteen games. Sam Allardyce, the new Sunderland manager, took control in the same week that Jürgen Klopp arrived at Liverpool. He too started well, but as at Liverpool, recent results have tailed off. Tonight's game is of critical importance to both teams. It would be sad to see a big club like Sunderland relegated, if that is what transpires, but in truth they have yo-yoed too many times between the Premier League and the Championship and have changed managers more often than can be good. Like Newcastle, they need a period of stability, investment and security.

Liverpool and Sunderland have plenty of shared history, most notably an FA Cup final that saw Liverpool beat the Black Cats 2–0 in 1992, after goals from Ian Rush and Michael Thomas. In 1999 both teams were invited to play in the Football League's Centenary Celebration Game, held in the Stadium of Light with Sunderland being the most recent champions (second tier) and Liverpool being the most frequent champions (first tier). Liverpool won 3–2. There was even one infamous encounter at the Stadium of Light when Liverpool lost a game 1–0 to a goal scored by a beach ball! A red beach ball somehow made its way onto the pitch and proceeded to bounce around the Liverpool penalty area. Darren Bent of Sunderland took a shot from the edge of the box that Pepe Reina, Liverpool's goalkeeper, looked to have covered. As he crouched to save, unfortunately for him, the football struck its lightweight beach cousin and bounced over his arm and into the net. A rare specimen indeed, defeat by beach ball. Ironically for Liverpool the offending inflatable had come from its own supporters.

On this the penultimate day of the year 2015, the 7.45 p.m. kick-off approaches, and the teams are announced over the loudspeakers. The crowd respects a minute's silence in honour of those connected with Sunderland Athletic Football Club who have lost their lives in 2015, a nice tribute. My mind wanders too, to those I have loved and lost and still love.

The dead remembered, football commences. Klopp asked his players for more fight and grit following the Watford game. He wants them to learn to win ugly. The pitch is much better than the bobble fest at Vicarage Road, so at least passes can be attempted and completed, but this is a tough no nonsense affair and hard tackles abound. It will be a night for cool heads and steady minds. The half ends with Liverpool much the better team and the only regret is that the scoreboard is bare.

The second half kicks off and within twenty-three seconds Liverpool are ahead. It's a goal made by Klopp proving that pressing can be a creator. Determined harrying in the middle of the park by Can sees the Reds win the ball. Coutinho releases Clyne on the right who plays it forward to the edge of the box where Lallana and Firmino are hunting in a pack. A fortuitous touch by Lallana bounces past the Sunderland defence and in a flash Benteke has accelerated free and steers the ball calmly past the advancing goalkeeper and into the bottom left corner of the net. The less time Benteke has to think the more instinctive and better a finisher he is. This is true of many strikers, their art based upon instinct. Predators not planners.

The rest of the half is hard to watch as Liverpool struggle for fluency and fail to create enough clear chances to put the game to bed. Both sides miss opportunities before the final whistle blows, but when it does, the Reds have managed back-to-back 1–0 victories. So, as the wind howled and the storm blew, Liverpool learned to win ugly and they finish 2015 on a high.

AULD LANG SYNE

'Maybe this year, we ought to walk through the rooms of our lives not looking for flaws, but looking for potential.' — Ellen Goodman

It's approaching noon and I'm still in bed. It's the last day of the year. At Sunderland, we observed a minute's silence in commemoration of those who had lost their lives over the preceding twelve months. In 2015, Liverpool lost former heroes Gerry Byrne and Brian Hall. Back in the day when substitutions were not allowed, Byrne wrote his name into Liverpool and FA Cup folklore, when playing nearly the entire game and extra time too with a broken collarbone as Liverpool beat Leeds 2–1 in their inaugural FA Cup Final win in 1965. Brian Hall may have been one of the only qualified scientists to don the red shirt, and he played an important role in the 1974 FA Cup final when Liverpool beat Newcastle 3–0. Everton said goodbye to a legend of their own in Howard Kendall, who won the League title once as a player and twice as manager with the Toffees. My own thoughts drift closer to home and to my eldest brother Eugene, who we lost in September. With my two other brothers we carried his coffin from the church as, 'You'll Never Walk Alone' was sung by a solo female soprano.

With mortality on my mind, a thought comes to me and I wonder, as I have done many times before, why do I go to football games? Why as a grown man do I roar at other not-so-grown men, as they kick an inflated ball around a green? Why do I sign up to become part of a grand collective, one that I cannot control? Generally speaking, I loathe tribes and how they can help tempt individuals to lose their personal responsibility and do or say things they wouldn't if they stood alone. I hate the confrontational scenes I witnessed at both the Manchester games. I despise football chants solely directed at deriding and goading opposition fans. I am only interested in supporting my own, in endorsing positivity, not negativity. I love how, at an American NFL game, the most passionate of fans from opposing teams can sit side by side in a stadium, without full scale war breaking out. There will be banter, sometimes raucous, but rarely does it turn as ugly or nasty as the football variety.

Football has a long history of tribalism and some of that sense of belonging is what drives the passion and the colour, and that's good. Attending games these days is a more enjoyable experience than it was in the unpleasant seventies and eighties, but mindless taunts and gestures and, let's face it, ugly people, still exist. Yet, there is great good too. As fans we are part of a collective. We share remembrances of the past; glory, defeat, and tragedy. Having collectively lived this history, it then binds us. Every new day we commit again, of our own free will, to stride forward with our nation, our brotherhood, for we share the same goals, the same ambitions, the same hope. Yet with every new day that I pledge my allegiance, the knowledge grows stronger in me that we, the tribe's citizens, need to help shape its future – make it one that we can be proud of. We share a responsibility and an accountability, as too do those that act in our name. These duties should not be forgotten as we make our daily vows. Being part of our nation becomes part of us. It forms part of our identity. We know that our nation, our brotherhood, will outlive us and, in some way as we pass our allegiance down, we ourselves become part of its immortality and we live on, as do all who went before us. Shankly remarked, "Liverpool is not only a club, it's an institution. Wives brought their late husbands' ashes to Anfield and scattered them on the pitch. So, people not only support Liverpool when they are alive, they support them when they are dead. This is the true Liverpool." Liverpool was Shankly's life, his religion, and he understood acutely how important a role the club played in the lives of others, how it provided a meaning, an attachment, where maybe few others were available. His words not only reflect this but also his and our immortality as part of the Liverpool brotherhood. He would say "Some people believe football is a matter of life and death, I can assure you, it's much more important than that."

Yet, I am not just part of the Liverpool nation, more so I am part of the footballing world. I love the game. I still play as I approach the big five-zero. Once football gets under your skin, you can't shake the infection. Even now, as I journey through my old neighbourhood, I will park my car if I see two teams running around a field of green, nets falling back from white posts, grass mown, white lines marked. The sight of a football game, even at this most basic amateur level, stirs a joy and an excitement. I watch to see how the average person plays, what the coach calls, what the eager parents shout. I watch to observe the 'footballing brain' in action, which players read the game best, which players see what is about to happen, before it actually does. Who has the proverbial eyes in the back of their heads? I watch to see the beautiful fluidity between movement, body, foot and ball. I watch it because it is football, played by everyone, in every corner of the globe. The common game, the beautiful game. The art form. Klopp's words come back to me, "if we don't have fans and stadiums, we play with jumpers in the park." I smile and think of my brother. He would have loved our new German manager.

Shankly loved the Scottish poet Robert Burns, who came to such prominence in the eighteenth century, seeing him as a champion of the common man. Burns was born only twenty-six miles from where Shankly grew up in the small mining village of Glenbuck. Shankly would say of him, "he murdered those people, the big people, the lords. It was not hard for us to grow fond of a person who saw things that way". A Burns lyric, written in 1788, comes to my mind given the day that is in it.

Should auld acquaintance be forgot, and never brought to mind?
Should auld acquaintance be forgot, and days of auld lang syne?
And days of auld lang syne, my dear, and days of auld lang syne.
Should auld acquaintance be forgot, and days of auld lang syne?

I hum it softly as memories of childhood football games, of laughter on the green, of family, come floating and as tears of love well in my eyes.

Premier League Table – 31-12-2015

		Played	Won	Draw	Lost	GF	GA	GD	Points
1	Arsenal	19	12	3	4	33	18	15	39
2	Leicester City	19	11	6	2	37	25	12	39
3	Man City	19	11	3	5	37	20	17	36
4	Tottenham	19	9	8	2	33	15	18	35
5	Crystal Palace	19	9	4	6	23	16	7	31
6	Man United	19	8	6	5	22	16	6	30
7	**Liverpool**	**19**	**8**	**6**	**5**	**22**	**22**	**0**	**30**
8	West Ham	19	7	8	4	28	23	5	29
9	Watford	19	8	5	6	24	20	4	29
10	Stoke City	19	8	5	6	20	19	1	29
11	Everton	19	6	8	5	35	28	7	26
12	Southampton	19	6	6	7	26	23	3	24
13	West Brom	19	6	5	8	18	24	-6	23
14	Chelsea	19	5	5	9	23	29	-6	20
15	Norwich City	19	5	5	9	22	32	-10	20
16	Bournemouth	19	5	5	9	22	34	-12	20
17	Swansea City	19	4	7	8	16	24	-8	19
18	Newcastle	19	4	5	10	19	34	-15	17
19	Sunderland	19	3	3	13	19	38	-19	12
20	Aston Villa	19	1	5	13	15	34	-19	8

EASTENDERS

'I like the dreams of the future better than the history of the past' — Thomas Jefferson

What do a bankrupt Icelandic businessman, a pornographer, Anne Boleyn, a World War II bomb, blowing bubbles and the Olympics have in common? If you are from East London you will have guessed straight away, why it's West Ham United FC of course.

It's the morning of January 2nd and my brother and I are at Upton Park for the first Premier League game of 2016. It only seems like hours since the Reds saw out the old year and, as befits their congested fixture list, here they are, already, ringing in the new. Although I believe I am at Upton Park, it seems in recent times everybody has started to call this place 'the Boleyn Ground' in some fit of nostalgia. Upon browsing various West Ham supporter forums online, the jury is out as to when and why the Boleyn version started to be used. The Upton Park title derives from the name of the local borough and underground station so its provenance is at least clear. The exact source of the Boleyn name seems unsure, but it is believed that the basis for its use came from a nearby building that the West Ham Club took over in its formative years, and which was situated on lands believed to have been owned by the Boleyn family, or where the Boleyn family stayed. I have seen this building referred to as Boleyn Castle and also Green Street House. One source suggested that Henry and Anne 'got it on' in the castle and given the lack of any evidential thread for the name, I suppose anything is possible. Of course, Anne Boleyn would become Queen of England and subsequently lose her head at the Tower of London at the kindly behest of her good King Henry.

How West Ham's strip came to be coloured claret and blue also seems shrouded in conjecture, with one story suggesting that in the summer of 1899, Bill Dove, a sprinter of national repute and a coach of the Ironworks team, was challenged to a race with four Aston Villa players at a fair in Birmingham. Dove won but the Villa men couldn't pay the wager so one of them pinched a set of claret and blue shirts from their club to settle the bet.

What we do know is that West Ham United was formed from the remnants of the Thames Ironworks team, hence their nicknames 'the Hammers' and 'the Irons'. The Thames Ironworks and Shipbuilding Company was a shipyard and ironworks straddling the mouth of Bow Creek at its confluence with the River Thames, with Leamouth Wharf on the west side and Canning Town on the east. The company produced ironwork for Brunel's Royal Albert Bridge over the Tamar in the 1850s and for the world's first all-iron warship, HMS Warrior, launched in 1860.

Today is the last time that Liverpool will play West Ham in the League at the Boleyn Ground, for just like Anne, the stadium is getting the axe. Facing us are the twin turret castle structures that are built into the Green Street entrance. The words 'Academy of Football' are written above the doors. West Ham have always fostered a philosophy of technical football, for playing the 'right way'. Through the years a lengthy cast of players have lived up to these values. Billy Bonds, Trevor Brooking, Alan Devonshire and Frank Lampard to name but a few. A statue of their 1966 World Cup winners Martin Peters, Bobby Moore and Geoff Hurst evokes the golden days of the Academy, when world beaters hailed from the East End.

In the car park are two spaces both marked 'Chairman', where side by side, sit two gleaming Rolls Royce Phantoms, one silver, the other purple. Maybe I'm colour-blind and these are coloured claret and sky blue, which would make more sense. The licence plates read D GOLD and DSIO WHU. West Ham United is owned by two men with characters as colourful as the club's history. David Gold and David Sullivan gained control of the club in January 2010, after then owner Björgólfur Guðmundsson, an Icelandic banker and businessman, was forced to sell up, having seen his personal fortune collapse in value from $1.1 billion to $0 within the space of nine months, following the crash of Icelandic financial institutions amid the global banking meltdown.

This was the second time that local-kid-made-good David Gold had tried to gain control of his beloved West Ham. David's father 'Goldy' spent time in prison for robbery, and the dyslexic Gold was raised in poverty on Green St, only a few hundred metres from the Boleyn Ground. Gold himself played for the club's youth team as a teenager and, growing up nearby, he witnessed first-hand the destruction caused by a German Doodlebug shell that landed on the old stadium during a Second World War bombing raid. Undeterred by his meagre upbringing, Gold would work his way up from scanty surrounds, honing his youthful business acumen and street smarts at the nearby Queen St markets, buying and selling, amongst other items, fancy buttons. After upgrading to a shop at Charing Cross, Gold discovered that one stock item seemed to grab the customers more than others; racy censored books. And so it passed that, from humble beginnings, Gold would build a raunchy business empire which included soft-porn publications such as *Rustler* and *Raider*, the saucy *Sunday Sport* tabloid (which he later sold for £50m), and the Ann Summers lingerie and sex-toy chain. Whilst publishing his productions, Gold struggled with the distribution market, as a particular competitor kept fouling his path, one David Sullivan. Sullivan did more than distribute naughty magazines, he also dabbled in the hard-core movie business and dated a notorious porn star of the time, Mary Millington, who years later committed suicide. Late one evening Gold received a call. It was Sullivan proposing a merger. Why beat each other up, when they could make twice the money working together? Gold loved the idea and so formed a pairing that would one day own West Ham United.

Upon taking over West Ham in 2010, the club were playing second tier football and were laden with debt. Within two years the 'top shelf' partnership oversaw a third return to Premier League football for the EastEnders, with a 2–1 victory over Blackpool in the Championship Play-Off final at Wembley Stadium.

West Ham had been to Wembley before, a long time before. They contested the first ever Cup Final at the famous stadium in 1923. Then, the Empire Stadium at Wembley had just been completed and had a stated capacity of 126,000. Problems arose though, when over 240,000 people arrived on Cup Final day. The game was in danger of being abandoned, as thousands of fans spilled onto the pitch before kick-off, with no sitting or standing room available in the stands. A majestic white police horse named Billy would take to the field and cleared the crowd. Billy had secured a place a history, with the game being remembered as 'The White Horse Final'. West Ham would lose 2–0 to Bolton Wanderers. The Hammers would go on to contest a further four FA Cup Finals, winning three. Their other defeat came at the hands of Liverpool in the 'Gerrard Final' of 2006. They would also lose to Liverpool in the 1981 League Cup Final with a replay at Villa Park deciding the tie. Success in the 1964 FA Cup saw West Ham gain entry to the European Cup Winners Cup and in 1965 at Wembley they would become only the second English team to win a European trophy, beating TSV 1860 Munich 2–0 (Moore, Peters and Hurst would go back to Wembley a year later to beat the Germans again, this time with England in the World Cup Final). In 1976, West Ham reached the final again and travelled to Brussels to play the Belgians of Anderlecht. This time they would lose 4–2. West Ham's highest ever League finish was third place in 1986 and they have never played below the top two tiers of English Football.

Sullivan and Gold are ambitious, they see the huge potential of being London's fourth big team. It's a city that can manage that number comfortably. Sullivan has a vision. "Long-term, there's no reason why we can't be one of England's leading six clubs, pushing for the Champions League. You have to dream. Otherwise what's the point of being an owner or supporter? And we are both owners and supporters."

It's wet and windy as we take our places in the lower section of the Sir Trevor Brooking Stand. On the ticket face is a depiction of the ornate iron John Lyall Gates, with the words 'Farewell Boleyn' 1904–2016. The gates have formed the ceremonial entrance to the ground since 1956 and were renamed in 2009 in Lyall's honour. The farewell sentiment confirms that today will see Liverpool's final League game at this famous old ground. Football evolves at breakneck speed and with more and more money flushing around, clubs' ambitions soar higher and higher. Gold and Sullivan, along with their business manager Karren Brady, have secured a ninety-nine year lease as anchor tenant in the brand new Olympic Stadium, home of the 2012 London Olympics, which sits about two kilometres as the crow flies from where we stand. West Ham's new home will house 54,000 fans, 19,000 more than are packed in today. When asked could West Ham fill the new Olympic stadium, Gold pointed out that in the 1981/82 season the Hammers average crowd was bigger than Arsenal's. Ambition unbridled is the Premier league. It's like the Californian Gold Rush again.

Kick-off approaches as liquid bubbles float across the ground and the home fans sing their glorious anthem.

'I'm dreaming dreams, I'm scheming schemes, I'm building castles high.
They're born anew, their days are few, Just like a sweet butterfly.
And as the daylight is dawning, they come again in the morning.
I'm forever blowing bubbles, Pretty bubbles in the air, they fly so high,
Nearly reach the sky, then like my dreams, they fade and die.
Fortune's always hiding, I've looked everywhere,
I'm forever blowing bubbles, Pretty bubbles in the air.'

West Ham are always tough opposition, particularly on their home turf, and having already lost 0–3 to the Hammers at Anfield earlier in the season, Liverpool will have to be at it from the off today. A good result would cement the momentum that saw 2015 end with successive victories over Leicester and Sunderland.

Liverpool are not at it from the start. Again the concession of an early goal sets the low tone and the notes only fall flat from there. Ten minutes in and Antonio scores, heading into Mignolet's net from an in-swinging cross. The Liverpool fans behind Mignolet's goal sigh and settle in for another long afternoon. Liverpool are not pressing hard enough anywhere on the field and West Ham have it easy. The half continues with possession veering feverishly back and forth between the teams. It is a game of high endeavour, but low skill. Both sides hit the woodwork before the break, but in truth it is Liverpool who are happy to get to the dressing room with the score still only 1–0 to the home team.

The second half sees Liverpool lift their game early on but with no real signs of a breakthrough. On fifty-five minutes, five statuesque Liverpool players fail to prevent a Mark Noble cross into the box and the six foot three inches former Liverpool player and the most expensive Reds signing ever, Andy Carroll, rises high, to gleefully nod the ball into the bottom comer; 2–0 to West Ham. Liverpool huff and puff and late on Lucas and Allen both miss headers that they should score. Many Liverpool fans stream out with five minutes to go, as today it seems clear that there is no way back. I can't blame them, it's a long and expensive journey down to London to endure this feeble offering. When the end does arrive, 2–0 is a fair result and again the bubbles float and singing rings around the old ground. Fair play is all I can think. West Ham are a club on the rise, with what could be a very bright future ahead. They have astute and business savvy owners, who have made their money the hard way (excuse the pun) and who possess a concrete plan to be one of the top clubs in the country.

From a Liverpool perspective, the day has been as flat as it could possibly be, worse than Watford. Later Klopp is livid and declares that it is a time to be angry, not disappointed. He accuses the players of only giving 80 per cent. He is visibly furious. Thank God he is not making apologies for the team, for a performance like this deserves only anger. The fans need somebody to vent our feelings. Statistics can lie and distort yet, some tell a tale like no other. Liverpool's goal tally is just twenty-two from their opening twenty Premier League games, officially the worst in the club's 124-year history.

On the journey back into central London, I can only muster disappointment, I'm too downbeat to stoke anger or lividness. After a defeat, there is nothing worse than the post-match journey, those lifeless hours when emotions lie on the floor. The future always seems bleak, nothing immediate to lift the gloom. All you can do is endure.

THE BLEAK MIDWINTER

'Youth is easily deceived because it is quick to hope.' — Aristotle

There is little or no time to lick wounds after the West Ham fiasco, incredibly five more January games await in what could become the bleakest and busiest of midwinters. With the bodies mounting on the treatment tables, the media smells a story that Klopp is pushing his troops too far in training, his Geggenpressing heavy metal crescendo is breaking the strings. This angle is chased down with glee by a snarling press pack, always sniffing for any scent of blood. When Klopp points out that the team had only time for rest and recovery between the hectic fixtures and that they don't train, it is clear that there is no meat on this bone. Two problems are evident though. Liverpool are ahead in two tables that no team wishes to lead. They top the Premiership for injuries suffered and they surpass all teams in the top European Leagues for the frequency of fixtures that they play. In simple words, no team in England or Europe is being asked to do so much, with so little.

Three days after Liverpool's mini winning bubble was popped in London's East End the Reds head once more for Stoke, a fixture which is becoming synonymous with this transitional period in the club's history. It helped define Rodgers' end and it could do the same for Klopp's beginning. Every manager likes to win a trophy early in their tenure. It sends a message to their players, to their bosses and to their competitors. We are winners. We are coming. We are growing. Winning is a habit, winning breeds winners. The lack of a trophy hung heavy over Rodgers. These days they are harder than ever to win. Three trophies are available domestically and one can be won in Europe. That doesn't leave a lot to go around and it guarantees infinitely more losers than winners, leading to the inevitable ripping up of plans and resultant job losses.

So despite the League Cup being the least important of the trophies on offer, its significance quite often exceeds its own rank. It's nice to lock up silverware early, it buys time and patience and carves another entry in the history books. The great teams want to win everything on offer. Look at Barcelona. Look at old Liverpool, who collected the League Cup a record eight times between the years of 1981 and 2012.

It's the first leg of the two-legged League Cup semi-final and after demolishing Southampton in the last round, Liverpool are at the Britannia Stadium to face a Stoke team that are on a high. With the Potters in red hot form and with Liverpool floundering on the pitch and in the treatment room, incredibly it is Stoke who are the favourites to reach the final. But if Klopp can't find consistency he can still find a reaction. The anger festered since West Ham is now channelled into this crucial game. By full-time Stoke are happy to have lost by only one and the tie remains delicately balanced for the second leg at Anfield three weeks later. The result comes with a heavy price though, Lovren and Coutinho are both substituted with hamstring injuries. Soon the Reds will find it hard to field eleven experienced first team players.

When it rains it pours and three days later Liverpool must face third division Exeter away in the third round of the FA Cup. Klopp and team go into emergency mode and Liverpool youth players, who had been on loan at other clubs, are now recalled from all around the country. Sheyi Ojo (18) returns from Wolves. Ryan Kent (19) is recalled from Coventry, Kevin Stewart (22) returns from Swindon and Tiago Illori (22) returns from Aston Villa. It is all youthful hands to the pumps. This is the day in the football calendar put aside for 'giant killing'. With Liverpool facing both Arsenal and Manchester United within ten days of the tie and with half of his squad on crutches, Klopp fields the second youngest team in Liverpool's history with a combined age of 247 years, and an average age of 22.5.

In a surreal but brilliant scene, he performs his obligatory pre-match TV interview in Exeter's cubby-hole kitchen, as two tea ladies look on. Klopp is all smiles and you sense he is enjoying the occasion. He remarks that this confined space is bigger than the changing room. Exeter's home ground, St James Park, as described by their manager Paul Tisdale, is a little spartan. A cracking game finishes 2–2 and a replay will be required.

Another game for Liverpool's congested fixture list and another chance for the kids to learn their trade.

Wednesday 13th January, five days after Exeter, league leaders Arsenal visit Anfield. Wenger expects a 'ferocious encounter' as is typical of these meetings. Two years previously, with Arsenal again on top in the League, the Gunners left Anfield on the receiving end of a 5–1 hammering. This time, if the result isn't quite the same, the spectacle turns out to be just as bright and the entertainment levels just as high. Liverpool's Joe Allen scores a stoppage-time equaliser in the falling snow to earn a 3–3 draw. Both Klopp and Wenger are a little disappointed in their post-match interviews not to have won. Klopp describes the game as 'a spectacular', and it sits high in the long list of classics between the two great clubs. Liverpool dominated throughout and created most chances, controlling the possession at 59 per cent. But for the now trademark-poor defending, it would have been victory. Still, it's most definitely a step forward. Klopp is slowly curing one of the Achilles heels, home form. The Anfield crowd and the home team are growing in confidence, together.

Four days later, sixth-place Man United, who sit three points ahead of Liverpool, arrive at Anfield to test that burgeoning confidence. Liverpool continue their good form and dominate from start to finish, but a handful of good chances go to waste. Can goes closest but De Gea is a world-class keeper and close is not enough. Liverpool press and press for a winner but then, calamity strikes. The Reds fail to clear a corner kick, despite the box containing eight Liverpool defenders and only four United attackers. In the ensuing mayhem Rooney pounces for United to score. Liverpool controlled possession with 53 per cent, had nineteen shots to United's seven, four on target to United's one, yet the Reds still lose. Man of the match goes to United's goalkeeper De Gea.

It is the week that the world mourned the passing of the enigmatic genius that was David Bowie. He might have been referring to Liverpool when he once quipped, *'I don't know where I'm going from here, but I promise it won't be boring'*.

DO DIFFERENT

'You either get Norfolk, with its wild roughness and uncultivated oddities, or you don't. It's not all soft and lovely. It doesn't ask to be loved.'
– Stephen Fry

It's a mild Saturday morning, just past noon and over my shoulder, high up to my right, a handful of people are leaning out of broad windows, gazing down to the green turf below. We are stood on the Jarrold Stand, in the away corner of Carrow Road, home to Norwich Football Club. The windows form part of the rear wall of a Holiday Inn hotel, which acts as one corner of the ground's structure. A room with a match view is certainly a unique stadium offering, in keeping with a Norfolk propensity for uniqueness, for being different. The hotel wall is just one small idiosyncrasy of what is otherwise a very smart stadium. Tight, compact and always full. Norwich fans are all-weather fans.

I peruse the match programme and the League table inside tells the story of two clubs struggling for points. Liverpool have collected only one from their last three League games whilst Norwich are coming off the back of three big defeats to Man City, Stoke and Bournemouth. For Norwich, sitting in 16th, only two places and two points from the drop zone, life is precarious. Liverpool just need to find a way to win in the League, having played well against both Arsenal and Man United but for scant reward. The haunting memories of away trips to Newcastle, West Ham and Watford still linger and it's hard to know which Reds team will turn up today. The hungry team that mauled Arsenal and outplayed United or the limp, sleep-inducing West Ham variety.

The match programme notes that Norwich have dedicated the game to the work of the anti-racism football charity 'Kick It Out', which tries to assure that people of every background are welcome in the football community. Norwich itself has a proud tradition of welcoming all and sundry that goes back to its very foundation. The Region's motto is 'Do Different' and that is what the locals have aspired to down through the ages. Stranger's Hall, a restored Tudor home, nestles in the heart of the town and it honours the many welcome 'strangers' that came to live and trade in the City of Norwich during its long history. The medieval period was a prosperous one for the region and the main industry was the wool trade. Large numbers of skilled Walloon and Flemish weavers came to Norwich from the Low Countries, often to escape persecution at home. It was Spanish immigrants who carried with them the hobby, popular with Spanish and English Kings of the era, of breeding and keeping canary birds. The pastime soon flourished and left such a mark that Norwich City Football club adopted a home kit of canary-yellow jerseys, green shorts and yellow socks and have been known as 'the Canaries' ever since.

Founded in 1902, Norwich Football Club, having previously played in a disused chalk-pit called 'the Nest', found a new home in 1935 to the city's south east, close to the railway station. It is there at Carrow Road that they have stayed till this day. As we wait for kick-off, I tell my son that another establishment that he knows well, grew up around these very same streets. Jeremiah Colman established his mustard and flour business in 1814 in Stoke Holy Cross, a village four miles south of Norwich. In 1858, his great-nephew, Jeremiah James Colman developed the production factory at Carrow Road which still exists today. The Colmans were conscientious employers who cared for the welfare of their workers, establishing company housing, healthcare benefits and a school for their children. Mustard seeds came from crops grown locally and the business became a major economic bedrock for East Anglia. In Colman's Mustard we find a fascinating example of the early days of brand power. The yellow badge, bull's head and red lettering have survived to this day. Colman's also pioneered the concept of 'product placement' and 'endorsement' with Shackleton taking supplies on his Antarctic expeditions aboard the Discovery and with local doctors extolling the health benefits of the yellow mixture.

Between 1650 and 1750, Norwich was second only to London in terms of importance and prosperity. Today, Norwich feels far removed from the major cities and international commuter trails, nestling happily and quietly in the Norfolk Broads. It feels like a small market town and everywhere is walkable. The city's medieval street structure, the largest in Europe, survives to this day offering quaint charms and a link to a storied past. Everywhere one looks, your eye will fall upon a church or a cathedral. 'A religious lot,' I suggest to my son on our walk to Carrow Road, silently hoping that it will not be the Reds in need of prayer.

***

Football can invariably conspire to make a lovely trip miserable, but we hope for happy tidings as kick-off approaches. One can only be impressed as the Norwich fans lustily sing their anthem, 'On the ball, City', believed to be the oldest football anthem in the world:

> *'Kick off, throw it in, have a little scrimmage,*
> *Keep it low, a splendid rush, bravo, win or die;*
> *On the ball, City, never mind the danger, Steady on, now's your chance,*
> *Hurrah! We've scored a goal.*
> *City!, City!, City!'*

Norwich feels like a club in touch with its community and fans. In many ways it is a throwback to the old days of English Football. Local celebrity chef Delia Smith is the major shareholder and native luminaries such as Stephen Fry are ambassadors.

Today, Klopp reverts to the senior players, just three days after the Liverpool youths dispatched Exeter 3–0 in the FA Cup replay. Firmino is preferred in the striker's role to Benteke, who must again wait his turn on the bench. Lallana is carrying a knock, so Klopp's trusted lieutenant is replaced by Ibe. Norwich have delved deep into the January transfer market spending £9 million on Naismith from Everton, £9 million on Klose from Wolfsburg and £3 million on Pinto from Dinamo Zagreb. Naismith and Klose adorn the programme cover, and inside, Norwich manager Alex Neill comments, "the fact that Steven Naismith and Timm Klose are the second and third biggest signings in terms of transfer fees in Norwich's history underlines our determination to keep pushing on." It is a vicious battle at the bottom of the Premier table to maintain survival. The stakes are so high, the Premier League riches so immense. Should one fall, bouncing back from the Championship is no easy task, with only three gaining promotion each season from twenty-four hopefuls. That is not a jungle that anybody wants to stray into.

It must be a curiosity for footballers to deal with the odd assortment of kick-off times that have become a facet of the modern game to satisfy demanding TV schedules, where it seems every hour of the day must be filled with live action. In any given week a team could start a game at 12.45 p.m., 1.30 p.m., 3.00 p.m., 4.00 p.m., 5.30 p.m., 7.45 p.m. or 8.00 p.m. The midnight slot still seems to be open. The last people to be consulted on these times are the travelling fans, who must organise their respective assortment of trains, planes and automobiles. Add to that, the expensive ticket prices ranging from forty to sixty pounds for an away ticket, and it is clear to see that following your team is not a task to take lightly. So for those hardy souls who have visited Newcastle, Watford and West Ham with the Reds, medals should be awarded for sheer perseverance through suffering. Today, kick-off is 12.45 p.m.

Liverpool start sluggishly and fans around us grumble that the team are still asleep. The fans seem to be too. Games can be funny like that. At some matches you can sense that the travelling end are up for it from the start, regardless of what's happening on the pitch. They are vocal and supportive. Alternatively, the group can be subdued as if collectively anesthetized. The team on the pitch always have the antidote though, show a little, give a little and fans will respond. Go missing and they will rip you asunder, tear you to shreds. Football is no place for the light-hearted. Everybody loves football, but football loves nobody.

Norwich are in the ascendancy but they are not making any headway in the final third. Both teams lack poise as possession is squandered time and time again. Then, incredibly, a move of pure quality and it's from the Reds. At least twenty intricate passes moves the ball from one side to the other and gradually Liverpool eek out some space. Milner slides a ball through the defence for Firmino to run onto. Firmino gets there first and directs a dribbling left foot shot goal bound. Norwich goalkeeper, Rudd, advances but can only manage a fingertip touch and the ball trickles off the post and into the net. The away fans are now awake and roar their approval. It seems Liverpool must go behind in every away game, so to start this one with a lead, whilst not playing particularly well, is a welcome bonus. 0-1 after eighteen minutes.

Liverpool don't build on the platform that the goal provides and it's Norwich who are back on top again. On twenty-nine minutes they win a corner and the away end collectively emit an audible groan. After a few hashed clearances the ball lands to Mbokani inside the box. Sakho hustles him, but he is too weak and Mbokani back-heels a powerful bullet into the Reds' net. 1-1, and Liverpool have now incredibly gifted a goal to the first corner kick conceded in four of their last five games. Norwich are well on top and the best Liverpool can hope for is to get to the break on level pegging. They don't. On forty-one minutes Naismith sends an arrow into the Liverpool armory. A neat one-two wall pass with Hoolahan sends the Scottish dynamo free into the box, leaving a bevy of cement-legged Liverpool players in his wake. From an acute angle, Naismith powers a low drive through Mignolet and into the back of the net. 2–1 to the Canaries.

The second half brings a more energetic Liverpool, ears obviously ringing from a Klopp roasting. It amazes me that professional footballers need rousing speeches or half-time scoldings. Despite Liverpool's solid efforts to get back on level terms, disaster strikes, or maybe better described, stupidity strikes. Moreno lunges at Naismith inside the Liverpool box and the ex-Evertonian goes down. Remarkably the ref waves play on. Not to be undone, Moreno kicks Naismith again as he tries to get up and this time the referee has no choice and awards Norwich the penalty. Liverpool's Spanish left back has suffered a momentary loss of blood flow to the brain and when he recovers lucidity Norwich are 3–1 up, after Hoolahan puts the spot kick away.

Now the home fans are letting us know in no uncertain terms who is on top. Up again goes a chorus of 'On the ball, City'. Yet Liverpool's Captain does what Captains do and within one minute of the restart Liverpool are thrown a lifeline. Clyne sends an arcing ball across the box, which is cleverly tipped on by Firmino into the path of Henderson. He swivels and sweeps the ball home past the outstretched right arm of the diving Rudd; 3–2. Both Henderson and Firmino chase after the ball into the net, eager to restart the game. Carrow Road crackles with excitement. I can see trepidation and doubt creep into the faces of the Norwich fans that are visible to me. I understand their plight completely. They have a team, just like us, that can't be trusted, you just don't know what's coming next. It makes for an exciting roller-coaster ride, but it's not good for the heart. I don't even cheer Henderson's goal myself, I'm still recovering from Moreno's slide into temporary insanity.

Eight minutes later we are cheering though, as loud as our vocal cords will allow. Lallana, having only entered the fray four minutes earlier, chases onto a Milner pass and then lofts a superb ball into the Norwich danger zone for Firmino to chase onto. Somehow Firmino is alone, Norwich's defence having taken a break, and as he bears down on the advancing Rudd he clips the bouncing ball over the keeper's prone leg and into the empty net. It's 3–3 after sixty-three minutes and incredibly Liverpool are back on level terms.

On seventy-five minutes, Milner takes a chance. On the blind side of defence, he gambles on a mistake, on intercepting a back pass. He wins. He rounds the keeper and bangs the ball home. The comeback of comebacks has been achieved. From 3–1 down, Liverpool now lead 3–4. The clock ticks past ninety minutes. However, the electronic board goes up and reveals five minutes extra time.

Benteke is caught offside on ninety-two minutes, when he shouldn't be and the Liverpool fans shudder as one, everybody knowing what is to come from the ensuing free kick. A high ball into our box. Our consistent undoing. Norwich oblige and hoof it long. The ball hangs forever in the air until gravity sets in and it lands around the edge of our eighteen-yard line. Sakho is pushed away too easily by Jerome and the ball bounces loose. Onto it leaps Bassong and he unleashes a daisy cutter that manages to evade an array of Liverpool legs and bodies. It fizzes towards goal. Low, fast and hard. Mignolet dives but he can't reach it. The Norwich fans behind the goal go crazy as the ball crashes into the back of the net. 4-4, Liverpool have blown it and Carrow Road goes bananas.

Ten red-shirted players trudge towards the centre circle as the sound of Norwich's triumphant goal music ('Chase the Sun' by Planet Funk) belts out of the PA system and the stadium goes into celebratory meltdown. Liverpool have only themselves to blame. There is no feeling worse in football than the gut wrenching concession of a last minute goal. My son looks at me and I have nothing to offer, my eyes tell it all. What a letdown. What an anticlimax. What a game.

Lallana talks to the ref on the half way line, waiting for the yellow-shirted Norwich players to get back into their own half for the restart. The ref gestures to his watch, time must be up. Yet play goes on and Liverpool win the ball near the Norwich box. Red shirts flood forward. Can lofts a ball towards goal and Benteke wins the header, knocking the ball down towards centre-half, now makeshift striker, Caulker. He shoots, but his goal-bound rocket is blocked and the ball ricochets up high. Caulker jumps and wins the header and the ball bounces loose. Three Norwich defenders converge towards it, but it's the on-rushing Lallana who gets there first. He connects and the ball powers down into the ground and then bounces up and over the legs of the Norwich defenders. From the other end of the ground we can see the flight path of the rising ball, but from our position it's hard to tell the trajectory or pace. Time stands still. Ninety yards from us the ball keeps spinning and turning as it passes limbs and bodies until all that will stop it is netting. The net duly obliges and three thousand Liverpool fans, lost in a moment of disbelief and sheer outrageous joy, go bonkers. It can't be true. It is true. Its 4–5 to the Reds with the very last kick of the game. Lallana wheels away, peels off his red shirt and spins it above his head. After him chase the other ten Liverpool players. Klopp sets off down the touchline to greet them and together they pile into a mass of joyous and delirious bodies. In the commotion Klopp's spectacles are broken but it's a small price to pay. The referee blows the whistle and the game is over. Liverpool's players make their way to the away fans and Lucas and Henderson give their shirts to some children. You can see how happy they are, how much it means to them and you wonder why we ever doubt them, ever doubt that they do their best, but we do. They have proven to us that this Liverpool team know how to 'Do different' too.

Klopp would describe it as an all-time classic while also describing his team's defending as 'complete rubbish'. Norwich manager O'Neill had a similar verdict for his own charges – 'garbage'. The press would call it one of the best Premier League games ever, one of only four 5–4 results in the League in the last twenty years.

Later in town, I fulfill a promise to my son. In celebration we treat ourselves at the Grosvenor Fish Bar, having passed it the evening before when the smell lingered and stayed in our senses, urging a return. Maybe it's just the taste of victory, or the light-headedness of disbelief, but we unanimously agree, these are the best fish and chips we've ever had.

THE RISING KINGS

'Now is the winter of our discontent, made glorious summer by this sun of York' – William Shakespeare, *Richard III*

If you go digging in Leicester you are sure to disturb all manner of brics and bracs, fragments of days long gone. Leicester is an ancient city and has seen settlement since before the days of Christ. In 43 AD, following the invasion of the Romans, the town was settled as *Ratae Corieltauvorum*. Two thousand years later the remains of a Roman town house were found at Vine Street. On the east side of Highcross Street the old walls of a Marcellum (market-hall) were discovered, built in the same manner as the walls of the nearby Jewry Wall. The Jewry Wall is the only visible reminder of Leicester's Roman past. After the Romans, Leicester fell under the control of the Anglo Saxons and eventually it would become one of the five fortified towns (Boroughs) of the Danish Vikings. Then came the Norman Conquest in 1066 and Leicester's emergence as a county town.

Leicester is also the home of Royalty, albeit dead Royalty. On October 2nd, 1452 with war brewing in the English heartlands, a baby named Richard was born to the Duke of York. After King Henry VI of Lancaster suffered a breakdown, the Duke of York seized control of the throne as Lord Protector of the Realm. The years that followed would see Henry attempt to reassert control against the will of York, leading to the many battles now known as the Wars of the Roses, the wars between the red rose of Lancaster and the white rose of Yorkshire. Eventually, after the capture of Henry VI by the Yorkists, and following the death of the Duke of York at the battle of Wakefield in 1460, the Duke's son Edward would become King Edward IV of England. Edward had two sons, both deemed too young to rule by Edward in his will, so when he died in April 1483, his brother Richard became Lord Protector. The mother of the two young boys refused to accept Richard as Protector, instead preferring to see the country ruled by a boy king, her own son, Edward V. Thus would commence an ugly drama that has divided opinion to this day. Richard would declare Edward V illegitimate on the basis that his father Edward had a pre-existing betrothing to a Lady Eleanor Butler. To protect his office, Richard took the prospective boy-king and his younger brother, his nephews, into custody to suppress a rumoured uprising and soon after he was crowned Richard III. The boys were sent to the Tower of London and their eventual fate remains a mystery. In 1674, workmen, whilst demolishing a staircase at the Tower, unearthed the bones of two children. This grim discovery seemed to bear truth to the words of Sir Thomas More who wrote that the boys were killed and buried "at the stair foot, meetly deep in the ground under a heap of stones".

Richard's treatment of the boys, their ensuing disappearance and the manner in which Richard himself had become King, did not sit well with many. Two years later, in 1485, Henry Tudor and his army landed in South Wales and marched inland to confront the King. Richard sent word to his noblemen to rally their troops in Leicester. On August 22nd 1485, Richard's troops marched west from Leicester and encountered Henry's army near Market Bosworth. Despite a numerical advantage, it would be here that Richard would meet his end and become the last English King to die in battle. Following his victory, Henry returned to Leicester and placed Richard's naked body on public display at Greyfriars Church, proof for any doubters or conspiracy believers that the king was in fact dead. It would be the last we would see or hear of the King, or so we thought, his body going missing as the decades and then centuries passed.

Richard's legacy saw him assume the role of the malignant villain king, a twisted power-hungry despot (Richard had scoliosis), a treacherous scoundrel and for this reason the loss of his remains seemed to perturb few. Shakespeare turned him into a hunchback and in 1995 when the actor Ian McKellen played the King, the portrayal was of a Hitleresque fascist, complete with Nazi-style uniform. Even wicked Lord Farquaad of the Shrek movie series, took his inspiration from poor King Richard. "A horse, a horse, my kingdom for a horse" is an oft-quoted line from Shakespeare's Richard III, and suggests a cowardly King, attempting to flee his fate. To the contrary, history researchers accept that Richard was a capable and brave warrior.

In 2004, writer, researcher and Richard III enthusiast Philippa Langley came to Leicester in search of the lost King. The Greyfriars Church had long since passed by the way and the exact location of Richard's corpse remained unknown. Previous searches had found no trace. Legend suggested that the body may have been thrown into the River Soar. However, upon examining the documentation of these previous hunts and having toured what existed of the old sites, Philippa became convinced that they had all been looking in the wrong place. Confident that together she, and historian John Ashdown-Hill, had found the location of the old friary, they persuaded Richard Buckley, the Director of the University of Leicester Archaeological Services, to embark on a new dig. He agreed, if not a little reluctantly. Incredibly, in August 2012, on day one of the dig, human skeletal remains would be found. Suddenly the world's attention was drawn to Leicester. After days of clearing mud and matter from the site, a full torso and skull were exposed. Not long after, the dig site manager, Mathew Morris, would make a phone call to Richard Buckley:

Morris – "You really need to come look at the skeleton."
Buckley – "Look, I really am a bit busy, I've got guests... I can't talk now."
Morris – "You really need to go and look at it now. The burial's got curvature of the spine, and trauma to the head!"

And so it came to pass that in 2012, after 527 years at rest, the remains of King Richard III would rise from the ground in Leicester, from under the car park of a local civil services centre. In 2015, the coffin of Richard III, covered in the white roses of York, would make its way from the University of Leicester, past Fenn Lane Farm near Bosworth and on to Leicester Cathedral, to where the King rests today.

***

Leaving the King and Cathedral behind, I make my way down towards the river and the old Norman castle. From there it's on through the grounds of De Montfort University and the Royal Infirmary Hospital. It's a bitterly cold evening and I'm wearing my winter warmest – two pairs of socks, two T-shirts, two jumpers, hat, gloves and coat. Call me soft, but standing for two hours on a cold terrace sends my blood temperature level to sub-zero.

Walking along the industrial units on Burnmoor Street, I pass Filbert Street, where for 111 years Leicester City played, until 2002, when their new 32,500 all-seater stadium opened nearby. The old stadium has now been replaced by student accommodation. The gathering crowd passes Lineker Road and eventually we reach the junction with Raw Dykes Road, where before us lies the new home of the Foxes, the King Power Stadium. The stadium's title owes nothing to King Richard III, but instead it is named after a Thai based Duty Free retailing empire, King Power, a billion dollar business, founded by Thai businessman Vichai Srivaddhanaprabha, now Leicester City's owner and Chairman.

Srivaddhanaprabha's plans for the Foxes are ambitious. The primary objective is to avoid fighting relegation on an annual basis. After that, who knows? In Summer 2015, he oversaw the arrival of sixty-four-year-old Italian Claudio Ranieri as new manager, a veteran of many campaigns with a roll call of top clubs that include Juventus, Atletico Madrid, Inter Milan, Valencia and Chelsea. English pundits often frown when continentals get domestic managerial jobs, yet more often than not these experienced, intellectual and technical football men could buy and sell their home-grown equivalents.

Predictably, not everybody was impressed. Former City legend Alan Smith tipped the Foxes for the drop and moaned that, "the appointment of Ranieri will prove counterproductive". Gary Lineker complained of "an uninspiring choice" and expressed his frustration at "how the same old names keep getting a go on the managerial merry-go-round". The *Telegraph's* Liverpool correspondent Chris Bascombe called the appointment "a calamity". It seemed most observers predicted a troubled time for the Midlanders, suggesting miracles don't strike twice, the Foxes having escaped relegation the year before against all probability. Odds of 5,000–1 were available if you wanted to give your money away and bet on the Foxes to win the League. However, the people that mattered most, the players, seemed to be energised by the appointment. Midfielder

Jeffrey Schlupp recalled the Italian's unveiling. "We were all gathered in a room and he walked through and it was; 'Wow, it's Ranieri, he's a big name!' It was just excitement." Ranieri himself remained unmoved by all the fatalism and spoke with steely determination of the season that lay ahead. "Nigel made a fantastic foundation here, well done to him. I have to carry on that job. We are a little club, we will fight against everybody." And fight they did.

By the time Liverpool arrive at the King Power Stadium on February 2nd 2016, a second footballing miracle is in the offing. Leicester and Ranieri have the opportunity to eclipse Pearson's relegation Houdini act, to eclipse everything that has passed in 132 years of existence. The home team sit top of the table after twenty-three games, three points clear of Manchester City and Arsenal, four points ahead of Spurs, with a large gap to the rest.

In their entire history, Leicester have won three League Cups. They have won no Leagues titles, with the closest finish being second in 1929, and no FA Cups, having lost four finals. The wait for a big trophy success has seemed infinite. To win the League this year would be one of the biggest events not just in English football history, but in world sporting history. Today, in the era of big club power and money, if lowly Leicester can claim the title, few superlatives would be adequate. It seems all of football (except for Man City, Arsenal and Spurs) is behind them as they continue on their remarkable journey. With every passing game, the unachievable, the unthinkable, gets a little bit more achievable, a little bit more thinkable.

Tonight's programme rightly points out that the Foxes, named after Leicestershire's association with the outdoors and hunting, have been a bogey team for Liverpool through the years. On January 31st, 1981 they were the team that ended the Reds' incredible record of not having lost at home for eighty-five games. The programme also shows a photo of Leicester's FA Cup semi-final win over Shankly's Liverpool in 1963. In the shot, Mike Stringfellow rises to head the ball into Liverpool's net. I notice that, eerily, behind the goal to which he heads the ball is a Hillsborough stand absolutely stuffed to the brim full of standing fans, in a crowd of 65,000. Even then the overcrowding of stands was evident to the naked eye.

For a club with only three major honours, compared to Liverpool's forty-four, the Foxes' head-to-head record with the Reds is admirable. In 102 clashes, Leicester have won thirty-five to Liverpool's forty-three. The teams leave the tunnel to the live blast of the 'Post Horn Gallop', a traditional bugle call heard at local fox hunts. The eleven who line up against Liverpool cost, in their entirety, £18 million in transfer fees, compared to Liverpool who weigh in at hundreds of millions. Benteke who sits on the bench cost £32 million alone. The difference in return on investment is startling. What Leicester have achieved couldn't be scripted. Well maybe it could, given that a Hollywood movie director has travelled to the game to meet with Jamie Vardy, Leicester's record-breaking striker, to explore the idea of a rags-to-riches movie. Only three years previously, Vardy was playing non-League amateur football with Fleetwood Town at the age of twenty-five, an age that normally dictates that things are not going to get any better. Not so. Today's Vardy would appeal to most clubs across Europe and, in the summer of 2016, he can look forward to donning his country's white shirt at the European Championships.

Leicester have been fortunate to have kept all of their key players fit for nearly every game. The team has rarely changed and familiarity has bred contempt for others. With Leicester's aggressive style of chasing the ball down and punishing retreating defences, they have proven that city foxes are hunters and not prey. Only one home defeat all season (this back in September 2015, 2–4 at the hands of Arsenal) proves the point. It is a style that Jürgen Klopp says he admires and indeed is reminiscent of the 'geggenpressing' of his best Dortmund teams.

Oddly enough, for once I'm feeling confident. Leicester's other defeat this season came at Anfield on Boxing Day and I am optimistic that we might have the measure of the Foxes again tonight. The atmosphere in this bowl of a stadium is raucous. The home fans make a deafening sound waving their club-issued cardboard 'clappers' in the air. It's a bit artificial, but it makes for a great noise. Elsewhere a drummer beats loudly, drowning any of the Liverpool fans' attempts to out-sing the home town majority. Away fans silenced, the drumming continues and rouses the local support into song. On the large TV screens a motto is displayed – 'Foxes never quit'. We shall see.

The first half ends at 0–0 and Liverpool have played okay. The consensus around me, however, is that these are our worst back four players ever, and that Liverpool won't be able to keep a clean sheet. We'll need to score two to win. I think we have a goal in us tonight so a 1–1 wouldn't be too bad. Liverpool fans, rightly or wrongly, expect a win at a club like Leicester. It comes from a history of dominance. Listening to the half-time banter, I have to remind myself that we are the underdogs and Leicester are the League leaders.

The opposing fans are having a right good go at each other but it is all light-hearted and in good spirit. Leicester fans chant, *'you're not famous anymore'* and the Liverpool's travellers reply with, *'we won it five times'* in reference to the European Cup and Istanbul. Leicester retort with the reminder that, *'we are top of the League'*. Liverpool reply with the *'going to Wembley'* song, now that the Reds have booked a place in the League Cup Final after defeating Stoke on penalties in the semi-final return leg at Anfield. Leicester fans then win the songfest with their chant of *'Leicester, Leicester, staying up, Leicester, staying up'*. It's self-deprecating and very funny. Only the season before staying in the Premier League was the sum of their wishes, now, glory awaits. Will they keep their nerve where Rodgers' Reds didn't? Will a slip prove the downfall? Tonight I cheer for the Reds, but from tomorrow I'll also be cheering Leicester in their search for the Holy Grail.

The deadlock is broken by a wonder goal. On sixty minutes, Mahrez plays a fifty-yard pass upfield to Vardy, who is outnumbered by two defenders. As Lovren stands off him and waits to see what happens, Vardy doesn't, he acts. He catches the ball first time and smacks a thirty-yard half-volley over the retreating but defeated lunge of Mignolet and into the back of the Liverpool net. It's a world class goal worthy of any team on any stage. The King Power erupts. Belief courses through every Blue man, woman and child in the arena. Leicester are the real deal. 1–0 to the Foxes. On BBC Radio Leicester the commentator describes the goal as outrageous, the goal of the season and the goal of Vardy's life. Hollywood indeed. Vardy says later that he had noticed Mignolet repeatedly straying too far from the safety of his line and that he had decided to go for it if the opportunity arose and go for it he did. By full-time it is 2–0 to Leicester, Vardy having bagged a second. Liverpool haven't played badly, but they have been blunt upfront and porous at the back, a terminal combination. Klopp has been bestowed with a squad of non-performing strikers and soft defenders. His team looks devoid of characters, particularly with the continued absence of Sturridge and Coutinho.

When the Roman artifacts were being unearthed on Vine Street, archaeologists discovered two thin sheets of lead both inscribed in Latin. They were the first written texts found from Roman Leicester. Upon examination they were declared to be 'Curse Tablets', which were typically small sheets of metal with an inscription to a god or spirit, wishing harm or retribution upon a named individual. In Roman times these would then be thrown into a sacred pool or hidden in the fabric or wall of a building. In one hundred years' time when Anfield is being rebuilt again, it will hardly be surprising if future custodians of our great club find just such a curse tablet or two, requesting retribution on the fabled Transfer Committee.

As I leave Leicester by train the next day, I think again of Leicester City FC's assault on the Premier League crown. Incredibly, if they pull it off, it would be a story every bit as incredulous, unbelievable and far fetched as finding a King under a car park after 527 years.

RAMPANT LIONS

'It's not a day to sing songs or things like this for us… we keep it for bad times.' – Jürgen Klopp

We disembark at Aston station and make our way along Grosvenor Road past nondescript blocks of flats and some very uninspiring industrial warehouses. The area feels neglected and rundown. But as you walk up the Queen's Road and pass under the overhead A38 Motorway onto Witten Lane, a Narnia moment occurs. Suddenly you have passed through the Wardrobe and have been transported back in time. To your right sits the beautiful sandstone structure of the Aston Parish Church of Saints Peter and Paul. This site was referenced in the Domesday Book, the book commissioned in December 1085 by William the Conqueror to document the settlements of England, and here a church has stood for over three millennia. The enormous Gothic structure with tall spire, that stands today, dates back to the fifteenth century. The old church graveyard contains many graves of the Holte family, former owners of the nearby Aston Hall. The Domesday Book tells us that, in 1086, there was a full-time priest in Aston and that the area was valued at 100 shillings, with the nearby village of Birmingham valued at only twenty shillings. Then began a tale of shifting fortunes. Today Aston is one of the poorer addresses of England's second city.

Further, and to your left, stands the Holte Hotel, a beautifully ornate three-storey building. The historic Holte was restored to its former Victorian glory in 2007 after Aston Villa owner Randy Lerner poured £4 million into the refurbishment. This unique landmark dates back to the nineteenth century. With time to spare, we stroll through the rolling grounds of the adjacent park and up towards the enormous Jacobean mansion that is Aston Hall. In 1874, not far from here, four friends from the Villa Cross Wesleyan Chapel cricket team, Jack Hughes, Frederick Matthews, Walter Price and William Scattergood, met under a gas-light and decided to form a new football club, to be named Aston Villa. Villa would lift the League crown in 1894 and 1896. In 1897, only seven days after completing the double of winning both League and FA Cup, a sports stadium built on the lower grounds of the Hall would become the new home of Aston Villa Football Club and would be identified simply as 'Villa Park'.

By the turn of the century Villa had lifted two further titles to bring their tally to five, this making them the best and most successful club of the league's first era.

Leaving Aston Park, we veer left at the Holte Hotel and walk along Trinity Road, passing the impressive external façade of the rebuilt Holte End Stand, replete with its gold lettering and swirls, its red-brick frontage and stained-glass windows. Further on, at the back of the Trinity Road Stand, we enter through ornate claret and blue iron gates that hang from pillars upon which sit proud stone lions. The Rampant Lion of Scotland forms part of Villa's crest and soon we find out why. We've come across a strong and impressive figure, glinting in the cold winter sunshine. A bronze statue of a fully bearded, broad-shouldered man, dressed in a three-piece suit over which is worn a long, open overcoat. In his right hand he holds a walking stick. His left arm is held outwards, his hand holding aloft a letter, proffered it seems to all.

"Do you know who that is?" I ask my son.

"Ehr no," he replies, with just a hint of derision, which rightly asks unspoken – "How would I?"

"That's William McGregor,“ I tell him, but unsurprisingly, the look I get back is blank. So I tell him the story, the story of how it all began. In 1877, Aston Villa invited a Scot, a William McGregor of Perthshire, a Draper who had moved to Birmingham seven years previously, to join its committee. McGregor was a keen football supporter and also a great administrator. At this time most games were local games and were friendly in nature. The only formal nationwide competition was the FA Cup which had been established in 1871, mostly for universities and colleges to compete against each other. McGregor found that Villa's fixtures were being regularly cancelled for a variety of reasons which included their 'friendly' nature and also due to tournaments like the FA Cup taking precedence. Clubs in the South had little desire to formalise matters, being happy with their amateur status. In 1888, McGregor would send this letter to various Northern clubs in the hope of concreting a more formalised structure within which to play games:

> *'Every year it is becoming more and more difficult for football clubs of any standing to meet their friendly engagements and even arrange friendly matches. The consequence is that, at the last moment, through cup-tie interference, clubs are compelled to take on teams who will not attract the public. I beg to tender the following suggestion as a means of getting over the difficulty: that ten or twelve of the most prominent clubs in England combine to arrange home-and-away fixtures each season, the said fixtures to be arranged at a friendly conference about the same time as the International Conference. This combination might be known as the Association Football Union, and could be managed by a representative from each club. Of course, this is in no way to interfere with the National Association; even the suggested matches might be played under cup-tie rules. However, this is a detail. My object in writing to you at present is merely to draw your attention to the subject, and to suggest a friendly conference to discuss the matter more fully. I would take it as a favour if you would kindly think the matter over, and make whatever suggestions you deem necessary. I am only writing to the following – Blackburn Rovers, Bolton Wanderers, Preston North End, West Bromwich Albion, and Aston Villa, and would like to hear what other clubs you would suggest.*
>
> *I am, yours very truly, William McGregor (Aston Villa F.C.)'*

And so it would come to pass that in 1888, the Football League was formed consisting of all of the clubs addressed in McGregor's letter. It would also include Accrington, Burnley, Derby County, Everton, Notts County, Stoke City and Wolverhampton Wanderers. My son touches the man's bronze foot, an acknowledgment that the story interested him.

When McGregor died in December 1911, Aston Villa had already lifted six league titles. It would not be until 1981 that they would lift another. That 1981 title victory saw Villa qualify for the European Cup for the first time and would lead to their most famous night. On May 26th, 1982 at De Kuip stadium in Rotterdam, Villa would defeat the mighty Bayern Munich 1–0 and write their name alongside the list of greats and become one of only five English teams to win the Cup (Liverpool five times, Man United three, Nottingham Forest two, Aston Villa once, Chelsea once). After the highs came the lows. Villa would be relegated to the second division in 1987. They would bounce back immediately achieving promotion under the guidance of Graham Taylor, the former Watford manager. Villa have remained in the top flight since, but from the turn of the new millennium their fortunes have waned. In the last five years their average finishing position has been fourteenth and in 2014/15 Villa finished seventeenth, one place out of the drop zone. This year it seems that their luck will finally run out. Villa are a big club, with a great history, a great stadium and great supporters. To see them fall will be sad but by the time Liverpool arrive to Villa Park the die already seems cast. The claret and blues sit in last position, a full eight points from safety.

We gain entry to the ground early. It's a cracking arena and everywhere you look you see the Villa colours of claret and blue. It's a ground that has been kind to Liverpool in the Premier League era, with the Reds having suffered only one league defeat at Villa Park in the last fifteen years. Liverpool know Villa Park well, having played here seven times in FA Cup semi-finals, when the ground was used as a neutral venue. The first of those was against Everton in 1906 and the last was against Wycombe Wanderers in 2001. Seven semis would yield four trips to the final and four cup wins. Today, the pitch looks in pristine condition. A low winter sun shines brightly from above the opposite Trinity Road stand and it forces us to cover our eyes. The long days of winter are nearly gone.

With fifteen minutes to the kick-off time of 2.05 p.m., we stand inside the advertising hoardings at the halfway line to catch a close-up view of Klopp who is positioned about fifteen feet away. He pays no attention to the Liverpool players who are going through their warm-up to our right. Instead he stares at the Villa players. Although he knows the line-up, he watches to see the combinations. Who links with who? Do certain players stay together, pass to each other only, practise certain routines? Can any hints be gleaned as to what shape the opposition might adopt or what tactics they could employ? Any morsel might prove valuable. He shares a few words with Buvac and only then does he change his focus to his own team. I like this man, he watches everything. The teams are announced over the PA system. Both Sturridge and Coutinho are fit and are in the starting line-up. We smile at each other. It's the first time all season that Liverpool have been able to name Sturridge, Coutinho and Firmino in the same team. At last our three best attackers are together.

It being Valentine's Day, the stadium's pre-match playlist is loaded with love songs. 'I Get a Kick Out of You' by Frank Sinatra and then 'Sway' by Dean Martin fill the air. Next up is 'Je T'aime' by Serge Gainsbourg, sung as a duet with his then lover Jane Birkin. It is said that the heavy breathing that can be heard was recorded mid-coitus but, I decide, Valentine's Day or not, my son can wait to learn this juicy little fact when he's older. I point up to the North stand where a long banner runs from one side of the upper tier across to the other. My son reads the words written across it; 'Shaw, Williams, prepared to venture down the left. There's a good ball in for Tony Morley. Oh, it must be and it is! It's Peter Withe'. I explain to him that these are the words spoken on television by Brian Moore as he commentated on Villa's European final triumph over Munich. The word 'prepared' adorns the Villa club crest below the rampant Scottish lion. Next to the lion's head shines one white star to signify Villa's proudest day. Liverpool have five of those stars and I wonder, does that protect them from Villa's current fate? Could Liverpool one day find themselves on the brink? For much of the season our League position and also our standard of play has been closer to the bottom teams than to the top. When does a slide become a fall?

Instead of buying just the match day programme for £3.50, we go crazy and splash out on the lucky bag for £5, which contains four additional Villa programmes from seasons past. I browse these and immediately the reason for Villa's plight becomes evident, they can't hold onto their better players. The August 2009 version has then manager Martin O'Neill hailing Fabian Delph – "Fabian played exceptionally well and I'm totally convinced he will make a major impact for Villa." Delph now plays for Manchester City. In the August 2010 version, Marc Albrighton talks about having another chance as a Villa player and of "wanting to make up for lost time", and has ex-Villa player Stan Collymore hailing Albrighton's "impressive performances". Albrighton now stars for table-toppers Leicester. A glance to the Liverpool team sheet and you will see the names of two of Villa's better players of the last ten years now wearing red, Milner and Benteke.

Villa have remained unbeaten in their last four home league games, winning two and drawing two, including a 1–1 draw against league leaders Leicester. Maybe ex-Lyon boss Remi Garde is starting to turn things around, having replaced Tim Sherwood as Villa's manager in November. The bookies got it right with both Sherwood and Rodgers after all; both have long departed. Conversely, Liverpool haven't won since the circus at Norwich. Funnily enough, I think that in their last ten games the Reds have at last started to find a little bit of form and consistency. There have been no stinkers, West Ham away on January 2nd being the last of these. West Ham would beat Liverpool Youths in an FA Cup replay five days before the trip to Villa.

In the chilly Valentine's Day sunshine it is the lions of Liverpool who run rampant. Come the final whistle Liverpool have bagged six and conceded zero. The hosts have been massacred. This was not one of Liverpool's best performances of the season, however, nine shots on target produce six goals and that type of efficiency will win games. It seems the players have been listening to Klopp's demands that they improve their decision-making in the attacking third of the pitch. To shoot at the right time; to pass at the right time. When crossing into the box, to pick a target instead of offering a general invite. Liverpool have punished a very poor Villa side that lacked structure, skill and heart. It's their biggest home defeat since 1935. Most of the 36,000 crowd have left for home long before the end but the Liverpool fans stay en masse to applaud their team. Again, some of the players, including Henderson and Milner, give their shirts to young fans. I was beginning to think Liverpool would never win a league game in their all-white kit but that little jinx has now been thoroughly exorcised.

After the game, Klopp is effusive in his praise for Sturridge describing him as a 'real striker'. Klopp continues, "It's really good to see. When he hides himself on the pitch it's really difficult to defend." Klopp also shows respect for shattered Villa, "It's not a day to sing songs or things like this for us. That's part of the respect for Aston Villa, a great club in a difficult situation. If one team wins 6–0 another loses 6–0 and that's not too nice for them. It's not too often in a manager's life, we keep it for bad times."

On our walk back to town we drop into the Crown pub on Corporation Street and soon we feel warmth return to our frosty toes. Here we have a bite to eat and watch the second half of the late kick-off from Manchester. Spurs beat Man City 2–1. Earlier, in the morning kick-off, Arsenal beat Leicester 2–1. It seems certain that the title will go to one of these four but, at this stage, it's anybody's guess who. What is clear though, is that the trophy will not be making its way to McGregor's beloved Aston Villa or, for that matter, to any of their fellow eleven league founders for some while to come. With time, everybody is eventually left behind.

FINIS

'The feeling is less like an ending than just another starting point.'
— Chuck Palahniuk

It is midday, Saturday, February 27th at Liverpool's training ground Melwood – the eve of the Final. The day before, thirty first-team players trained hard, all hoping for a place in the first eleven or at worst for a place on the substitutes' bench. It is the most players that Liverpool have had fit and available all season and only the two long-term injured, Ings and Gomez, are unavailable. One could be forgiven a rueful grin at how the treatment tables empty so quickly when the possibility of a winner's medal comes around. It's what players play for and manager's manage for. Medals are legacy. They are the shiny metal that can be held by a wide-eyed son or daughter. They are the stories that can be told again and again in quiet retirement. A fourth-placed qualification for the Champions League is less tangible, how do you touch that twenty, thirty, fifty years from now?

"Actually going to a final and winning a trophy, in front of all your fans at Cardiff or Wembley, those are the days. You keep those forever." says Michael Owen. As scorer of Cup Final goals for Liverpool in both the League Cup and the FA Cup, he knows what he is talking about. "It's the stuff of dreams, isn't it? That's what I used to imagine when I was running round the garden as a kid."

During the week Klopp talks of moments that should be savoured and relished, he talks of his hunger. "I am long enough in the business to know that I am greedy for success. Lots of managers work their whole life and never get the chance to win trophies. After a short time we have that chance. Of course I will enjoy it with all I have, everyone will give their all. Clubs with a big history like Liverpool, it is always the same problem if they are not successful in the present. With the right decisions and then the right patience you can get back on track. With all the clubs around with a lot of money, we should not go the same way, we have to go our way, how Liverpool always did. It's a big chance for us. It's a chance and that's all I need. You should not waste opportunities of winning cups and I'm ready for winning something."

Klopp's first trophy opportunity arrives 143 days into the job, yet his finals record isn't great. He's been to four, yet tasted victory only once. In fairness, on three of those occasions his team were major underdogs, the plucky Dortmund taking on the Bavarian might of Munich. The odd one out was his very last game with Dortmund where he hoped to leave with a trophy win, only to lose the German Cup Final to Wolfsburg 3–1.

The players gather in a circle as Klopp and his management team reveal the team selection on a screen display. It is the moment of truth for many. Particularly for the Brazilian, Lucas, Liverpool's longest serving squad member. He missed Liverpool's last final victory in 2012, when the Reds defeated Cardiff on penalties, also in the League Cup, and is yet to play at Wembley. "It feels so special," he says. "The final is the biggest game and you want to be involved and that is why everyone is really working hard to get a place in the team."

Lucas's efforts have paid off, he is picked at centre-half alongside Mamadou Sakho with thirty-five-year-old Kolo Touré, Liverpool's most senior squad member, dropped to the bench. Dejan Lovren and Martin Skrtel, Liverpool's two other centre-halves, have both just returned to training after injury, but the game arrives too soon for either to be considered. Mignolet starts in goal and Clyne and Moreno fill the right and left-back roles. In midfield there are no surprises with Can, Milner and captain Henderson all included. Upfront the Brazilians Coutinho and Firmino flank Sturridge who, remarkably for him, has remained fit. Lallana must feel most aggrieved of those who take the subs' roles, but he too has only just returned from injury, and it would be hard for Klopp to pick him. If you gamble on the fitness of a player, you could be replacing him after only five or ten minutes. With the possibility of extra-time and penalties, the ability to use your subs at the right time is an important strategic weapon. Origi, Benteke, Flanagan, Allen, Toure and reserve keeper Bogdan fill the remaining places on the subs bench.

"We don't tell the players individually or write it on a board, we have it on a screen," says Klopp. "When I started as a manager, I told every player individually and after that I said 'never again' because everyone I told before my first game, that they were in, were like 'yeesss!' And the rest were like miserable. There is no explanation, that is how it is. Any player can talk to me all the time, only not before the game, because nothing will change. It's like a referee with his decision. Afterwards we can talk, before the game, no."

On Saturday afternoon the Liverpool squad travel from Merseyside to London by train. Late that night Klopp meets the club's American owners. It's near midnight and around a table sit John Henry, Henry's wife Linda Pizzuti, Tom Werner and Klopp. They sip Peroni beers and contemplate the events that are about to unfold. Klopp wasn't appointed to win League Cups, but then again he wasn't appointed not to. To win a trophy within five months of arrival would make a statement. It would set the bar, build confidence. That said, Kenny Dalglish won the League Cup in 2012 but it wasn't enough for him to keep his job following a lowly eighth place finish in the Premier League. As the key men plot and plan, Liverpool sit ninth in the table. So winning won't be the be-all and end-all, but as Klopp says one should never turn down the opportunity.

Captain Henderson agrees. He was in the team that beat Cardiff but that success proved an oasis, a false dawn. The hope is that under the new regime of Klopp, albeit still very much with the squad of Rodgers, this might be the start of a new voyage of success. Henderson wants to be the captain of that ship. Most Liverpool captains' homes are adorned by at least one grinning photograph, a silver trophy held aloft, their place in the club's annals secured. Yet Henderson may find it harder than those who went before him, now that Liverpool look up to the best and not down at the rest.

"As a captain you will be judged on what you win basically. If you are doing well and the team is winning everything, you become a very good captain. At the other end if you're not playing so well, if you're not winning trophies, you will be judged in a different way. I knew that before I took the role and it's a big occasion, not only for me, but the players and the club." Speaking about his manager he says, "I think if we can win on Sunday and lift the trophy then that will be a great platform for him to start a new reign if you like, a new team to go on and win many trophies in the future. We've got a lot of potential in the group and we've got a lot of talented players, a lot of young players as well, who have a lot of personality, and I feel with the experiences we have had and the longer we play together the better we will get, and I'm hoping we can kick on from there."

Liverpool have won more League Cups than any other team, eight in total. It provided Roy Evans with his only silverware as Liverpool manager and it kick-started the success of Gerard Houllier in 2001. Reds fans are hoping that it can prove a similar catalyst for Klopp's reign.

Henderson is clear that big-spending City are the favourites and he states that Liverpool will have to 'work harder, run harder, win the battle'. "In a Cup Final it's just about giving your all and making sure you leave everything on the pitch as individuals and as a team."

Great upsets of the past inspire Klopp. "Sometimes it is the quality of one player who decides the game, but it is more about the performance of the whole team. If you look at big titles in the past; Denmark were European Champions in 1992. That is the best I ever heard about. They met each other at McDonalds then they heard they had to go to the European Championships and they won the title. That is cool. Greece too. It is not always the best team that should win. Everybody can win if you have the right idea and if you are full of trust. The most important thing is to win the final. I don't care how. I care before the game, but after, if we win with a lot of luck 1–0, I wouldn't care."

Klopp has been to Wembley before and lost, Dortmund losing the Champions League final to Bayern Munich in 2013 with Arjen Robben snatching the late, late winner. "The name is a really good sound. Wembley," says Klopp. "Going there is one of the best things you can do in life – sports life – and one time is not enough."

The stage is set. It is Final time. Final from the Latin *finis*, the end, the limit. Come Sunday night it will be all over and only the victors will remain standing. The winner takes it all.

THE HOTTEST FIRE

'We are past the end of things now, but I don't want to leave.' —
Richard Ford, *The Sportswriter*

My son and I board the tube at Paddington and ride the Bakerloo line to Wembley Central in north-west London. We disembark and join the mass walking east along High Road. The village of Wembley grew up on the hill by the clearing with the Harrow Road and its name derives from the Old English word 'Wemba' and 'Lea' for meadow. After about five hundred metres we turn left along Wembley Hill Road and the new Wembley Stadium comes into view. Built on the site of the old stadium and opened to the public on March 9th 2007, it is the biggest stadium in the United Kingdom and the second-largest in Europe. High above the North stand curves an enormous metal arch traversing from one side to the other. This marvel of modern engineering, which rises forty stories in the air and has a span of 1,000 feet, offers a clue as to how this 90,000 seater stadium cost a colossal £798 million to build.

Sir Norman Foster designed the arch and the roof structure. With a sixty-eight degree tilt from the horizontal, the arch supports 5,000 tonnes of roofing and allowed designers to eliminate the need for columns within the interior, which importantly for fans means that every seat has both a covered and unobstructed view of the pitch. The arch fulfils another function aside from supporting the majority of the roof. It also provides a beacon for the stadium, a tube of light illuminating the north-west London sky on match days. Later it will be lit in the colours of the victorious team. We hope for a red sky at night.

Crossing the White Horse Bridge that spans the railway tracks below, we enter the stadium via turnstile N. Today Liverpool's fans will fill the western half of the large bowl, with Manchester City's fans to the East.

We are early and an hour remains to kick-off at 4.30 p.m. It's February 28th, the penultimate day of a leap year winter and even though the afternoon is bright and sunny, I can feel my extremities starting to numb. It is bitterly cold.

My son browses the £10 match program as I scan the variety of Liverpool flags that are draped across the stands to my left. There are over one hundred. To my right I can only make out two uninspiring St. George's cross flags at the City end. No team does flags like Liverpool. They are part of our culture and heritage, symbolic displays of our community.

Closer to kick-off the stadium starts to fill as the players go through their warm-up on the pitch. When they vacate and return to the dressing rooms for final instructions and encouragement, the pre-match pageantry begins. The crests of both teams are displayed on one hundred foot-high sheets which float above the pitch, attached to long cylinder-shaped balloons. The League Cup trophy is placed on display by a military officer as jets of fire spurt high into the air from pedestals placed the length of the pitch side. Fireworks spray into the afternoon sky and the atmosphere in the now full stadium ratchets a few notches higher. The teams emerge from the players' tunnel and enter the arena. The sound of 'You'll Never Walk Alone' greets the Reds and Man City's fan's respond with 'Blue Moon'. It's game time.

The first half speeds by in a blur, the pace furious with neither team showing timidity in the battle. The teams leave the pitch with no goals scored. Neither has been on top with both sides keen not to make early mistakes or allow too much space to the opposition. Yet it has been enjoyable fare with plenty of determined endeavour and no little skill. The brightest moment involved a flash of brilliance from both sides. On twenty-three minutes City's talisman, Sergio Aguero, skipped past both Liverpool centre-halves as he made his way into the danger zone. Free from pursuers he sent a curling shot low to Mignolet's left and a goal beckoned. Incredibly Mignolet managed to stretch far enough and tip the ball onto his left-hand post, off which it cannoned to safety. Moments later Liverpool's Sakho, still dazed from an earlier head collision, was substituted and Kolo Touré took to the fray, to face his brother, Yaya, in the City side.

City start the second half brightly and it's not long before they are ahead. A Liverpool move inside their own half breaks down after a poor pass from Henderson. Moreno, the Reds' left-back, is now stranded ahead of the ball. The Liverpool midfield are slow to react and it is City's Fernando who chases towards the left edge of the Liverpool penalty box and into the gap vacated by Moreno. Can he find a man now with Liverpool in disarray? No, instead he drills a hard shot towards goal from an acute angle. It's a shot that every top keeper should save. Rule number one in Goalkeeping School is never get beaten on your near post from an acute angle, block the path. Mignolet has time to see it all happen, but the ball goes through his body as he falls backwards and rockets into the Liverpool net. Forty-nine minutes and it's 1–0 to City.

Liverpool respond bravely and start to knock the ball around with more deliberation and desire. On fifty-six minutes, Sturridge and Milner interlink brilliantly but Milner's shot misses. City retreat in numbers and soak up the pressure. But a team of their class is always dangerous on the counter. Can loses the ball and City break with pace. The ball is played across the Liverpool box to the unmarked Raheem Sterling. The headline 'Sterling Sinks Pool' must have flashed before his eyes, blinding him, for he miscues badly and the ball bounces wide. Liverpool escape, just. Within minutes Aguero breaks free in the Liverpool box with only Lucas to beat. Moreno flicks out his leg and seems to foul the Argentinean but the referee waves play on. Nine out of ten times that's a penalty, but not today.

On the relentless pace of this enthralling final goes. Lucas, at the heart of the Liverpool defence, is having a man of the match performance, breaking up attacks, distributing the ball with intent, driving his team forward in search of an equaliser. Firmino gets behind the City defence on seventy-two minutes but he is offside. Liverpool's creator of recent weeks has had a quiet game. Lallana is introduced to the action as Moreno is substituted and Milner drops back to left-back. Lallana's verve and tenaciousness immediately provide a lift. Firmino is caught offside again and is replaced by Origi on eighty minutes. Sterling misses another sitter for City and it seems that this is not to be his day.

On eighty-two minutes the Reds push forward once more, attacking the end that houses their loyal fans. In the inside right channel Sturridge finds Coutinho who plays the ball onto Origi. Sturridge continues his run forward and the ball finds him again on the left edge of the City box. It's close and intricate play from the Reds, who are surrounded by defenders in sky-blue shirts. Sturridge beats his man inside the box heading for the end line. He whips a brilliant pass which flashes across the face of the City six-yard line. Lallana arrives late at the back post and stretches to meet the ball. He gets there and directs his shot goal bound. It must be the equaliser but no, it crashes off the post and is sent careering back into the melee of players that have gathered inside the danger zone. Fortunately it falls to the one who will not panic, the one with ice in his veins. It falls to Philippe Coutinho, 'El Magico'. With one deft touch he controls the ball and with the next he fires it home. With only seven minutes remaining, at last a richly deserved equaliser. My son and I dance up and down with joy and elation. Coutinho runs to those that love him and is lost in a mass of delirious fans. The game is alive again and is there for the winning.

Liverpool push forward in search of the decider, but so do City. It is City who go closest and come the full-time whistle Liverpool are hanging on and glad of the second chance that their dogged play has afforded them. The final is going to extra time. The players gather at the centre circle and take instructions from their managers and coaches. They take on fluids and energy supplements. It has been a gruelling duel under the cold February sun.

City make their first substitution of the day with Zabaleta replacing Sagna. This ability to bring on fresh legs may prove telling. Daniel Sturridge, only just returned from a lengthy injury, looks out on his feet, but he can't be replaced. Liverpool have used all their subs. Toure's entry was forced and Lallana and Origi's introductions were tactical as the Reds chased an equaliser. Both have helped turn the tide, particularly the gifted Englishman, but Klopp has no more aces up his sleeve. The game flies by with no let-up. On 104 minutes Aguero breaks free in the box with only Mignolet to beat. He attempts to flick the ball up and over the keeper's left hand but Mignolet makes a fine instinctive save and keeps the Reds' hopes alive. The second half of extra-time sees Liverpool in the ascendancy. On 107 minutes Origi crosses into the box but Sturridge and Lallana only manage to get in each other's way and the chance goes a begging. Minutes later Henderson surges forward and sets Milner free but his shot is weak. City are wilting now and in the stands the Red fans can sense glory. Moments later it seems to have arrived. Milner floats a cross invitingly into the City penalty area and Divock Origi rises to win it. From point blank range he sends a powerful header goal bound. It must be, but it's not. Cabellero flings out a hand and somehow saves his team from going behind. My son and I exchange open-mouthed glances and no words are needed. Liverpool push again and Sturridge and Origi have shots saved. Then, as it was at the end of normal time, it is again in extra-time with City finishing strongest. Fernando rises to head the ball home in the final minute but misses. Nobody can find the elusive winner and the game finishes 1–1 after extra-time. Penalties will decide the final.

The two managers embrace in the middle of the pitch. They both know that, whatever happens from here, the outcome is in the lap of the gods. Ask Northampton or Stoke, both beaten by Liverpool on penalties on their route to the final. Liverpool's record in penalty shoot-outs is incredible, fourteen won from seventeen contested. Yet it is exactly this that worries me. Fifty-fifty odds have a way of balancing out over the long run and I can't help feeling that today might be the start of it.

But maybe I'm wrong. Fernando steps up to take City's first spot kick and he hits the post. Emre Can takes Liverpool's first and scores. Advantage Liverpool. Next up, Navas makes it 1–1. Then the momentum shifts as it often does in these affairs. Lucas, probably Liverpool's best player on the day and so beloved of the Red fans, misses and it's back to square one. Aguero takes the next for City and the outcome is never in doubt. Up steps Coutinho to take Liverpool's third. I'm nervous about this one. Even though the kid is a magician, quite often his brilliance is instinctive. Give a genius time and he might think too much. The memory of Roberto Baggio at the 1994 World Cup finals springs to mind, not to mention Shevchenko in Istanbul. Coutinho misses and my worries have found life. Yaya Touré scores the fourth City spot kick and now it's 3–1 to City and Liverpool are in mortal danger. Lallana steps up to take the next and it's very simple, he must score to keep the game alive. He drills a hard shot to Cabellero's right but it's a little too high and too close to the diving keeper who parries it to safety, to glory, to victory. I hug my son and we smile at each other, resigned smiles, yet smiles infused with pride. Liverpool have contributed to a great game, a ding-dong encounter. On balance City deserve their hard-fought victory, just. We'll take the rough with the smooth and we'll move on.

If City's players won the game it was Liverpool's fans who could be heard loudest in the stands. Even in defeat they sing vociferous approval of their team. Mike Walters would write in the *Mirror* newspaper, "*In the days of the old twin towers, Liverpool fans used to refer to the national stadium as Anfield South because it was their second home. Trips to Wembley have been less frequent, and less kind this century – but emissaries from the Kop always lend a vibrant atmosphere to the place. And in one respect they remain unrivalled among supporters across the land, in lean times, and there have been plenty of those. In the twenty-six years since Liverpool were champions, they have never turned on their own players. Grasping American owners, yes, but never the team.*"

Later we hear some of the post-match comments and it is clear that the players and manager are as gutted as we are. Captain Henderson comments, "At 1–1, I felt that the momentum was with us. We were winning the ball back in crucial areas and we were getting the ball up the field quickly, causing them problems, but it wasn't our day. It's hard, but I don't think we could have given more. We said before the game we needed to leave everything out there and we certainly did that." My son and I exchange glances and we both nod. We concur fully. As fans we couldn't have asked for more from our team. They sweated blood.

Later we watch Klopp's post-match interview. It's the most dejected I have seen him. The effervescence is gone. He looks drained. I know how he feels, we all do. Emotionally sapped and caught in the vacuum of a loss, a horrible place where nothing more can be done, no effort can be raised to change the irreversible.

"You need a little bit of luck in penalty shoot-outs, but of course you need to shoot a little bit better than we did. They know how it works usually, but today was not too difficult for the goalkeeper, but we were not lucky. Simon was two or three times really close to the ball so that's how it is and at the end we have to accept that we lost. At the moment I don't feel the positives, I'm a human being, after all. It's not my first big defeat, I've had defeats before and I've had wins before. I know how it goes."

Indeed it's Klopp's fourth cup final defeat in a row, yet he remains defiant. Like any winner he knows that you must mix the rough with the smooth. The toughest iron goes through the hottest fires.

"Do you think I will go home now, close the door and stay there for the next four weeks? Yes it's normal to be down. But it's okay. You have to feel a defeat, you can't say 'oh it wasn't important' because it was. We lost a Final, so it's not too good. But you always have to fight back. We can say all these things, but you know you are always going to fall down. You have to stand up, that's the truth. Only silly people stay on the floor and wait for the next defeat. Of course we will strike back, 100 per cent. We were down in this game and we struck back. The next time you are in a final you have to feel how it is to lose. Then you can feel how it is to win. It was a great day until the last shot of the shoot-out. It was perfectly organised, it was the perfect atmosphere, a really great experience. But I feel rubbish. Am I allowed to say? … I feel shit."

We feel for Klopp, he looks deflated. He keeps meeting gorillas with bazookas. It will take every ounce of his talent to become a winner at Anfield. He continues to talk on the TV screen and we continue to listen. My mind drifts to the winning shot in the wildlife photographer exhibition at the National History Museum, which my son and I visited that morning. At first glance it is a simple yet powerful image, a red predatory fox holds a white arctic fox in its teeth, clenching tight into the prey's blood-soaked neck. The colours are visceral, the foxes' deathly embrace framed by a blanket of white snow. I think of Man City captain Vincent Kompany's comments about this being 'hunting season'. The time to take scalps and win prizes. Yet the photograph tells another tale. Red foxes don't normally hunt their own breed and certainly not so far north in the domain of the arctic fox. But everything is changing. Increasing temperatures in the Arctic have allowed his range to extend northward. Conflicts between the two will now be more common. All has altered in the footballing ecosystem too. No longer are Liverpool's territories protected and the battle now is for their very survival at the top table of English and European football, the hunter now very much the hunted.

PART V

EUROPEAN ROYALTY

THE IDES OF MARCH

'Hunting. One thing it is not is a sport. Sport is when individuals or teams compete against each other under equal circumstances to determine who is better at a given game or endeavour '
— R. Lerner

'Hunting season' is how Vincent Kompany, Manchester City captain, described it. He's not the first to make reference to how important this time of the year is, the time when titles and destinies are decided. City, when winning their recent two titles, proved particularly good at putting together runs of form from March to May that would see them chase down the leaders and claim glory. Their last day of the season, last seconds of the game victory over QPR in 2012, which saw them claim their first title since 1968, may never be matched for drama or emotion. It was the most incredible finish to a League campaign ever, bar none (although Arsenal fans might disagree given their last-minute title-winning goal at Anfield in 1989). United had effectively won the title by April but managed to let a large lead slip to allow their 'noisy neighbours', as Ferguson had described City, to pilfer the crown. The same fate awaited Liverpool in 2014, as the Reds faltered close to the finish line and again City would sneak in to claim the glory.

The great teams come alive at this time of the year. Like top racehorses they finish with power and strength leaving the also-rans in their wake. It's the climactic stretch, the time to stand up and be counted. The time for winners. It's the first day of March and four teams remain in the title hunt, with the table as follows:

		Played	Points
1.	Leicester	27	56
2.	Spurs	27	54
3.	Arsenal	27	51
4.	Man City	26	47

9.	Liverpool	26	38

In their heyday, Liverpool under Paisley, Fagan and Dalglish, would only now begin to hit their stride, everything to this point being the preamble. The Reds were practically guaranteed involvement in the title shake-up every year. In the eighteen years from 1973 to 1991 Liverpool FC would finish outside the top two places only once, lifting eleven titles in the process. Now Liverpool fans can only hope to still be in the hunt come spring. It hasn't been all bad news, with the last ten years bringing two second and two third place finishes and an average finishing position of 4.8th. The period since 2010 has seen the alarming decline, the one that Klopp has been hired to halt. In that time, Liverpool have finished 7th, 6th, 8th, 7th, 2nd and 6th. It is during this time that Spurs have moved ahead of Liverpool in the pecking order, with the Reds now outside the big five in the form guide. That said, Spurs have not truly challenged for the title in my living memory, and not since their second and last victory in 1961. In more recent times they have never led the League after March. This season is their equivalent of Rodgers' 2014, their chance to end a League title drought of fifty-four years. Leicester, the leaders, haven't ever won it and Arsenal's last winning campaign was in 2004. Trying to lift the crown will be a new experience for all of City's competitors. No wonder Kompany is preparing the dogs.

Every game at this time of the season is critical, as much so at the bottom as at the top. It is widely accepted that this is the worst possible year in history to fall into the Championship. Season 2016/17 sees the mammoth new Premier League TV deal kick in and the gap between the top table and the scrap eaters below will widen even further. To fall now might be akin to a life sentence without parole. The bottom of the table looks like this:

		Played	Points
14.	Crystal Palace	27	32
15.	Bournemouth	27	29
16.	Swansea	27	27
17.	Norwich	27	24

18.	Newcastle	26	24
19.	Sunderland	27	23
20.	Aston Villa	27	16

Villa look dead and buried unless they can pull off a Leicester 2015 type revival but, having witnessed the Valentine's Day massacre, that seems unlikely. The big two from the North East are teetering on the precipice. Palace would seem to be above the safety line, yet with no wins recorded since the turn of the year, they need to arrest their slide.

For Liverpool, fresh from the heart-breaking defeat at Wembley, twelve games remain in the League. Spring 2015 proved a downfall of sorts for Rodgers, with back-to-back insipid displays at home to Man United (1–2 defeat) and away to Arsenal (4–1 defeat), putting paid to any Champions League top-four hopes. This would lead to an end of season capitulation with further demoralising defeats to Hull and Palace, not to mention the 6–1 Stoke thrashing. Throw in one of Liverpool's worst ever performances at Wembley in the semi-final loss to Villa and the writing was splashed all over the wall for anybody to read. Prior to that dreadful run, Rodgers had outperformed. Things can go pear-shaped very quickly in the world of football.

Klopp will know it's important to finish this season well, it's the foundation for the hard pre-season training of July and August, it's the feel-good memories players take into a new season. It's a momentum thing. These are mostly the same players that trailed off abysmally the previous season under Rodgers so it will be interesting to see what Klopp can extract from disappointed minds and tiring legs as the finishing line approaches. Many of these players have never won any silverware of any type. It's one of the reasons, repeated over and over, why they signed for the Reds – the club's track record of lifting trophies. The chance to win.

But no divine right exists, you have to earn it. The defeat at Wembley will have hurt many. Now we will see how they respond as individuals and as a unit. At Wembley, Liverpool proved they can compete on a one-off basis with big spending Man City, toe to toe. The challenge now will be whether they can go on a run and challenge for the final Champions League spot? In 2001 Gerard Houllier's team went on a late, late surge, winning six of their last seven League games to secure third place on the final day of the season. It would prove the springboard to Cup victories in both the FA and UEFA Cups in the weeks that followed, to add to the League Cup already collected earlier that season. The season after would see Liverpool finish second to Arsenal in the League. Confidence builds momentum. Momentum builds confidence. That third-place finish was three years into Houllier's reign, so to expect Klopp to engineer a similar run would be foolhardy, not six months into his tenure. However, with a full squad of players now available and fit and with an easing fixture list, Liverpool fans will be hoping for a bit more of that much dreamt of quality – consistency. Henderson has spoken of the need for it and Klopp has insisted that the team make 'consistency a habit'.

But if a top four finish looks out of reach in the League, there is still much for Liverpool to play for in Europe. In the week leading up to the Wembley final Liverpool overcame plucky Bundesliga outfit FC Augsburg 1–0 on aggregate over two legs. If the final defeat had left anybody thinking that the season might peter out, a bomb landed when the draw was made for the last sixteen of the Europa League. Liverpool would play their bitter rivals Manchester United for the first time ever in European competition. Losing a League Cup Final was one thing, but the thought of losing to Man United in Europe, with the eyes of the world watching, well that would be unbearable. The testing challenges don't stop there. Three days after the Wembley defeat, Liverpool play Manchester City again, this time at home in the League. March would also bring two tough away fixtures at Crystal Palace and Southampton, both bogey teams of a sort and both grudge games. It could prove a make or break month.

Not surprisingly Klopp would remark, "it seems like it's Liverpool versus Manchester, like always." And so it has been. Historically just the Red half, but now if Klopp's time is to prove successful at Anfield, he will need to conquer both the Blue and the Red. That's before he even sets his sights on the London boys of Chelsea, Arsenal and Spurs. The gargantuan scale of his task must have come into clear focus, high definition. Yet, Klopp's ebullient and charismatic character is not one to lie down to a challenge or to betray any sign of weakness. Brazenly, he tells the media that he had hoped for the Man United draw in Europe. He gives a broad smile and two thumbs up, "Ask my staff," he instructs before continuing, "we have to clear something. In the League game we lost 1–0, it was not what we deserved. This gives us a chance to make it better."

In the tunnel after the match at Wembley, Klopp's shoulders were sunken, his trademark smile was gone. He wanted to be anywhere but there but, as was required, he answered the TV reporters' questions politely, obligingly. Still it was clear to see he was devastated, sunken. The German is a walking billboard of body language and just minutes after a demoralising defeat the message read 'broken'. A few days later, with Liverpool's conquerors arriving with blood in their nostrils once more, Klopp is galvanised and defiant. "I am 100 per cent excited about the challenge. It gets better and better by the way. Why? Because I know more. I am not the cleverest but I love the challenge. I like to change things and help if it's possible. It's a hard way to go. I don't know what other names FSG would have taken but I think I am a really perfect solution. I like this. I am patient enough to work for the moment and then we can change things. On Sunday, with a bit of luck, we could have won the game. If Divock Origi makes that header, it's 2–1. To become successful in the future we need to learn a lot of things. The first thing is that you really need to work to get there. We can't be successful just because of the history of the club or the name of the manager or the name of the players. The way we play football is influenced by a few things, how we train and which players we have. We have to change a lot of things to be successful."

The warning seems clear to his players, their Liverpool careers are on the line. Performances from March to May would decide which of them would still be sitting in the dressing room come August 2016 and the start of Klopp's first full season in charge.

"It's not possible in this world to be successful in England five or six years in a row. Nobody can win the League five or six years in a row because the financial potential of all the teams is too big. But always to be a part of this and to be a challenger is possible. That's what we have to be in the future. To do that we have to make decisions. I feel absolutely perfect here, not after losing a final, but the next day because I know everyone here is working so hard. They need a bit of help. And they need a big hand from someone who is patient enough and can handle the pressure from the outside. I can handle this. I am only interested in Liverpool FC. If I had gone to another club would it have been easier? They would have other problems. We have problems here but we are in a good way to solve them. How long do we need for this? Time is very important. All we can change to become a good side we will do."

The Cup Final saw the end of a dream-like period where most Reds fans drifted on a wave of hope that somehow their new manager would incredibly lift silverware within five months of his arrival. What a statement that would have been. However, winning the League Cup is not why Klopp is at Anfield, it is not his objective, nor that of the owners. Don't get me wrong, anyone and everyone connected with Liverpool wanted that trophy. In many ways the League Cup has become a harder trophy to win and maybe a more important one than the FA Cup. With the importance of the League and the top four and also of late season European campaigns, the bigger clubs want the calendar as free as possible come April and May. The League Cup affords an opportunity to put a trophy in the cabinet early before the bigger hurdles come along. It is the lowest hanging fruit. City and Liverpool played pretty much full strength teams from the quarter final onwards. Yet both clubs fielded weaker, understrength, and in Liverpool's case a youth side, in the FA Cup. Whether this becomes a trend or not will remain to be seen.

Klopp had said in the programme notes for the Wembley Final – "In many ways I feel like we have ridden on the journey with the team and the supporters in this competition. The team had already progressed through one round when we arrived." With the final now gone, that dream sequence, that journey has ended. Now it's down to the real stuff. Can Liverpool climb the table to a respectable top six League finish? Can they win the next and even bigger final and vanquish the Red Devils of Manchester? Can they lay down a marker for the following season and send a message out to players around Europe; come and have a look at this project, it could get exciting? The month ahead would tell us much. Beware the Ides of March.

BOOM CITY

'Courage is being scared to death and saddling up anyhow.' –John Wayne

To meet again so soon after a competitive Final is unusual, but for Liverpool the visit of Man City to Anfield three days after the Wembley showdown offers an opportunity for absolution of sorts. A victory won't see the Cup handed over but at least it will inflict damage on an opponent while pushing Liverpool forward with positive momentum again. Straight back on the horse.

In his programme notes Klopp congratulates City and Pellegrini on their victory. For Liverpool he explains that the "pain is still very real and the hurt has not gone away from the outcome and nature of the defeat on Sunday. It feels raw in this moment and will probably feel this way for a while. This is healthy and is part of being involved in professional sport at the highest level. If we didn't feel pain after losing a final I would be very worried. But, what is absolutely not allowed, is that we allow that pain to be negative and affect us in a way that means we don't learn from it. The attitude, collectively, we must show now is that the pain, hurt and disappointment from Sunday will drive us on and make us bigger, stronger and better as a group. Falling down is okay in life; it is expected. But you have to get up and keep going forward. I said to the players before the game that this is hopefully our first final, and not our last. These words are more important now, having lost the game."

As ever, it is important for Klopp to build unity with the fans, as he did in Mainz and Dortmund. "The backing you gave the side from the first minute, until beyond the 120 minutes to the final penalty, was incredible. The reason, for me, the players and the staff, it was so painful on Sunday at the end was because we didn't reward your support with the win, I will never forget the atmosphere you created and you have given me some special memories. Hopefully, in the days, weeks, months and years to come, we can have more special moments and enjoy them together. You'll never walk alone. Jürgen."

Klopp is in a belligerent and irritable mood. In the pre-match interview it's clear to see that anger still simmers. Losing does not sit well with him. He talks like a fighter, not willing to be prey to City twice in quick succession, warning, "If somebody wants to be Champions, they should be Champions without our help, without our points. That's a real Champion. I don't think about who can win the League, I only think about – can we win? It is not possible to change history, if we win the game nobody will give us the League Cup. We have to show now that we are more greedy than before. This game is very important for them, it is very important for us too."

From the off it is Liverpool who are up for it more. On his first return to Anfield, Raheem Sterling is welcomed unceremoniously by a ferocious tackle from Flanagan, a true native son of Liverpool. Steven Gerrard always did it when the big matches came around. Hit them hard and early, set the tone, draw the crowd into the game. Flanagan achieves his objective, the Kop roar, baying for retribution. By half-time Flanagan has marked, hassled and hustled Sterling out of the game and the former Liverpool man is replaced at the break by striker Bony. City need a striker, they need goals, for they trail 2–0 to a rampant Liverpool after goals from Lallana and Milner. It could and should have been more, such was their dominance.

The second half sees no let-up from the Reds. Lallana and Firmino combine in the fifty-seventh minute and Firmino calmly dispatches the ball into the net for a 3–0 scoreline. It could have been five or six, but by the final whistle 3–0 does nicely and Liverpool close the gap on fourth place to six points. With so many teams ahead of them it is a long shot, but at least it's a target of sorts, something to fight for over the remaining eleven League fixtures.

Klopp is ebullient – "Tonight I told the lads, we have to be angry, angry in a positive football way. They take the Cup we want, now they want the points that we want to keep, this was our best home game, the only word I can describe this was...", he pauses, sentence unfinished and a broad smile breaks out on his face, a full mouth of teeth showing, eyes glistening in mischievous delight. He looks away from the TV interviewer, and stares directly into the camera, into the eyes of the watching audience and declares …

… "BOOM!"

THE NORWOOD ADVENTURE

'To give and to take, to accept success modestly and defeat bravely, to fight against odds, to stick to one's point, to give credit to your enemy and value your friend – these are some of the lessons which true sport should impart.'
— Sir Arthur Conan Doyle

Trade fairs are big business and not surprisingly the market seems cornered by the large industrial and manufacturing behemoths that are Germany, America and China. From the Beijing Auto Fair to the Munich Property Exposition, the range of events seems endless. Vegas is always a popular destination for the poor businessman, seeking inspiration. The construct is normally the same – enormous warehouse-type buildings containing numerous large halls, these hosting hundreds of stalls, each displaying goods and wares for trade. England is poorly positioned in this lucrative marketplace, but this wasn't always the case. In fact the very first World Fair was held in London in the nineteenth century, the Great Exhibition of 1851. This was a showcase for technologies and products developed in the Industrial Revolution. Some 100,000 items were to be displayed by over 14,000 contributors. Such an event needed a grand home and so it came to pass that the historic Crystal Palace was constructed in Hyde Park. Effectively the Palace was a building made of glass, maybe the largest greenhouse the world had ever seen. A team of eighty glaziers fitted 18,000 delicate panels and the final structure was over half a kilometre long and fifty metres high and included 84,000m^2 of glass. The exhibition opened on 1st May 1851 and closed its doors five months later on 11th October 1851.

Now, a conundrum existed. A big glass conundrum. What to do with an enormous greenhouse sitting in the middle of London. It was decided that the Palace would be taken apart and re-erected south of the Thames on

Sydenham Hill in Penge, some twelve kilometres from its former home. And so, the Crystal Palace was rehoused on a large estate of a few hundred acres, which included a Victorian theme park, all dedicated to the greater glory of the British Empire. The theme park included and does to this day, thirty-three life-sized dinosaurs sculpted by Benjamin Waterhouse Hawkins. A sports stadium would also be developed and this would host the FA Cup Finals from 1895 to 1914, before Wembley was built. The owners of the venue wanted a professional team to use the grounds and so Crystal Palace FC was formed. Appropriately, the club would adopt the nickname of 'the Glaziers' and the image of the Crystal Palace would form its crest. The outbreak of the First World War led to the Admiralty requisitioning the Crystal Palace and the club was forced to move to the home of West Norwood FC on Herne Hill. By 1924, the Glaziers had moved to their own purpose-built stadium named Selhurst Park and it is here that they have stayed to this day. In 1936, the glass palace would burn to the ground in a massive inferno which it was said could be seen from eight counties. The cause of the fire was never established. One hundred thousand people came to Sydenham Hill to watch the blaze, among them Winston Churchill, who remarked, "this is the end of an age".

If trade fairs where invented to peddle wares, then the Premier League has turned into one big international investment fair, masquerading as a football tournament. Palace have become the eleventh of twenty clubs to agree an overseas investment deal and Steve Parish, their charismatic and media-hungry chairman, was the deal-maker. Discussing the transaction he remarked, "You have to kiss a lot of frogs, that's really the art of it". The chosen frogs, whom all Palace fans hope magically morph into Princes, are Americans Josh Harris (co-founder of private equity investment giant Apollo, and said to be worth $1.4bn) and David Blitzer (senior executive at Blackstone Investment). The Palace deal is said to involve an investment of somewhere between 50–100 million pounds into the club for the issuance of new shares and leaves the new owners with a combined 36 per cent stake. It is said that this injection of cash, along with some bank debt, will be used to modernise the stadium, expanding its capacity from 26,000 to 40,000. Funds will also be available for players and squad development. In this bold age of ambition Palace see a bright future ahead. Parish explains, "There's only one Premier

League club south of the river. No club south of London have ever really stamped their authority on the League or been considered a big club. I've supported the club since I was four years old. It has been a rough old ride and I've always felt it had unfulfilled potential." In an interview with Jonathon Northcroft of the *Sunday Times,* Parish further outlines why the Premier League is so alluring to foreign investors. *"The Premier League's a success story. I hope nobody's stupid enough to mess with it. To think Crystal Palace (next season) might have more TV revenue than Barcelona. A higher wage bill than Atletico Madrid. It's insane. We had an Italian club visit us when we got promoted. A club I remember, as a kid, winning UEFA Cups. The meeting was basically, 'Which of our players do you want to buy?' And then you look at our turnover and think, 'Wow, we have twice theirs'."*

It's another Sunday in London, one week on from the Wembley Cup Final defeat to Manchester City. Instead of my son, this week I'm accompanied by my lovely fiancée. A London overground train from Whitechapel takes us south to Norwood Junction where we disembark. Norwood today is a residential suburbian borough of London. In days of yore, it served more as a tranquil rural retreat. The great impressionist painter Camille Pissarro painted one of his masterpieces here in 1871, titled 'Lower Norwood under Snow'. He wrote, "Monet and I were enthusiasatic about the London landscapes. Monet was working in the parks while I, staying in Lower Norwood, then a charming district, studied the effects of fog, snow and spring."

At the top of Station Road we find the ornate cast-iron Norwood clock tower where we turn left onto Selhurst Road. It is a bright and chilly early March afternoon. After a few hundred metres we turn right onto Park Road. A left turn here, and you are on Tennison Road, home from 1891–1894 to Sir Arthur Conan Doyle, author of the Sherlock Holmes stories. One of those, *The Adventure of the Norwood Builder,* would involve an elaborate subterfuge only a mastermind such as Holmes could solve – a murder that wasn't a murder at all. Doyle's Norwood story was written in the 'Return' series. Holmes and his nemesis Dr James Moriarty had seemingly died at the Reichenbach Falls in the 1893 publication *The Final Problem*, but, due to public demand, Doyle reprised the character in 1903 in the 'Return' series and continued to write the Holmes stories until 1928.

We ascend Park Road up to the crossroads where it meets Holmesdale Road, which may or may not have been named in honour of the great detective, and here at the top of the hill you suddenly encounter the stadium. To our left is the back of the Holmesdale Road Stand, wherein Palace's most vociferous fans congregate behind the south goal. The stand is no taller on the outside than the terraced houses that face it. We continue to walk through the junction and down the declining gradient that runs to the bottom of Park Road. We enter the Arthur Wait Stand which houses both home and away fans. Inside, it becomes clear how the stadium holds 26,000 people. It is built down and into the hill that falls from the junction above. It's quirky and a little disorientating, but after a quick vote we decide unanimously that we like it.

The game has already started and the Liverpool fans are in cracking form with song after song being belted out. The Palace fans are up for it too, they normally are, particularly against Liverpool. This rivalry has developed an edge of its own. Palace like to burst Liverpool's bubble and, in fairness to them, they've been quite good at it. A trip to Anfield in September 1989 saw Palace lose 9–0 (a record defeat), so when the clubs met again the following April in the FA Cup semi-final, any neutral would have been forgiven for expecting an easy ride for the Reds (or the greys with red stripes as they were that day). In a spectacular barnstorming match, Steve Coppell's Palace team would beat Liverpool 4–3, with a winning goal in extra time from their current manager Alan Pardew. In the final, Palace would fail in their attempt to win their first ever major trophy, losing in a replay to Man United. Their trophy cabinet remains bare to this day. Palace would again confound Liverpool under Brendan Rodgers in that ill-fated push for glory in 2014. In their penultimate game, Liverpool still had a slim chance of winning the title but needed to beat Palace by six or seven goals to enhance goal difference and keep destiny in their own hands. At 3–0 up it looked like the Reds would push on and get more goals, but eventually Palace showed their resolve and in a late surge they incredibly penned Liverpool back to 3–3. Palace fans now ironically call it Crystanbul, a witty jab at Liverpool's own comeback from three goals down in Istanbul.

Today Liverpool are in all white and Palace wear their home kit of blue shorts and stockings, topped by a red and blue vertical striped jersey. It's the only home colours that I've ever seen Palace wear, so I'm surprised to learn that, prior to the arrival of manager Malcolm Allison in 1973, Palace had been a claret and blue team, just like Villa and West Ham. Thank God, I think, there are enough claret and blues about. Not only did Allison change the strip he also changed the nickname and today Palace are known as the Eagles and not the Glaziers. Allison then quickly presided over further change, the relegation of Palace from Division One (now the Premier League) to Division Three. Palace defender Jim Cannon, who played under Allison, would say – "Malcolm Allison put Palace on the map. No other man could single-handedly take a club from the First Division to the Third Division and still become an instant hero." Allison had his hands full, on and off the pitch. He was a notorious carouser and he liked the ladies. Brian Clough called him "the Errol Flynn of football, who was too handsome for his own good." Don Revie dismissed him as "an embarrassment to the game." As ever, Clough and Revie rarely saw eye to eye. Christine Keeler, the woman at the heart of the Profumo affair, a scandal which brought down a government, was a lover of Allison's. If you visit the National Portrait Gallery in Trafalgar Square you can view Lewis Morley's iconic and provocative photographs of Keeler, sitting naked the wrong way around on a wooden chair, legs spread to either side. The Gallery describes how the photographs, taken in 1963, "offer a combination of pin-up and icon, suggestive both of sexual liberation and at the same time of the penalties of sexual exploitation, and of how they occupy a morally ambiguous universe." Allison knew the terrain, being neither the first nor last football man to occupy morally ambiguous universes.

On the pitch both teams are showing their boldness, it's end to end. Liverpool have started brighter but they don't really threaten, the play is too slow and intricate. The Reds dominate possession but despite a few blocked attempts they rarely look dangerous. On the break, Palace look lively as they attack into the Whitehorse Lane end. Ten minutes in and Palace striker Adebayor fires at goal. Mignolet saves low to his right. A minute later Lovren fluffs his clearance and when the loose ball is crossed back into the box, Adebayor rises to head the ball goal bound. It crashes off the Liverpool crossbar, another let-off. At half-time the game is tied at 0–0. Liverpool have been far from their best and hardly resemble the team that hunted down City only four days before.

Three minutes into the second half and disaster, an old fault line reappears. Liverpool can't clear a corner kick and from the resultant scramble Joe Ledley fires home from the edge of the box and it's one-nil to the hosts.

The response is good though, immediately Liverpool are on the attack and with numbers in the Palace box, Lallana nearly prods the ball home. It breaks loose and after two further blocked attempts, Origi blazes wide. On sixty-two minutes disaster strikes again. Milner gets a second yellow card and receives his marching orders. That's game over. Ten men at Palace, 1–0 down. A point would be a great result now. The problem with ten men is not attacking, you can always score a goal if you push everybody forward. The difficulty lies with the gaps that this leaves behind. In today's league of counter-attacking teams, a ten-man team are sitting ducks. Easy prey for hovering Eagles. Liverpool revert to a back three with Lovren now on the right, and they hope for the best.

The Reds get plenty of the ball but you can see Palace are waiting for the breakdown, waiting for the chance to pounce and kill. But maybe Palace are giving Liverpool too much breathing room. Origi goes very close and it's nearly an equaliser. The ten men are showing more drive than when the full complement was on the pitch. The shackles are off. On seventy-two minutes Palace goalkeeper Alex McCarthy makes a hash of his clearance. The ball breaks to Firmino who is loitering outside the penalty area. He beats a defender and bears down on goal. McCarthy comes out to meet him, to try and rectify his mistake. Firmino curls the ball past the keeper with ease and amazingly ten-man Liverpool are level. It's been coming and is richly deserved.

The ten men are not reading the script, they are not trying to hold on, instead they are threatening the shocked Eagles with wave after wave of attack. On eighty minutes Lallana drifts a ball across the box but it's between two Liverpool players and gets cleared for a corner. The corner swings in and is flicked onto the back post where it is met with a low drive from Benteke, who has replaced the tired Firmino. It's straight at McCarthy though and the keeper gratefully gathers it up. From twenty-five yards Moreno unleashes a left foot rasper. It beats the diving McCarthy to his left, cracks off the bottom of the Palace post, rebounds along the line behind the splayed and prone keeper and rolls out to safety. Three minutes to go and incredibly the ten men have nearly won it. On eighty-eight minutes Klopp puts on defender Kolo Touré to shore up the back and protect a well-earned point, it would be heart-breaking to concede now after such a valiant display.

But Klopp's soldiers are still not playing time out. They still believe something heroic can be achieved in south London. The ground buzzes in expectation. On ninety-three minutes, deep into injury time, Can strides forward out of his own half. He feeds Coutinho vertically, up the gut of the Palace team. Liverpool have no width, not with ten men. Coutinho plays the ball to Benteke on the edge of the box. The big Belgian curls it homebound but McCarthy saves well. It's hard to believe we are watching this, but it's enthralling, swashbuckling stuff. The clock ticks on and so does the game, ninety-four minutes.

Once more Can wins the ball and strides over the halfway line. He has been immense. He feeds Henderson who springs forward and plays an early ball to Benteke. Benteke lets the ball beat him and runs after it into the Palace penalty box. Delaney comes over to meet him and goes to ground with a sliding tackle. Benteke goes down under what seems like contact and the Liverpool end erupts all around us with howls of 'penalty'. Referee Andre Marriner waves away the Liverpool protests, no penalty. Captain Henderson leads a group in protest, they are furious.

But in front of where we are stood, not ten feet away, the linesman is flagging. Liverpool players can see him and now, so too can Marriner. He turns away with whistle to mouth and I know what's coming next. A rush of adrenalin engulfs me. He points to the spot. Penalty. Nobody can believe it. Grudge game at Palace. Ten men. 1–0 down. An equaliser, 1–1. Now, last kick of the game to win it. It was the reverse fixture in November where Klopp questioned Liverpool fans for leaving early, doubting that something could happen. "I felt pretty alone," he said. Palace won 2–1. Now, in the ninety-sixth minute everything has come full circle. Anything can happen! I turn to look. Benteke accepts the burden. He steps forward, feigns to shoot, stops, draws the keeper's dive and then calmly rolls the ball into the bottom right corner of the net. Game set and match. Cue the unbridled delirium of Norwich multiplied by two. What a comeback. Wow! Or as Klopp would say, 'Boom!'

Later I learn that it's the first time in Liverpool's long history that they have turned around a deficit with ten men to win the game, incredible indeed. A storm rages about the penalty decision, was there contact or not and was it enough to award a spot kick? Opinion seems to be 60/40. More say yes it was, but a lot disagree. Palace manager Pardew moans vociferously. Palace's offender Delaney addresses the issue later in the evening. He writes: "I can honestly say I didn't make contact with Benteke today." But then in classic football doublespeak he adds, "and if there was slight contact I didn't impede him and certainly didn't feel there was enough to award a penalty in the ninety-sixth minute… if a penalty is awarded that late it has to be unequivocal". Palace are unfortunately not accepting defeat bravely. Maybe with TV replays and some crime scene analysis, Sherlock Holmes could solve this mystery of the penalty that wasn't a penalty. Without him the TV pundits are called to investigate. The verdict arrives. When you have eliminated the huff and puff, what remains are the facts. Penalty! Case closed.

Liverpool have won three League games in a row under Klopp for the first time. Two words are starting to spring to mind, two words not associated with the Reds for well over a year; momentum and consistency. This time it is a perfect day in London and the tune of one of my favourite songs comes to mind as we make our way back to the city.

'Oh, it's such a perfect day, I'm glad I spent it with you,
Oh, such a perfect day, you just keep me hanging on,
You just keep me hanging on,
You're going to reap just what you sow
You're going to reap just what you sow.'

THE MOTHER OF ALL GAMES

'Cry havoc and let slip the dogs of war!' — William Shakespeare

The time has come. It's here, the clash of the titans. Klopp is not long to these parts but he understands the significance, describing the game as 'the mother of all football games'. He's right. It is.

Liverpool versus Manchester United, it's the first time that these arch rivals, these most bitter of enemies, will meet in European Competition. The retro style Match Programme sets the stage as if for a heavyweight boxing bout.

******* PRESENTING THIS EVENING'S MAIN EVENT*******

THIS IS

ANFIELD

Featuring KLOPP *as LFC boss*	*Featuring* VAN GAAL *as MUFC boss*
INTRODUCING THE ONE AND ONLY...	AGAINST THE MEN FROM OLD TRAFFORD...

LIVERPOOL FC VS MANCHESTER UNITED FC

LFC WEIGHING IN WITH ELEVEN EUROPEAN TROPHIES VS FIERCE RIVALS AND FELLOW GIANTS ON THE EUROPEAN STAGE

PLAYING AT THEIR MYTHICAL HOME OF ANFIELD ROAD IN A TIE TO DECIDE WHO STAYS IN EUROPE AND WHO GOES.
UEFA EUROPA LEAGUE. ROUND OF 16 FIRST LEG.
THURSDAY 10TH MARCH 2016. KICK OFF 8.05 P.M.

All around the ground you can feel the feverish buzz of tense and nervous anticipation. Electricity surges in the chilly night air. The chatter comes fast, loud with excitement, arms waving in animated gestures. Dads and sons run, hands linked, when maybe a walk would do. This game is not fun, it's never fun, it's too important to be fun. Heartbeats will gallop tonight. This is a tie you can't afford to lose, for if you do, it will rot away and fester for an eternity, with no chance of atonement, not until the next time the teams meet in Europe. Tonight has been 124 years arriving, so when will that chance come again? You'd rather not play at all. When the draw was made, I was hoping for a trip to Spain, but then United's name came out of the bowl and the mix of dread and excitement set in.

On form and on player talent Liverpool should be good enough. United don't have the strength in attack that Liverpool do. The fearsome foursome that are Coutinho, Lallana, Firmino and Sturridge are as good as any attacking line up in English football when fit and primed. The biggest worry is Liverpool keeping a clean sheet in the home tie, as somehow United seem to always steal a goal at Anfield, good performance or not. An away goal could be crucial, with these counting for two if the outcome is a draw over the two legs.

This is a second cup final of sorts for Klopp, and in some ways it is just as important as the League Cup. Liverpool and Anfield are made for these European occasions. It is this European standing that attracts managers like Klopp to Liverpool and Van Gaal to United, they understand these are jobs with a global audience. It is a heritage that the Reds have built ever since their first foray into Europe in 1964/65 saw them lose in the semi-final of the European Cup to the then reigning champions Inter Milan. On that occasion the atmosphere and noise created by the record 54,082 crowd set the tone for every big European night at the old stadium since.

Tonight, United chase a record fifth win in a row against Liverpool and Klopp is asked pre-match whether that puts him under pressure. Defiantly he reminds the reporters "I was only part of one of these games."

Klopp is informed that United manager Van Gaal has said "Liverpool are not the enemy," and is asked, "Are United the enemy?"

"I don't believe in enemies, I believe in real, real, *real* opponents. I have no problem with Louis Van Gaal, but the last thing I want, is he win." He adds, "Everything else can happen in the world, but you only talk of this game. It is very important to go to the next round, we have to beat them, that's it!"

That is it, he has summed up perfectly the feelings of the Liverpool fans that converge on the stadium. I'm worried. This group of players have folded too many times against United, mostly under Rodgers it must be said. In fairness to Klopp, his sole attempt did see Liverpool outplay their foes, but still lose 1–0. On a positive note, Sturridge and Coutinho are back fit, with neither having played in that loss. That sets the balance more in the Reds' favour. Klopp agrees in his programme notes – "We are certainly in a better moment as a team and a squad as we have been for any period during my time at Liverpool. By this I mean availability of talent and players. You only had to look at the substitutes' bench on Sunday at Selhurst Park to see the quality that we can now pick from. And it's not just having them available – it's having them fit and available."

It's twenty minutes to kick-off and we are eager to get into the ground. So is everybody else. Normally the stadium fills in the last five minutes, but not on a big night like this. Already we can hear singing from within. Helicopters buzz overhead, either police or TV, maybe both. Inside, the atmosphere sizzles. We are in the Kop and it's a sea of flags, many paying homage to our European legacy. 'European Royalty' reads one, 'European Elite' another. A long red banner stretches lengthwise, the images of five European Cups emblazoned across it. Another displays three UEFA Cups. The Kop is going through its repertoire of songs. The sound is deafening. I haven't experienced this type of raw power since the great European Cup campaigns of 2005 and 2007. It's electric, spine-tingling. The teams have lined up to face the Main stand and the Kop sings 'You Never Walk Alone' at its cacophonous best. I can see the heads of some of the United players turned, not facing their own fans, but looking our way. They know it and we know it, there is nowhere more intimidating than Anfield on a big European night. The great George Best recognised this, saying, "When the Liverpool Kop sang 'You'll Never Walk Alone', I'd look up from the pitch and see them swaying in time to their singing, which had the force and emotion of a massed cathedral choir."

It's what Klopp asked for – "Everybody needs to be in best shape. The crowd needs to be involved. You know I believe in the influence of the crowd, that we enjoy the relationship with the crowd. It is very important, decisive for sure. Hopefully we can set a new level in this young history of LFC."

The fans have set the tone and are fulfilling their side of the bargain. Shankly described these Euro nights as having 'heat in the air' and he was right. Tonight it is red hot, searing. The game begins. Less than a minute in and United nearly have the precious away goal. A long diagonal ball is played and United's tall Belgian Fellaini wins it easily. He finds Memphis Depay who gets to the Liverpool end line, attacking the Kop end. His whipped cross manages to evade the entire Liverpool defence and there to greet it is United's eighteen-year-old home-grown prodigy, Marcus Rashford. In only his fifth senior game the youngster has the chance to put Liverpool to the sword, but in front of the Kop, the occasion gets to him and he misreads the flight of the cross only managing to knee the ball wide. The Kop exhales in relief and immediately bursts back into rapturous song. This is a night to be bold and to lift the team, the finger biting and head wringing, if needed, can come later. I am now convinced that we will not make it through ninety minutes without conceding, so it's up to the boys upfront. With Milner out injured, the fearsome foursome all play. Can and Henderson shore the midfield behind them and the back four are Clyne, Sakho, Lovren and Moreno. Mignolet minds goal.

On two minutes Henderson is deemed to have posed a threat to United midfielder Morgan Schneiderlin's health and earns a yellow. The captain does like to make a mark hard and early, educated by Master Gerrard, but maybe this time he should have trodden more carefully. Spanish referee Carlos Velasco Carballo is a staunch disciplinarian with a card-happy reputation, brandishing no less than sixty-six yellow cards in his last ten games. Since the start of the season ten have been banished by his red. This is one of the idiosyncrasies of European football, referee approach and quality can vary widely from game to game. On these fine margins destinies can rise or fall. Henderson will now run the gauntlet for the next eighty-eight minutes.

Play moves swiftly from end to end, but it's scrappy and tense. The initial skirmishes in these battles normally produce a high-octane tempo with players relentlessly hounding, harrying, and hunting down the opposition in the fight for early ascendancy. The start of this game is no different. Later, as legs tire and lungs burn, space unfolds and then the chess moves can be made. Firmino collects the ball halfway into the United half and plays it wide to Clyne. Clyne cuts in and plays it to Henderson who lurks on the edge of the United box. Henderson cuts it backwards to Firmino, who with a clever forward pass into space, with the outside of his right boot, finds Clyne who has continued his onward progress. It's classic triangular football from Liverpool at pace and speed, with each corner of the triangle moving, creating new angles. New triangles create space, space to run into, space to wreak damage. The ball splits the defenders and now Clyne has managed to get goal-side of Depay. Moving at speed towards the danger area Clyne's progress is halted, firstly by a pull of the shirt, and finally by a clip of the heels. He goes down under Depay's clumsy challenge. Is it inside or outside? From where I'm standing eighty yards way I've no idea, but regardless I'm shouting loud for anyone to hear – Penalty!?! The referee, unmistakeable in his luminous sky-blue shirt, takes his time. He looks again and then with decision made, he walks stridently into the box, right arm pointed outwards, whistle blowing. Penalty to Liverpool.

Sturridge, who has never scored for Liverpool in Europe (having been injured for most of the campaigns) steps up. He couldn't take one at Wembley, as he couldn't walk, but tonight he's recovered and ready. He paces up, pauses, and then left footed he sends the ball wide to his left. De Gea, the United goalkeeper and the best player at their club, dives to his right, gets a hand to the ball, but it's not enough and it's 1–0 to the Reds on twenty minutes. Anfield erupts in ecstasy.

Liverpool are emboldened by the goal. The shackles are off. Now they are at United's throats, wave after wave of attack, running the Red Devils ragged. It's too good to be true. The Kop bellows from behind, putting wind into their sails. Within three minutes comes a moment of poetic movement, pace and skill. Sakho finds Firmino in the left channel just inside the United half. Firmino turns inside and strides away from Varela, the young right-back who is enduring a torrid time trying to keep the ever-mobile Brazilian in check. Firmino finds Lallana in a central position, who immediately shifts it out to the right edge of the box to Sturridge. Five Liverpool players are bearing down on goal and United are all over the place. Sturridge moves into the box, beats his man and pushes the ball across the front of the goal with his right foot, past De Gea and into the path of the oncoming Coutinho. Open goal, poke it in with the outside of the right foot, it must be. No, incredibly the magnificent De Gea has managed to scramble back and claws an outstretched hand to the scuffed shot, somehow scooping it to safety. A golden opportunity goes a-begging.

Liverpool brush off the disappointment and keep driving forward. Firmino skins his man and lofts a ball across the box that evades the United defence. On the six-yard line Sturridge meets it full force but again it hits the wall that is De Gea, and still the score line is only 1–0. On forty-two minutes another golden chance arrives. Henderson finds the effervescent Firmino and his cross finds Lallana, six yards out. From point blank range, his first-time shot bullets towards goal but De Gea flings an arm out and the ball ricochets away once more. This game should be over. Unfortunately for Liverpool, who ride the crest of a wave, the referee blows his whistle for half-time.

Van Gaal won the European Cup and the UEFA Cup with Ajax, managed Bayern Munich and also led his country, Holland, to the semi-final of the 2014 World Cup. He is nobody's fool. He makes changes at half-time, he has to. Veteran midfielder Michael Carrick replaces the youthful Rashford. United's team shape changes to three at the back and five in midfield and immediately they start to retain the ball better and keep possession. They needed to, Liverpool amassed an incredible 70 per cent possession in the first forty-five minutes. Liverpool lift the tempo once more. Coutinho and Firmino combine beautifully with a Brazilian one-two. The ball sits up invitingly on the edge of the box and Coutinho sends a pile driver goal bound. It swerves and moves, but it's at a nice height for De Gea and he palms it over for a corner. That's better from the Reds as they start to reassert their dominance. On sixty-three minutes, Klopp sends midfielder Joe Allen on for the tiring Sturridge. Allen's impact is immediate, his sure-footedness allowing Liverpool to retain more possession. Firmino is pushed forward to chase down United's three-man defence. A rare United foray sees a good cross that

Martial rises to meet six yards out, but Mignolet is brave and decisive. He punches both ball and man and the danger is snuffed out.

Soon after, Clyne sends a ferocious shot goal-bound but again it's at a nice height and angle for De Gea and he fists it away. Then, on sixty-nine minutes, a move of great artistry. Triangles at work again. Moreno is first to the ball before Martial. Liverpool are first to every ball. He plays it forward to Henderson who passes a lovely ball deep into the United area for Lallana to run onto. He gets to it, looks up and then slots it back to Henderson who has advanced to the edge of the United box. Henderson side-foots the ball with power goal-wards. It must be? It's not. The ball sails agonisingly wide. It should be 2–0. It should be 5–0. Twenty minutes to go. The unvoiced doubts in my head nag – 'We'll regret this next week in the return leg'. Quiet!

Liverpool continue to push forward. Clyne wins the ball in his own half and finds Lallana, who sets Henderson scampering down the right wing. His cross isn't great but makeshift centre-half Carrick, makes a hash of the clearance and it only reaches Lallana, who is loitering with intent inside the box. Lallana does what Lallana does, he keeps his cool, while everybody else is losing theirs. He doesn't snatch at it, or mishit it, or make the wrong decision. He makes the right decision. One touch to control the ball, a look up, second touch to Firmino who stands on the six-yard line. Left foot, side of the boot… Goal! De Gea is beaten at the Kop end. Seventy-three minutes gone, 2–0 to Liverpool. At last, just reward for the dominance, the passion, the skill. Klopp, whose touchline exuberance had been questioned pre-match by Van Gaal, trots past the United bench and punches the air to the Liverpool fans. This is a time to be exuberant! The two teams have somehow managed to replicate their coach's demeanour in their displays. Van Gaal's, austere and slightly dour. Klopp's, a passion play, all high energy. Football by osmosis.

Liverpool don't really threaten again, they don't need to. They do need to keep a clean sheet. Sakho and Lovren have been resolute throughout at the centre of Liverpool's back four so my early worries have proven wholly unfounded. Fellaini sends a weak header wide on eighty-six minutes and that's it. Game over. A resounding home win for the Reds and a strong lead to take to Old Trafford for the return leg one week later. The roof is lifted with a rousing YNWA.

Earlier in the season, an Achilles heel inflicting Liverpool was their struggle to perform at home; Anfield was engendering an opposite-than-intended effect on its own troops, intimidating them, stifling their expressiveness, pouring nerves into their veins. Dr Klopp has cured that ailment, not fully, but damn close. Impressive home displays against Leicester, Arsenal, United twice, Augsburg and City have all been recorded. Even the Sunderland performance was imposing but for the last twelve minutes. Against United, Liverpool achieve 56 per cent possession and amass eight shots on target to United's one. Five hundred and fifteen passes versus four hundred and ten. Telling statistics and more signs of progress. Yet tonight wasn't about progress or the future, it was about standing your ground, securing your heartland and fending off the invaders. Next week it will be unto the breach at Old Trafford.

Klopp is in positive mood after the win. He thanks the crowd, "The atmosphere tonight was *unbelievable!*" he states, dragging out the word slowly and loudly, accentuating his meaning, eyes glistening, chest puffing.

Van Gaal does what no United fan would want him to, he praises the Liverpool fans and asks for his own to match them in the return. "Liverpool created an atmosphere that was fantastic." He continues, "we need to copy them at Old Trafford." Liverpool's captain Henderson says that the special atmosphere, conjured up pre-match, had contributed to the Reds' whirlwind first half performance. Klopp was right, the crowd does matter.

We leave Anfield and walk back into Liverpool city centre and I can't help thinking that this was a very important night in our evolution. Bigger than the game, the scoreline, or whether we go through or not. It's the first time that Klopp has seen the Liverpool fans in their full resplendent glory. It's the first time he's heard that deafening noise from every corner of the ground, seen all of those flags fly, smelt a night reminiscent of the past. He says so himself after the game – "That was Liverpool as I knew it before I came here, so thank you for this."

But it's not the past, this is the era of Klopp and the start of the "young and new history of LFC" as he described it. It is the start of building memories associated only with Klopp's team, his Liverpool. In this new future, this has been a red-letter day, a milestone, a foundation block. Klopp is starting to build a reservoir of shared experience, positive experience, experience that will stand the club, the fans and the players, in good stead for when the bigger and more important occasions hopefully arrive. But for tonight, there was nothing more important than beating United, in Europe. Round one over and Liverpool lead convincingly on points. United are still standing, there's been no knockout, but let's not be in any doubt, they are on the ropes and puffing hard.

THE FULL PACKAGE

'By failing to prepare, you are preparing to fail.' — Benjamin Franklin

You can tell that Klopp relishes these titanic tussles, he knows that they come to define a manager. Tonight brings his first trip to Old Trafford as Liverpool boss and he's keen to relish the occasion, soak it all up. UEFA rules decree that the away team must stay within a radius of thirty miles of the club or city whom they are visiting to play. The governing body also instructs the home team to make their ground and pitch available to their visitors on the eve of the tie for training and preparation. Van Gaal requested a remission of these rules for United before the first leg (Manchester being thirty-four miles from Anfield). UEFA agreed and United stayed at home. The Manchester press, benefitting from their privileged hindsight, pounced on this decision suggesting it was a contributing factor to their defeat. The argument goes that United, having treated the tie like any of the previous eighty-nine games they played at Anfield, failed to recognise the uniqueness of this particular clash, it being played out for the first time on the European stage where both teams had built their heritage. They argued that, in making his decision, Van Gaal failed to recognise that many of his young players had never played at Anfield before and that many others had not played there under floodlights. He failed to allow his group to experience the atmosphere and anticipation that enveloped the city as it awaited the arrival of their great foes into the Red cauldron. Maybe these factors did contribute to United freezing on the big occasion, allowing Liverpool to run them ragged, maybe not, we will never know for sure, but what's clear is that Klopp sees things differently. Liverpool hold their pre-match press conference in the bowels of Old Trafford and the team train on the famous turf on the Wednesday evening, twenty-four hours before the second leg.

Klopp explains, "I always enjoyed it with my former clubs in European tournaments, to breathe the stadium where you play the next night, I like to imagine what can happen. I really enjoy this, there was no doubt we would take this opportunity. I don't think one second about it. We come one day early to Manchester, not for feeling comfortable, we could sleep at home. I'm really looking forward to it, one of the best things in football you can do is to play against Man United, especially when you are manager of Liverpool. We wanted to take the 'full package', so we come here today."

On match night, Old Trafford is on fire and the thought of letting the tie slip from our hands doesn't bear consideration. If United manage to salvage this wreck, it would be one of their most famous comebacks in European history – at Liverpool's expense. That would never be forgotten. The stakes couldn't be higher, Liverpool must get through this game, by hook or by crook. Klopp goes with a bold side, again favouring four attacking players in Lallana, Coutinho, Firmino and Sturridge. The only change from the first leg sees Milner slot into an unfamiliar left back role to replace the injured Moreno.

As expected, the game starts at a frenetic pace and United have the edge, their red shirts getting to every second ball first, winning all the fifty-fifty tackles. But Liverpool, all in black, are up for it too and they scrap for their lives, desperately fighting not to concede early and hand the impetus to the home team. Shots on target are few and far between, but endeavour is high, as play moves in hasty waves back and forth. On eighteen minutes, a clear chance is created, United's Argentinian left-back, Rojo, lofts a high swirling ball into Liverpool's box. Mignolet, caught in two minds, hesitates and gets stranded in limbo, a few yards from goal. Lingard rises unchallenged near the penalty spot and heads the ball towards the left corner of the net. Mignolet, now retreating, manages to fling his right hand towards the ball and palm it out for a corner. It should have been a goal, but somehow it isn't and Liverpool survive the scare. From the resulting corner the ball bounces and ricochets around the Liverpool area and finally it falls to the trusted left foot of the unmarked Mata, only six yards from goal. He can't miss, but again somehow he does, and he screws his shot wide of Mignolet's left post. Liverpool are on the rack and leading a charmed existence, yet somehow their two goal advantage from the first leg remains intact.

On twenty-eight minutes, Liverpool come close to putting the tie beyond United, but Coutinho's low stinger is saved superbly by the world class De Gea. Only four minutes later, Coutinho plays a silly ball across the front of his own box that leads to mayhem. Mata feeds the ball to Martial, who faces up to Clyne one on one and takes him on. Clyne swings a boot out but connects with leg, not ball. Penalty. Martial takes it himself and unerringly he drills it to Mignolet's left as the keeper dives the other way. 1–0 on thirty-two minutes, 1–2 on aggregate. United have a foothold in the tie, and a ladder of belief to scale the mountain. It's backs to the wall time now for Liverpool as Old Trafford goes berserk and I'm starting to worry that our worst nightmares are about to be realised.

United drive forward in search of a second but manfully, Liverpool's black shirted wall blockades the siege. Liverpool need to get to half-time without conceding another. But Klopp's charges have other ideas, they don't just sit back and park the bus, instead they take the fight to United. On thirty-five minutes, Sturridge sends a curling left foot free-kick over De Gea, heading for the roof of the net. Instead of a soft landing, the ball smacks with a crack off the crossbar and the sound reverberates all round a stunned Old Trafford. Liverpool seize the initiative and push forward, knowing an away goal will leave United needing to score three more times to win the tie. Ten yards out, unmarked, and with the goal at his mercy, Henderson is through on De Gea. His right foot connects sweetly but there's too much venom and, agonisingly, the ball curls inches over the bar. Henderson holds his head in his hands in disbelief as Klopp shakes his in despair on the sideline.

It's nearly half-time and now both sides will be happy to get to the sanctuary of the dressing rooms, to recharge the batteries, regroup. Play goes on and Milner finds Can, who spins away from his marker and plays a lovely ball down the left wing for Coutinho to run onto. Taking the ball in his stride, Coutinho bears down on the right edge of the United box forcing his marker, Varela, to retreat backwards, eyes glued to the Brazilian's feet, hoping to read the movement, the feint, the bluff when it arrives. He can't. Coutinho breezes by him as if he's not there and cuts inwards acutely towards the United goal. He looks to his right to see who has supported his foray forward, who can he find with a pass inside. Four black shirts have joined the attack, tracked by five defenders. De Gea spreads himself to block the pass but it never comes. Instead, Coutinho scoops the ball impudently over the keeper's head and into the back of the net. Time seems to pause, nobody quite believing what they've seen. It's such a delicate chip, that the net hardly moves as the ball nestles, and it's difficult to know that he's actually scored. But only for a brief moment and then realisation arrives, the little magician has actually just gone and scored a wonder goal with the last kick of the first half. It's a knife wound to United's dreams and the air gushes from a deflated Old Trafford. Klopp punches the air in the direction of the now delirious 3,000 travelling fans who are jumping up and down jubilantly in a fog of red smoke gushing from celebratory flares. It's the golden away goal, United will now need a miracle in the second half. With the tie at 3–1 on aggregate, and with Liverpool possessing an away goal, United now need three goals without reply to triumph 4–3. It must be too much to ask.

And it is. United toil valiantly, creating a few half-chances but, as the second half unfolds, it is Liverpool who come closest to another goal and come the final whistle, but for the wonders of De Gea, it could have been a rout. As it is, the match ends 1–1 on the night and 3–1 over the two legs. Liverpool have vanquished their nemesis and rarely has victory tasted so sweet.

FAIRY TALE

'Fate is like a strange, unpopular restaurant filled with odd little waiters who bring you things you never asked for and don't always like.'
— Lemony Snicket

My son looks to me and says with a smirk that suggests he knows something I don't – "You know it's going to happen, don't you?"

It's Friday morning, March 18th, only thirteen hours after Liverpool's triumph over Man United and we're glued to the TV. It's the draw for the quarter finals of the Champions League and the Europa League live from Nyon, Switzerland. In the main event some tasty ties await;

Barcelona vs Atletico Madrid
Paris St Germain vs Man City
Wolfsburg vs Real Madrid
Bayern Munich vs Benfica

Next is the draw for the Europa League. In the wide glass vase lie eight plastic balls, each containing the name of one of the remaining challengers for the trophy. Of these, three are former Champions, Sevilla having won four times (2006, 2007, 2014 and 2015), Liverpool three times (1973, 1976 and 2001) and Shakhtar Donetsk once (2009).

I laugh back at him and smile a little at the innocence. Of course Liverpool being drawn against Dortmund would be the romantic fairy-tale story, Klopp returning to his former home, new team versus old. It seems like predestined fate, as if it is meant to happen, and for this reason my son believes it's a sure thing, nailed-on. He's seen too many movies, I think. I don't believe in predetermined destinies, but now he has me wondering, what if?

First out of the bowl are SC Braga of Portugal. They will play the first leg at home to the next name out, which proves to be Shakhtar Donetsk. The names of Villarreal CF and Sparta Praha quickly follow. My son's prediction now looms, surely not. Next out is Athletic Club Bilbao. To play… breathe… Sevilla FC. My son roars with laughter and I join him, what else can you do. It may prove to be the end of the road, but what the hell, it will be a great road to travel.

"So, are we going?" he asks, smiling, eyes wide, expectant. He knows what it means. He loves playing with the Dortmund team on his games console, and week in, week out, all I hear is how amazing their front trio of Reus, Aubameyang and Mkhitaryan are.

"Definitely… we can't miss this one."

We set about our preparations. Flights and hotels get booked up fast, so without delay I am on the laptop scheming the mission to Dortmund. Four days later, on March 22nd the city of Brussels is attacked by ISIS terrorists with nail bombs exploding at Zaventem Airport and Maelbeek Train station. Thirty-two victims and three suicide bombers lie dead. Thoughts of football subside for now.

HEARTLAND

'It is a mistake to try to look too far ahead. The chain of destiny can only be grasped one link at a time.' — Winston Churchill

It's roughly midday, German time, Thursday 7th April and we have arrived at Flughafen Dusseldorf. We make our way to the station, from where we'll catch the train to Dortmund. After a six a.m. rise, I'm tired. My son is perky enough, considering the paucity of shut-eye achieved the night before. Three times I thought he had gone to sleep only for him to rise again. "One last thing," he'd declare each time as he checked his bag, his ticket or something else. He's been buzzing all week in anticipation of the trip and for good reason, it's his first Euro adventure with the travelling Reds.

Bags dropped in our hotel, we take to the streets. Founded around 900AD, Dortmund first came to prominence in the thirteenth and fourteenth centuries as a member of the Hanseatic League, Hansa being the German word for Guild or Association. The League came to dominate commercial activity in Northern Europe during the latter medieval period, protecting and securing trading interests for its members all along the Baltic shores. Albeit a German organisation, the League established permanent commercial enclaves in a number of foreign countries, notably Bruges in Flanders, Bergen in Norway, Novgorod in Russia and the Steel Yard in London. Trade commonly comprised products such as grain, timber, furs, tar, honey, flax, minerals and fish. In the fourteenth century the League claimed membership of 100 towns, mostly German. In all this time Dortmund was never a large conurbation, its old walled city little more than one kilometre wide by one kilometre in length.

Dortmund came to prominence again during the Industrial

Revolution due to its central European location and also because of the rich seams of valuable minerals lying below its soil. As the principle city of the densely populated Ruhr region, it became a trading powerhouse in the mining of coal and iron and in the brewing of beer, its zenith arriving before the First World War. Two wars later and following the Euro-wide collapse of the mining industry, it is now a very different city. Where before stood Medieval-walled boundaries, now the city is circled by a ring road. Inside this most areas are pedestrianised and large communal squares dominate. Shopping streets and galleries are modern but the city's architecture is uninspiring. With 95 per cent of the city destroyed by Allied bombing in World War II, Dortmund is not a beautiful city, more a functional one. These days its name has become synonymous with football and with the rise of the 'Schwarzgelben' (the black and yellows).

This industrial North-West region was the birthplace of the working man's game in Germany and accounts for no less than six major German clubs including FC Schalke 04, Borussia Monchengladbach, Bayer Leverkusen, FC Cologne, Hannover 96 and of course BVB Dortmund. Dortmund's closest rivals and derby opponents, Schalke 04, are a team founded by the sons of miners. In days gone by, industrial heartland equalled football heartland. Dortmund have the same number of European Cup wins as Chelsea, Arsenal and Spurs all put together, one. Borussia Monchengladbach have played in five European Finals, winning two trophies. That's more finals than affluent Paris St Germain or any of the above three London giants. In the future will trophies only be won by clubs based in the massive metropolitan and cosmopolitan cities such as Paris, London, Madrid, Barcelona and Munich? Hopefully not, for the colour and passion is still strongest in the heartlands. We walk back towards the train station and visit the National Football Museum. It is no surprise that it is housed here in this football mad city. In the room reserved for the greatest managers, we watch the video of Klopp on the tactics wall. My son is impressed to see how honoured and revered the bespectacled one is, with only the very best afforded a berth.

The score predictions from the local media have the home team as overwhelming favourites for tonight's game: 3–1, 3–0, 3–1, 2–0 – few in Germany give the Reds much chance. With Dortmund having dispatched title-chasing Spurs with ease in the last round, the prevailing consensus seems to be that Liverpool won't prove any harder. The Reds' two league ties since knocking Man United out of Europe would seem to validate these views. A 3–2 defeat away to Southampton and a 1–1 draw at home to Spurs have not left Dortmund running scared. My son is not too perturbed one way or the other by the ominous predictions. He likes Dortmund and can't wait to see their star players in the flesh. That said, he feels Liverpool can challenge and he predicts either a 1–1 draw, or a 2–1 victory to Dortmund.

The more I consider this game the more I realise how high the stakes are for one man in particular, Herr Klopp. Despite having built the Dortmund team that he will face tonight, and having developed them into winners, a narrative is now forming amongst pundits and anybody connected with the Dortmund club, which suggests that new boss Thomas Tuchel has taken the team to a new level. Instead of playing helter-skelter ball under Klopp, Dortmund now retain possession better and are more tactically astute. So the story goes. This slant suits some, particularly Dortmund. German-based journalist, Jonathan Harding, says "Tuchel has taken Klopp's concept and made it Bundesliga-proof, demonstrating the kind of dominance only on display in Munich." Former Dortmund European Cup and League winning boss, Ottmar Hitzfeld, agrees saying, "Dortmund have become more stable, harder to work out for opponents and more flexible."

One player in particular has jumped on this bandwagon, Mkhitaryan, Dortmund's fantastic playmaker, signed by Klopp for £21 million in the summer of 2013. He goes further and slights his former coach's reputation. In an interview with *Gazzetta dello Sport* he whines – "With Klopp, he was a football madman; pressure and counter attack. Instead Tuchel has changed our lives. Now we command the game and I have more freedom to attack. Thanks to him I now make myself more useful." I wonder how many of the Dortmund players share the Armenian's view? Are memories that short? Prolific striker Aubameyang seems to have clarity of recollection. He reminds us that Klopp made him into the striker he is today, one of the most feared in world football. Mats Hummels, the towering centre-half, is equally effusive about Klopp remarking that it will, "be something special for the players to meet him again." Maybe someday Tuchel will join Klopp as a Dortmund great, as Paisley joined Shankly. Maybe both clubs have found the right man at the right time, only time will tell.

Tuchel, to his credit, speaks only in respectful tones, "Borussia Dortmund is what it is now because of Jürgen Klopp, anything but a great welcome would be a surprise. If it's eight months or eight years, Klopp's input will still stand."

Dortmund, as a club, are keen to accentuate that this is business as usual. "Our friendship with Jürgen will be put on hold until the second leg," says BVB Managing Director Hans-Joachim Watzke. He continues, "I am afraid that Klopp is trying to lull us, that he will draw the fans on his side which will create a friendly atmosphere. There must not be an amicable reunion. We are very clear opponents. We have sympathy expressions only after the game. These are two special games, because both teams are great, because they both represent pure footballing history."

Klopp, too, is keen to play down the building media storm. He says, "I love this place, a few of the best things in my life happened here, so of course I am looking forward to it. But on the other side, I hate the hype around my person in these matches." He manages to convince a local German TV station not to run a 'Klopp-Cam' showing pictures of him and him alone during the game. Klopp is cautious, for who would know better than he, the scale of the task that awaits. He describes the tie as "a story only football can write". Analysing his old team, he warns, "They're a really strong opponent. But we are not bad too. Everybody knows our best games have been against really strong sides, so we know how to play this, we know how to handle it and we know a lot of the Dortmund players – not all, but 98 per cent. So, it's open, and two games that I think the whole world will watch. We have the highest mountain to climb, but it is possible. Dortmund are a very strong side in Germany and probably in most Leagues in the world, they would be champions this year. Going to Dortmund and playing in Dortmund is one of the best things you can do in football. And then, they are all 100 per cent looking forward to coming to Anfield. It's football at its best and how it should be. Everybody is looking forward to it."

Behind all the chatter and the noise, it's the statistics, the hard facts that show the scale and enormity of the mountain to which Klopp has referred. Dortmund are unbeaten in seventeen games since December 2015. They have scored 114 goals to Liverpool's 72 this season. Indeed Dortmund's three main attackers surpass Liverpool's entire team total by three, having notched an incredible seventy-five goals, Aubameyang having bagged thirty-six all by himself.

Statistics, damned statistics!

FORZA LIVERPOOL

'It's a thing to see when a boy comes home.' — John Steinbeck

We are in our seats an hour before the 9.05 p.m. kick-off. This is a dark stadium, a brooding gothic arena. Vertical walls of black and grey seats rise steeply into the gloomy night sky. Only the pitch offers respite, the green grass illuminated in a fluorescent floodlit radiance. There is very little that is soft about the design inside or out. Concrete, steel, grey plastic seating – they all serve their function. Yet it is beautiful in its stark dystopian power. The purpose is undeniable, everything focuses you to the glowing rectangle below. This is unashamedly a citadel of football, a cathedral for its worship.

Klopp takes to the pitch to supervise the pre-match routine, and is greeted by the home fans who have arrived early. The applause is less than euphoric, more warm and respectful, there is a game to be won. Liverpool's fans are in great voice and they greet their leader with bellowing lungs. It is clear to all where allegiances now lie. Liverpool flags and banners abound as they always do on these European odysseys. 'Scouse Nicht English' reads one, 'Forza Liverpool' another. A large flag depicts Coutinho and Firmino celebrating together and is titled 'Magicos'. Next to us are sat three Liverpool fans from Russia and two from Scandinavia. This game has whetted the appetites far and wide. Three lads in front of us have travelled via Hull and Rotterdam. As kick-off approaches the stadium fills and the famous SüdTribüne, the Yellow Wall, is now awash with huge black and yellow flags. 66,000 have gathered to witness the spectacle. The stage is set.

Dortmund start on top, but Liverpool are able to contain the threat comfortably and thankfully we survive the first fifteen minutes without conceding. On seventeen minutes Weigl, Dortmund's bright young midfielder, sees space behind Liverpool's back four and dinks a pass over the head of Moreno, for the onrushing Schmelzer, who traps the lofted ball, pulls it back for Mkhitaryan, who shoots from eight yards out. It looks a certain goal but Sakho flings his body in front of the shot and the ball is cleared. The scare seems to wake Liverpool who are soon on the attack themselves. A floated free kick is met by Lovren who can only head straight into the hands of Dortmund's grateful keeper Weidenfeller. A golden chance for a crucial away goal is missed. It's hard to see the Reds getting many better chances than that. However, Liverpool steadily grow into the game and possession and control of the ball starts to balance.

Mkhitaryan is finding space behind the Liverpool midfield and a few half chances come and go. On thirty-six minutes Moreno advances on the left and chips a delightful ball forward towards the head of Milner, who has pushed into the Dortmund half. Milner beats Subotić and his header sails over the Dortmund back four and into space. Now it's a foot race to see who can get there first. Time for Divock Origi to show his pace and speed. He does, winning the contest against two pursuing Dortmund defenders. The young Belgian is free and closes in on goal. The ball gets caught under his feet, but he digs it out with a scuffed strike that sees it beat Weidenfeller to his right hand side and roll into the bottom left of the Dortmund net. Liverpool lead 0-1. This is more than we could have imagined, an away goal, a lead against the might of Dortmund.

Liverpool weather the whirlwind Dortmund response. In first-half extra-time Mkhitaryan probes again and sends a delightful through-pass to Aubameyang, deep inside the Liverpool box. The tall and athletic French-born Gabonese striker pulls the trigger, but Lovren flings himself in front of the shot sending the ball ricocheting to safety. From the resulting corner kick Liverpool fail to clear their lines and the ball bounces to Marco Reus, who is unmarked three yards from goal. This time it is Mignolet who spreads his body wide and Reus's shot is deflected onto the roof of the charmed Liverpool net. Still in injury time, Liverpool break forward with Moreno at speed. He plays a delightful pass and Origi is through once more. Weidenfeller darts from his goal to confront the young Belgian and manages to block the attempted lob. The referee blows his whistle and a breathless first-half comes to an end.

Worrying news reaches the terraces. Henderson has sustained a bad knee injury and Joe Allen takes his place at the break. Three minutes after the restart Dortmund draw level. After forty-seven minutes of top drawer defending, Liverpool fall asleep. Following a quick short corner, Mkhitaryan crosses and Hummels, from the identical spot where Lovren missed for Liverpool earlier, nods home with ease. After all the heroics, it's a soft goal to concede, however, at 1–1 the scoreline now fairly reflects the balance of the game. Liverpool respond well to the setback and Origi shoots wide on forty-eight minutes. The young Belgian is coming of age tonight. On fifty minutes he breaks down the left wing and finds Allen inside the Dortmund box. Allen flicks it to Lallana who back-heels it to the awaiting Coutinho, just inside the eighteen-yard line. The Brazilian unleashes a pile driver that seems to beat Weidenfeller, but incredibly the German keeper manages to reach low to his right and, with all his strength, block the shot when it seemed impossible to do so. What a goal that would have been. Liverpool keep pressing hard and now it's Dortmund who are on the rack. Clyne shoots from distance and once more Weidenfeller saves low to his right. The ball breaks and finds its way back to Coutinho who from inside the box unleashes another rocket. Again the German stopper finds a part of his body to block the effort. Single-handedly he is stemming the Red tide. Dortmund rally and push forward. On fifty-eight minutes Reus curls a central free kick goalwards but Mignolet gathers low, danger averted.

The final thirty minutes can't match the relentless pace of what went before and with few clear chances, the game eventually peters out to a 1–1 draw. It is a hugely satisfying result for Liverpool and with an away goal in the bag, it sets the tie up perfectly for the second leg at Anfield. Klopp's homecoming has gone perfectly to plan. Mission accomplished.

Klopp echoes all of our moods after the game when he remarks, "We could have won the game. A lot of people thought we would lose 2-0, 3-0, 4-0." The TV reporter asks him, "Can his team do it again next week?" Without missing a beat Klopp replies, "Or better!"

Better will be needed I feel. The Reds were excellent tonight, but Dortmund didn't seem to find top form, maybe the occasion unnerved them after all. It's hard to imagine them being as lacklustre a second time. Next week, with everything on the line, Liverpool may need their best performance of the season.

'Or better…'

THE MAGIC CAULDRON

'Magic is believing in yourself, if you can do that, you can make anything happen.' — Johann Wolfgang von Goethe

Fans stand on walls and hang from windows, some have even taken to the top of a scaffold-clad building. Thousands have gathered all along the Anfield Road in the bright evening sunshine. Flags are draped on every surface. A flare is set off, then another and plumes of red smoke rise gently on the soft breeze. The crowd is twenty deep on both sides of the narrow road, leaving just enough space for a bus to squeeze through. The Liverpool team bus. It approaches through the slender passage afforded by the faithful for their warriors. Dortmund fans look on, expressions of disbelief and awe abound. If this is the reception for the bus, what will the match itself behold? Once more I hear the words of Klopp "Or better..." and my pulse quickens just a little.

Inside, the Kop is full in number and voice with thirty minutes to kick-off. I'm in the Anfield Road end, Liverpool section, but there are plenty of Dortmund fans sat amongst us. There is a friendly bond between these fans. This is how football should be, fans of all creed and persuasion stood together. Rivals, yet friends with a unified love, football. Civil, respectful, dignified and passionate. 'Give peace a chance,' as John Lennon said.

The evening sun starts to set but the floodlights are not yet needed. Above and behind the old Main Stand we can see the skeletal frame of the new stand as it undergoes frenetic construction to be ready for the next big kick-off in August. Its 650-tonne roof truss towers high and proud over the old stadium and gazes out over the port-city to the Irish Sea. It is the future, this is the now. There is always a particular excitement about a big European game late in the season, which kicks off in daylight and ends in darkness. To be competing in these games at the business end of the fixture list underscores that a positive campaign has being waged. The smell of fresh cut grass comes to my senses, a spring feeling of renewal, the sun shining, feeding life and hope. That's how these games start, but then the sun sets and darkness falls and the great stage lights go on, the final dramas illuminated in fluorescent searing wattage.

The teams line up and all four corners of the ground rise for 'You'll Never Walk Alone' as they did a week previously at the Westfalenstadion. This time we are led by Gerry and the Pacemakers and not the Pur Harmony version of Dortmund. The fans on the Kop hold coloured sheets aloft to form a mosaic which spells out the number ninety-six, in memory of the Hillsborough victims who died this week, twenty-seven years ago. Dortmund fans do likewise, again showing a ninety-six, this time in yellow and black. A gracious and notable gesture from a super club. When the anthem finishes, the crowd applaud and we are ready for battle to commence. But the singing doesn't finish. The chorus of the great song continues over and over, again and again, sung by what seems to be every single Liverpool fan in the stadium. They sing as a war cry, a salvo of undiluted and unlimited support. They also sing for the memories of those that cannot be here, those that can never be here again. The chorus reverberates for what seems an eternity, bellowed out like few times before. Dortmund and other clubs around Europe have borrowed our great anthem, but when chanted like this, in this stadium, with this intensity and poignancy, it finds its true home, the home that it is synonymous with in the hearts and minds of the footballing world.

The Liverpool crowd rise instinctively to the occasion on these big European nights. Roy Evans said, "European football without Liverpool, is like a banquet without wine." Similarly, Anfield without European football is like an ocean clipper, moored in dock sails down, gazing longingly out to sea. They should never be apart. This blanket of scarves, banners and flags is a glorious sight to behold. We are a proud bunch. Tonight, we know the world is looking on, eyes and lenses focused, and we remind those millions that this is what Liverpool FC is all about, this is what the sleeping giant can look and sound like. Have you missed us? When Anfield is this noisy, this colourful, this passionate, then special things can happen. The coliseum has seen so many glory nights filled with epic drama and nail biting tension. Inter Milan, 1965. St Etienne, 1977. Auxerre, 1991. Barcelona, 2001. Roma, 2002. Olympiakos, 2004. Chelsea, 2005 and Chelsea again in 2007. The list goes on and on. Now it's Klopp and his team's chance to write another chapter, a chapter in their own legacy.

Liverpool start brightly, but anytime they lose the ball, Dortmund do what Dortmund do best, they break at speed and with a cutting edge. The pattern of the game sets early. Dortmund execute a rapier counter attack when Liverpool concede possession. Aubameyang's shot is well saved by Mignolet, but Mkhitaryan is there to drive the ball goal-bound. Sakho makes a lunging dive to block but this time he can't match his Dortmund heroics, 0–1 to Dortmund. Within five minutes, Dortmund have taken the lead and all the hard work exerted in Germany now seems worthless. Klopp had argued that the away goal was not important, not unless it was 0–0 with five minutes to go. Unfortunately, he is proven right, now it is irrelevant. The task is laid bare, Liverpool need to score more goals than Dortmund on the night to go through. Any other outcome and it is curtains.

The pattern is not just set, on nine minutes it is cast in stone. Game, set and match Dortmund. Liverpool are sloppy in possession and Aubameyang races clear of Sakho and closes in on goal. Before Mignolet can fully advance, the striker unleashes an unstoppable blast into the roof of the Liverpool net. 0–2 to Dortmund and Liverpool's worst fears have been realised. All the storm in the Liverpool fans' sails has deflated. Recognition sets in and spreads like a virus amongst the crowd. This is how a world class team can punish you. 0–2, and Liverpool, after only nine minutes, have been set an insurmountable hurdle. To score three goals without reply.

One word races through my mind over and over – salvation. Salvation of pride, salvation of respect. To lose by a landslide, here at Anfield, after such outpourings of emotion. To lose abjectly to Klopp's old team, as his successor celebrates gleefully on the Anfield touchline in front of him, validating all of the whispers from Germany that he was somehow an upgrade to the man who had rebuilt their club, that would be demoralising, gut-wrenching. Memories of what half-time at Istanbul felt like come flooding back. Jamie Carragher described it – "There was a sense of shame to go with my sorrow. I almost began to regret reaching the final. Keeping the score at 3–0 and at the very least restoring some respectability was all that mattered to me." Now, all around me Reds must be feeling the same. We must go out fighting, we must show the spirit of Liverpool FC, the spirit that pulled this great club back from the brink so many times. When the celebratory noise from the visiting fans ebbs a little, Liverpool's fans step in and try to lift their team's drooping heads. It's certainly not every voice in the stadium, but more than enough to remind the team and ourselves, that we are still here, still present. The Red men do lift themselves from the floor. Wave after wave of Liverpool attacks follow. The play is intricate and skilful. Time after time, the ball flashes across the face of the Dortmund goal below us, but it seems that tonight will not be our night. Lallana mistimes his connection inside the box and only scuffs the ball. Origi goes close twice. Corner after corner come and then go, but no breakthrough. Dortmund counter with real threat and, just before half-time, Mkhitaryan misses narrowly. It looked all the world a goal, but somehow Liverpool escape; 0–3 would have been truly unbearable.

The half-time whistle blows and both teams are applauded from the field after a breathless, high quality forty-five minutes. On the whole, I think a 1–2 score would be fair, but Liverpool have not managed to gain any reward for their sterling efforts. Three goals will be needed after the break to win through. Against a side like Dortmund, the odds are negligible. Tuchel said before the game that he had no doubt that Dortmund would score an away goal and was at pains to stress that they wouldn't stop there. They wanted two, three if possible. He has been true to his word. The Yellow and Blacks look dangerous every time they go forward. When Liverpool attack, as they must, the back door will be wide open. I fear the embarrassment of a rout.

A call comes in on my phone, it's my daughter. She's forgotten about the game and is just calling to say that she's off to bed, as she does every evening that I'm not with her. We chat about the game and she sends her commiserations and reminds me that it is only football. That doesn't help but I don't tell her. Then my son comes on the line. "What a disaster," he exclaims and I concur. He's been listening on the radio and quite often that's worse for the nerves, every miss seems a shocker and every opposition attack sounds like a certain goal. "Can we get back into it?" he asks and in honesty I reply that it's very, very unlikely. "Remember Istanbul," he chides.

"I do, I do," I tell him, reminding him that it was me who preached that miracle to him. He laughs.

"It can happen again," he says with that 'anything is possible' belief that kids possess until the world knocks it from them.

"I suppose so," I agree, "they are weak at the back every time we attack," deciding not to mention that Liverpool look just as, if not more, porous themselves. Around me, the Anfield crowd must be having the same thoughts, the same conversations, the same memories. For, just as in Istanbul, a rendition of 'You'll Never Walk Alone' starts to ring around the stadium. It's being sung for the team sitting below the stands, the Red team sitting heads down in the dressing room. 'Listen to us,' it implores, 'we still believe, do you?' My son listens on the other end of the line and then we say goodbye and get ready, many miles apart, for the second half to commence.

Liverpool are at it from the restart, frenzied harrying of the yellow shirts, snapped tackles, bolting runs forward. The game moves at break-neck pace. Emre Can, an inspiration for Liverpool since the New Year, bursts through the midfield ranks leaving two Dortmund players in his wake. Without hesitation and with an economy of touch, he threads a pass intersecting the Dortmund back-four for Origi to run onto. Roman Weidenfeller, the giant Dortmund goalkeeper and hero of the first tie, sprints out to meet the ball. Can's pass is dead weight, the perfect pass and Origi will only need one touch if he can get to the ball first. He does. He toe-pokes it. It beats Weidenfeller and finds its way into the back of the net in front of a delirious Kop. Three minutes after the restart and it's 1–2. At last we have a game worthy of the introduction and build-up. Scarves unfurl over heads and Liverpool's supporters jump up and down singing, roaring, hugging one another as they do. My overriding feeling is one of pride, Liverpool don't roll over, we don't do surrender. Even if it ends this way, honour has been restored. But we hope for more, all around I see fans looking into each other's eyes, asking the unspoken question. Can we do this? Really? The Dortmund fans amongst us are gracious and they nod in approval. It is clear they have not reached worry level yet, they know that the mountain is still above Liverpool and that all that has been achieved is base camp.

The Reds pile forward relentlessly, caution thrown to the wind. A Clyne shot is blocked. Origi shoots from outside the box but it sails high and handsome. Then on fifty-seven minutes, danger. Hummels advances confidently from Dortmund's defence and makes ground on Liverpool's right side. Marco Reus, who has been quiet till now, makes an instinctive striker's run in and behind Clyne at right back. Hummels sees it and threads a delightful pass for Reus to chase onto. The German gets there first and advances on Mignolet's goal from an acute angle. This proves no problem as he curls the ball deliciously above and beyond Mignolet and disaster strikes home as the ball settles into the back of the Liverpool net. Reus turns and trots the few yards to where the away Dortmund fans are going berserk. Normal service has been resumed for this German juggernaut and it's 1–3 after fifty-seven minutes. An avalanche has swept through Liverpool's base camp and again they have Everest to climb. But now, the enormous ascent is not the only problem, time is also running out fast as the night draws in. Only thirty minutes remain and three Liverpool goals are needed once more. The momentum has shifted too, both on the pitch and in the stands. The oxygen that Origi's goal provided has gone and Anfield now feels like a vacuum of despair, but for the yellow and black enclave that celebrates what must now be a definite path to the semi-finals. Yet if any team have cornered the market for incredible comebacks, then it is Liverpool. I think of Newcastle 4–3 all those years ago. I think of Olympiakos at Anfield when Gerrard grabbed improbable late glory. I think of the Arsenal Cup final at Cardiff and the two glorious goals from Michael Owen. I think of the West Ham Cup final, when the game was lost twice, only for the Reds and more specifically Gerrard, to find a way. Most of all I think of that balmy night in Istanbul when three goals were needed, as they are here. So, we sing and we sing and our friends from Germany look on with a mix of respect and bemusement.

On sixty-two minutes it is Klopp's turn to do what he can do. Till now he has been an electric dynamo on the touchline, encouraging his charges, extolling the crowd for more fervour. Now he plays his strategic cards. He sends on Sturridge and Allen to replace Firmino and Lallana. Both have been quiet by their standards. The fresh faces make an immediate impact with both Allen and Sturridge sending in shots from outside the box. They are speculative efforts, but it's progress and it lifts the crowd's spirits. The clock ticks on.

On sixty-six minutes Coutinho advances from midfield with determination. He springs a forward pass to Milner, who is lurking on the edge of the German box. Coutinho races forward for the return pass. There are defenders all around, so Milner will need to play it perfectly. He does. The ball sits up for el Magico to hit. Twenty yards from goal. He connects sweetly, perfectly. The ball curls towards the bottom right corner. Weidenfeller stretches to save it, but it's too good, Coutinho is too good. It's a goal to Liverpool. 2–3. Can this possibly happen? I can't even start to consider the thought. I get a text from my son. One word – *'Believe.'*

The Dortmund faces around me now look a little bit more apprehensive than before, it's game on again. Liverpool push and push. Klopp gesticulates with his arms on the line. Attack he exhorts. Liverpool win a corner on seventy-seven minutes as Tuchel plays one of his cards, replacing attacking midfielder Kagawa with the more defensive Ginter. Play resumes and the corner whips in from Coutinho. It beats the first line of defenders and bounces in front of the goal, three yards out. Sakho stoops and prods his head to the ball. He connects and sends it home. What is happening? It is 3–3. Anfield is bouncing, the stands reverberate under the seismic release. The crescendo is overwhelming. Something strange is occuring in this old ground, another spell is being spun and mystical particles of magic dust fizzle into the floodlit night. The Dortmund fans are now wringing their hands, shaking their heads. They look to the clock, as do I, as do we all. Twelve minutes to find one more goal, twelve minutes for the players, the fans, the manager, to write another famous chapter in our club's history. It was twelve minutes in that Palace game too, when Klopp was left alone. Not now. We are as one now. He has taught us to trust again. I now believe it can be done, actually that's not true. I believe it will be done. It seems that if we will it to happen, then happen it will. Now I'm buying into this fate business. A text arrives, this time three letters. 'OMG!' I respond, the non-religious person that I am, 'Pray'. To whom, to what, I have no idea, but now I'm praying big time.

On the men in red push and further and further Dortmund retreat. It's a siege. Liverpool win a free kick, but Coutinho shoots over. Even Serbian centre-half Dejan Lovren has pushed forward, but he shoots speculatively from inside the box, when he should cross and it's lost in the Kop behind the goal. The clock strikes ninety. Five minutes of injury time is announced and a roar goes up urging the final surge. Clyne wins a free kick inside the Liverpool half on the right side. With no time to waste, he plays a ball down the line for Sturridge who has broken wide into a good position. Sturridge miss-controls the ball and it seems the advantage is lost. But then he turns cleverly and jinks a pass between defenders for Milner to run onto. Milner gets there first. He turns one way and then the other and from the edge of the Dortmund box he sends an inviting lofted cross into the danger zone. It's a clever ball, a hanging floater that has 'if you want this enough, then it's waiting for you' written all over it. The area is full. Liverpool have piled everybody forward. Lovren leaps salmon high at the back post. Hummels springs with him. Lovren's climb is the highest and he sends a powerful header goal bound. It's unstoppable. Goooooaaal. Tooooooooor. 4–3.

It's seconds before I can fully comprehend what has happened; my heart pounding at one million beats per minute. Liverpool lead 4–3 and time must be nearly up. 'You'll Never Walk Alone' rings around the ground. It has to be over. But on the match goes. Dortmund now attack. If they score, they go through. Allen tackles rashly and the Germans have a free kick on the edge of the Liverpool box. Reus stands over it. I remember my son's words when he played with this team on his console, as virtual Reus curled goal after goal in from free kicks just like this. "He never misses," I can't watch the real Reus and I turn and look behind me to where three Dortmund fans are stood. I will know by their reactions. And soon they come. Deflation. He has missed. That must be it. It is. The referee puts an end to the game and the historians start to make the entries. This will never be forgotten. All around there is the sense that we have witnessed something special, otherworldly. I feel in my pocket to make sure I have my ticket stub and program, they are for my son.

In that programme Klopp stated, – "Tonight promises to be a very special occasion, with two of Europe's biggest clubs playing in a special ground in front of two groups of amazing supporters." How right he was.

I shake the hand of the Dortmund fans around me, offer my commiserations. They wish us luck and comment on how incredible Anfield was, how it lived up to the mythical stories. It doesn't always, but on these rarefied nights, these special occasions, more often than not it takes on a charmed and magical spirit. A rush of pride overwhelms me, pride for this place, these enchanted stands, this green field. This home. Tonight, it seemed like an army of one hundred thousand manned the stands, but the official attendance is 45,848. That should have read 45,848 plus 96.

Afterwards Dortmund manager Tuchel is in a state of shock. He rested most of his team the weekend before, for the Ruhr derby versus Schalke, where a 2–2 draw put an end to their chances of beating Munich to the Bundesliga title. All their remaining hopes for the season had rested with this trophy and now, they too had evaporated, their eighteen-game unbeaten streak broken, all to a fairy-tale comeback from Liverpool. "I can't explain it, it was not logical," he says. "It was very emotional. At the end, at 3–3, everyone here believed it was meant to be, it was destiny. If you have such a strong belief, then things can happen."

Klopp had felt it too. "Something happened in the stadium. You could hear it, you could feel it and you could smell it."

In Germany, *Spiegel Online* are effusive and gracious with their praise –*"Among the football-faith community, the legendary Anfield Road stadium is not considered a sacred site for nothing, and on this memorable night everyone felt what mighty magic can be summoned here."*

I call my son and he asks what it was like, the game, the atmosphere. "Magical," is all I can say, over and over. Magical.

Mourinho spoke of it when Chelsea fell. Ferguson lauded it too. Van Gaal had called for his fans to copy it. But if you can't explain it, then how can you copy it. It is ethereal, spiritual, otherworldly. Impossible to repeat. Not even the Anfield faithful know when it is going to happen, but when it does, batten down the hatches and let history unfold.

IN MEMORY

'Fly, fly, fly high against the sky, so high I almost touch the sky. Thank you, thank you, thank God for you, the wind beneath my wings' – The Wind Beneath My Wings, – Jeff Silbar, Larry Henley.

The mood is sombre below a hanging grey sky. Where the night before, thousands scampered and scuttled in anticipation of the big match, smiles wide on excited faces, scarves and flags aloft, a loud buzzing noise of expectancy in the air, today, the faces are drawn and respectful as those who have gathered walk slowly, steadily. Younger folk help their elders from cars, offering strong arms as support for the less firm. Families gather; generations pulled together. Some carry flowers, others carry private personal mementos. In the pubs and cafes the voices are low, the eyes are soft and the faces are filled with kindness and reverence. All who come are bonded in grief and love. Each has been touched in some way. Each has shed tears of anguish and despair. Some more than others. It is the day after the epic Dortmund game. The LCD screens on the stadium's exterior walls display the message 'Never Forgotten'. Across from the Albert pub a fifty-foot-long flag is draped across two buildings and reads 'To the victims of Hillsborough'. At the gates outside the Kop, three fans huddle together for a photograph. One wears a Liverpool shirt, the second an Everton shirt and the last a Man City shirt. At the Hillsborough memorial, now positioned behind the Kemlyn Road Stand, hundreds gather to lay wreaths and scarves in honour and respect. A Scottish flag is pinned to the wall, it reads 'Bravehearts 96'. Below it lies a sprawling bed of flowers. Various scarves have been left in a show of unity and fraternity from the footballing community both near and far. I see the colours of Dortmund, Hearts, Celtic, Everton, Aston Villa, Dumbarton, Bristol Rovers and Esbjerg FB amongst many others.

It is Friday, April 15th 2016, twenty-seven years to the day of the Hillsborough disaster, and inside Anfield, nearly 30,000 people have gathered for the final public anniversary service for the ninety-six dead. The mass begins with the singing of 'Abide With Me' and then, one by one, the names of the ninety-six are called out to deafening silence. As each name is read a single light is illuminated in a large silver band, a memorial sculpture that signifies eternal life and love, representing the bond between the families, friends and fans who were brought together in a time of great grief and suffering. All that can be heard is the soft patter of rain over our heads as it falls on the roof of the stand. Angels weep.

At 3.06 p.m., the time that the fateful game was halted, a minute's silence begins and it spreads from the ground all the way back into the city of Liverpool, where people stand still and silent on the main streets and shopping thoroughfares. Flags hang at half-mast and public transport comes to a halt, all buses carrying the message 'Remembering the 96' on their displays. The bells of Liverpool's Metropolitan Cathedral toll ninety-six times. In the stadium, Kenny Dalglish reads from the Gospel of St John as Jürgen Klopp and his team look on from the stands. Trevor Hicks, whose two daughters, nineteen-year-old Sarah and fifteen-year-old Vicki, died in the tragedy speaks to the congregation and describes how 'unbelievable' the club was with the families. He comments on the irony that we all feel. "Last night Anfield was a cauldron, today it is a church." Margaret Aspinall, whose son James died at Hillsborough, is last to speak and she asks the crowd to arise and sing 'Wind Beneath my Wings' as ninety-six white doves are released into the grey sky above.

A final song, 'You'll Never Walk Alone', sends us back out into the world to carry on with our lives, clinging to our memories of those who have shared our days but who now rest in peace.

THE MONSTER IN RED

'You may say I'm a dreamer, but I'm not the only one,' — John Lennon

Say the name of these cities – Liverpool, Dortmund, Manchester, Glasgow – and one of the first associations that might enter your thoughts is football. Each of these were industrial towns at one time or another, each with large working class conurbations, each fanatical about football. Say the name Bournemouth and most likely an image of a trip to the seaside will spring to mind. Deckchairs, ice creams and fish and chips by the shore. Football might be the last thought that pops up and given Bournemouth's history, that is not surprising.

Before 1810, Bournemouth, as we know it today, didn't exist. Back then the only people hazarding this particular piece of coastline were fishermen and smugglers. Then a Captain Lewis Tregonwell and his wife Henrietta passed by and fell in love with the tranquil and unspoilt location. They decided to settle and build a house. An early visitor Mrs Arbuthnott wrote in 1824 – "I rode one day to a place called Bournemouth – a collection of hills lately planted by a gentleman by the name of Tregonwell, who has built four or five beautiful cottages which he lets out to persons who go sea-bathing. I was so charmed by the beauty of the situation that Mr Arbuthnott and myself agreed to take one next summer."

As Bournemouth's popularity as a seaside resort grew, its accessibility became an issue. It was difficult to reach by road or rail, so most people arrived by sea. Landings were difficult with the long, shallow and sandy shore. By the middle of the century it became clear that a pier would be needed. The first Bournemouth Pier opened to much fanfare in 1856, but by 1861 it had been largely dismantled due to storm damage. An improved, stronger and longer version would be needed. Eventually, in 1880 the new 755-foot-long pier was opened by Sir Francis Wyatt Truscott, the Lord Mayor of London, who described Bournemouth as "the garden city of the south".

The walk from the pier uphill into the city, through the Lower Gardens and then the Central Gardens is a tranquil and lovely experience. Grey squirrels run along the Bourne River (which gave the town its name) as it flows through the park down to the sea. Families stroll in the slightly chilled spring sunshine and the overall mood is one of serenity and relaxation. Overhead a large hot-air balloon rises, a permanent feature of the Gardens, as it lifts day trippers into the sky. It's not surprising that, historically, Bournemouth earned the reputation as a retirement destination, selling tranquillity by the sea. Later that night I question whether this is still the case. After dark, the streets are mobbed by young party people on their way to and from the plethora of late bars and clubs that populate this university town. I spot long queues outside a number of venues and it's not yet midnight. I can only imagine how raucous the place gets in the summer and a large part of me is thankful that my dancing shoes are consigned to the retirement press.

For 116 years AFC Bournemouth dreamed of playing at the elite level of English football and finally in 2015 that moment arrived. Promotion followed from 2014/15's victorious Championship campaign, when Bournemouth won the title on the very last day of the season, defeating Charlton Athletic 0–3 away. Now Bournemouth are one of the elite, yet their story could have been so different.

Go back in time six years to the 2008/09 season. Once more it is the last day of the season and Bournemouth are at home to Grimsby. Bournemouth started the campaign with minus seventeen points, following a Football League penalty for entering into financial administration the year before. Defeat will spell demotion to the non-professional leagues and most likely the death of an only recently resuscitated club. Yet somehow, with thirty-year-old manager Eddie Howe at the helm, Bournemouth survive, coming from behind to win 2–1. Seventeen points adrift in August before a ball had even been kicked in anger, incredibly the sea-siders manage to cling onto their footballing lives. Last-day drama seems to be the fashion on the south coast.

Fast forward to today and it is easy to see that the rise of Bournemouth has been meteoric, promotion through the divisions achieved within six years of that pivotal Grimsby game. 'The Cherries' (named after the cherry orchards that were once located next to their home stadium) have finally made it to the big time. They have achieved the dream. But dreams can turn to nightmares in a blink. The glamour and polish that pervades the top of the table, the chase for places in Europe and for the title itself, is countered by the ruthless and vicious battle to the death at the bottom, where clubs will rip each other apart to stay inside these exalted feeding grounds. Lose your berth and you might never get back. Avoid eviction and the rewards are limitless.

Many clubs have found the air at the top too rarefied and after brief dalliances with glory the descents proved rapid. On the way down the ride is always faster and more precarious. The fall can prove more perilous than ever imagined. Inflated wage bills still need paying, expanded stadiums are harder to fill, expensive signings are harder to shift out to other clubs. Queens Park Rangers, relegated in 2014/15, are a good example of what not to do. Don't buy ageing players on huge wage bills for big transfer fees from clubs who don't want them anymore anyway. Don't buy mercenary footballers who are happy to sit on the bench and collect the cash instead of moving on to a club where they will get playing time. Don't let your manager buy in the transfer market with the same policies adopted by children in sweetshops. A glance at clubs like Wimbledon, Coventry and Swindon should prove sobering, all adrift for some time now from the top tier, their wings having burned in the sun's fire. In 2013, Wigan Athletic won a first major trophy after eighty-one years of existence, when beating Manchester City 1–0 in the FA Cup final. That same season they were relegated from the Premiership after an eight-year tenure. Now they fight a relegation battle in League Two (the third tier of English football). Old money often scoffs and sniffs derisively at new brash wealth and sometimes for good reason. But it's not only the upstarts who can fall quickly. The once mighty Leeds United bet the kitchen sink on becoming Premier and European elite. The journey was glorious for a few brief years, but then came the fall and, to this day, they are still paying for their financial hubris. 2015/16 will be their twelfth successive season looking up at the Premiership, praying for a return. So, tread carefully whilst enjoying the view from the summit.

In the Premier League everything is bigger, the crowds, the worldwide audience, the media attention and not least, the financial commitments and rewards. It is easy to lose one's head amongst the bright lights, amid the sea of money. Given Bournemouth's recent history of recovery from financial doom and elevation to lofty footballing heights, they are as well positioned as anyone to juggle the contrasting needs of, on one hand, maintaining their new-found Premiership status and on the other, assuring their long-term financial stability. For guidance, they could do worse than look to coastal neighbours Southampton, now enjoying their fourth successive campaign at the top, having finished in seventh the season before. Southampton appear to be the model club, playing quality football, developing young and technically gifted players, achieving results and making profits as they go. Yet, that's a high standard and living the dream is never easy. Yet it is okay to dream, to hope, for what are we without dreams?

From all soundings, it seems that Bournemouth have solid plans to hang around. Their Chairman, Jeff Mostyn, understands the financial pitfalls. "We are in a really good position to learn from the mistakes of other clubs that have been promoted. What we've been offered and what we don't want, are the so-called prima donnas and the aged of the Premier League all believing that they can find one final payday. The phone never stops ringing. We won't be signing those guys."

For some reason I don't think we will hear thirty-seven-year-old Eddie Howe, Bournemouth's bright young manager, complaining. He understands what's at stake and prefers, it seems, to go about his business quietly and keep progressing under the radar. Veteran of over 250 appearances as a player for Bournemouth he summarises the club's objectives better than anybody: "The challenge is trying to get the balance right, between having a go and being competitive, but also not risking the long-term viability of the club. But, we are going to be brave!" Wise words.

It seems Bournemouth have worked out what it takes not to shoot themselves in the foot.

★★★

Today as Liverpool visit the seasiders, Bournemouth sit in eleventh place and another season in the top flight in 2016/17 is already assured. What an incredible achievement that is for a small and unheralded club, which only seven short years ago had been at death's door. In August I was convinced that, if the Cherries did manage to stay up, it would be the biggest story of the season. But for the unfolding drama at Leicester, I might have been right. The Foxes are fast becoming the biggest footballing and sporting story of the century, possibly of all time and, in some ways, they have stolen the thunder of the smaller clubs such as Bournemouth and Watford who are managing to survive the shark infested waters of the Premier League.

This trip to the seaside comes only three days after Liverpool's awe-inspiring, but energy-sapping, comeback against Dortmund and only two days after the emotional outpouring of the final Hillsborough Anniversary Mass at Anfield. In many ways Bournemouth, with its southern tranquillity, seems to me to be the perfect antidote to what has been a tumultuous week on Merseyside.

The setting is peaceful, green and serene at Bournemouth AFC's Vitality Stadium. Set in lush green parkland, this is nice football, community football. Around the back is the visitors' section in the East Stand. Past that lie the home team's training pitches and in the past at some time the cherry orchards from where they picked their nickname.

Before kick-off, Bournemouth present a flowered wreath to Liverpool in honour of the ninety-six who died at Hillsborough. It reads 'AFC Bournemouth Remembers'. It's a lovely warm touch. Then the PA system plays Liverpool's anthem and both home and away following sing 'You'll Never Walk Alone' as one. Respect to Bournemouth.

Not surprisingly Klopp has shuffled the team and it is unrecognisable from the one that played less than three days earlier. Three young Liverpool players make their League debuts. Ward in goal, Randall at right-back and Smith at left-back. Other Academy graduates, Stewart and Ojo, play in midfield and Ibe gets a return to action after a lengthy spell out of favour. The senior players include Lucas and Touré in central defence, Joe Allen in central midfield and Sturridge and Firmino up top. For me, the pressure is off. I'm happy to watch these young players cut their teeth, whatever the outcome. Of course you hope for a win, but the decision to rest the senior players makes sense.

It seems that Bournemouth's mid-table security has seen them switch into summer holiday mode a little early. Liverpool's youngsters are bright, inventive and have the total run of the pitch. Rarely have I witnessed such an easy forty-five minutes. At half-time Liverpool lead 2–0 through goals from Firmino on forty-one minutes and Sturridge in stoppage time. The kids have looked bright and sharp and Klopp must be delighted with this glimpse of the future. Sheyi Ojo in particular has the appearance of a star in the making. The second half sees Bournemouth battle back into the game but it is the Reds (in all-white) that go closest with Sturridge hitting the woodwork twice. It's not until the ninety-third minute that the net rustles again, this time for a Bournemouth goal. But it's all a little too late for the home team and Liverpool deservedly leave the south coast with a 2–1 victory and three valuable points in the search for a place in Europe next season.

Before leaving the seaside town, I take time to visit the beautiful old spired church of St Peter's beside which rests a small tiered graveyard of yesteryear. Impressive granite tombs rise from the lush green grass, backed by thorny bushes and tall trees. Here Bournemouth's founding father Captain Tregonwell lies in his grave. However, I did not come to see the Captain, instead I stand over the tomb of a brilliant woman named Mary. In 1818 she wrote a novel that still to this day retains the utmost relevance. Now and into the future, her work will tax man's moral compass about creation, science, prejudice and the debate between nature and nurture. Having eloped with Percy Bysshe Shelley on a European vacation, Mary Godwin and Shelley would join the company of Lord Byron and John William Polidori. This young, anarchic and illustrious group of poets, authors, agitators and philosophers found themselves holed up for days amid a terrible storm in a Gothic Swiss castle. Lord Byron would write, "I was half mad… between metaphysics, mountains, lakes, love inextinguishable, thoughts unalterable and the nightmare of my own delinquencies." Huddled by candlelight in the dark of night, the castle dwellers decided to each create a ghost story. Polidori would write a short story called 'The Vampyre', the original tale in English of the genre. Mary Godwin, later to become Mary Shelley, took days to think of hers, but at last in a series of dreams it came to her. Frankenstein was born and so too, a horror story to live through the ages. I doff my metaphoric cap to the great lady and take my leave of quaint and lovely Bournemouth.

The bus home meanders through the rolling valleys of the New Forest, passing grazing horses and quaint thatched cottages. Everything in life seems good after a relaxing weekend by the sea. A semi-final in Europe awaits, our emerging crop of kids exude quality and the senior squad that Klopp inherited, instead of being the worst ever, is now starting to look like a battle-hardened, never-say-die band of warriors. Speckled sunlight glints through the trees dazzling the inside of my closed eyelids and I drift softly into a warm contented sleep. A dream comes. Before me stands a giant of a man. He wears glasses and bears a manic toothy grin, wild hair spiking from his head. All the while he laughs aloud and kicks a ball back and forth shouting 'Boom, Boom'. On his white-scientist jacket a name tag announces 'Dr Kloppenstein'. As I look on, he slowly assembles a machine from the various spare parts that he can find at his disposal. Then he infuses the form with his own blood, power and energy, all the while shouting and roaring at it, encouraging it to become all that it can be. It takes life. Time passes, but after years of painstaking lessons and devotion, his finished creation becomes an unstoppable force. A monster in Red.

TRUTH AND JUSTICE

'At his best, man is the noblest of all animals; separated from law and justice he is the worst' — Aristotle

Some days will always be etched in the mind, when momentous events stop you in your tracks. They can be sad, heart-breaking or joyous occasions, but they are always seismic. The Berlin Wall would fall on November 9th, 1989. On September 11th, 2001 we watched in surreal shock as planes flew into buildings. On July 7th, 2005 buses and underground trains exploded. Saturday April 15th, 1989 was another one of those days, a black day when the harrowing tragedy that was the Hillsborough disaster unfolded to widespread disbelief and numbness. Ninety-six souls would be lost and a city would unite in grief.

Within days, heinous lies would be spread that would only compound the anguish. The dead would be accused of being criminals, louts and contributors to their own demise by the *Sun* newspaper. *The Guardian* would report as follows: *'According to Peter Chippindale and Chris Horrie in their definitive history Stick it Up Your Punter – the Rise and Fall of the Sun, Kelvin MacKenzie, the Sun's Editor at the time, spent an unusual amount of time deliberating over the fateful headline for that day's paper. "MacKenzie then did an enormously uncharacteristic thing. He sat for fully half an hour thinking about the front-page layout." According to the book he pondered two headlines, one that was rejected, reading 'You Scum', and the one that was eventually used and was to prove the biggest disaster for the paper's reputation and sales: 'The Truth'. A team of about eighteen journalists and photographers had been sent to cover the story, and although reporter Harry Arnold sought out MacKenzie to caution against reporting allegations as truth, MacKenzie pressed on. Having decided to lay the blame on the fans' doorsteps, there was no stopping him. Under the headline 'The Truth' there were three subheadings: 'Some fans picked pockets of victims – Some fans urinated on the brave cops – Some fans beat up PCs giving the kiss of life.' The story read as follows: 'Drunken Liverpool fans viciously attacked rescue workers as they tried to revive victims of the Hillsborough soccer disaster, it was revealed last night. Police officers, firemen and ambulance crew were punched, kicked and urinated upon by a hooligan element in the crowd. Some thugs rifled the pockets of injured fans as they were stretched out unconscious on the pitch. Sheffield MP Irvine Patnick revealed that in one shameful episode a gang of Liverpool fans noticed that the blouse of a girl trampled to death had risen above her breasts. As a policeman struggled in vain to revive her, the mob jeered, throw her up here and we will ★★★★ her.' The story went on, 'One furious policeman who witnessed Saturday's carnage stormed, "As we struggled in appalling conditions to save lives, fans standing further up the terrace were openly urinating on us and the bodies of the dead"'. A high-ranking police officer was quoted as saying: "The fans were just acting like animals. My men faced a double hell – the disaster and the fury of the fans who attacked us."*

The country was reviled at the shocking revelations, but in Liverpool anger was rising to match untold grief, for this was not the truth, not a bit of it. In fact, it was a blanket of lies concocted to shroud the day's events with innuendo and slander. The families would bury their dead with grace and respect, but then would begin the fight for justice. Incredibly it would take twenty-seven long years for that fight to eventually reveal to everyone the real truth of that sad day long ago.

On 25th April, 2013 (twenty-four years after the disaster) Lord Justice Goldring would summarise the chain of events that had culminated in the longest judicial process in the history of the British judiciary and which had led to the second Hillsborough Inquest, over which he now presided. Here is an excerpt from his summary:

'Inquests into the deaths resulting from the Hillsborough Football Stadium Disaster

1. *Much has been said and written over the course of the past 24 years concerning the events of 15th April 1989 at Hillsborough Stadium which led to 96 deaths.*

2. *On that day, 95 spectators of the football match who had travelled to Sheffield to enjoy what should have been one of the high points of the season suffered fatal injuries; one young man, having been so injured that he was left in a persistent vegetative state, died some years later, in March 1993. The disaster claimed men*

and women, boys and girls. The youngest of those who died was only 10. The oldest was 67. Some families suffered the loss of more than one of its members. I echo the words of the Lord Chief Justice, Lord Judge that each death was, and remains, the source of anguish and grief to those to whom they were precious. I acknowledge that, for all that has been, or will be, said and written concerning the disaster, nothing will remove or lessen the private individual grief for those intimately concerned.

3. *The disaster has been the subject of many investigations in the past. I shall sketch only the outline now. I shall do so with little comment.*

4. *Within a few days of the tragedy on 17th April 1989 the then Home Secretary asked Lord Justice Taylor to conduct a public inquiry. The West Midlands police were appointed to investigate, gather evidence for the Inquiry, and to assist the South Yorkshire Coroner who was to conduct the inquests in due course. Lord Justice Taylor reported on an interim basis in August 1989 and produced his final report in January 1990. He heard evidence from a large number of witnesses on a wide range of issues and received submissions from interested parties.*

5. *Preliminary inquest hearings, the so-called "mini inquests," were conducted in Sheffield between April and May 1990. Following the decision of the Director of Public Prosecutions not to institute criminal proceedings, the so-called generic inquests began on 19 November 1990. On 28th March 1991, the jury returned verdicts of accidental death in all 95 cases it was considering.*

6. *Between 1992 and 1993, some bereaved families sought to quash the verdicts and obtain new inquests, first by an application to the Attorney-General and then by judicial review proceedings. They did not succeed. All of these legal processes ran in parallel with civil proceedings and investigations into possible police disciplinary proceedings.*

7. *In June 1997, the then Home Secretary commissioned Lord Justice Stuart-Smith to undertake a scrutiny review of new evidence. His report was published in June 1998. He advised that there was no basis for a further judicial inquiry, new inquests or new criminal charges.*

8. A private prosecution of two of the senior members of the South Yorkshire Police led to their trial on charges of manslaughter in Leeds Crown Court in June and July 2000. One was acquitted. The jury did not agree in respect of the other. An application for a re-trial was refused.

9. A second application to the Attorney-General seeking a new inquest was commenced by Anne Williams, the mother of Kevin, in 2006. This unsuccessful application was considered by the European Court of Human Rights in 2009.

10. In December 2009, the Government waived the 30-year rule protecting public records from disclosure. The Hillsborough Independent Panel was appointed to oversee the disclosure of records, and to produce a report on their work. Their report was published on 12 September 2012. It sought to explain how the wider body of material available to the Panel may add to the public understanding of the tragedy. Following the publication of the Panel's Report, the Attorney-General commenced statutory review proceedings. On 19th December 2012, the Divisional Court presided over by the Lord Chief Justice quashed the inquests which had been held in 1990. It ordered that fresh inquests be held into each of the deaths arising from the disaster.

11. Throughout the course of these many investigations, inquiries and reviews, the bereaved families have not ceased in their pursuit of a full understanding of the events of that day.

12. This is the first preliminary hearing of the fresh inquests. The purpose of these inquests is to examine fully and fairly how each of the victims of this terrible disaster lost his or her life. The inquests will seek to ensure so far as possible that the full facts are brought to light; that any culpable or discreditable conduct is exposed and brought to public notice. However, it should not be forgotten that an inquest is a fact-finding investigation. It is not a method of apportioning guilt. There are no parties, no indictment, no prosecution and no defence. In other words, an inquest is not a trial but an inquiry to establish the facts.

13. The original inquests were, as the Lord Chief Justice said, scarred by degenerating into a kind of adversarial battle. This will not happen with the new inquests. There will be a determined search for the facts in which the process is fair and balanced. For my part I shall try to ensure that they are conducted in as open and inclusive a way as possible.

14. *It is with this task ahead of us that we meet today. The enormity of that task and the work involved must not be underestimated. The very fact that these inquests have been preceded by a raft of earlier investigative processes means that there is a very large volume of documents (to be counted in the hundreds of thousands) which require collation and organisation in a form suitable for disclosure to, and use by, the interested persons. This is an urgent, significant and substantial task.*

15. *One of the topics for discussion today will be the timing of the inquests in relation to the other investigations currently being undertaken by or on behalf of the Independent Police Complaints Commission and the Home Office. I understand that if these inquests are deferred until those investigations have been concluded, we may be unable to start for at least another 2 or 3 years. Whatever my decision on that issue, I bear in mind that 24 years have elapsed since the deaths occurred and that over that course of time some of the bereaved have died, most recently of course, Anne Williams. Her death is a powerful reminder, if one were needed, that there is an urgency attaching to the commencement of the inquest hearings as well as a need for that investigation to be as full as possible.*

16. *I shall now invite Counsel to the Inquests to make submissions on the procedural matters to be addressed today. Lord Justice Goldring, 25th April 2013'*

On March 31st 2014, the new inquest into the Hillsborough disaster began. Two years later, on the morning of April 26th 2016, the families of the bereaved would take their seats in Warrington crown court. Just after 11 a.m. the verdicts arrived. A jury of nine people, six men and three women, had been asked to provide a Yes or No answer to fourteen questions (along with any elaboration as to the reasons for the answer). The jury read their answers aloud from the General Questionnaire for Jury Determinations (reproduced below);

1. Basic facts of the Disaster: Do you agree with the following statement which is intended to summarise the basic facts of the disaster; Ninety-six people died as a result of the Disaster at Hillsborough Stadium on 15 April 1989 due to crushing in the central pens of the Leppings Lane terrace, following the admission of a large number of supporters to the Stadium through exit gates?
   YES

2. Police Planning for the Semi-Final Match: Was there any error or omission in police planning and preparation for the semi-final match on 15 April 1989 which caused or contributed to the dangerous situation that developed on the day of the match?
   YES – (*No specific instructions were issued to manage the crowds outside, on how the pens were to be filled and monitored and as to who was responsible for those actions.*)

3. Policing of the Match and the Situation at the Turnstiles: Was there any error or omission in policing on the day of the match which caused or contributed to a dangerous situation developing at the Leppings Lane turnstiles?
   YES – (*Police response was slow, un-coordinated. A road closure and sweep of fans exacerbated the situation. No filter cordons were used. No contingency plans existed. Attempts to close perimeter gates were made too late.*)

4. Policing of the Match and the Crush on the Terrace: Was there any error or omission by commanding officers which caused or contributed to the crush on the terrace?
   YES – *(Commanding officers should have ordered the closure of the central tunnel before the opening of gate C, as pens 3&4 were full.)*

5. The Opening of the Gates: When the order was given to open the exit gates at the Leppings Lane end of the Stadium, was there any error or omission by the commanding officers in the control box which caused or contributed to the crush on the terrace?
   YES – *(Commanding officers did not inform officers in the inner concourse prior to the opening of gate C and failed to consider where the incoming fans would go.)*

6. Determination on Unlawful Killing Issue: Are you satisfied, so that you are sure, that those who died in the Disaster were unlawfully killed?
   YES – by a majority of 7 to 2 – *(To reach this answer the jury was satisfied that it was sure that Chief Superintendent Duckenfield owed a duty of care to the 96 people who died in the Disaster, that he was in breach of that care, that that breach caused the deaths and that that breach amounted to gross negligence.)*

7. Behaviour of the Supporters: Was there any behaviour on the part of football supporters which caused or contributed to the dangerous situation at the Leppings Lane turnstiles?
   NO

8. Defects in Hillsborough Stadium: Were there any features of the design, construction and layout of the Stadium which you consider were dangerous or defective and which caused or contributed to the Disaster?
   YES – *(Design and layout of crush barriers in Pens 3 and 4 were not fully compliant with the Green Guide. The removal of barrier 144 and the partial removal of barrier 136 would have exacerbated the 'waterfall effect' of pressure towards the front of the pens. There were too few turnstiles for a capacity crowd. Signage to the side pens was inadequate.)*

9. Licensing and Oversight of Hillsborough Stadium: Was there any error or omission in the safety certification and oversight of Hillsborough Stadium that caused or contributed to the Disaster?
   YES – *(The Safety Certificate was never amended to reflect changes at the Leppings Lane end, therefore capacity figures were never updated. The capacity figures for the Leppings Lane terraces were incorrectly calculated when the Safety Certificate was issued. The Safety Certificate had not been re-issued since 1986.)*

10. Conduct of Sheffield Wednesday FC before the Day of the Match: Was there any error or omission by Sheffield Wednesday FC (and its staff) in the management of the Stadium and/or preparation for the semi-final match which caused or contributed to the dangerous situation that developed on the day of the match?

YES – *(The club did not approve the plans for dedicated turnstiles for each pen, nor agree any contingency plans with the police. There was inadequate signage and inaccurate/misleading information on the tickets.)*

11. Conduct of Sheffield Wednesday FC on the Day of the Match: Was there any error or omission by Sheffield Wednesday FC (and its staff) on 15 April 1989 which caused or contributed to the dangerous situation that developed at the Leppings Lane turnstiles and in the west terrace?
NO – As this answer was NO, a further question was asked –

12. Was there any error or omission by Sheffield Wednesday FC (and its staff) on 15 April 1989 which may have caused or contributed to the dangerous situation that developed at the Leppings Lane turnstiles and in the west terrace?
YES – *(Club officials were aware of the huge numbers of fans still outside the Leppings Lane turnstiles at 2.40 p.m. They should have requested a delayed kick-off at this point.)*

13. Conduct of Eastwood & Partners: Should Eastwood & Partners have done more to detect and advise on any unsafe or unsatisfactory features of Hillsborough Stadium which caused or contributed to the Disaster?
YES – *(Eastwoods did not make their own calculations when they became consultants for SWFC, therefore the initial capacity and all subsequent capacity figures were incorrect. Eastwoods failed to re-calculate capacity figures each time changes were made to the terraces. They failed to update the safety Certificate after 1986. Eastwoods failed to recognise that the removal of barrier 144 and partial removal of barrier 136 could result in dangerous situation at the game.)*

14. Emergency Response and the Role of the South Yorkshire Police: After the crush in the west terrace had begun to develop, was there any error or omission by the police which caused or contributed to the loss of lives in the disaster?
YES – *(The police delayed calling a Major Incident, so the appropriate emergency services were delayed. There was a lack of co-operation, communication, command and control which delayed or prevented appropriate responses.)*

15. Emergency Response and the Role of the South Yorkshire Metropolitan Ambulance Service (SYMAS): After the crush in the west terrace had begun to develop, was there any error of omission by the ambulance service (SYMAS) which caused or contributed to the loss of lives in the disaster?
    YES – *(SYMAS officers at the scene failed to ascertain the nature of the problem at Leppings Lane. The failure to recognise and call a Major Incident led to delays in responses to the emergency.)*

As the verdicts were read, the families of the bereaved shouted for joy and wept in relief as twenty-seven years of betrayal, cover-up and intransigence were at last purged by justice. In Liverpool, hundreds would gather at the St George's Hall as the cathartic group-healing of a city began. John Aldridge, a Liverpool footballing great would describe the verdict as, "the biggest victory in the history of the club". The next day newspapers in England and across the globe would lead their front pages with the remarkable story of this struggle for truth and justice. Not surprisingly there would be no reference to the verdicts on the front page of the *Sun*.

Labour Party leader Jeremy Corbyn would demand that those who peddled "vile and malicious lies'" be held to account and he paid tribute to the "passionate and dignified" campaign of the families. South Yorkshire Police said it, "unequivocally accepted the decision" and chief constable David Crompton said, "I apologise unreservedly to the families and all those affected. The force failed the victims and failed their families." Prime Minster David Cameron said, "Today is a landmark moment in the quest for justice for the 96 Liverpool fans who died on that dreadful day in April 1989. It is also a long overdue day. The bereaved families and survivors of the Hillsborough disaster have had to wait for twenty-seven long years for the full facts of what happened. And it is only due to their tireless bravery in pursuing the truth that we arrived at this momentous verdict. All families and survivors now have official confirmation of what they always knew was the case, that the Liverpool fans were utterly blameless in the disaster that unfolded at Hillsborough."

The footballing world rallied. Celtic FC would send a message of support to the club. They and their fans had been a rock of support in

1989 and now once again they were stepping up to the plate. Countless clubs, the length and breadth of the land, followed suit. Newcastle and Coventry vowed to sing 'You'll Never Walk Alone' before their forthcoming games.

In Liverpool, once more flags flew at half-mast and again ninety-six bells tolled. The clock at town hall stopped at 3.06 p.m. On the M62, traffic signs showed the words 'Never Forgotten'. That night buildings all across the historic city were bathed in red light in solidarity with the families. At St. George's Hall ninety-six candlelit lanterns would glow illuminating a large banner, inscribed with the names of the ninety-six, hung between the tall pillars of the old building, reading simply 'Truth' and 'Justice'.

AMONG THE ORANGE GROVES

'I believe that in a great city, or even in a small city or a village, a great theatre is the outward and visible sign of an inward and probable culture'
— Laurence Olivier

Dry Spanish heat bakes the barren landscape as I drive further from Madrid. I'm headed for Castellon de la Plana, located between the eastern sea ports of Barcelona and Valencia, some four and a half hours away. My tired and aching eyes squint in the glaring afternoon sun after an undesirable 5 a.m. rise to catch the flight to Spain's capital. As always, I'm working out what can go wrong and tiredness only adds to an overall feeling of unease. Tonight brings Liverpool's biggest European tie for six years. Six years since another Spanish club, Atletico Madrid eliminated the Reds at this same semi-final stage. Following the drama of vanquishing reviled foes Man United and the emotional tsunami wherein Klopp and his warriors saw off our Dortmund soul-brothers, what is left in the tank? Now we face Villarreal.

Villarreal don't hold the same glamour as a United or Dortmund, even in Spain they are not an elite name. However, what this small club from the Valencian province lack in size and glitz, they make up for in spades, with cleverness and determination. Domestically they fill the role of the 'model club', run within budget, operated to a distinct plan, possessing of a unique identity. Villarreal as a city has just 50,000 inhabitants but every two weeks 25,000 of those fill the El Madrigal stadium. Formed in 1923, the Yellow Submarine, as they are affectionately known, only climbed to the top tier of Spanish football in 1998. Since then the Yellows have been a semi-permanent fixture at the elite level both at home and in Europe. Second and third place finishes in La Liga speak to their incredible rise, as do three European semi-finals. Incredibly, the small-town club reached the last four of the Champions League in 2006, only to lose 1–0 to Arsenal over two legs. They would also make two Europa League semi-finals, losing the first to provincial rivals Valencia in 2004 and the second to Porto in 2011. It hasn't all been plain sailing, though. Villarreal would be relegated in 2012 and then one month later, within 24 hours of his appointment, new manager Manolo Preciado died of a heart attack, aged fifty-four. Current manager, fifty-year-old Marcelino would take the helm and guide the Yellow Submarine back to the top flight. Today they lie in fourth place in La Liga, within sight of a return to the Champions League. This season, no team from outside of Spain has defeated a Spanish side in a knockout tie and remarkably Spanish sides have won forty-five from their last forty-eight ties in Europe against non-La Liga sides. Spanish football is the overwhelmingly dominant force on the European landscape. Liverpool need to treat Villarreal as if they are Dortmund, it's that simple.

Arriving in Castellon de la Plana, a feeling of tranquillity and of time slowing pervades. The rural landscape offers a mix of orange groves and low green shrubbery, broken by taller Van Gogh cypress trees. I need sleep and decide on a power nap after arriving at my hotel. When the Chemical Brothers wake me to the sound of *'Go'* at 7 p.m., it takes a few minutes to work out where I am and why. Then it comes to me, it's match night. Fifteen minutes later I cross the Mijares River that separates Castellon from Villarreal and park my rental on Avenue Castello, at the edge of town. That should be easy to remember, the road home. My phone rings and I answer the call from my son as I walk.

"What's the atmosphere like Dad?" he enquires

"Nothing yet, I've only just arrived. It's very quiet."

I keep walking towards the centre and pass the beautiful old church of St Pascal and the Basilica of Saint James. People are scarce, bar a few old ladies leaving prayer time. Maybe it's like that scene from the *Magnificent Seven* where all the town folk are hiding from the marauding invaders. When I reach Carrer Comte Albay, I hear the singing voices before I see the bodies. Songs of Spanish Reds of yore drift on the cool Mediterranean air, the rain having ceased, an evening chill now settling. Songs of Torres and Garcia and of how he drank sangria. Now I see some of the locals as they drift away home. This is where the life is.

More people pass, these all in yellow, walking in the opposite direction to me, towards the stadium. I turn another corner and I'm in the heart of it now, Plaça de la Vila. Hundreds of Liverpool fans fill the square, sitting and standing, flags draped from every possible surface, red and white all around. Across from the travelling hordes, a little café hides under the arches, wherein the locals watch, with a mix of fascination and bemusement, the antics of the foreigners as they reel off their anthology of songs and some local beer to boot. Near to me are a collection of young teenage girls who laugh and giggle as they gaze at the new arrivals. Behind them three old ladies chat to each other, I've no idea what they might be saying or thinking. Spain doesn't really do travelling away fans, so this is not a familiar sight. Inside I feel stirrings, the first awakening that a huge game awaits.

Further up at Plaça Major is the Town Hall. Over the entrance hangs a banner that reads, 'Vilareal, Ciutat d'acollida, per una Europa més solidária I en defensa dels drets humans – Villarreal, host city, for a Europe of solidarity and defence of human rights.' Next to the entrance sits a statue of King Jaume I of Aragon, who afforded the city its Royal-*Real* status in 1274 during his campaign to regain Muslim territories in the long and bloody Reconquista. I look from the crowned King to the banner and I wonder about humanity and how little it learns.

It's time for football. I walk along the narrow warren of cobbled streets flanked by tiled paths on either side and closed in by low rise apartment blocks. The buildings are typically Spanish, plastered wall finishes, old wooden doors, slatted window grills. From these city homes, the inhabitants of Villarreal emerge one by one. Fathers, sons, mothers, grandparents. All ages. All bedecked in yellow. The people of this small village live on its streets, they work and celebrate as families together and they all support the Submarine, young and old. On Calle Santa Anna a second floor window shows a display of yellow sunflowers complete with flags of Villarreal C.F. A clear sense of local pride pervades. The town, its people and its football club seem as one. Close to the ground, it is carnival central. I shuffle through the crowd and past the monument which depicts local farmers shifting a very large boulder, as they dig a well for water. To my right the stadium appears, El Madrigal, named in respect of this agricultural background.

I make my way under the south stand and come to Carrer Blasco Ibanez. The street is packed with hundreds of Villarreal fans waiting for their team to arrive. Police on horseback control the good-humoured hordes. Eventually the bus passes but the crowds don't part. Next comes an inflated yellow submarine, held aloft by reverent fans and trailed by two dancing brass bands. I speak to an old man next to me who is visibly moved by the celebration unfolding before him. 'Fiesta' he says to me with the thumbs up sign. I agree and shake his hand before I follow the crowds along the side of the stadium.

After the most rigorous body search I've ever experienced, I scale the many flights of concrete steps that lead to the away seats. The stadium is an even height rectangular box, except at the North Stand, where atop the box sits a further tier of 2,000 near vertical seats that rise into the sky. These seats are for the away fans, separated from the rest of the stadium by a heavy-duty glass wall, itself topped by a wire mesh that stretches all the way to the roof above. No messing here. From this elevation, we are afforded views out across the town, which rests five kilometres inland from the Mediterranean. To my right smoke rises from the stacks of the Pamesa Ceramica plant. Where once, orange groves and agriculture were the primary employers, now it is the ceramics industry. Fernando Roig, billionaire owner of Villarreal C.F. also owns Pamesa, a €450 million turnover business and sponsor of the Yellow Submarine. I wonder for how long you can buck the trend and my mind wanders to the glory days enjoyed by Parma of Italy, who now sadly nestle in the Italian fourth division after financial mismanagement. I hope the hands of Senor Roig prove more able and secure.

A rousing rendition of Yellow Submarine greets the teams as they take to the pitch. To see this Spanish side adopt the Beatles tune as their anthem and hear it sung with such passion feels, if a little surreal, completely uplifting. The Liverpool fans join the party and sing along too. El Madrigal is an ocean of yellow scarves held aloft, brighter than the Yellow Wall of Dortmund, just smaller.

Some rumblings of discontent are voiced among the travelling contingent when it is discovered that despite Origi being injured, fellow striker Sturridge remains amongst the substitutes. I think it's wise. Villarreal are a tight outfit, tough at the back and free scoring going forward. Why risk too much when it's only leg one of a two-leg tie? There's a saying in golf that goes, 'you can't win the tournament on day one, but you can certainly lose it'. For me Klopp is astute to adopt a little of that logic here. Speaking at his press conference he says, "We saw Villarreal five or six times. They defend in a very organised way, they are patient enough to wait for your mistakes, and then use the mistakes."

The game starts with both teams moving the ball sharply and with precision. Clyne collects a breaking ball on five minutes and feeds Lallana down the right wing. Lallana's cross into the Villarreal box is deflected and the ball breaks invitingly free near the penalty spot. Joe Allen gets to it first and fires a side footer towards goal, but into the gut of keeper Asenjo, who makes an easy save. A firmer strike to either side and it's the dream start for Liverpool, an away goal and the home crowd silenced. It's a chance you have to take in these big games, a golden opportunity spurned. On eleven minutes a quick free kick is lofted over the head of Liverpool left-back Moreno and Soldado, the former Tottenham Hotspur striker, runs onto the landing ball. He connects with a downward right volley and the ball flashes across Mignolet's goal and goes narrowly wide. It's a good response from the home team. Gradually the game settles into cat and mouse possession and it is clear that Villarreal are a cautious chess playing side. Deliberate, stealthy, cagey. Few further chances arrive before the break and at half-time, it's 0–0. So far, so good, I think, Klopp's guarded game plan is working.

At half-time Liverpool suffer another setback to the roster, when Coutinho, who has fallen sick, has to be replaced by Jordan Ibe. This explains a quiet display from our talisman. Now Liverpool are without five outfield starters and the strength of Klopp's management abilities are being tested to the full. Sturridge continues to sit restlessly on the bench as Liverpool continue with Plan A, to stifle and suffocate.

Both sides are cautious and the game drifts towards a goalless draw. Each has survived a scare or two and both are afraid to make a killer mistake. Late on, Mignolet makes a great stop from Bakumba. From the resultant corner kick, Liverpool head the ball clear and counter at speed. Moreno goes through on goal but he can only find the net via the advertising boards behind it.

We are into injury time but Liverpool still push forward. Lallana loses control of a Benteke headed pass and Villarreal take possession. Lallana is Liverpool's 'first press', the man that runs first to close the opposition down. He breaks and closes, but Villarreal's left-back plays the ball past him. Milner breaks next, but further slick Villarreal passing leaves him stranded too. Pina plays it forward to Lopez who is ten yards inside his own half. He flicks it over the advancing Moreno, who is now woefully out of position and lost in no man's land. Liverpool's Lucas rushes to help, but Lopez beats him too and now it's red lights flashing – Danger, Danger. Liverpool's defence is badly exposed with eight outfield players stranded behind the ball in the opposition's half. Bruno Soriano looks up and lofts a beautifully weighted pass over Kolo Touré's head and Suarez runs onto the free ball. He bears down on Liverpool's goal and Mignolet comes to meet him. With calm and poise Suarez plays the ball to his left, a slide-rule pass to the advancing Lopez, who has outrun the retreating Moreno. From seven yards out he can't miss and he doesn't, as he side-foots the ball home. Marcelino and the entire Villarreal bench run onto the pitch in celebration and from our elevated position they resemble a swarm of manic, swirling bees. The stadium has gone bonkers and I can't remember when I've seen such wild celebration during a game. Klopp's words of yesterday come to haunt – "they are patient enough to wait for your mistakes, and then use the mistakes," – and I feel nauseous, as if the wind has been knocked from me. The final whistle blows. Sucker punch.

The players and staff come to the away end, heads bowed, disconsolate. They receive our sympathetic applause and trudge away. Before he leaves the pitch, Klopp turns again, looking up to the dimly lit section. He swirls a clenched fist above his head, two, maybe three times. His message is clear. We are still in this, keep believing. In a post-match interview, he is unbreakable, unequivocal.

"Half time," he says frostily.

As we leave the stadium the Liverpool fans sing *'Don't worry about a thing'* from Bob Marley's *'Three Little Birds'* and it helps lifts the mood somewhat. Yet I find it hard not to worry, or to shake the horrible feeling you get when something you want was within your grasp and you let it flit away, needlessly. Liverpool may not have deserved to win this one, but then neither did Villarreal, it was a 0–0 all the way. Until it wasn't.

I know Klopp wants us to remember his clenched fist wave and not the Villarreal goal and wild celebrations, but I am only human. It will be a long journey home and an even longer wait until the second leg a week from now.

Back in the dejected Liverpool dressing room, still in the lair of the noisy celebrating victor, Klopp is rallying his troops. The fight back has started. "The manager told us: 'do not worry, be disappointed for five minutes but no longer – wait until we get them back home'," says Lallana. "He told us that we have got the fans and then he said: 'we will make it another magical night next week'."

Half time indeed.

THE GREATEST VICTORY

'This land of my fathers is dear to me. Land of poets and singers, and people of stature.' — Land of my Fathers, Welsh National Anthem

Wales gets more rainfall than most places in the United Kingdom with its westerly geography and its valley and mountain topography. As we walk north from the city of Swansea (Abertawe in Welsh – 'mouth of the Tawe') and out towards the Liberty Stadium, the rain falls incessantly. It's that misty, fine rain that wets you through and through. Above there is no sunshine, no sky even, just a heavy grey blanket that hangs so low it seems almost touchable. At the top of Neath Road we turn right along the steamy sodden hedgerow that smells of wet and country life. Across from us, Swansea City's Liberty Stadium comes into view. On first gaze it disappoints, its façade resembling a conventional office building with each of the three storeys lined by neat rows of small windows. Here it is not alone, much of Swansea's architecture is uninspiring. The three night German Blitz in February 1941 decimated most of the city and what has replaced the old town is functional and lacklustre. Walking among the blitzed ruins in 1941, Dylan Thomas, maybe the greatest Welsh poet and a native of Swansea, would comment, "Our Swansea has died". Dylan saw both the beauty and the less than beautiful in his home town – "an ugly, lovely town… crawling, sprawling… by the side of a long and splendid curving shore". In his radio play *Return Journey* he describes the changes wrought upon the city by the savagery of the bombings. "It was a cold, white day on High Street, and there was nothing to stop the wind slicing up from the docks, for where the squat and tall shops had shielded the town from the sea, lay their blitzed, flat graves, marbled with snow and headstoned with fences. Dogs, delicate as cats on water as though they had gloves on their paws, padded over the vanished buildings."

The Welsh are proud of their culture and particularly their unique language, yet they do not actively seek independence, unlike their Celtic brother Scotland. Wales' relationship with England is a little dichotomous, on one hand their cultural and ethnic differences seem huge, Wales revelling in being different to their border cousins, yet on the other they have assimilated with relative placidity into the life of a broader United Kingdom, with England as the totem leader. In a 1979 referendum, 80 per cent of the population voted No to having its own Political Assembly away from London rule. Yet there are significant differences between the Welsh and the English, as attendance at any sporting occasion between the two in Rugby or Soccer will bear testimony. The legend of the Red Dragon of Wales finds its roots in this very rivalry. The Red Dragon featured in one of the oldest pieces of literature in Europe, the collection of Welsh myths written and collected under the title the Mabinogion. In these tales, the Red Dragon was released from captivity and vanquished the White Dragon of Saxon England. When Henry VII, head of the house of Tudor, and his army marched north from Wales to confront the hunchback king Richard III at the Battle of Bosworth in 1485, they carried flags displaying the Red Dragon of Wales standing proudly against a backdrop of green and white representing the house of Tudor. This image of the dragon sitting to the forefront of two horizontal green and white halves would become the Welsh flag that we know today.

If Welsh identity seems somewhat ambiguous to some, well then so too is their football. The country's first love is Rugby Union, and not until 1991 did a national Welsh Premier League come into existence. It's not surprising therefore that the two largest Welsh football clubs, Cardiff City and Swansea City play in the English leagues.

Liverpool legend John Toshack didn't just play under Shankly and Paisley, he absorbed their techniques; their knowledge. In 1978, he grabbed an opportunity to return to his native Wales and become player-manager of Swansea City. Swansea were marooned in the Fourth Division and had average attendances of no more than 2,000. Miraculously, Toshack led the Swans all the way to the First Division for the first time in the club's history, following three promotions in four years. Shankly remarked, "John Toshack has done a remarkable job at Swansea. He's taken a team from the Fourth to the First Division. Turned 2,000 gates into full houses. What he's done is miraculous." When asked had he spoken to Toshack about management, Shankly would reply, "Yes, we've been in touch constantly." Toshack revered the man he called 'Boss'. Only one day after Shankly's funeral in 1981, with his Swansea team lined up on the pitch at Anfield ready to play Liverpool in the League, Toshack would remove his tracksuit top to reveal his old red Liverpool shirt underneath. A wonderful mark of respect and honour to the great man from a grateful pupil.

For Swansea, the First Division dream didn't last and the decline that followed was dramatic. Relegated in both 1983 and 1984, Swansea City were formally wound up on December 20th 1985. They had reached the point of no return. At the gates of oblivion, a group of directors put together a rescue package and permission was granted for the club to continue its fixtures. For twelve months the future of the club hung in the balance and, unable to sign or borrow new players, Swansea were relegated to Division Four in 1986. However, the High Court finally approved the new board's salvage plan and the club survived. By 2005, there were new owners and new optimism as 'the Swans' prepared to leave their home of more than ninety years, the Vetch Field (Vetch meaning a cabbage-like plant used for cow feed), to move into the new purpose-built Liberty Stadium. The move from the Vetch was completed in style, with the club securing promotion to League One. Further progress in 2007/08 saw the club promoted, as Champions, to the Championship.

Swansea's nickname is 'the Jacks' and derives from a dog named Swansea Jack. Jack was a black retriever who lived in the North Dock / River Tawe area of the city with his master, William Thomas. In 1936, he won the *Star* newspaper's 'Bravest Dog of the Year' award. For good reason too, legend has it, that in Jack's lifetime he saved twenty-seven people from a wet demise on the river's bed. In May 2011, 40,000 'Jacks' saw Swansea, under the managerial guidance of Brendan Rodgers, beat Reading 4–2 in the Championship Play Off Final at Wembley to return to the top flight for the first time in thirty years. Then in February 2013, Swansea won its first major trophy, the League Cup under new manager Michael Laudrup. An incredible turnaround had been achieved. The Jacks had never had it so good.

It's been a week of high emotion on Merseyside, where a city stood shoulder to shoulder, united, as the verdict of the two-year Hillsborough Inquest was released and Liverpool fans and their families were fully and finally vindicated. Today, Swansea City show their class. They present Liverpool with a bouquet of red flowers that spells out ninety-six. It is greeted by appreciative applause from the travelling contingent, which is matched respectfully by the home fans. The bouquet is placed facing the Liverpool fans behind the away goal.

The match day program is the only one in the League to feature two languages, Welsh and English. 'Croeso I Stadiwm Liberty' is printed on the cover page 'Welcome to the Liberty Stadium'. Inside is the following tribute; *"We Salute You. Swansea City Football Club pays tribute, respect and love to the Hillsborough families, whose twenty-seven-year fight for justice has finally delivered The Truth. Your display of courage, strength and spirit through such heart-breaking times has been truly heroic. Vindication is irrefutable and the whole world knows it. We Salute You. Fighters for Justice, for the greatest victory in the history of the greatest game and remember the ninety-six loved ones who tragically and unlawfully lost their lives. You will always be remembered. RIP the ninety-six."*

These words remind me of what I already know to be true. The vast majority of people that follow this fantastic game, both here and all around the globe, are wonderful, warm and passionate people. It can't be repeated enough but somehow this spirit of positivity and love for each other and the game itself needs to be tapped more often. It is all of our duties to try and do so. Once more I hear the voice of Lennon and I nod to myself in agreement.

The Swansea game comes sandwiched between the two legs of the Europa Semi Final versus Villarreal, and as such, it's hard to muster much enthusiasm, beyond enjoying a nice, albeit very wet, weekend trip to the land of song. Put clearly, I am not up for this game at all. A twelve noon kick-off doesn't help. My son moans that he's soaked and I remind him that he is in Wales, it goes with the territory. I have no doubt that Klopp will rest many key players with an eye to Thursday evening and the Euro return leg. When the team sheet is announced, it transpires that the Liverpool team will become the youngest starting eleven in Premier League history with an average age of just over twenty-three years.

For the record the line-up is as follows: Ward, Smith, Lovren, Skrtel, Clyne, Ibe, Chirivella, Stewart, Ojo, Coutinho, Sturridge.

The Liverpool team don't just look young, they play young. They are last to every loose ball, slow to react, timid in the tackle. Ball possession is non-existent with nearly every Liverpool player either dwelling too long or giving it away too easily. By half-time the Reds have hardly strayed from their own half and Swansea lead comfortably 2–0. It could have been more. Liverpool's Welsh goalkeeper, Ward, has been our best player. It's cold now as well as wet. Liverpool finish the game with ten men after Brad Smith is sent off, and by full-time Swansea have recorded as effortless and easy a 3–1 victory against Liverpool FC as they are ever likely to manage.

The highlight of the game for Liverpool arrived on twenty-seven minutes when the entire stadium stood and applauded as a message of support to the families of Hillsborough filled the large screens positioned at both ends of the ground. The applause rang loud and long for a fight for justice that took an equivalent number of years.

Despite the thumping, we've enjoyed this visit to Wales. Great stadium. Great fans. Great singing from those sing-song Welsh vocal cords. Not for the first time the words of Dylan Thomas come to mind. The poet who died at just thirty nine years old, his tender age still much older than so many of the ninety-six. The poet who wrote his words to be revered and spoken aloud, words that resonate and move us still.

'And death shall have no dominion. Dead men naked they shall be one
With the man in the wind and the west moon;
When their bones are picked clean and the clean bones gone,
They shall have stars at elbow and foot; though they go mad they shall be
sane, Though they sink through the sea they shall rise again;
Though lovers be lost love shall not;
And death shall have no dominion…'

FAMILY

'In every conceivable manner, family is the link to our past, bridge to our future.' — Alex Haley, novelist

I wake on match morning and almost immediately I can see it, that goal, the goal that has haunted me for a week. I can't imagine what it must have felt like to the players. To have performed so professionally, to have defended so well and then, defeat. One moment of madness. A moment of madness that might end up eclipsing the unforgettable nights that preceded it, beating United 2–0 when it should have been more, the miracle that was Dortmund at Anfield. I can still see Marcelino sprinting twenty yards onto the pitch to wheel wildly in celebration, arms outstretched, manic grin flashing. Fair play to Villarreal, but you shouldn't enter the field of play, never mind twenty yards in. No wonder a rueful Klopp had looked on, bemused, a wry smile appearing on his face. He might even have seen a little of himself in the exuberance.

At times like these, a team needs a leader to take the bull by the horns. Klopp is that leader. Speaking after the defeat, the pain and frustration of the loss still fresh and visibly etched on his face, he stood firm, resolute. "It is 1–0, but it is only the first leg and they have to come to Anfield, where we know how strong we are. This race is not over. We showed against Dortmund we can respond. We know we can do it, we just need to believe."

Nearly a week later, on the eve of the return leg, Klopp is asked whether Villarreal's celebrations were excessive, did they feel the tie was already over. "You are right," he replied. "My first thoughts after they scored the goal, when I saw all of them celebrating, was; 'Sorry to say, but you have to come to Anfield'."

So, another huge occasion awaits and Klopp summarises the mood perfectly – "To be honest it's one of these things in life, you cannot buy feelings like this, it is most special. That's the main thing of football, these moments when you really know we are all together. I don't want to make it too big to be honest, it's only football I know, but it is a moment for the whole of the Liverpool world and all the fans around the world. If we have a television, we will watch it on television, if we have no ticket, we will listen on the radio. If we have no radio, we will follow it on the Internet. That's how it is. We will do everything for all of us. Let's do something special."

Before the first leg, Liverpool's players were falling like swatted flies. Now, at last, some good news. The dynamo Emre Can is fit. "I put in a lot of work, I didn't have one day off in three weeks," he explains. "Every day I was at Melwood for seven or eight hours, doing everything I could to get fit for this game. I am so happy that I can play. The manager spoke with me and asked me if I was fit. I told him I was ready."

Villarreal are hopeful of breaking their semi-final duck, but they know the job isn't fully done. Their captain Bruno Soriano comments, "I don't know that we are owed a final, but we have that ambition and we really want to play in one." Statistics suggest that Villarreal may have to wait though. This tie is Liverpool's seventeenth European semi-final, the Reds reaching eleven of those finals, winning eight. Of those seventeen semi-finals, nine saw the second leg played at Anfield. Liverpool won eight and drew one of those nine games, all nine results leading the Reds to a final.

Liverpool's players warm up in front of the Kop and again the stand is full early, flags flying, songs sung. It's the first home game for Liverpool since the verdict was released from the Hillsborough inquest. In memory of the departed, and for those that helped the families in their struggle for justice, the fans hold aloft cards that together form a red and white mosaic covering three sides of the stadium. To this backdrop, the famous anthem is given one of its finest and loudest renditions. The Mosaic reads – '96. The Greatest Football Family'. The programme notes include the following message:

'THE GREATEST FOOTBALL FAMILY. In this most extraordinary of seasons the families of the 96 Liverpool FC supporters who died at Hillsborough, along with those who survived, have made

the most remarkable achievement. After 27 years, against all the odds, their courage, resilience and above all love never wavered, and last week the Hillsborough Inquests returned a determination of unlawful killing of the 96 on 15 April 1989. The city of Liverpool and the football family have been overwhelmed by the subsequent response, at home and abroad, and wishes to thank everyone – particularly the great family of Liverpool FC fans, and also the staff and supporters of Everton FC – for their compassion and solidarity in recent times and over these long years. Above all it is the families of the 96 to whom this city owes the greatest debt. Their conduct throughout this prolonged process has been truly inspirational, and for that we should all feel extremely proud. You'll Never Walk Alone."

Klopp has changed his team. Needing goals, Sturridge has been introduced upfront. Can is back in midfield and Allen and Lucas drop to the bench. It's an attacking line up, with Firmino, Coutinho and Lallana all on the pitch. As Klopp said, "if you are going to lose in a semi-final 'then go out kicking and screaming'."

Liverpool attack from the off and in front of a fervent Anfield, Villarreal are no match for the swarming Reds as they hunt and pillage. At full-time the Reds have won 3–0 with goals from Sturridge, Lallana and an own goal from Bruno. After only seven months in the job Klopp has steered his team to a European Final. In the other semi-final Sevilla see off Shakhtar Donetsk and it is the reigning Champions who Liverpool will face on May 18th in Basel, Switzerland.

Post-game, Klopp is ecstatic and can't praise his team enough for propelling him back into the global limelight. "I have not the right words for this performance so maybe you can find a few. It was nice to watch, be part of it, the whole performance from 6.45 when we drove through the road again. The first half-hour was power, the will was obvious, but for the fifteen minutes when we lost patience. The second-half we were back to the plan. We were very emotional plus very smart and scored some wonderful goals."

Sturridge spoke of harnessing the power of the home crowd. "It was about soaking up the atmosphere and putting on a performance." David Maddock of the *Mirror* wrote of the Liverpool fans, "*Yes, yes, I know it's a cliché, but really, you had to be there to understand just how intimidating, how emotional, how goddam scary they can be*." A twelfth European final awaited.

Klopp had been right, it hadn't been over and it still wasn't. One final journey remained.

THE BLACK COUNTRY

'It was my father who taught us that an immigrant must work twice as hard as anybody else, that he must never give up' — Zinedine Zidane

It's the last weekend of the season and a trip to West Bromwich Albion sees Liverpool conclude their Premier League campaign, not far from where it started way back in August with the revenge mission to Stoke. Prior to 1974, Stoke-on-Trent and West Bromwich both resided within the county of Staffordshire. Now West Bromwich sits in the new county of West Midlands. Less than ten kilometres to its east, sits the major city of Birmingham. However, West Bromwich is closer in ties to the collection of small towns that sit to its west and north; Dudley, Smethwick, Tipton, Wednesbury, Walsall, Sandwell and Wolverhampton. These towns and lands form what is collectively known as the Black Country.

The expression 'Black Country' dates from the mid-nineteenth century when used as a term to describe land that held a thirty-foot deep seam of coal. In many parts the seam, the thickest in Britain, would rise from the ground, black coal deposits in clear sight. With the area a hotbed of industry during the Industrial Revolution the term also described the blanket of soot which seemed to cover the land, emitted from the collieries, the coking plants, the iron foundries and the steel mills. A breath of fresh air would have been hard to find.

Elihu Burritt was appointed United States Consul in Birmingham by Abraham Lincoln in 1864, and in his book *Walks in the Black Country* he spoke of the region being, '*black by day and red by night*'. An 1851 guidebook for the London and North Western Railway included this description – "*In this Black Country, including West Bromwich, Dudley, Darlaston, Bilston, Wolverhampton and several minor villages, a perpetual twilight reigns during the day, and during the night fires on all sides light up the dark landscape with a fiery glow. The pleasant green of pastures is almost unknown, the streams, in which no fishes swim, are black and unwholesome; the natural dead flat is often broken by high hills of cinders and spoil from the mines; the few trees are stunted and blasted; no birds are to be seen, except a few smoky sparrows; and for miles on miles a black waste spreads around, where furnaces continually smoke, steam engines thud and hiss, and long chains clank, while blind gin horses walk their doleful round. From time to time you pass a cluster of deserted roofless cottages of dingiest brick, half swallowed up in sinking pits or inclining to every point of the compass, while the timbers point up like the ribs of a half-decayed corpse."* It seems that tourism wasn't high on the list of local industries.

As my son and I travel the region, these descriptions seem outlandish. Long gone are the thriving coal and iron works, the soot shrouded labourers, the stack chimneys rising into the smog. Today we are surrounded by a rural green landscape, which nestles tranquilly below a clear blue sky. The closest we can get to experience the days of smoke and smog, involves a visit to the Black Country Living Museum in Dudley. Here we find an entire 1850s landscape recreated meticulously from original buildings and works, set over twenty-six acres, including previously used mineshafts, coal works, metal work plants and an entire village including shops and dwellings. If strolling through the Forum transports you back to the days of the Roman Empire, then this museum does likewise for the Industrial Revolution.

For lunch, we treat ourselves to cod and chips cooked in beef dripping from the on-site Hobb's 1930s fish and chip shop. The Black Country is well known for its unique dialects, accents and the continued use of a variation of ould English vocabulary. We are told by our server that our food is 'Bostin Fittle' (smashing food) and she is right, it is truly Bostin. As we devour our indulgent lunch, I tell my son how, in the early 1900s the nearby village of Netherton was the anchor capital of the world and how a local company, Noah Hingley and Son, which employed over 3,000 men, built the then largest ever anchor for the *RMS Titanic*. A single piece of steel weighing five tonnes was super-heated until red hot, to form the anchor's six-metre long shaft. The ten tonne pointed flukes which dig into the seabed were cast in a giant mould with the entire anchor forming sixteen tonnes of high-grade steel. This was then attached to 603 metres of steel chain. Titanic indeed.

West Bromwich (named to avoid confusion with the town of Castle Bromwich which lies to the East of Birmingham) houses a population of 75,000 people. Today this population is growing, as is the population of many of the Black Country towns as they creak under the wave of migration that floods through Britain and Europe. Indeed immigration has become the key vote driver and hottest topic of the soon to be held referendum that will decide if Britain stays in the European Union or leaves. If Britain decides to exit (Brexit as the event has been coined) then the border walls will rise and the immigrant surge will dissipate, so goes the logic anyway. The local *Express and Star* newspaper releases the findings of its own poll – "*In April's online poll, more than 10,000 readers took part, with 76 per cent indicating a preference for leave and just 22 per cent saying they wanted Britain to continue as a member of the union.*" These figures fly in the face of the majority of national polls, which put the remain side up by ten points as the referendum debate enters the final straight. The findings from the *Express & Star* polls give credence to claims that parts of the Black Country and Staffordshire are some of the most Eurosceptic areas in the country.

Previously the same newspaper had reported how more than 56,000 immigrants had registered to work in The Black Country in the six years from 2008–14. In 2014, the region saw a rise of 39 per cent in applicants versus a national average of 26 per cent. In many areas that are already unemployment blackspots, the paper wondered how local services and jobs could sustain the influx. Wolverhampton Councillor, Wendy Thompson, complained, "How do we build communities when we have people coming in and out all the time? Not many migrants that come to Wolverhampton are going to walk straight into a job."

This is not the first time that the Black Country has been at the heart of a British debate on immigration and race. In 1968 Enoch Powell, the then Conservative Member of Parliament for Wolverhampton South West, gave what became known as his 'Rivers of Blood' speech in Birmingham, in which he criticized proposed Commonwealth immigration and anti-discrimination legislation. The infamous speech derived its title from its reference to a line from Virgil's *Aeneid* – "As I look ahead, I am filled with foreboding; like the Roman, I seem to see 'the River Tiber foaming with much blood'." The speech caused a political storm, making Powell one of the most talked about and divisive politicians in the country, and leading to his immediate dismissal from the Shadow Cabinet by Conservative Party leader Edward Heath.

However, the Black Country is not the epicentre, nor the beginning or end of this debate, one which will rage on for as long as borders exist. Brexit is the conversation that fills the news-sheets and airwaves of Britain, with the vote less than two months away. Across the water in the United States, the same debate rages as businessman Donald Trump campaigns in the Republican Primaries. He proposes building a long and high wall along the US/Mexican border, having described Mexican immigrants as criminals and rapists. Incredibly Trump's ratings and number of followers have soared and it is not inconceivable that he could succeed Barack Obama, the first black president of America, he himself the son of immigrants. How regression can follow progress so quickly.

West Bromwich Albion go by the nickname 'the Throstles', the throstle being a songbird of the thrush family, many of which were to be found among the hawthorn bushes which populated the rural countryside where the stadium was built in 1900 and from which it derived its name. Since then 'The Hawthorns' has seen rebuild, facelift and refurbishment. Today, it is an impressive 27,000 all-seater facility. Like many teams, West Brom have more than one nickname. They are also known as 'the Baggies'. The story goes that this name derived from the loose 'baggy' clothing that local workers would wear in the coal mines and iron mills as they toiled in the sweltering heat. On match day they would head straight from the workplace to the stadium and, after a time, the supporters came to be described after their working apparel. West Brom, like their near neighbours Aston Villa, Wolverhampton Wanderers and Stoke City, were all founding members of the very first English League in 1888. It seems that this region did not only help revolutionise global industry during the Industrial Revolution but it also laid the foundations for the global business that is football in the twenty-first century.

Yet sadly, just as the local economy dwindled in a post-industrial world, similarly these Black Country and West Midlands teams have all seen better days. At least West Brom will play Premier League football in 2017, but their heyday is long in the past. A League title win in 1920, now nearly one hundred years ago, was their proudest day. One League Cup and five FA Cups have also been won, but the last major trophy celebrated was in 1968, when Jeff Astle scored the only goal to see the Baggies beat Everton at Wembley in the FA Cup Final.

Under manager Tony Pulis, West Brom play a tough no-nonsense style of football. This pragmatic approach provides a fighter's chance of avoiding relegation. Many points can be collected by being stubborn and hard to beat. Yet on the downside, it's not pretty and it's not expansive enough to make the fans dream of ever lifting trophies again. West Brom don't seem to be as ambitious as similar size clubs such as Southampton, Crystal Palace or of course, Leicester. Maybe that's a location issue, I'm not sure. Maybe they are too conservative or wise to gamble. It's a conundrum for sure, damned if you do, damned if you don't. WBA's chairman, Jeremy Peace, writes in the match day programme – *"Leicester City have written the football story of the season and they have effectively challenged all like-sized clubs to match their performance on and off the pitch."* What road this Black Country club decide to travel will be intriguing to watch.

The 3 p.m. kick-off approaches for the last league game of the season and again, to be honest, there is nothing much to play for. Since the Swansea trip, Liverpool finished their home league fixtures with a 2–0 win versus Watford followed three days later by a 1–1 draw against Chelsea. Even a win today at the Hawthorns will not secure automatic qualification to the Europa League for next season, with the Reds needing various unlikely results and scenarios to go their way elsewhere. West Brom sit in fifteenth place, eight points clear of the relegation zone so they are packed and nearly ready for their summer break. It's last day of the season weather too – warm, sunny and muggy. The atmosphere inside the stadium is languid and easy-going, betraying a distinct lack of tension. This is the proverbial dead rubber.

In the programme, WBA chairman Jeremy Peace greets the visitors. *"We will be honouring a pledge we made a fortnight ago when, in the wake of the Hillsborough inquest verdicts, Premier League clubs came together to show the unity of the wider football family with the victims and their families of that terrible, terrible day. Albion and Liverpool have a rivalry which dates back to 1894 since when we have contested nearly 150 games. For a few moments this afternoon we will be as one and remember the context Hillsborough makes of our daily struggles.*"

Prior to kick-off, two West Brom players walk to the away end with a floral wreath in honour of the ninety-six dead. One is former Liverpool player Rickie Lambert and the other is former Man United centre-half Johnny Evans. Both are very warmly greeted. In addition to this, WBA have replaced ninety-six blue seats (West Brom play in blue and white vertical stripes) in the away-end with red seats. With a backdrop of blue, the new red seats spell out the number ninety-six. On each seat is a silver plate upon which are inscribed the badges of Albion and Liverpool and the name of one of those that was lost. These seats remain unsold and vacant for today's game. At the end of the row where my son and I are located, is the seat left vacant for James Gary Aspinall. At the Hillsborough Inquest, James's brother David read a pen portrait of his brother. It included these words –

"Growing up, I remember our 'Ja' doing the usual boys' things that included playing football, cricket and bike riding, although football was his real passion. This love for football came about on 2 September, 1978 when James attended his first ever football match at Anfield with Dad. Liverpool went on to record an impressive 7-0 win against Tottenham Hotspur and this left an indelible mark on James for all things LFC... at Hillsborough, Dad could only watch from the side pen of the Leppings Lane terrace as his eldest son's future disappeared in such harrowing circumstances, powerless to help his son when it was most needed. Dad has never attended a football match since that day. If there was one word to describe our Ja, it would be 'selfless'. His love for his family always shone through, especially towards his two younger sisters Kerry and Louise, whom he idolised. They still have the last gifts that James bought them. A few weeks before Hillsborough, James also bought his dad a guitar from one of his first pay packets in his new job and this guitar still gives Dad much comfort each time he plays a tune... James has been carried in our hearts every day for the past 25 years. He will always be loved for who he was and what he meant to each and every one of his family."

This is just a part of one of ninety-six stories that will always be remembered. Margaret Aspinall, mother of James and David, would act as Chair of the Hillsborough Family Support Group and for 27 years would lead the fight for Justice.

***

Today's game lives up to the billing, it's pedestrian. After ninety minutes we are all happy to hear the final whistle of what was a turgid and irrelevant affair. The record books will record a 1–1 draw.

In a season where Liverpool used thirty-four players, four more than in any previous campaign, they finish in an uninspiring eighth position. In any other year that would spell disaster with heads rolling, but not this year. This year has been about next year and then the one after. It's been about Mr Klopp and his ever-improving impersonation of one Bill Shankly. Klopp is not Shankly, and nor does he want to be, he is in every way his own man. Yet there are remarkable similarities between the two. Shankly had an ability to lift and inspire a team, a fan base, a city. Klopp too is rekindling the fires, the enthusiasm and the belief. It's early days, but very exciting ones.

Klopp and his players congregate in front of the away end and thank the Reds fans for their season-long support. The mood is buoyant and we lustily serenade our team with one of our European songs in anticipation of the final that awaits;

'Bring on your Internazionale, bring on your Roma by the score, Barcelona, Real Madrid, who the hell you tryna kid, Liverpool are the team that we adore'.

Rolling Stone magazine voted Led Zeppelin's 'Stairway to Heaven', written by West Bromwich native Robert Plant and lead Guitarist Jimmy Page, as the thirty-first greatest song of all time. Will it be Liverpool or Sevilla who make the heavenly footballing ascent in Basel? Soon we will know. The big event is now just three days away. There is nothing else that needs doing now, no more dead rubbers to count down. The League campaign may have ended, but this season is far from over.

THE EIGHTH WONDER OF THE WORLD

'Miracles are not contrary to nature, but only contrary to what we know about nature.' – Augustine of Hippo

And so it came to pass. A true bona-fide miracle occurred right before our eyes. Nobody can say it didn't happen, it did. It is now written in the annals of history. Leicester City won the 2015/16 Premier League title. In the end it was a landslide, ten points separated the Foxes from the pack. They were not for catching.

It was the biggest football story of this century, and of the last century, and the one before that too. It was maybe the biggest story in the history of sport. We may not fully realise how incredible the achievement was, not yet. Of course, there have been similar stories, Nottingham Forest, the last first-time winners, did it in 1978. Back then though, there wasn't the financial imbalance that exists today. For Leicester to win with a squad that equalled the cost of one discarded loan player from either Chelsea or City beggars belief. To win the league with terrible possession and passing statistics does too. But what Leicester did have, a strong spine and backbone, will get you most places. An excellent goalkeeper in Schmeichel. Two towering centre-halves in Huth and captain, Morgan. The beast, Kante, in the middle of the park and up front the electric pace and incredible finishing of Jamie Vardy. Throw in Mahrez to add a bit of guile and pizazz. Ride the luck of suffering nearly zero injuries and what do you get? Champions!

Yet Leicester did manage to hide in the eye of a perfect storm that was obliterating all competitors. Manchester City would announce in January that they were changing manager at the end of the season and, in doing so, effectively put paid to their title hopes. Mourinho's return to

Chelsea brought divisive in-house squabbling and the team turned on a manager beloved of the fans. With civil war raging the Champions would slide to tenth place and mid-table obscurity. Arsenal did what Arsenal have done for a decade now, flattered to deceive. The Gunners would never contest for the title, but still end up in second place. Spurs would be for a long time the only real challengers to Leicester but would fall away near the end, a 2–2 draw at Stamford Bridge proving their undoing. This was no 'Spursy' though, more a case of time expiring before they could hunt the Foxes down. Under manager Pochettino, a powerful force is rising and the Argentinian's new version of the Hotspurs looks like having more steel than any Spurs team in the last fifty years. A title might wash up at White Hart Lane sooner rather than later. Under Van Gaal, United stuttered and stalled, the players never quite understanding the Dutchman's dour tactical conundrums, with a fifth-place spot the resulting outcome. Success would arrive in the FA Cup with victory over Crystal Palace. It wouldn't be enough though for the Dutchman to keep his job. And as for Liverpool, well a poor start, a new manager and a new playing style resulted in a campaign that constantly faltered in the League. Eighth place would be the culmination of a year in transition.

Yet none of this should take away from Leicester's feat. Without the distractions of Europe or lengthy cup campaigns, the Foxes raided the coop and put all their eggs into one basket, the title chase. Key players stayed fit and displayed champagne form, dazzling the stadia of England, as Leicester blew through in a whirlwind of counter attacking, fast paced football. Manager, Ranieri, proved a joy, constantly smiling and belittling his own mastery. Since the 2009/10 season the Champions of England had retained on average 57.5 per cent possession. In 2015/16 Leicester managed only 44.8 per cent, the third lowest in the league. Put simply, they won the league by letting the other teams have the ball. It's not surprising that they rarely had possession, as at 69.3 per cent, their pass completion rate was the lowest in the Premier league and the fifth lowest of any team in the top tier of Europe's top five leagues. So much achieved, with so little.

A miracle had been performed and the League crown secured by the wiliest of all the foxes, Claudio Ranieri, but not in a way that we had seen before, nor most likely one that we will ever see again. All hail the Champions!

2015/16 Premier League

Final Standings

		GP	W	D	L	GF	GA	GD	PTS
1	Leicester City	38	23	12	3	68	36	32	81
2	Arsenal	38	20	11	7	65	36	29	71
3	Tottenham	38	19	13	6	69	35	34	70
4	Man City	38	19	9	10	71	41	30	66
5	Man United	38	19	9	10	49	35	14	66
6	Southampton	38	18	9	11	59	41	18	63
7	West Ham	38	16	14	8	65	51	14	62
8	**Liverpool**	**38**	**16**	**12**	**10**	**63**	**50**	**13**	**60**
9	Stoke City	38	14	9	15	41	55	-14	51
10	Chelsea	38	12	14	12	59	53	6	50
11	Everton	38	11	14	13	59	55	4	47
12	Swansea City	38	12	11	15	42	52	-10	47
13	Watford	38	12	9	17	40	50	-10	45
14	West Brom	38	10	13	15	34	48	-14	43
15	Crystal Palace	38	11	9	18	39	51	-12	42
16	Bournemouth	38	11	9	18	45	67	-22	42
17	Sunderland	38	9	12	17	48	62	-14	39
18	Newcastle	38	9	10	19	44	65	-21	37
19	Norwich City	38	9	7	22	39	67	-28	34
20	Aston Villa	38	3	8	27	27	76	-49	17

DESTINY

'Life has no meaning a priori… It is up to you to give it a meaning, and value is nothing but the meaning that you choose.' — Jean-Paul Sartre

Klopp's journey mirrors that of the Rhine, upstream from Mainz to Basel, the hard way. On the path to this final, signs have appeared, linked destinies, a sense of fate convening. A river runs through it. Was this always to be? In the centre of Basel, atop a high hill overlooking the murky Rhine below, stands Munster Cathedral, its two spires reaching to the heavens. Inside, we gaze at a tall granite tomb and its Latin inscription – Desiderius Erasmus Roterodamus. I explain to my son that he stands in the presence of greatness, albeit long-dead greatness.

Erasmus and the Humanist movement have a lot to be thanked for. Today, in an age where liberal western Europeans take free speech and autonomy of thought for granted, we can hardly imagine Europe any other way. But for a long period in history, free thought of any kind was frowned upon, particularly thought that questioned the powerful ruling bodies of Church and State. During these dark Middle Ages, incarceration, torture and even execution were common punishments for nonconformists. Life counted for little if you didn't abide by the rules. If you stood up for what you believed in, you might just lose your head. Alas, Erasmus's good friend Sir Thomas More proved the point.

In the early sixteenth century, Martin Luther's religious reformation was on the rise. Luther's principles were narrow, the Church and God ruled all men and their actions. Luther believed in predestiny, God governed and foresaw all outcomes. Man had no free will, no recourse to shape his own fate. Erasmus couldn't countenance that, this was not what his studies had taught him, nor his readings of the Bible. He believed in God, but also in man. Man could shape his own destiny, for good or bad, he had free will. Erasmus would become the founding father of Humanism, of free thought and speech. His work and the work of like-minded academics laid the foundation for the Renaissance, 'the Rebirth'. Da Vinci, Michelangelo, Copernicus, Galileo would all flourish in this new age of reason, culture and discovery.

'Destiny' is a peculiar concept, the belief that a predetermined map guides us to an already chosen destination. Some football men believe in destiny, Shankly did, saying, "I felt that somewhere along the line I was being guided. I believed I had a destiny." After one of many setbacks at Mainz, Klopp too felt he was being tested at times, directed even, "Yesterday I asked myself what it all means, and then I realised; someone has decided that it's necessary to show people that you can really get knocked down, once, twice, three, four, five times, and still get up again." If 'Destiny' exists, then someone, somewhere already knows who will win the 2016 Europa League Final. Probably a bookmaker. With Sevilla the bookie's favourites, that doesn't bode well for the Red masses that have engulfed picturesque Basel.

In 1987, the EU introduced the 'Erasmus' programme whereby students would travel to other countries to expand their knowledge of foreign cultures and ideas, much as Erasmus had wandered 500 years before. Long before the Erasmus programme sent students in search of their travel guides, football fans were traipsing back and forth across Europe discovering new exciting cities, cultures and languages and embracing the spirit of discovery. It was with the advent of the European Cup in 1955 that this football revolution began. Ever since, expeditions into Europe and the stories of these travels have long been the stuff of legend. Liverpool have acted as the English flagbearers to a continent, eleven finals reached, eight trophies won. Countless cities visited and loved. In Basel, the revolution story awaits its latest chapter.

The streets are busy with fans and it's still over twenty-four hours to kick-off. Reds fans seem to outnumber Sevilla by three or four to one. Most fans scheme their travel plans before they even know they have a ticket, hope springing eternal in the search for the golden papers. This time they will be harder to get than ever before. The ground, albeit perfectly formed and very atmospheric, is small. It holds only 37,500 people and in the build-up UEFA have been criticised heavily. Liverpool could have sold four times that number of seats alone. Sevilla only manage to sell 8,000 of their 10,000 allocation and the balance go back on resale and into the hands of Liverpool fans. It does little to quench the unsatisfied demand. Reds come from all corners to be in Basel. On ferry and train from Rotterdam. From Milan by car. From Germany and then over the border. We managed to book flights directly to Basel, arriving on the eve of the game, but we'll have to go home via Geneva which is three hours away by train. That's not too bad and thankfully we have the two slips of gold paper. Black market prices have reached £5,000 and more. Ours are hung around my neck in a 'money bag'. I'm thinking it's a bit over the top, but hey, it's a final, so safety first.

After a nice meal downtown, my son and I jump on one of the trams that traverse the old city to make our way home. We are tired and our beds are calling. We are staying near the ultra-modern exhibition and theatre area. Basel is compact and walkable and the trams make it easy to whizz around. It's been less than forty-eight hours, but here in Basel, West Bromwich and the Black Country seem like a different universe.

Game day arrives and, as ever, I wake up worried. I'm not the only one. Steven Gerrard says aloud what we are all dreading inside as he contemplates the match ahead, "Then there is the darker road, the one none of us who love Liverpool want to contemplate. It is a second final defeat in a matter of months, disrupting the feel-good factor achieved in securing that flight to Switzerland, undermining the meaning of all those notable wins over Man United, Borussia Dortmund and Villarreal. Not just another year without a trophy, but no European competition at all next season. That will have an impact on the quality of players Klopp can attract, the financial rewards for the club and the morale of the squad. Despite all the positives that would be taken from getting so far, there would be a hangover. There always is when you lose a game of this magnitude, but the difference between a memorable season and one that could take a long time to get over is immense." All or nothing might not do this game justice. It's all or less than nothing really, defeat signalling a step backwards again, a spear of doubt plunged into the heart of the renaissance.

Klopp is personally under scrutiny in the pre-game press conference, his poor record in finals is questioned. He's lost four on the bounce. I've rationalised this before. He's rarely had a team, if ever, that could enter into a final and say to themselves – 'We are favourites, we *should* win this game and we will find a way because we are better and we are good enough'. No, he's been manned with the opposite task, pitting the wits of the underdog against the bigger beast. This affair is much closer, but given their winning track record in this tournament, if I was a bookie I'd have Sevilla as favourite as does the clever money. Still, five out of five would be near unbearable, even for a man of Klopp's resolve and enthusiasm. Klopp prefers to look on the positives. "It is a very important stage, but we can do better. In any part of life, it feels wonderful to be a champion. It is a wonderful story to tell your grandchildren when you are old about being a Liverpool legend. How it feels to be a Liverpool legend, I have no idea, but it must be one of the best things you can feel in football. I would be really pleased for the boys if they can do it."

While the Sevilla manager, Unai Emery, is respectful and complimentary about Liverpool, he exudes inner confidence – "Liverpool are among the best ten teams in the world. They are pure football, real football, they have a great history – they have won five European Cups, won the UEFA Cup and leagues in England. This is an opportunity for us to play in a third final and win it to change history and to have our names recorded for ever and ever. We are winners, we are champions and we have the possibility to defend our title. Sevilla does not fail when we are really focused."

When asked about Liverpool fans outnumbering their Spanish counterparts Emery is ebullient – "We are not really worried by the fact there might be more Liverpool supporters in the stadium. Maybe more of them are here tomorrow, but it doesn't really matter. We know Sevilla fans regard the club as their second wife."

Once again, the stage has been set. 'Destiny' awaits.

FINAL

'I am the master of my fate and the captain of my destiny'
— Nelson Mandela

There are at least five Liverpool fans to each one of Sevilla on the streets of Basel. Most of those who have travelled will not make it to the game and will have to make do with the big screens in the city centre fan zones. It's a warm muggy day, the air heavy and moist. A quick scan of the skies tells me that the weather forecast may be right after all. Thunder and lightning and heavy downpours are expected. Above us gathers a dark sodden blanket waiting to break its load. Another sign – the same weather that prevailed in Dortmund in 2001 when Liverpool won their last UEFA Cup beating Alaves. As the rain is somehow holding off, I've convinced my son that walking to the St Jakob-Park stadium is the best option. That way, we'll be able to breathe in the atmosphere, enjoy the colour and the singing. However, by the time we reach Elisabethenanlage square we have to take shelter. The thunder which rolls and roars above us is soon accompanied by incessant vertical sheets of rain. We take cover in the small café bar on the green. Twenty minutes later, it seems safe to start walking again. We pass the Bahnhof SBB train station on our right and take Nauenstrasse and then Grosspeterstrasse out of town. The rain comes again, lighter this time, but with no cracks in the brooding dark sky, it's here to stay. After a police security check to make sure that only those with tickets continue, we walk along the rail-tracks, off limits for trains, and make our way east. The track walls are splashed with graffiti, slogans and rallying calls to FC Basel, who call St Jakob-Park home. The rain keeps falling. Bells ring from a small church situated beside the stadium. For whom do they toll?

Organisation at the stadium is haphazard and it's hard to know where to enter. The sodden crowd gathers in their thousands, patiently attempting to gain access to narrow passages flanked by crash barriers. These funnels are much too short in length to thin the crowd at the entry points, and only for the excellent behaviour of frustrated fans, who stand without shelter in the incessant rain for well over thirty minutes, crushes at the entry points are avoided. Direction or assistance from the security personnel on duty or the UEFA officials is non-existent. After forty minutes of inching toe to heel in the downpour, we pass through the final ticket and bag checks and at last we are inside. This is the best moment of the day, unless of course you win. But the feeling of winning is different, it is a mixture of relief, satisfaction and achievement. The excitement before the game is more exhilarating, the nervous anticipation of what will unfold.

My phone lights up with team news from my brother back home. Sturridge starts upfront, Henderson only on the bench, not deemed fit enough by Klopp. No surprises there I think, it's all about performances now. Can the Reds find one more gladiatorial heave for the season's final call to arms?

The team picks itself with Henderson still injured. It is unchanged from the eleven that beat Villarreal and had its final warm-up at home to Chelsea in the league. The teams line up as follows;

Liverpool: Mignolet, Clyne, Lovren, Touré, Moreno, Milner (C), Can, Coutinho, Firmino, Lallana, Sturridge.

Sevilla : Soria, Mariano, Carrico, Rami, Escudero, N'Zonzi, Krychowiak, Coke (C), Banega, Vitolo, Gameiro.

Sevilla start brightly and control the early exchanges. Liverpool seem to be suffering from stage fright, but ever so slowly they ease their way into the game and it is the Reds that have the first sight of goal, a long-range effort from Can pushed away sideways by Soria, the Sevilla keeper. Liverpool pick up the pace and attack again. Clyne makes a strong run down the right and swings a looping ball, curling towards the back post. The keeper is caught in two minds, whether to make a flap at the ball, or stay on his line. Instead, Sturridge rises and loops a header back over

Soria's head. Unfortunately for the Reds, Carrico has tracked back sensing the danger and he clears the ball off the line from under his own crossbar. Now Liverpool are dominating. They press forward once more down the right-hand side. Milner plays a perfect pass for Firmino to run onto. The Brazilian flicks the ball inside his marker but a flailing hand stops his progress. It's a clear and intentional handball in the box. It must be a penalty but incredibly no, the Swedish referee, Jonas Eriksson, waves play on. What a poor decision, that was blatant. Liverpool don't lick their wounds though, they keep pushing, tails up. On twenty-five minutes, Lallana feeds Sturridge through on goal, but the angle is tight and Soria saves with his knees. Just after the half hour, Sevilla threaten for the first time. Gameiro tries an ambitious overhead kick inside the box and his effort flies narrowly wide. It's a near miss and a clear sign that Sevilla are dangerous upfront.

Liverpool push forward again. Firmino finds Coutinho, who in turn finds Sturridge at the corner of the box. Moreno sprints past him, overlapping, looking for the pass, but Sturridge has other ideas. He feints inside and then a delicious flick, with the outside of his left boot, sends the ball curling right to left, past three Sevilla defenders, past the goalkeeper and into the left hand corner of the net. It's an absolute cracker of a goal, a goal to grace any final and it's richly deserved. Liverpool lead 1–0. The Reds can now smell blood. Forward they surge from the restart. From a corner kick, Lovren rises, and just as he did against Dortmund, he powers his header into the opposition's net. 2–0 to Liverpool but no, Sturridge was in an offside position and deemed to be interfering with play. It's chalked off and the score stays at 1–0. It's a contentious call and it could be crucial. On the stroke of half-time Clyne again races down the right wing. His cross flashes across the face of the Sevilla goal to where both Sturridge and Firmino await, but incredibly neither can connect to poke it home. The ref blows for half-time and Liverpool leave the pitch rueing the fact that they lead by only one goal.

Liverpool are made to wait on the pitch as Sevilla emerge slowly after the break. Their manager, Emery, must have been reading them the riot act for a first-half no-show. They form a huddle near the centre circle as Liverpool's players look on. Inside the small circle of heads, the Sevilla players urge each other to evoke the spirit of previous triumphs, to not miss out on their chance of an historic three successive victories. Within seventeen seconds of the kick-off, they are on level terms. Moreno makes a poor headed clearance from the box, straight to Mariano, who picks the ball up and darts towards the errant Liverpool left-back. Moreno moves to meet the attacker but is exposed awfully by a deft nutmeg, the ball flicked through his legs, leaving him for dead. Mariano advances on the Liverpool six-yard line and then calmly passes the ball across the face of the goal to where Gameiro awaits, unmarked at the back post, to tap the ball home. It's 1–1 and all Liverpool's first half dominance is undone before much of the crowd have even returned to their seats.

It's a soft goal for the Reds to concede and now we fear the momentum might start to drift towards the Andalusians. It doesn't shift, it tsunamis. Sevilla maraud forward and only minutes later Touré makes a last gasp dive to block a Gameiro blast on goal. On sixty minutes Gameiro finds freedom in an acre of space, where Moreno should be located, but amazingly Mignolet saves his point-blank shot and keeps Liverpool in the game. But not for long, four minutes later Vitolo and Banega cut open the Liverpool midfield with a couple of wall passes. Vitolo nutmegs Lovren and, as the ball runs free, Coke, who is drifting in from the left edge of the box, in a similar position to where Sturridge opened the scoring, curls an unstoppable shot into the same corner of the net. 2–1 to Sevilla.

Liverpool are on the ropes now and the body language looks awful. Heads are down, shoulders slumped. Changes are needed and Klopp sends on Origi for Firmino. My son and I shake our heads, we want Joe Allen in the middle to shore up a midfield which is being overrun. Origi hasn't played since the derby against Everton and from his movement, he looks only half-fit. The logic must be to use his fast legs to stretch the play and try to push Sevilla back, but Liverpool can't get hold of the ball to feed their attacking players. For the first twenty minutes of the second-half, Lallana, Coutinho, Firmino and Sturridge have all been onlookers, passengers. Can and Milner are being overrun and Liverpool's defence is exposed every time Sevilla break. On seventy minutes the ball ricochets to the left of Liverpool's box and again a Sevilla player finds himself unmarked. Coke fires home past an unlucky Mignolet and it's 3–1 to the Spaniards. However, the referee doesn't give it, offside, the flag is up. But wait, after a delay and much deliberation, he changes his mind again, the goal stands after all, it is 3–1 and Liverpool are going to need another mercurial comeback reminiscent of that famous night versus Dortmund. But this isn't Anfield and both the Liverpool players and support seem deflated. The huge Red balloon, filled with hope and dreams, which took over this picture-postcard town in the heart of Europe, has been pricked and the air billows out at a speed of knots.

Allen replaces Lallana but it's hard not to feel that Klopp got his substitutions in the wrong order. On eighty-three minutes, Benteke replaces Toure in a last throw of the dice. But nothing works and by the time the final whistle blows, I can't remember a dangerous Liverpool attack in the whole second-half. Incredibly, after a season filled with endless heroics, the team ends on a whimper, outplayed, outfought and outwitted by the Europa League specialists Sevilla. Yet the victors rode their luck too – bad refereeing decisions cost Liverpool dearly and a deflected ball set up the fortuitous final goal. To coin the old football adage, if ever there was a game of two halves, then this was it. Liverpool won the first comfortably but didn't score the goals their play deserved and Sevilla punished them gleefully with a second-half siege.

We don't stay to watch Sevilla lift the trophy for a record three years in a row, or to hear their fantastic fans sing their hearts out, or to watch their wonderful white-shirted players soak the applause and adulation. I'm decimated, growing tired and weary of defeat and the horrible numbness it brings. I'm not sure I've ever felt lower after a loss and recently there have been many. Athens and a 2–1 defeat to Milan in the 2007 European Cup Final. Losing to Chelsea when Gerrard slipped. Another defeat to Chelsea in the 2012 FA Cup Final. League Cup Final defeat to Man City. Klopp knows how we feel, he's becoming a serial second-place man too. This was to be the start of something and maybe it is, but tonight it feels like a depressing end. A horrible finale. The way back from here is long. No catapult to recovery, no easy road. It's going to be the long hard way. Fortunately, it's the way that Klopp knows best and thank goodness we have him to lead us from this darkness. My son offers me some of his remaining sweets. He knows how hard I take it, so I cheer up a little, for him, for sanity. There is nothing else to be done.

We walk back along the dark tracks in silence. Rain still falls incessantly adding to the mood of mourning. Normally fans talk feverishly after a game, as they make their way to where they have to go. Why did we lose? How did we win? Who did well? Who was terrible? Tonight, in the gloom, it's near silence. A few grumbles, a few growls, but mostly muted dejection. The manner of defeat will be the hardest thing to forget and surely the biggest worry for Klopp. To not go out fighting, to not even threaten a comeback, that's the stain that clings and can't be washed off by the rain of this black Basel night.

After the game, Klopp bemoans the poor refereeing decisions and he is right to do so but, having watched the tame and inexplicable collapse of the second-half, it is hard to believe that better refereeing would have changed matters. Liverpool were ahead and had their chance but didn't take it. "Today there were four decisive, obvious decisions and all were against us. In a final when it's close you need a little luck and we didn't have it," he would tell the gathered media.

But Klopp does not lie down for long and he continues, "now we are frustrated but tomorrow or in a week we will see more clearly and we will use it. We will come back stronger for sure. There were a few moments we've over-performed and the boys have been great. But you need consistency, you need more. Someday people will say Basel was a very important moment for the future of Liverpool FC."

It's how Shankly saw it too, when the Reds crashed out, humiliated by Ajax 7–3 over two legs in the European Cup in 1966, just a few short months after losing the Cup Winners Cup final to Dortmund at Hampden Park. "We were out of Europe again, but we were undeterred. We were too busy to let setbacks like that bother us, we were examining the team and planning ahead."

Rafa, too, found solace in 2007 as he walked the sodden streets of Athens until dawn with his chief scout Eduardo Macia, "discussing the future, the players we were considering signing, how we hoped to develop the academy, what we needed to do to assure we could reach another European Cup final, and win it. We talked about staff, how to organise the club, about our vision, our project."

Only a fool lies on the floor, yet the weight of another final defeat hangs weary on Klopp's shoulders. He must believe that he is not predestined to this outcome, to defeat. He must believe that he can affect his own future and forge success from failure.

"There are more important things in life than football, I don't think God had a plan with me to go to the final and always have bad luck. I've had a lot of luck in my life. I sit here as manager of Liverpool. I don't think I am an unlucky person or life has not been good to me. I will carry on and I will be in another final – and you'll tell me I lost the last five finals. I will try to reach the next final even when I know I can lose it."

Both Klopp, his team and Liverpool FC are becoming well versed in defeat in the last ten years. The taste of it can be malignant, spreading doubt into every cell and fissure, a cancer corroding confidence. Confidence breeds winners. Klopp's job at Liverpool has somehow been made even harder by the 'near victories' experienced so early in his reign. Once more he will need to mould tougher steel from the hottest and harshest of fires. He may be right. In the future Basel may be seen as the turning point, as a crossroads in the history of our famous club. A night when defeat redoubled our efforts, and helped shine a light on our future, a beacon to the path forward, the path home.

As we leave Basel and speed by fast train to Geneva, Klopp's words ring in my ears. "I don't think God had a plan for me to lose these finals." My mind drifts to Erasmus and his debate with Luther about Free Will and predetermination. I heard many Liverpool fans declare, prior to the final, that it was our destiny to win the trophy, 'our name was on the cup'. This belief had been fostered by the nature of the journey, the incredible comebacks, the never-say-die approach. Somehow it just had to be. Of course, it was proved that it didn't have to be and instead, if one believed in fate or predestiny then the reverse was true, a cruel trick had been played on us. Believing in predestiny can be a self-fulfilling prophecy, the loser learns to be a loser and starts believing it, it is predetermined. The winner keeps winning, confident that he has the favour of the gods. For me, I don't believe in predetermination or a prescribed fate, I'm a humanist in the spirit of Erasmus. I believe in people and their ability to forge their own destiny, I must, otherwise this journey might prove unbearable.

PART VI

ALLEGIANCE

THE TASTE OF DEFEAT

'I never thought of losing, but now that it's happened, the only thing is to do it right. That's my obligation to all the people who believe in me. We all have to take defeats in life.' — Muhammad Ali

Fast Eddie is a whizz-kid pool player, but when the chips are down and the going gets tough, he folds. Bert Gordon, his unscrupulous manager tells it to him straight.

"Everybody's got talent. I got talent. You think you can play big-money straight pool, or poker, for forty straight hours on nothing but talent? You think they call Minnesota Fats the best in the country just because he's got talent? Nah. Minnesota Fats's got more character in one finger than you got in your whole skinny body."

Both characters populate the world of Walter Tevis's *The Hustler*, a novel first published in 1959. *The Hustler* was an original, a ground breaker, a bleak soul-torturing tale of how we can learn to hate ourselves. A dark study of the human psyche. The book won solid acclaim and later a movie of the same name starring Paul Newman and Jackie Gleason proved a critical and box office success. *The Hustler* focuses on a tortured character, Fast Eddie Felson (Newman), a poolroom hustler who moves from town to town conning strangers into thinking they can beat him, when in fact Eddie can play, and then some. Fast Eddie is a shark, but even sharks need to be wary. Eddie eventually meets his match in Minnesota Fats (Gleason), the true king of the baize. Fats teaches Eddie that talent alone is never enough. Winners need more than that. Tevis's novel is a classic and authentic tale of one man's inner struggle to fight his demons. Bert explains to Eddie that winning can be harder to bear than losing.

"And winning; that can be heavy on your back, too, like a monkey. You drop that load too when you find yourself an excuse. Then, afterward, all you got to do

is learn to feel sorry for yourself - and lots of people learn to get their kicks that way. It's one of the best indoor sports, feeling sorry... A sport enjoyed by all. Especially the born losers."

Brendan Rodgers was bang on. With all the mindless derision he received every time he referred to the need for 'character', the point may have been lost; without it you are nothing. Without it you are Fast Eddie, never quite getting the job done. Sometimes it's easier just to lose. You have fought so hard, touched glory, but still can't get it over the line. It's easier to let go, switch it all off – the anxiety, the pressure, the overwhelming desire. The awareness of what victory looks like is scary. You admire the winners, the legends, envy them even, with their awards and their immortal epitaphs. Success can never be taken away. We only remember the winners. The fear of defeat can overwhelm the will to win, smother it. The moment we consider the consequences of losing, the game is up. The moment we look down, we slip and fall. Tennis-great Billie Jean King captured the event horizon with clarity, the difference between glory and the black hole. "A champion is afraid of losing, everyone else is afraid of winning."

Is this what happened in Basel in the second half? Forty-five minutes from glory, on top in the game, the summit in sight. The referee hadn't awarded two stonewall penalties – the gross unfairness of that must have rankled. Gilt-edged chances had been spurned. If taken, it would have been game, set and match. Sevilla made Liverpool wait for the restart and emerged late from the tunnel. They had not given up, they were not defeated. They huddled together on the pitch before the ref called time, as the Reds players watched idly on, hoping, wondering – why won't they just lie down?

Sevilla didn't lie down, they rose up like warriors and within minutes the die had been cast, as Liverpool's resolve vanished along with their lead. That's what happens when you don't know how to win. You react badly. Sure you've been unlucky, sure you could have led 2–0 and it's now 1–1. But heh, it's only 1–1, still all to play for, still over forty minutes to go in a cup final. Still time to win. But too many Liverpool minds had drifted to the prize, too eager to get there, unable to lift their heads when Sevilla mounted a fightback. The easiest thing was for Liverpool heads to fall. And fall they did. All that effort and emotion as the Reds soared to beat their nemesis Man United, and then fought like lions to overcome Dortmund. The vanquishing of King James's Villarreal too – was all that for nothing? Nothing for the losers, had we not learned that lesson at Wembley versus Man City in the League Cup? No. Go out fighting they say, not with a whimper, but never was there a sorrier second-half display in a final from a Reds team, ever. Most unusual was the nature of the collapse. It didn't sit right with what we know of this team. It just didn't tally. They had proven themselves to be fighters, never-say-diers. The comeback kings of Norwich, Palace, Dortmund and Villarreal. It wasn't just once. Yet the smell of victory can be overpowering, it can weaken the muscles, tie the legs, freeze the mind. Fast Eddie knew that.

We would have all summer to mull it over. That's the horrible thing about the last game of the season going foul on you. Even the 6–1 at Stoke wasn't this bad. A ninth European trophy would have been a glorious way for Klopp to begin his tenure. A major stepping stone towards an assault at ending the drought and restoring the Reds to the European elite. To become the ninth set of Reds players to triumph in Europe, that would have meant something for the boys too, something to be proud of, particularly given how magnificent the journey had been. Winning builds reserves of steel that can be called upon when the going gets tough. Winning is a bank that can be dipped into, invested in future campaigns. However, all of that was gone now, opportunity lost. Summer tasted sour, it tasted of defeat.

Most worrying of all is that this is a familiar taste. A decade of sliding has passed by in a blink. Just one victory in the League Cup in 2012. Losing finalists in the Champions League in 2007, the FA Cup in 2012, the League Cup and the Europa Cup this 2016. Two second-place finishes in the Premier League in 2008/09 and 2013/14. Always within touching distance. Always the bridesmaids. Leaving the Olympic Stadium in Athens near midnight, having lost the European Cup Final 2–1 to Milan, for some reason life didn't feel as bad as it did in Basel. For sure I was dejected and demoralised, unable to stomach a late beer. Instead, straight to bed and then an interminable wait at Athens airport the next day as our exorbitant flight negotiated a much delayed departure slot. Back then though, the team had given it a go, a late goal from Kuyt had provided hope. Consensus said we were the better team that night, but as sport will have it, that is not always enough. Istanbul had proven that. Leaving Athens we had a strong team, built over a three year period by Rafa Benitez. Alongside Milan and Chelsea, Liverpool were the best in Europe. Soon, we hoped, Rafa would be able to cement the domestic form and bring the League title home. A positive future seemed mapped, the prospects of winning were tangible, Istanbul was still fresh in the memory. But, as we know, life doesn't do mapping. Random events and chaos is the more natural order and soon entropy took hold. Now, after ten years of losing, the taste of victory is but a distant memory. Leaving Basel, one wondered when the next chance for glory might come. As Klopp said, you have to grasp your opportunities when they present themselves. We didn't.

Liverpool and Klopp can draw cold comfort from knowing that they are just another name to be added to a long list of the defeated that populate the football annals, some glorious, some less so. For many, it's the only taste they've known. In defeat one is never alone. One need only look to the Anfield record books to see titles lost, some on the very last day of the season. On 29th April 1899, Tom Watson would take his Liverpool team to play Aston Villa on the final day for a winner take all tie. Villa triumphed, and then some, pulverising the Reds 5–0. Salvation would come for Watson though when, two years later in 1901, he became the first ever Liverpool manager to win the title. Paisley recalled being held to a goalless draw at Arsenal in 1972, when a win would have secured the crown. "To add to our frustration John Toshack had the ball in the net but it was ruled offside. If the goal had been given we would have been champions!" Derby County under manager Brian Clough would lift the crown. So near, yet so far. In 1989, Arsenal again would prove Liverpool's nemesis, winning 2–0 at Anfield in the final game to steal the crown and deny Liverpool a double. Yet coming so soon after the Hillsborough tragedy, it didn't really matter, nothing did.

All winning teams have tasted bitter defeat on their path to glory. Some never quite reached the summit of their potential. The great Leeds team of the sixties and seventies knew more about defeat than most. In an era of iconic players and great teams, they went so close, so many times. With Don Revie as manager and with fantastic players such as Johnny Giles, Billy Bremner, Peter Lorimer and Alan Clarke, Leeds were an awesome outfit, capable of winning with skill or aggression. Yet the battlefield was littered with mighty armies – Shankly's Reds, Busby's reborn United, Brian Clough's Derby County. In a ten-year spell from 1965 to 1974, Leeds would never finish outside the top four in the League. Five second places would be achieved but only two titles. To say 'only two' seems harsh, but most feel they should have won more. A chance to put the record straight and to crown a wonderful decade of brilliance and earn the title of 'Europe's best' arrived on 28th May 1975. Leeds would meet Bayern Munich in the European Cup Final in Paris. Europe had proven a mixed bag for Leeds, with two UEFA Cup wins from three Final appearances, one European Cup-Winner's Cup final defeat and one European Cup semi-final defeat. Leeds would dominate the game but, after having what seemed to be a perfectly good goal by Peter Lorimer disallowed, Bayern would go on to win 2–0. It was a deflating end to the club's golden era. To this day Leeds fans sing in defiance – *'We are Champions, Champions of Europe'*, in honour of a victory that they believe was stolen. Leeds have only lifted one major trophy in the 41 years since that night in Paris. We never know when the opportunity lost is the last we might get.

Newcastle's second-place League finishes in 1996 and 1997 must feel like an eternity ago as they look ahead to life in the Championship. As for Arsenal's European Cup Final defeat to Barcelona in 2006, when next will such an opportunity present itself to the Gunners? The Eagles of Lisbon, Benfica, last won a European trophy in 1962, losing eight finals since. Borussia Monchengladbach lost three out of five European finals in their greatest decade, the seventies, two of these at the hands of Liverpool. Valencia lost two European Cup Finals in a row in 2000 and 2001. Atletico Madrid have been to three European Cup Finals and have lost them all, two to their bitter cross town rivals Real. Holland have lost all three World Cup finals that they have played in, in 1974, 1978 and 2010. In both 74' and 78' they were widely regarded as the better team. Sometimes a strange solace can be found in defeat. On rare occasions the defeated are remembered more than the winners. "Maybe we were the real winners in the end," Cruyff would say of his Dutch side, "I think the world remembers our team more." Keegan's Newcastle and Rodgers' Liverpool are two similar cases. Yet solace can never feel as good or shine as brightly as glory.

If Klopp looks carefully he will also find stories of great resilience. Tales of teams who rose from the ashes and fought back from hardship. Brazil blew the chance to lift the World Cup for the first time in 1950, when they lost the final on home soil to hated foes Uruguay. The football-mad country fell into a state of national mourning for years. The loss even resulted in an exorcism of sorts; the changing of their strip from white and blue to the now familiar yellow jersey with green trim, blue shorts and white socks. Brazil would rise again to win the World Cup in 1958, 1962, 1970, 1994 and 2002 and become the most successful soccer nation in the history of the game.

When Matt Busby arrived at Old Trafford after the Second World War he set about awakening a sleeping giant. In the League, three consecutive second place finishes, followed by a fourth place and yet another second place would arrive over a five-year period. Always within touching distance, but never winning. United had been waiting since 1911 for a title victory. Busby could have been excused for throwing in the towel. Instead, hard work produced success, with United eventually triumphing in 1952, securing their first League triumph in forty-one years. Two more League crowns would follow in 1955/56 and 1956/57. United would also compete in two European Cup semi-finals, the first ten months before, the second three months after the tragic Munich Air disaster in 1958. Although grief-stricken, Busby, the man who Liverpool's Bob Paisley proclaimed to be the game's greatest manager, would not lie down. He would rebuild, literally from the ashes and United would become the first English team to win the European Cup ten years later.

Bill Shankly, too, would suffer setbacks before success arrived. It took three attempts for the indomitable Scot to lead Liverpool from the Second Division to the promised land in 1962. Two years later, the Reds would be crowned champions and in 1965 Shankly would end the Reds' seventy-three year wait to lift the FA Cup for the first time. However, glory in Europe eluded the great man, a bitter and disputed defeat in the semi-final against Inter Milan in 1965 being the closest Shankly would get to steering the Reds to the biggest prize of them all. Defeat at the hands of Dortmund in the 1966 European Cup Winners Cup proved a chastening experience. Finally, in 1973, Shankly would lift European silver, with Liverpool winning the first of three UEFA Cup crowns.

History's lessons were clear. Sometimes you have to lose before you win. Sometimes you have to lose a lot, to win a lot. Sometimes you just lose. Never do you only win.

With Reds fans now all-too accustomed to the taste of defeat, they were not alone, it had also become very familiar to Klopp himself and his players. Basel marked five Cup Final defeats in a row for the German. Two with Liverpool. Against City at Wembley the Reds only succumbed, somewhat unluckily, on penalties. Basel was different, there were no excuses to be found. Sevilla were beatable and Klopp will have left Switzerland with that knowledge gnawing a hole through his skull. Defeat too, has become a constant companion for many of Klopp's inherited side. Mignolet, Coutinho, Henderson, Allen, Touré, Sturridge, Sakho, Leiva, Flanagan and Smith all watched on as Gerrard slipped. All were present for the losses in the FA Cup, to Villa in the semi-final and to Chelsea in the final. Now they had joined Klopp in defeat at Wembley and St Jakob-Park. All opportunities wasted, nobody knowing, Klopp included, when the next golden chance might arrive. If any comfort was to be found, it would be in the knowledge that the best leaders learn from their setbacks and grow stronger. It was Shankly who said, "more is learned from defeat than victories."

With the club season over, Euro 2016, the competition for European national teams, would see France host twenty-four nations. Remarkably, for a squad so derided for long parts of the season, Liverpool would see fourteen of its players represent their countries, more than any other team in Europe. The Olympics in Rio also brought welcome relief and perspective. It would prove refreshing to see the drive, dedication and commitment shown by mostly amateurs in the pursuit of excellence. Their humbleness in victory, respect and dignity in defeat, helped some of us take our mind off football, if only for a short while.

For Klopp, though, there would be no wallowing in self-pity, no time for distraction. 'Only a fool stays down' he proclaimed. He might have understated the case, sometimes the broken and cheated do too. Yet Klopp is none of these, nor are Liverpool. Klopp arrived in Liverpool on October 8th, 2015, his first game at Tottenham coming nine days later. That would see the start of an incredible and relentless run of matches, whereby the Reds would play fifty-two times in 215 days, a game every four days. This unbelievable schedule played out against the backdrop of one of the worst injury crises the club had ever witnessed. At times ten or more first-team players would be missing. Kids were recalled from far-flung loan clubs and Klopp would field the Club's youngest ever side, more than once. All this time, he watched his inherited players closely; scrutinising, analysing, planning. Some wouldn't be around when autumn's green fields arrived. Who had the mettle for the battles that lay ahead? Who could shake off the taste of defeat? Now the real work would begin.

MIND THE GAP

'The greater the obstacle, the more glory in overcoming it.' — Molière

If Liverpool had developed the losing habit, then shaking it off and becoming winners was going to prove harder than ever. Yes, Leicester had achieved the miracle and for sure, escalating TV money had made more teams more competitive. However, repeating Leicester's heroics would prove difficult, if not impossible. Rarely, if ever, have all the big teams been in such a state of flux at exactly the same time. This instability resulted in the Foxes triumph more than the rising financial tide. Upon any objective analysis 2015/16 had been an inauspicious season from a footballing standards perspective. Leicester won the title with a total of eighty-one points, however, since the turn of the century, only Man United (in both 2001 and 2011) had won the Premier League with fewer points – eighty. Since Liverpool last lifted the crown in 1990, the average winning total has been eighty-four points (adjusted for a forty-two game campaign from 1992–1995). Yet that only tells half the story.

Before Wenger's arrival at Arsenal, the first four Premier League crowns were won with an average of only eighty points. Wenger's Arsenal raised the bar and an average of eighty-three points was required to win the League over the next eight seasons. When Abramovich and Mourinho took up residence at Chelsea, followed years later by Sheikh Mansour and his oil money at Manchester City, the bar was raised even higher. For the next eleven seasons, until 2015, an incredible eighty-eight point tally became the average League winning total. Steven Gerrard would remark with not a little regret, "There are two major reasons why I didn't win at least one title with Liverpool, Roman Abramovich at Chelsea and Sheikh Mansour at Manchester City. The memory of Abramovich arriving at Chelsea is still raw. At first you think, will this last? Will he get bored or is it real?' Then Mourinho arrives and the question has been answered." It was then that Gerrard realised he was in his own words "fucked as far as winning the league was concerned". And so it proved.

Can Leicester's tally of eighty-one points in 2015/16 become a new lower norm? Will more teams be truly competitive and level the playing field, or will the arrival of a new wave of elite and hungry managers mean that nothing short of excellence is needed to lift the crown? The trends of recent history suggest the latter.

One way or the other, Liverpool and Klopp will have to make some enormous catch-up strides to compete. Liverpool finished eighth in 2015/16, gathering sixty points from thirty-eight games, losing ten times along the way. If this hadn't been Klopp's first term in charge, and with the German only taking up the reins eight games into the campaign, then these statistics would have had the axe sharpeners at the ready. It's shocking form for a club like Liverpool. Only five times during the long twenty-six-year drought have the boys in Red performed worse and fallen below sixty points. On each such occasion the manager would be fired or had only just been hired – divorce or honeymoon. Of course, Klopp is allowed his soft introduction and for sure Liverpool's cup runs, which became the season's priority, provided compelling reasons for hope, but now, as the new season approaches, significant improvement will be expected.

An analysis of Liverpool's form during the waiting years shows just how big the task will be for Klopp and his team. In those twenty-six years Liverpool finished in an average position of 4.7, collecting on average sixty-six points. Anything less than seventy points and you are not really challenging for the top four spots, never mind hoping to win the title itself. To be challenging in the title race, eighty-plus points are needed. In 2013/14, Rodgers' Reds amassed eighty-four points but lost out to Man City's eighty-six. In 2008/09, Rafa Benitez did even better, his team securing eighty-six points but still losing out to United with ninety, and in 2001/02, Houllier would also finish second with eighty points, beaten to the line by Arsenal with eighty-seven.

Many of these barren Liverpool teams had been very pleasing on the eye, with daring attacking play from players such as Saunders, Fowler,

Owen, McManaman, Collymore, Heskey, Baros, Torres and Suarez to name a few. More often than not the problem has been keeping the back door shut. On average, Premier League winning teams concede thirty-two goals over a campaign. Crazy-Horse Hughes (if you are watching from above), Ron Yeats, Phil Thompson, Phil Neal, Alan Kennedy and Alan Hansen, all please look away now. Liverpool's average number of goals conceded per season since FSG took charge has been forty-six. The Americans, their managers and the statistics-loving transfer committee obviously don't get defence. Since last winning the title the number has been thirty-nine, still nowhere near good enough.

In these twenty-six years, Liverpool have lost on average three home games and seven away games, ten in total each season. Over the same period, the respective League winners have lost on average one home game and three away games, only four in total. Arsenal's 'Invincibles' lost none, going the full season unbeaten. Home is where the heart is and it is also where League titles are won. In ten of those twenty-six years, the title-winning team went the entire season without losing a home game. It's what Liverpool used to do when Anfield was a feared destination, a bastion. Remarkably, Liverpool went unbeaten in eighty-five home games from 1978 to 1981 under the management of Bob Paisley. How incredible, nay impossible that feat seems to Reds fans today. If the League trophy is to return to Anfield, it is on L4's hallowed turf that the battle must be waged and won.

If these figures are startling, and they are, well then so too is the realisation of how high the tide has risen. In the 2004/05–2015/16 Abramovich and Sheikh Mansour 'financial doping' era (as described by Arsene Wenger), the League winners have collected on average 77 per cent of all the points available to them (in a thirty-eight League game season, 77% = 88 points). As seen in the last twenty-six years Liverpool have been nowhere near this level of performance (collecting on average 58% or sixty-six points), very often the Reds' league challenge faltering before Christmas. Yet, even when Liverpool were the best in the land, when they were lifting eighteen League crowns, rarely did they achieve the same level of dominance that today's League winners have to achieve to lift the crown. In only one of those eighteen title winning seasons did Liverpool manage to collect more than 77 per cent of the points available. Bob Paisley's 1978/79 vintage, his double champions of Europe team, would collect a whopping 81 per cent of the points on offer (sixty-eight points from a total of eighty-four, in a forty-two game season with two points for a win). This doesn't mean that these Liverpool teams were poorer outfits than the League winning teams of the last decade or so, the fact that many of these Reds teams dominated in Europe tells its own story. You do what you have to do, to win the League you are in. You can only beat the opposition in front of you, particularly if you are thrashing all-comers on the continent too. Before the advent of the Premier League and Champions League, the divide between the haves and the have-nots was narrower, with more teams taking more points from each other. In that more competitive and 'level playing pitch' environment the Champions were less inclined to bolt away with the title. This is borne out by analysing the average points collected by the top four teams in the League in the following periods from 1960 to the present day.

Period	Average Points collected by top 4 teams
1960-69	71
1970-79	71
1980-89	71
1990-99	72
2000-09	78
2010-16	77

(all adjusted for 38 match
league and 3 pts for a win)

We can see that the average points collected by the top four teams has jumped dramatically since the turn of the millennium, directly influenced by the financial strengthening of the top clubs in their pursuit of domestic and Champions League glory. The gap between the top six and the rest has grown to the extent that often the reference is used that two, if not three leagues exist within one. The battle for the top four waged by six elite clubs, followed by the competition for the best of the rest, this tailing off to the scrap against relegation at the bottom. With the top four stretching their supremacy over those below, it is not surprising that the quantum of points needed to lift the crown has risen also. 'Mind the Gap' seems to be the warning for those wandering aimlessly below sixth. It should also be a warning to the custodians of English Football. Is this what we want? Is this what anyone desires bar the elite super clubs?

Some conclusions can be drawn from this array of data. Liverpool had a very poor 2015/16 season collecting a paltry sixty points, losing ten games, but with many mitigating circumstances absolving Klopp from any rush to judgement. Promising green shoots of hope have appeared, with two inspiring yet ultimately unsuccessful Cup runs enjoyed.

The scale of improvement needed to challenge for the title is stark. League winners don't often lose more than four games. Quite often they don't lose at all at home. Under Klopp, the Reds lost eight times in the League, mostly against the lesser sides – at home to Palace and United and away to Newcastle, Watford, West Ham, Leicester, Southampton and Swansea. Klopp will need to learn to motivate himself and his team to win when the world is not watching. Leagues are won by scraping out results in the less glamourous ties.

Klopp needs to solve Liverpool's poor defensive record. If you concede over forty league goals, you rarely win the league. Rodgers learned that, when his team shipped fifty goals. In the eighteen winning campaigns when Liverpool did scale the summit, an average of thirty-two goals were conceded. The Premier League winner's average is also thirty-two. Paisley said Liverpool's best ever team was the 1978/79 vintage, a team in which only fifteen players were utilised and one which allowed a mere sixteen goals to beat them and enter the Reds net. All this, while scoring eighty-five at the other end. It is obvious that the time has come to tighten up.

Klopp and Co may need to collect a higher percentage of points on offer than any Liverpool manager has ever achieved before. Now that is asking a lot. When Rafa Benitez's Liverpool side collected eighty-six points in 2008/09 and still only finished second, they equalled the second-best collection percentage (75 per cent) of points on offer in the history of Liverpool Football Club (in the top tier). Only Paisley's greats of 1978/79 would beat that with 81 per cent. Maybe Leicester's eighty-one points or 71 per cent will prove enough once more, but the longer run average of 77 per cent (since 04/05) suggests not.

The story is no different in the other top leagues in Europe. Over the last decade the average champion's percentage points won/available in Spain, Germany and Italy has been 81, 77 and 77 per cent respectively. It is clear to see that winning league titles is proving harder than ever, right across the continent.

To be successful at Liverpool, Klopp will most likely have to set new record performance levels for the club, coming from an eighth place starting position. The German will have his work cut out. A David and Goliath mission for sure. In one-off games, anybody can win as Cruyff observed wryly, "Why couldn't you beat a richer club? I've never seen a bag of money score a goal." But to win the League and then to win it again, to get back to the summit, that will take some doing. In his debut press conference, all the way back in October, Klopp himself dramatically described the task that awaited him as "The biggest challenge in world football." How true those words now appear.

(Note: Where relevant the data presented in this chapter has been adjusted pro-rata, to reflect a 20 team league, 38 game season)

CATCH 22

'It's hard to win when you always lose' —Tom Waits

On Saturday 15th December, 1959, Bill Shankly watched on from the Anfield stands as his new team Liverpool, players picked by the directors for the last time, were mauled 4–0 by Cardiff. The *News Chronicle and Daily Dispatch* outlined the scale of the task that awaited the man from Glenbuck. *"Bill Shankly, normally one of Soccer's most outspoken characters, was a very subdued man after sitting through his first match as Liverpool manager. Right from the start, Shankly was made to realise the tremendous task that lies ahead of him as this shabby Liverpool team was humbled by a Cardiff side wearing an unmistakable promotion look. The final blow for Bill Shankly was hearing the jeers hurled at the directors' box by the disappointed Anfield fans. Still, Shankly has never been afraid of hard work as a manager. I fear he's going to get plenty of it within the next few months."*

Shankly himself would remark, "Naturally I'm disappointed but it's just as well that I've seen the team give an off-form display in my first match. I've learned quite a few things this way." Shankly realised that he had to be ruthless. Upon reflection, he would say, "After the match, I knew that the team as a whole was not good enough. Within a month I wrote down twenty-four names that I thought should go and they went inside a year."

Shankly decided to rebuild from the back and then up along the spine. Driven by a desire to win, he would fight constantly with the club's directors for funding but each time they would refuse. However, Shankly had cultivated an ally in financial director Eric Sawyer. So next time, when the board said they couldn't afford a signing, Sawyer was ready, countering, "We can't afford not to." Having gone out of their way to secure Shankly's presence at the club, the Board now realised that they would have to back him financially too. The logic seemed irrefutable and with not a little reluctance they agreed. For the first time in forever, Liverpool FC were being managed to win, not just to make up the numbers. Shankly tried to sign Jack Charlton from Leeds but the Yorkshire club were fighting relegation and needed to hold onto their man-mountain. Instead, Scot Ron Yeats arrived from Dundee United. Shankly would growl to reporters, "Go on, walk round him, he's a colossus." Another Scot, Ian St John would arrive from Motherwell. These two would catalyse the team and Shankly's Reds would never look back. Ron Yeats, or 'Rowdy' as he was known on the Kop, would go on to become the first Liverpool captain to lift the FA Cup in 1965. Shankly didn't just have a knack for identifying and signing future greats, he also promoted promising youth prospects such as Jimmy Case, Tommy Smith and Ian Callaghan from the reserves. His eye for the game would also see him change the position of certain players such as Jimmy Melia and Alec Lindsay, recreating them as such, extending their usefulness to the squad and club, expanding the options available.

The success or failure of a manager can be influenced by a whole array of factors, some of these within their control, some not. Imposing a playing style and identity, along with preferred formations and tactics, are matters that a manager can control, and must. Building a squad of players that are suited to that style is next. Sometimes this happens in reverse, if the players cannot be changed, then maybe the style and formation will have to adapt to suit the raw materials. Above everything, managers will live and die by the quality of the performers at their disposal. Those not up to standard or that do not suit the playing style must go.

Successful managers nearly always have one thing in common, the signing of great, or soon to be great players. New recruits should be enhancements, not more of the same. No matter how good a manager is, if he doesn't have the players, he is goosed. Cruyff summed it up well, "If your players are better than your opponents, 90 per cent of the time you will win." It is interesting to note that Lionel Messi won the European Cup with three different managers. He was the constant. At Liverpool, Shankly bought Yeats, St John and Keegan. Paisley bought Dalglish after Keegan had left for Hamburg. Dalglish bought Barnes and

Beardsley. Benitez bought Alonso, Torres and Sterling. Dalglish returned and bought Suarez and Henderson. Although unsuccessful, Rodgers, let us not forget, did sign some quality additions in Sturridge, Coutinho, Milner, Lallana and Firmino.

Of all the greats, one name stood out for Bob Paisley, a name most Liverpool fans would concur with. "Of all the players I have played alongside, managed and coached in more than forty years at Anfield, he is the most talented. When Kenny shines, the whole team is illuminated." And boy did the King shine.

★★★

The summer of 2016 had arrived and at last Klopp had time to breathe, sit back and take stock. The American owners, too, had assessed the state of their nation and they liked what they saw, offering Klopp an extended six-year contract as a sign of their commitment to his appointment. Klopp had no hesitation in saying yes, the challenge hadn't scared him away, not yet. Now we would see the beginning of his long-term plan. It was time to inject fresh blood, introduce new talent. Liverpool fans waited eagerly to see what the profile of a Klopp signing would be. What type of players suited our new leader's eye? Legend Graeme Souness was unequivocal as to the scale of the task that awaited the German, lamenting, "There's not a single area of his squad he will be satisfied with. It's hard to look at any part of the team and think it could not be improved." Klopp would have to do a Shankly.

Klopp's first signing had in fact already been made the previous winter. A young unknown Serbian by the name of Marko Grujic had been snapped up from Red Star Belgrade for £5 million. He was immediately loaned back to Red Star, to assist in their push to win the League, which they duly did. With the season over, it was time for Grujic to head to Anfield. Early signs looked good. Goal scoring pre-season performances against Fleetwood Town and Huddersfield, whetted the appetite of Reds' fans to see more of the rangy and athletic box-to-box player. With excellent technical ability and standing 6ft 2in tall, it seemed there was little not to like about Klopp's first foray into the transfer market. At Dortmund, Klopp had earned a reputation for signing raw talent, such as Reus and Lewandowski, and moulding it into star quality. This allowed the Black and Yellows to be competitive on a tight budget. Klopp became renowned for giving youth a chance, for helping fledgling players to refine and hone their skills. Liverpool fans hoped that Grujic would be the first of many new examples of Klopp's transfer mastery at work.

Klopp's second signing of the winter transfer window had been to acquire Joel Matip, a 6ft 4in centre-back, on a free transfer from Schalke in Germany. Few in the English game, bar avid Bundesliga watchers, knew much about the Cameroonian, but reports would soon filter in that the Reds had got their hands on a Rolls Royce of a defender, a towering technical talent to make the fans dream of a new Alan Hansen in the back four.

Come the summer window, Klopp needed to strengthen his defence further. Kolo Touré at the age of thirty-five, had been allowed to leave on a free transfer and join old friend Brendan Rodgers, now manager of Glasgow Celtic. Fellow centre-half Mamadou Sakho was banished to the youths for falling foul of the club's disciplinary policy, Klopp sending a clear message to all that there would be no passengers or rebels. Veteran Martin Skrtel was sold for £4.5 million to Fenerbahce in Turkey. Incoming arrivals included defensive cover in the shape of Estonian Ragnar Klavan, signed from German side FC Augsburg. Again the early reports were good. A 6ft 1in defender, excellent footballer, good in the air. The only pitfall was Klavan's age at thirty years old. He was a fix for now and his arrival would allow young Joe Gomez, who was still recovering from his cruciate injury, to blossom at his own pace. With the addition of two tall, experienced defenders, both proficient with the ball at their feet and both crucially good in the air, Liverpool fans could hope for an improvement defensively for the seasons ahead.

Behind the two new centre-halves a new goalkeeper in the shape of twenty-three-year-old, 6ft 2in stopper Loris Karius would also arrive, a signing from Klopp's old club Mainz for £5.5 million. Who would become the number one was unsure, but at least now the erratic Mignolet had some real competition. Klopp was building from the back, strengthening his team's spine, just as Shankly had done before him.

A stellar campaign by midfielder Joe Allen at the European

Championships, which helped propel Wales all the way to the semi-finals, heightened interest in his talents, and when Stoke offered £13 million, Klopp accepted. Like Shankly, Klopp too was creating new roles for existing players. Thirty-year-old all-rounder James Milner would be asked to convert to the left-back position as a replacement for the error-prone Moreno. It was a role that we saw the ever-consistent Yorkshireman fill very competently at Wembley versus Man City and at Old Trafford versus Man United. In hindsight, had he played there in Basel, Liverpool might well have a Europa Cup in the trophy cabinet and be getting ready for a campaign in the Champions League. Alas, football, like life, is full of ifs and buts. Allen's sale and Milner's move from midfield left a gap for a younger, fresher set of legs and Klopp would look to relegated Newcastle to entice the twenty-five-year-old Dutch international Georginio Wijnaldum. The 5ft 9in midfielder wouldn't need to think twice and, carrying a price tag of £25 million, Klopp must see the new man as a starter in his preferred 4-3-3 formation.

Then came the signing that excited fans the most. Forward players grab most attention and always will. The previous March, Liverpool travelled to play Southampton in the League. Leading 2–0 at half time, the three points seemed secure, until the home team's Sadio Mane produced a cameo performance that blitzed the Reds and led Southampton to a remarkable 3–2 turnaround victory with the Senegalese striker scoring twice. That day, the speedy and agile Mane proved simply unplayable. Klopp had tracked Mane since his Dortmund days, but this performance only cemented his desire to acquire the young striker. Despite interest from United and Chelsea, it was Liverpool that Mane wanted. A £34 million deal was completed and a new attacking hero had arrived at Anfield. Christian Benteke was now surplus to requirements. Although a fine striker, Benteke's old-fashioned number nine style didn't fit with Klopp's all action, all running philosophy. Benteke would move to Crystal Palace late in the transfer window for £32 million, the same price that Liverpool had paid to Aston Villa for his services one year earlier. Instead of a tall muscular target man upfront, in Mane, Klopp had acquired a lightning-fast, superbly skilful goal-scoring dynamo, who could play anywhere across the attacking three positions, right, left or centre. Quite often Klopp played with no out-and-out striker, just a constantly shifting and swirling body of three. In this system, Mane would complement perfectly the existing attacking talents of Firmino, Coutinho, Sturridge and Origi.

More players would leave Anfield, but unlike the year before when it was Sterling forcing his way out the door, this time it was the manager deciding who would stay and who would go. Jordan Ibe would head to Bournemouth for £15 million. Brad Smith would follow him to the south coast for £6 million. Jerome Sinclair would move to Watford for £4 million. Klopp described these deals as good business. The club had blooded three young players, helped develop their careers and now it had moved them on for significant profits. If their path to the first team had been clear they would have stayed, but it wasn't, and in the end it was best to go. Luis Alberto would move to Lazio for £4 million and young Jordan Rossiter would head to Glasgow Rangers for a nominal fee. Lazar Markovic failed to convince in pre-season friendlies and would be loaned to Sporting Lisbon. Troublemaker Mario Balotelli, the bane of Rodgers' life at Anfield, would be transferred for free to Nice. No tears would be shed at the departure of the Italian man-child. Jamie Carragher would describe the zero price paid by Nice as "expensive". To take the place of the departed, some of the club's under-age talent would be promoted to the first team squad, in the shape of winger Sheyi Ojo, midfielder Ovie Ejaria and defender Trent Alexander-Arnold. The ever constant treadmill of football life continued unabated. As one door closed, another opened.

Since arriving at Anfield, Klopp had now signed seven players for a combined total of £76 million and sold six players for a sum of £78 million, a net profit of £2 million. While making for good financial business, whether or not Klopp now presided over a squad ready to win trophies, only time would tell. The additions highlighted a clear strategy. In defence height and strength had been added along with the ability to play the ball out comfortably from the back. This enhances the Reds' ability to counter-attack with fluency and retain possession which is crucial to the 'geggenpressing' style. The midfield had also been strengthened with younger legs and taller players. Taller players should equal fewer goals conceded to headers and set-plays, one of the Reds' Achilles heels from the season before. Upfront guile, pace and goals come with the signing of Mane. Youth, too, had been promoted and new roles had been created for some. The Klopp blueprint was already starting to take shape.

The German was ebullient about his summer business proclaiming the collection of players as 'his' squad and declaring that there now existed no excuses, nothing to stop the Reds from competing for silverware. Klopp had hardly spent any money on a net basis, yet he seemed convinced that Liverpool could compete with the big spenders. "You should try to be more independent of the money. Because in a world of money it looks like everybody in football has more than they need."

As Liverpool were busy evolving into a Klopp-shaped club, so too the competition were strengthening and once more the challenge ahead seemed harder than ever. These days, even Chelsea seemed to find it hard to match the oil flushing through Manchester City's veins. Since the arrival of Sheikh Mansour in August 2008, City have spent over £1 billion. Apart from a fabulous squad worth £500 million and more, the sky-blues have fifteen top players out on loan around Europe, these including Samir Nasri, Wilfred Bony, Eliaquim Mangala and Joe Hart, the first three signed in the last five years and collectively having a market value of up to £70 million. These stars proved difficult to sell because at City they earn astronomical wages that most clubs can't even dream of paying. With City packing off unwanted players to all corners of the continent, new signings John Stones, Ilkay Gundogan, Nolito and Leroy Sane amongst others, would arrive costing £181 million. Only £18 million would be recouped giving a net spend of £163 million. Add to that the hiring of one of the world's best managers in Guardiola and what have you got? A monster. But there were other formidable beasts stirring to life.

My son, genuinely delighted with Liverpool's business, could only look on in despair when I told him of the dealings in Manchester. And that was at United, not City. "What?" was his shocked reply when informed that Paul Pogba, the fantastic French midfielder and one time Manchester United youth player, had been re-signed from Juventus for the princely sum of £89 million, a world record transfer fee. That wasn't the end of the new arrivals at Old Trafford. United would also sign

Henrikh Mkhitaryan from Dortmund and Eric Bailly from Villarreal, both for £30 million each. Only £6.5 million would arrive from sales with the Red Devils closing the summer transfer window with a net spend of £143 million.

"Can they just spend what they want and buy anybody they like?" my son would ask incredulously, "What's the point for everyone else then? Why bother?" he continued, annoyed. This was before I told him that Chelsea had also spent a net £85 million and had sent a staggering thirty-eight players out on loan.

To be honest, I wasn't sure how to answer him, not with a straight face anyhow.

"Have you heard of Catch 22?" I asked him.

"No," he replied.

And so I recounted the tale of Yossarian, the hero of Joseph Heller's anti-war novel *Catch 22*. Yossarian, a bombardier, based on a small island off the coast of Italy during World War II, proves infinitely creative in his efforts to save himself from the horrors of battle. He wants to complete his tour of duty, go home but despite all efforts, he can't. The problem is his senior Officer, Colonel Cathcart. Cathcart keeps raising the number of missions the men must fly to complete their service. However, if a soldier makes an attempt to excuse themselves from the dangerous assignments, they fall foul of the Glorious Loyalty Oath Crusade, the administrative code which includes a clause called Catch 22. The clause is explained to Yossarian by Doc Daneeka:

> *'There was only one catch and that was Catch-22, which specified that a concern for one's safety in the face of dangers that were real and immediate was the process of a rational mind. Orr was crazy and could be grounded. All he had to do was ask; and as soon as he did, he would no longer be crazy and would have to fly more missions. Orr would be crazy to fly more missions and sane if he didn't, but if he was sane he had to fly them. If he flew them he was crazy and didn't have to; but if he didn't want to he was sane and had to. Yossarian was moved very deeply by the absolute simplicity of this clause of Catch-22 and let out a respectful whistle. "That's some catch, that Catch-22," Yossarian observed. "It's the best there is," Doc Daneeka agreed.'*

“Do you see the similarities?” I asked my son.

“Er yes, I think so,” he replied. “No matter what we do, they’ll just keep spending more and make it harder and harder. That it?” he continued.

“That’s it,” I said, “Catch 22.”

BRIGHT LIGHTS, BIG STARS

"I was never afraid of failure; for I would sooner fail than not be among the greatest." – John Keats

It wasn't just the big boys who were spending like there was no tomorrow, it seemed everybody else was too. The Premier League was awash with cash, all twenty of the Premier League clubs now ranked among the top thirty richest in the world. Yet, come the end of the summer 2016 transfer window, Liverpool were one of only four clubs to have a minus net outlay. In total, English club purchases topped £1.1 billion, a new record, up from the summer 2015 spend of £870 million. Thirteen of the twenty Premier League clubs broke their transfer record. However, it wouldn't be just new on-pitch talent that Liverpool would be facing in the season ahead, the riches of the Premier League were attracting the brightest and best managers to the sidelines too.

At the age of thirteen, a young Spanish boy, Pep Guardiola would leave home to take up residence at Barcelona Youth Football Academy, La Masia. Here he could be treated for the illness he had contracted, one described by his mother: "It's a virus, a virus that's in his blood. It's the football virus." The young Guardiola would grow and find a first team berth under the management of Johann Cruyff, going on to play for the Catalonians 263 times, whilst earning forty-seven international caps with Spain. He would return to manage Barcelona in 2008 and help develop the career of a rising star named Lionel Messi. In an incredible four-year spell, Guardiola and his Messi-charged team won all before them playing their famed tiki-taka style of short passing football. Former Chelsea manager Avram Grant believed it was Bob Paisley's Liverpool team that pioneered 'tiki-taka' football and the high press saying, "The way they [Paisley's Liverpool] played was unbelievable. I think people don't remember that, but he really changed football in England. Nobody before played like this. They played on the ground, not long balls and they won three European Cups. Since I was there I followed all the games and it was amazing to see them: tap, tap, tap, tap, tap. When you say 'tiki-taka', it starts with them."

After Barcelona, Guardiola moved to Bayern Munich. While the Bavarians continued to dominate at home, as they had before Pep's arrival, three semi-final exits in succession in the European Cup saw Guardiola's German residence deemed only a partial success. All the time Man City would call and call and Guardiola would say no and no again. Finally, feeling unloved in Bavaria, the ever sensitive Pep would succumb. At the age of forty-five, it was now Guardiola's job to sign Manchester City's blank cheques. The man widely regarded as the world's premier coach had arrived at the world's wealthiest team. Who could stop them now? I spoke to esteemed Spanish journalist Guillem Balague to enquire as to what we could expect from Guardiola's arrival. "As a coach he is brilliant. He is maximising what he has, to his idea, and the club has worked with that, with signings that make sense, the idea is much sharper now, much clearer, they get the players that they need, there will be the coaching, there will be the patience, there will be the idea, everything that you need to win things, so it's going to be difficult for everyone else to catch up."

At Man United, something had to give. They weren't catching up at all. Under Van Gaal they had headed in the opposite direction. Former player Steve Coppell's words rang true, "Success in football is relatively easy. If you spend the most money, then you have the best players and the best team. If that formula breaks down then a cog has gone wrong and the cog that has gone wrong appears to be the manager." And so it was. When Louis Van Gaal's neck was hooked at Old Trafford, it was hard for the United board not to offer the job to the most qualified man available, Jose Mourinho. The son of Felix Mourinho, a professional footballer and a goalkeeper who played one game for Portugal, Mourinho grew up in Setubal, Lisbon. Jose would attend his father's workplace and watch the team train, all the while unknowingly imbibing knowledge and a love for the game. He would also watch his favourite team on TV, Liverpool, and their great players Keegan and Dalglish. Privately educated, Mourinho excelled at languages and this ability would eventually land him a role as interpreter to manager Sir Bobby Robson at Sporting Lisbon, then Porto and Barcelona. Slowly but surely Mourinho's duties would evolve towards the footballing side and he would secure his first managerial role with Benfica in 2000, at the age of thirty-seven. Two years later he would take the top-job at Porto, later leading them to Champions League success in 2004. From there Mourinho would only know success. United have not challenged for the title since the departure of Alex Ferguson and now the man that seems capable of guaranteeing success wherever he goes steps into the big shoes. It's a funny fit in some ways, Mourinho renowned for his defensive, intransigent tactics, managing a club built on a reputation for free flowing, fearless, attacking football. United legend Eric Cantona found the appointment perplexing saying, "I love Jose Mourinho, but in terms of the type of football he plays, I don't think he is Manchester United." Mourinho doesn't seem to stay in any one place too long either, his authoritarian style lasting but a few years, until players and fans alike seem to grow tired of the relentless siege mentality that the Portuguese conquistador creates. But siege mentality often works, Ferguson himself managed to keep it going for nearly twenty-six years and, just like the Scot, regardless of his many failings, Mourinho is a winner.

Into the hot seat vacated by Mourinho at Chelsea steps a successful, likeable and passionate manager named Antonio Conte. That is the first time in a long, long time that I've found myself using the words 'Chelsea' and 'likeable' in the same sentence. For Conte, three straight title wins with Juventus, his team going undefeated in the 2011/12 season, would precede a spell as the Italian National team manager. Conte's 'Azzurri' would lose out on penalties to Germany in the quarter-final of Euro 2016, but not before entertaining all of Europe with their wholehearted, never-say-die approach. Before managing, Conte knew only success. At Juventus he played under two of the greatest ever managers in Giovanni Trapattoni and Marcello Lippi, becoming Lippi's captain and winning every trophy that could be won with the Old Lady. Conte looks like a clever signing for Chelsea. The great Andrea Pirlo agrees and fondly remembers Conte's message to his new team upon arrival at Juventus, "He needed only one speech with many simple words to conquer both Juventus and me. He had fire running through his veins and he moved like a viper. He said 'This squad, dear boys, is coming off two consecutive seventh place finishes. It's crazy. It's shocking. I am not here for this, so it's time to stop being so crap.'" Conte shook up Juventus for sure with his biggest attribute being his defensive coaching. His teams simply refused to leak goals. Over three seasons from 2011–2014 they would allow only sixty-seven, at an average of 0.58 per game. That type of defensive record wins you leagues, lots of them. So, it appears that Chelsea have bagged a younger, more energetic and infinitely more agreeable version of Mourinho. Maybe the Blue Flag of west London may once more be in the ascendency.

In North London, Wenger and Pochettino still rule over Arsenal and Spurs respectively. Gunners fans continue to call for a new man at the helm, but it's hard to see who is available outside of England that would be an improvement. Carlo Ancelotti took over from Guardiola at Bayern Munich. Tuchel is fully occupied building a youthful Dortmund team to compete with the ageing Munich. Sevilla's serial winner Unai Emery got lured by money-bags Paris St Germain. Diego Simeone has been linked and he, of all of the above, might just be the heir to Wenger's throne. At Tottenham, Pochettino's project goes from strength to strength and he may just be the godsend to break the Spursy jinx and end the Hotspur's fifty-five-year wait for a League crown and, in doing so, call time once and for all on St Totteringham's Day.

Ronald Koeman, another student of Dutch master Cruyff, would be enticed away from Southampton by Everton. Koeman captained Cruyff's European Cup winning team at Barcelona, scoring the winning goal in the Wembley final. Any final will do for the Blue-side of Merseyside, as the shrewd Dutchman sets plans for a new era of glory for the Toffees. With fresh shareholder investment and a new stadium mooted, Everton are starting to hope again.

And then there are champions Leicester. Claudio Ranieri continues to manage the Foxes and only Kante from the playing personnel has been lost, lured by Chelsea's gold. New signings have deepened the Foxes squad, which will be fully stretched on two fronts – the defence of their League crown and the club's first ever foray into the European Cup. It's hard to see lightening striking twice, but after last season's miracle, one should never say never. Leicester's win came amid a perfect storm amongst the big clubs. We will hardly witness such a confluence of implosions again.

So, the protagonists were readying for the battles that lay ahead. The new owners, the new players, the new managers. Only a few short weeks of gruelling pre-season preparations remained. Had Liverpool enough mettle to put up a fight in Klopp's first full season? Klopp and his troops would need to show marked improvement, the honeymoon period was ending. But it wasn't just manager and players who would face the scrutiny of the microscope. For the first time, Liverpool fans were looking with inquisitive eyes to Boston. After six seasons, did the Reds find themselves any closer to the prize under the ownership of FSG? Like everybody around L4, they too were now on trial.

THE TRIAL OF JOHN HENRY AND FENWAY SPORTS GROUP

'Judge: It's now your duty to sit down and try and separate the facts from the fancy.' – Twelve Angry Men. Sidney Lumet

Sometimes, as a parent, you might dismiss a child's question or reply flippantly without great thought, comfortable in your notion that they just don't get it, they're too young to understand. I try not to fall foul of this mistake too often, as one important role of a parent is to give your child a voice, a voice that is listened to.

So when my son asks me, "Why is it always Catch 22, why can't we spend more and buy Pogba like United did?" I have to pause and consider. For a while I find I'm stymied as I search for a good answer. My immediate reaction was, "because we don't have the money," but after a few moments I wonder is that really the truth of the matter. Is it money or ambition I question to myself silently.

"Well that's what we are told. We work within a budget. FSG say that the club spend what it has made from football operations. They won't put in funds, nor extract them." I continue.

"So we made no money last year, is that why we spent zero?"

"I think we clear roughly £30 million a year in profit which is available for transfers," I reply

"So, it was Klopp who decided not to spend?"

"Maybe," I respond, "he did say he only wanted a certain type of player. Those who wanted to be here and who could add quality."

"Adding quality wouldn't be hard," my son chuckles and it's hard not to agree with him. We still look weak at centre-half, left-back, goalkeeper, on the wings and up front.

“I suppose no European competition is forcing him to keep the squad tight with fewer games to play.”

“Fine,” my son responds, “but with all the new TV Money we could surely have bought one £50 million player. Arsenal spent £82 million net, Spurs and West Ham £30 million. We need more star quality.”

It’s a no-brainer really, the club is flush with new TV money and we are, and have been, short on star quality for some time. It’s one of the reasons we keep tasting defeat in the face of victory. Mane may prove to have gold dust sprinkled on his feet, but another magical assistant wouldn’t have gone amiss.

“Is it Klopp or FSG then?” my son continues, still gnawing at the bone.

Again I pause and Brendan Rodgers’ words about performing to par ring in my ears. “Give me the tools and I’ll do the work,” he told us a week before he was axed. If there is one thing we know, it is that FSG, and maybe all owners, are very precious about not being called out in public. It didn’t work for Rafa, nor Rodgers, yet when it has to be done, then it should be done and let the devil be badgered.

So what are FSG’s ambitions? They rolled into Liverpool nearly seven years ago in 2010. In their own words, financial growth was slowing at the Red Sox and in their other sporting businesses. Liverpool offered an opportunity to buy an underutilised global brand on the cheap. Fair enough, they are businessmen, not local owners with civic pride like previous custodians the Moores family. English football had already sold its soul, and now you just hope that the highest bidder for your given club possesses one themselves. But FSG said they wanted to win, didn’t they? Tom Werner had said clearly ‘we come to win’, yet under the stewardship of FSG Liverpool have experienced league finishes of 6th, 8th, 7th, 2nd, 6th and 8th. Add to that one solitary trophy, the League Cup won by Dalglish in 2012, and their reign hails as one of the worst in Liverpool’s long and illustrious history.

Has it been the fault of the managers? Hodgson, Dalglish, Rodgers all fired. King Kenny summoned to Boston for the axe. How dare they? If you want to chop our man’s head off, you should come to Liverpool, his home, our home. Rodgers dismissed by phone, not good. Or is there a bigger picture? Is meandering along acceptable if investment valuations are going through the roof regardless?

They say that over the longer run, where you rank in spending on transfers and wages correlates to where you finish in the table, more often than not. We saw how the Cleveland Cavaliers ended the long wait to win their first national title, so it was no surprise to see in an international sporting study that the Cavaliers ranked number one in the world for highest wage payments. When we look at Liverpool's spend under FSG in the table below and assess where they rank versus the competition it is easy to see what Rodgers meant by par. In 2016 Liverpool paid every first team player an average of £3.01 million per year. Man United paid £5.42 million. Since 2010 Man United have spent £545 million net in the transfer market compared to Liverpool's not meagre, yet paltry in comparison, £207 million. This is the course Liverpool and their custodians FSG have chosen. It may be sensible, but will it prove successful?

Liverpool's Spending under FSG – Mind the Gap!

2010 – 2016	Player Purchases £ STG M	Player Sales £ STG M	Net Transfer Spend £ STG M	2016 Player Average Wage £ STG M
Man City	914	229	685	5.77
Man United	750	205	545	5.42
Chelsea	777	300	477	4.51
Arsenal	415	186	229	3.70
Liverpool	591	384	207	3.01
Spurs	407	313	94	2.67

FSG arrived in Liverpool hell-bent on implementing the 'Moneyball' philosophy. Billy Beane, its greatest proponent, advised them that the best guy to pull it off in the football world was a man named Damien Comolli. Comolli had worked with Spurs previously and had advised them on the purchases of Gareth Bale and Luka Modric, two of the best players in the world today, both now playing for Real Madrid.

When FSG replaced Hodgson with Dalglish, Comolli was appointed alongside him as Football Director. However, upon his arrival, Comolli found that FSG's new guidelines for signing players weren't going to wash in the footballing sales. All signings had to be for less than £10 million. All signings had to be under twenty-one years old. This was the Premier League, not the Championship. Comolli broke the rules signing Andy Carroll for £35 million, Luis Suarez for £23 million and Jordan Henderson for £16 million. Carroll flopped and Liverpool recovered £15 million. Suarez became a global star and was sold for £75 million and Henderson remains as one of the first names on the team sheet and wears the band of Liverpool captain. For his troubles Comolli got fired. So too did Dalglish. John Henry subsequently admitted that 'Moneyball' and the statistical pinpointing of undervalued talent didn't work with football, 'the game was too dynamic'.

My son shakes his head and laughs. "So these guys knew nothing about football basically, and have spent the last seven years working it out on our time."

"Yep, that's about the sum of it. The Red Sox manager, Francona, he said they knew nothing about Baseball either, but hey, at least that worked."

"It's not working here though."

"No not yet."

"Have they done anything good for us?"

"They did sort the stadium out, for that they should be commended," I tell him, "and they have cleared the club of any debt, except their own that is. They hired Rodgers and Klopp too. They've also kept a low profile, too low maybe. So yeah, they've done good things too, but let's not forget someday they'll be very well paid for their troubles. I'm just not sure that it's not all business for them. Sporting clubs are built to compete, to win, not to make money for wealthy businessmen."

"Do you want them out?" he asks.

I pause for I've found myself pondering this question a lot recently. Over and over, and I can never settle on an answer, so I fudge it a little.

"Not yet. They've settled on Klopp and have signed him for six years. He must have been convinced by their marketing pitch. He could have gone anywhere. If we don't trust their motives, then Klopp's should be clearer I hope – to win! Let's see how the next few years go. Let's see whether both of them want to win as much as the fans do. Then we'll know…What about you?"

"FSG out," he chants over and over; the clarity of youth.

Hung jury.

"And Klopp accepts all of this?" he asks, chanting over.

And here I pause once more. Teeth on bone.

"There is the rub," I explain, "Klopp is manna for these guys. Klopp loves a challenge. He hates to do anything easy. He has a bit of the Wenger in him. He wants to build. Develop youth. Buy cheap, if at all. He wants to make players better, teach them on the training pitch. He is a match made in heaven for the tight-belted rich kids from Boston."

"Has that ever worked?" my son asks. "Have any managers been able to beat the banks, knock over the big boys?"

I smile, for at least here I have some good news to share.

"Yes," I reply, "do you want to meet some of them?"

THE MASTERS OF FOOTBALL

'I am not afraid of an army of lions led by a sheep; I am afraid of an army of sheep led by a lion.' — Alexander the Great

It's 1886. An eight-year-old North Yorkshire boy eagerly awaits the return of his father from the pits. He's late. Maybe he's been to the pub on his way home, thinks young Herbert, as the night creeps in amid the gaslight dimness. When John Chapman eventually arrives home, Herbert's suspicions are confirmed, as he observes the bloodied fists of his father. Bare knuckle fighting in the taverns brings valuable extra income for a family of originally eleven children, now only seven. Despite his youth, young Herbert recognises the sacrifice, as he queues for his hug. Some children of his age are working in the mines, but not he, his father has urged him to look beyond the pit.

Herbert heeds the advice and instead of venturing down the black hole he decides to study for a degree in mining engineering at Sheffield Technical College. However, the management training and industrial knowledge that Chapman learns, would not be put to great use in the mines, rather, it would find application in a profession closely related to the pits, football. Herbert himself was a decent player but had a modest footballing career. He could see that football teams were being managed by administrators and paper-pushers and was sure he could do a better job. And so was born the first football manager in the true sense of the word. A manager who would take control of footballing affairs, tactics, finances, club development and also, crucially, team selection.

I am telling my son of the great football men. The masters. The men who transformed the sport, bit by bit. Each of them a maverick, each a game changer. All, managers who succeeded against the odds. Chapman would be the first of these true pioneers.

After early stints with Northampton and Leeds City, Chapman found success with Huddersfield Town in the 1920s leading the Terriers to two League titles and one FA Cup win. Most teams focused on attack-minded formations, but instead, Chapman built from the back. A resolute WM formation saw three central defenders flanked by two wing backs. The system focused on breaking down opposition moves, followed by quick counter-attacking play. After Swindon Town lost to Chapman's team, their English international Harold Fleming complimented Chapman saying, "You have something more than a team, you have a machine."

Chapman was still hungry for progress, his keen eyes gazing southwards saying, "What a chance there is in London. I would like to build a Newcastle United there." Soon, fortuitously, an advertisement would appear in the *Athletic News* on Monday 11th May 1925;

'Arsenal Football Club is open to receive applications for the position of Team Manager. He must be experienced and possess the highest qualifications for the post, both as to ability and personal character. Gentlemen whose sole ability to build up a good side depends on the payment of heavy and exorbitant transfer fees need not apply.'

"That rules out Mourinho, Conte and Guardiola," my son jokes.

I smile broadly replying, "Exactly! That's exactly it!"

Chapman would apply and get the job. The Gunners had finished third from bottom prior to his arrival, yet by 1930, Arsenal would lift their first ever trophy, the FA Cup, and in 1931 they would become the first London side to wrestle the title away from northern dominance. Chapman's legacy had been cemented.

Chapman would regularly debate football matters with an old colleague, Jimmy Hogan, whom he had met at Spurs during his amateur days. Hogan, like Chapman, was a journeyman footballer. But Hogan's genius lay in coaching. In Austria, he acted as footballing consultant, a guru, to national coach Hugo Meisl and his 'Wunderteam' of the 1930s. Hogan advocated a more skilled game, with better ball control and slicker passing movements, the ball on the ground, not in the air. These technical skills combined with better physical training resulted in vastly improved performances and a style of play described as 'The Whirl'. A game based upon perpetual motion, a fluidity of positions and movement. Each player involved in defence and attack, and able to master all roles. In 1953 when Hungary humbled England 6–3 at Wembley, a fitting tribute was paid to Hogan by Gustav Sebes, the Hungarian manager, when he said of Hogan, "He taught us everything we know about football. When our football history is told, his name should be written in gold."

In 1925, another great footballing man was born, Ernst Happel. Happel, like most other denizens of Vienna, would do his thinking amongst the café society clatter of coffee cups, the serving of brandies and the smoking of cigarettes. Happel's haunt was Café Ritter, a traditional café replete with high ceilings, dark wood wall panels, crystal chandeliers and large windows contemplating the world outside. Happel had become a philosopher of one specific art form, football. Sitting in the Ritter, smoking one cigarette after another, the stocky Albert Finney lookalike contemplated how he would put his footballing philosophies into practice. A minor Dutch side, ADO Den Haag, were keen for him to join. It would mean leaving his beloved Vienna, but sacrifices had to be made, he felt. The move would see the swarthy Happel climb the first rung on the ladder to greatness.

ADO Den Haag were a mid-table side when Happel arrived in 1962. Quickly he would transform the sleepy team into real challengers, with top four finishes becoming the norm. Happel's philosophy was clear and echoed the club's unabbreviated title – Alles Door Oefening – 'Everything through Practice'. Train hard in a defined system and formation and the results would come. Happel preferred a fluid and flexible 4-3-3 formation which was new to the lowlands. Dutch football at the time was more familiar with winger based systems such as 4-2-4. His system echoed the perpetual motion of Meisl and Hogan's Austrian 'Wunderteam'. Happel led Den Haag to three Dutch Cup finals in four years, from 1963 to 1966, but all would be lost. Happel and his team must have felt that defeat would never turn to victory. But then in 1968 their luck changed. The mighty Ajax of Amsterdam, managed by Rinus Michels and led by Johann Cruyff, awaited in the final. At last ADO prevailed winning 2–1 and lifted their first silverware since 1943, after a wait of twenty-five years. The legend of Happel was born. It is believed by many that the defeat forced Michels' hand in adapting to a

4-3-3 formation and a move closer to 'Total Football'. Happel would go on to win the European Cup twice with unfancied sides Feyenoord in 1970 and Hamburg in 1983 (one of only five managers to do so with two different clubs). His Bruges team would lose both a UEFA and a European Cup Final to Liverpool, and in 1978 he led Holland, without Cruyff, to within the width of a goalpost from lifting the World Cup in Argentina.

Closer to home, Jock Stein became manager of Glasgow Celtic in 1965 – the catholic club's first protestant manager. Stein had already lifted the Scottish Cup with minnows Dunfermline and before long he would end Celtic's twelve-year wait for a title, by immediately leading his new charges to the 1965/66 league title, the first in an incredible nine-in-a-row sequence. Celtic would lose a European Cup Winners Cup semi-final to Shankly's Liverpool in 1966 but one year later they would meet Helenio Herrera and his 'Il Grande Inter' team in the European Cup final. Celtic ran out 2–1 victors and it was hailed as a triumph for attacking football over defensive dogma, with Celtic becoming the first British side to lift the coveted trophy. Stein had declared that, "the best place to defend, is in the opponent's penalty box", and his team played to this creed. Jock Stein would become manager of his country, Scotland, in 1978 and seven years later, he would die aged sixty-two in the place he knew best, the manager's dugout, as his Scottish team played Wales in Cardiff in a World Cup Qualifier.

For the Dutch, football is a cultural thing, every bit as beautiful and poetic as the artistry of Van Gogh and Vermeer. The credit for a lot of this must be laid at the door of Ajax and Rinus Michels, the man who managed Cruyff. Where their inspiration came from we shall never truly know. Maybe from Happel and his 4-3-3 formation? Maybe from the magnificent Hungarian Magyars or 'the whirl' of Austria's 'Wunderteam', both inspired by Jimmy Hogan? Maybe, as some people believe, Cruyff was the origin? Under Michels, Ajax would build a way of football that would transcend from the first team all the way down to the youths and the kids in the academy, some of these as young as ten and eleven years old. They would set on a 4-3-3 formation, whereby each part of the pitch could be accessed by a player quickly, movement conquering space, with complete fluidity, each player capable of transitioning into somebody else's role – 'Total Football'. The team moves forward and backwards in waves of relentless pressure, whether it be attacking or defending. The space becomes malleable and manageable, making the pitch as large or as small as possible, by exploiting all available space.

From 1965 to 1971, Michels developed and honed his philosophy and Ajax lifted trophy after trophy. Four League titles, three Dutch (KNVB) Cups and one European Cup victory in 1971 at Wembley. Cruyff was effusive when he spoke of his mentor Michels, "I always greatly admired his leadership. Both as a player and a coach, there is nobody who taught me as much as he did. I often tried to imitate him and that's the greatest compliment one can give."

Michels would leave Ajax for Barcelona after the Wembley triumph. Two years later after lifting two more European Cups, Cruyff would follow him. At Barcelona, Michels and Cruyff set about ripping the structure of the Catalan club apart and rebuilding it in the image of their Amsterdam Academy. Neeskens would join his Dutch compatriots to assist with the rebuild, the 'turning Barcelona Orange' project. A new powerful force in world football was being born. Barcelona had never dominated like their capital city rivals, Real Madrid. The Catalonians had still to lift a European Cup. Under the Dutch influence though, Barcelona would evolve into a possession-based football team built on the foundations of their youth academy – La Masia. It was Ajax Mark II. Michels would leave Barca in 1978 and would go on to lead his country, Holland, to their first ever international success at the 1988 European Championship in Germany.

In 1988 Cruyff would take the management helm at Barcelona and eventually become their longest serving coach. He would win four League titles in six years, and most tellingly, he would lead Barcelona to their first ever European Cup win in 1992, defeating Sampdoria of Genoa 1–0 at Wembley, with a goal from current Everton manager Ronald Koeman. It made sense that a defender would get the winner. Martin Jol remembered of Cruyff, "he wanted defenders who were footballers first. Creating an extra man in midfield was always essential to him. So many of the ideas were his. Even when he was twenty, thirty-year-old players at Ajax would sit listening to him."

One player in Cruyff's Barcelona team that night was a young Josep

('Pep') Guardiola. Guardiola, a disciple of Cruyff and of Total Football, would himself become manager of Barcelona in 2008. His Lionel Messi led team would lift three League titles and two European Cups in the space of three years. Guardiola would say, "Johann Cruyff painted the chapel, and Barcelona coaches since, merely restore or improve it." With Guardiola now at Man City it may be that Total Football, Mark 3 has arrived in Manchester.

"I didn't know that stuff about Guardiola," says my son, who has listened patiently throughout. "Do you buy into this 'Total Football' stuff?" he asks.

"Yes, but to a point. Every winning system needs players good enough to play it and make it successful. You don't get better than Cruyff, Neeskens and Co. Yet you can argue that the system makes the players too, it gives them confidence and confidence is everything. I think really good footballers can play in many roles. Great players can play anywhere. With all the pressing and with the fluidity of the attacking players and the wing backs that Klopp employs, you could actually call his tactics 'Total Football' just as easily as 'geggenpressing'. I think you can have hybrid systems, all kinds of systems. The key is that the players know the system, and have the discipline to carry it out, every time, to believe in it. That's why Klopp always bangs on about training. And what was Happel's first team called – ADO remember? Practice or training makes perfect."

"Klopp said that the players gave up on the system in Basel, in the second half. Is that what happened? Or were they tired?" he asks.

"It was probably a bit of both, but I think so many of them had not won and suddenly, when within touching distance, they wilted. Same in 2014 with Rodgers, the home stretch is the hardest. But you have to keep putting yourself there, in with a chance and then one day… it's gotta happen. The weight of history gives us this hope."

My son knows Liverpool's history, the story since Shankly anyhow. He knows how the great man from Glenbuck resuscitated a club floundering in Division Two and transformed it into the best in England, whilst laying the foundations for glorious European conquests. He has heard of how Shankly's disciples such as Paisley and Fagan built on these foundations. And he knows all about Dalglish and then years later Rafa.

So I'm telling him about the managers he doesn't know – doesn't really know!

"Did you know Alex Ferguson won a European Trophy?" I ask.

"Err, yeah… two, wasn't it?"

"No, I mean before United, with Aberdeen."

"What? No way," comes the reply.

And so, although I hardly want to, I tell him. He needs to hear it from me. The Ferguson story and of how an over-achieving career was built long before he ever reached Old Trafford. As manager of lowly St Mirren, Ferguson would oversee their promotion to the top tier of Scottish football in 1977. St Mirren would survive their season in the top flight, but Ferguson's constant fighting and wrestling with the board for complete control of the club, would see him sacked and leave prematurely. St Mirren chairman, Willie Todd, would issue what we now know is one of the most ludicrous statements in the history of sport, saying that Ferguson had 'no managerial ability'. It wasn't long before Ferguson would show everybody just how much ability he had. In the merry-go-round that is football management, Jock Stein was leaving Celtic to take the job at Leeds United. Aberdeen boss, Billy McNeill, the captain of Stein's Lisbon Lions, who lifted the European Cup in 1967, would leave Aberdeen and move to the vacant seat at Celtic. Ferguson would be offered McNeill's old job in the North East and he jumped at the chance. Aberdeen had a good team, but mentally they could never seem to break the stranglehold held by their bitter Glasgow rivals, Celtic and Rangers. One League title in eighty years attested to this. Ferguson knew he had to change that mindset and somehow create winners, not also-rans. In 1986, after an eight year reign, Ferguson's Aberdeen had won three League titles, four Scottish Cups, one Scottish League Cup and a European Cup Winners Cup, beating the mighty Real Madrid in the final. If he had never gone to Manchester, he would have been a managerial legend for this work alone. But as Liverpool fans know to our regret, his work was far from done.

"I didn't know that about Ferguson," my son exclaims. "Aberdeen beat Real Madrid in the final?"

"Yes, they did," I tell him, "In Gothenburg, 2–1. It wasn't Real's greatest team ever, but that's not taking away from the achievement."

Fergie used a psychological ploy suggested by his mentor Jock Stein, presenting Real coach, the great Alfredo Di Stefano, with a big bottle of whiskey the night before the game. "Make him think you are just happy to be there," Stein had told him. It worked.

I remind my son of Brian Clough. Together we have watched the two great movies about the enigma, *The Damned United* and *I Believe in Miracles*. For me, Brian Clough was possibly the best of them all. His feats were staggering. Dragging Derby County from the Second Division to the First Division, winning it and then leading the Rams to the semi-final of the European Cup. He then joined near neighbours Nottingham Forest. A team which was described as 'a mix of fresh and worn faces who ought to be slogging it out at the bottom of the table'. Few knew who any of them were, with the exception of goalkeeper Peter Shilton. Yet Forest possessed one gold star, Clough himself. And he wasn't shy about letting people know it, hilariously saying, "Did you know Sinatra met me once?" Known or not known, Clough guided his merry band of misfits from the Second to the First Division. Then they won the League first time out. And if that wasn't crazy enough, Forest proceeded to lift not one, but two European Cups. "I wouldn't say I was the best manager in the business, but I was in the top one", Clough would cheekily reminisce.

My son knows of how Rafa broke up the Spanish cartel of Madrid and Barça and how Simeone followed in his footsteps and still does. He knows about the English based managers – Wenger, Mourinho and Guardiola.

My lesson is nearing a close, with only a few names left on our list. The answer seems clear. History always throws up 'Davids' who can achieve what others can't, who can win against all the odds, slay the Goliaths.

"So where does that leave us?" he asks and once more we look down through the names of over-achievers, footballing mavericks, innovators, game changers and motivational magicians.

My son jabs a finger at the page and highlights one name – Guardiola, Man City's manager.

"If he is as good, or maybe even a better manager than Klopp, like they say he is, because everybody thinks he's the best, and if he has better players and more money to buy even better players again, well, what then?" he asks, once more gnawing away at the question that dogs us all – is the chase futile?

"I don't know, but remember what Atletico Madrid have done. Simeone took down Guardiola and Messi together, not to mention Suarez and Neymar too. Atletico also beat a Real Madrid team which included Ronaldo, Bale, Rodriguez and Kroos. So there is always hope. The thing is we just don't know how good Guardiola really is. Klopp too, for that matter, we can only hope that our man is maturing in knowledge, getting even better than his days at Dortmund when he felled the Gorilla with his bow and arrow."

"Maybe we are just cursed," he jokes, "and we'll never win it again." I laugh too, but as I chuckle, one last name springs to mind, a man I forgot. So I tell him the crazy story of Bela Guttman. And as I do, silently I pray. I pray that there are no such things as curses, for only a fool would believe in such nonsense... even after twenty-six years.

★★★

Over a period of forty years, Guttmann, a Hungarian Jew, would manage twenty club teams, in twelve countries, over two continents, never staying longer than three years in any one role. In 1953, he took charge of AC Milan and a team that included legend Nils Liedholm. Midway through his second season in charge, and with Milan on top of the table, Guttmann was fired. His fiery temper and penchant for arguing over the smallest of matters had been his undoing. At his parting press conference he stunned the waiting press with the outrageous comment: "I have been sacked even though I am neither a criminal nor a homosexual. Goodbye."

In 1957, Guttmann would find himself at the other end of the globe, in Sao Paolo, Brazil, and his time there would influence the national team towards developing a 4-2-4 system, one that would see them conquer the World at the 1958 World Cup in Sweden, Pele et al. That year, Guttmann moved to Portugal and so began the most successful spell of his career. He took charge of FC Porto and helped them overhaul a five-point lead enjoyed by Benfica, to win the Portuguese League title in 1959. Benfica responded by offering Guttmann more money to join them and without hesitation he did. Now at Benfica, Guttmann showed his ruthless streak as he promptly sacked twenty senior players, and promoted a host of youth players to the first team. Reports abounded that neighbours Sporting Lisbon had unearthed a jewel of a player playing for their feeder club in Mozambique. His name was Eusébio. Having got wind of the story, Guttmann flew to Mozambique, tracked the kid down and convinced him to sign for Benfica. A major row erupted between the two clubs. Fearing a kidnap attempt on the young Eusébio, Benfica clandestinely smuggled the young player into Portugal giving him a code name so that he would not be traced – Ruth Malosso. Such was the tension surrounding his move, the youthful Eusébio was forced to hide out in an Algarve hotel for a fortnight. Eusébio would go on to become one of the best footballers the world had ever seen.

Now, with a potent blend of experience and talented youth, the Eagles of Benfica soared and lifted the League title in 1960 and 1961. Benfica also won the European Cup twice in a row. In 1961 they beat Barcelona 3–2 and in 1962 they retained the title, coming from 2–0 and 3–2 down to beat Real Madrid 5–3. Guttmann had conquered Europe, twice, and beaten the best there was to beat. Things couldn't be better. He asked for a bonus for his fantastic work but was refused. Guttmann, if nothing else, was consistent. He walked. But not before issuing his infamous curse. He swore to the board: "not in a hundred years from now will Benfica ever be European champion." Since that fateful day, Benfica have reached no less than eight European finals, five in the European Cup and three in the UEFA/Europa League and have lost all eight. Before the 1990 European Cup final between Benfica and AC Milan, held in Vienna, where Guttmann was buried, his former great prodigy, the player he had smuggled in from Mozambique, Eusébio leant by Guttmann's grave and prayed for the curse to be lifted. As we know the prayers didn't work and Milan won 1–0. To this day the curse of Guttmann lives on.

THE DNA

'It is a cursed evil to any man to become as absorbed in any subject as I am in mine.' — Charles Darwin

In baseball we saw the 'Moneyball' story of the Oakland A's and Billy Beane. We saw how FSG would employ the father of Sabermetrics, Bill James, partner him with a college kid, Theo Epstein and together end an eighty-six-year curse with the Boston Red Sox. Epstein would do it again with the Cubs. The A's, the Red Sox and the Cubs couldn't outspend the Yankees, but they could try to out-think them. Outfox them. This side of the pond we witnessed the unleashed havoc caused by another skulk of foxes, Leicester City. Playing to their strengths of lightning speed, counter-attack and dogged defending, the Foxes beat all-comers and in doing so exploded a decade-long obsession with possession football, temporarily anyhow. Leicester proved to be a better team without the ball. So how did Liverpool plan to make the breakthrough? How was Klopp going to succeed against all the odds? He had done it before, but not against such overwhelming obstacles as those that faced him now. In Germany, there had been one beast, here there were many behemoths, all bigger, stronger and more ferocious. If one didn't get you, then another would. If he could pull this off and somehow succeed, defying all logic, a place amongst the legendary Masters awaited. A place alongside Stein, Happel, Guttmann, Chapman and Clough not to mention the Godfather himself, Shankly.

If Klopp is someday to walk in Shankly's footsteps then many already see a resemblance between the two. Ian St John, a player whom Shankly built his first Liverpool team around, sees Klopp as being as capable as any recent Liverpool manager. "Klopp is in the same mould as Bill Shankly, he has the same characteristics and enthusiasm." Steve Heighway, immortalised in the song 'Fields of Anfield Road', played under Shankly and also ran Liverpool's youth Academy for many years. He believes Shankly would approve of Klopp. "There has been enormous change at Liverpool, but when I see what is happening here now, I approve. And I think Shanks would approve too. He'd approve of the work rate. He'd approve of the way the first team are playing. And he'd approve of the way we are treating the youngsters. He would like that. He would like that a lot."

Where Shankly, Busby and Stein built their clubs from the ground up, including the facilities and stadiums, today's great managers are tasked with building an identity, a philosophy. Klopp has wasted no time. He has plans afoot to move from Melwood, Liverpool's training facility since the late 50s, to join with the youth Academy at Kirkby. Following that transition all will develop and train as one, in one location. From the seniors down to the underage children. All learning one system of play, developing a philosophical backbone that will spine through the club. Klopp explains why this is good for the kids. "Of course, it makes sense they get used to it as early as possible, but not too early. We don't have to talk about it with a ten to twelve-year-old. There has to be individual development. There comes a moment where you are to be involved in team tactics and all that stuff. We work very close together."

Klopp looks to the long term. He has signed a six-year deal, he can. FSG are delighted to have him tied down. "His leadership will be critical to everything we hope to achieve. The ideas and plans he has for the football infrastructure excite us," remarks John Henry. "When you have an individual of Jürgen's quality in the building it makes sense to secure that person for a long time. To not do so would be irresponsible." For Liverpool fans, having watched the manager's door continuously revolve throughout this recent period of American ownership, this newfound stability, which has always been the hallmark of the club, is a breath of fresh air. Klopp talks of patience to fulfil the dream, and in truth he needn't bother, Liverpool fans are as patient as they come. Once they see the club moving in the right direction that is. Even at the end with Rodgers, dissent came only in murmurs and grumblings.

Klopp explains the benefits. "I have always been longer term in my clubs. When I saw a sixteen-year-old player who was good, I could always wait for him." Gary Gordon, a youth coach under Klopp at Dortmund expands on Klopp's desire to develop youth. "He likes to make his own stamp and say 'I brought him through from the academy didn't I?' That gives the whole club a kick. If you just keep buying, then what does that say to the rest of the youth crews? There's no point in trying because nobody is coming through. He wanted fast players – they had to be fast. It wasn't worth picking up anyone who was slow. It doesn't matter how technically gifted they were, he didn't want a slow player. He also wanted hungry players, who didn't have to be pushed. He doesn't need stars, he needs hungry players. Stars are going to be difficult to deal with. Young players in their early twenties and taking them to the next level is his thing. That's what he's good at." Klopp wants the kids to believe that the path is open to the first team. He believes in a one-club approach at all age levels. In fact, he guarantees it pledging, "I can promise that before we sign a player which is not a lot better than what we have, we'll always use our own boys. That's how it is. That's how the future should be. Even in this crazy football transfer world, we want to be this special club."

Ferguson's experience at United was similar as he explained, "Because I was at United for such a long time, I could afford to plan ahead – no one expected me to go anywhere." Dalglish agreed with Ferguson's methods and went as far as saying, "Many clubs should look and learn. The way he came in and had a right good look at the youth side. He didn't gauge their success in terms of trophies but through progressing their ability." Giggs, Scholes, Neville and Beckham would emerge to justify the wisdom.

Klopp's passion and drive remind us again of the greats that went before him. Yet, his didn't emanate from a youth spent down the blackened mines. Instead, it seems an ultra-competitive father helped stir the fire within. When playing tennis, Jürgen's dad, Norbert, would win 6–0, 6–0. "Do you think this is fun for me?" Jürgen would shout in anger over the net.

"Do you think this is fun for me?" a furious Norbert would reply.

"He was ruthless," Klopp spoke of his father. "When we went skiing, I only ever saw his red anorak from behind. He never waited for me. It didn't matter that I was just a beginner. He wanted me to become the perfect skier." Klopp's father would die from cancer in 2000, not getting to witness Klopp's remarkable rise to success with Dortmund. Klopp, a religious man, states, "I firmly believe that he is watching from above." What Norbert bred was a fighter. Klopp junior would describe his playing days with Mainz – "I was a fighting machine with a will of iron." Now it is the son's ways that are hard and uncompromising. Tough love. He looks for players suited to the challenge. "For me, attitude is always more important than talent."

Klopp admits too, that the job becomes obsessive. "My car knows only one way – home to here, here to home. There are more exciting lives around." But if Klopp spends most of his waking hours scheming a path to Red's success then it is because the bug has caught him, he is hooked. "I think I am the right person for the job. I am not saying I am the best manager in the world, but I'm quite good and I am one of those managers who is really interested in structure. Here is the moment when the club needs consistency in this chair – they need the right person and I am the right person. It wasn't a big decision for me. It was the only club that could have broken up my holiday. I had enough offers, I was saying 'No, no, sorry, not now…' and then came Liverpool. And I know how this sounds, and what people will say, but I fell in love. I felt responsible really quickly. It's like if you are in my inner circle, my family, my friends. I felt Liverpool was both; family and friends."

He speaks with the conviction, singlemindedness and vision synonymous with successful leaders. He also carries that indefinable aura that cannot be faked. After meeting Klopp, Steve Gerrard said he left the room 'feeling ten feet tall'. One consistent feature of great and over-achieving managers is their very persona. Many seem to have been individual forces of nature. Their mere presence capable of silencing a room, a square, a city. German footballing legend Horst Hrubesch recalled meeting Ernst Happel for the first time when the Austrian joined Hamburg. "He came into the dressing room and I thought somebody had switched the light on. My teammates felt the same."

In the modern manager we find a different animal to the club-builders of old. It is not always a given that they are even the most important man at the club. These days, more often than not, the manager earns less than the star players. An average quality Premier League player can earn

£4 million per year. The best can earn £15 million or more. Rarely do managers' wages reach these heights. These players are often islands, removed from the reality of society, mollycoddled from a young age, constantly told that they are special and never in the wrong. The thought of 'respecting' their manager might never occur to them, never mind 'fearing' him. If one club doesn't work out, another will come along, there is no need to get too worked up. If the player fails, it wasn't his fault. 'I was played in the wrong position' or 'the manager didn't trust me' are popular refrains. Respect and deference don't come with the job anymore, they have to be earned. It was clear to anybody who looked in the direction of Klopp that he both demanded and commanded respect. There was only one boss.

All the great managers need control, Shankly wouldn't sign for Liverpool until the board agreed that he controlled all football matters and picked the team too. Finding the right type of character and style of player to fit the team and its philosophy is crucial. Get this wrong and you can have a mess on your hands. Rodgers never wrestled full control of which players were or were not recruited during his time at Anfield. It didn't help when he needed a striker and instead got a misfit in Balotelli, a player it seemed devoid of even an ounce of the thing Rodgers demanded most – character. Why Rodgers was derided for asking for this trait I will never know, for what more can we want of ourselves, our family, or even the team we support, than to have character? Arsenal legend of the thirties, Herbert Chapman, when discussing player recruitment observed, "I'm always sorry for clubs who have to act hurriedly, for under favourable conditions it is a tricky business. It is not enough that a man should be a good player. The longer I have been on the managerial side, the more I am convinced that an all-round intelligence is one of the highest qualifications. One of the first enquiries I make when contemplating the engagement of a man is 'What sort of a life does he lead?' I will never tolerate slackness". Cruyff would agree on the need for footballing intelligence, "You play football with your head, and your legs are there to help you." I'm doubtful if either would have signed or tolerated Signor Balotelli.

Where Rodgers had been undermined, Klopp stood firm, insisting on the last word on transfers. After nine months of assessing the squad inherited, it was time to begin moulding the group into the shape that he desired. Klopp described what he looked for in a signing, stating that he needed players who were interested, "in pushing the train, not jumping on board the running train. If you are full of motivation as a player, if you are full of concentration, I am open arms."

And he means it literally, the tall German's fondness for bear-hugging his players as often as possible has been well documented. Klopp is not the sergeant major type, instead he is a warm and tactile leader of men, a natural born motivator and intuitive man-manager. What at first seemed to be a gimmick, has over time borne fruit and trust amongst his charges. Adam Lallana explains "People speak about the hugs he seems to give everyone, but sometimes it can mean a lot to a player. It can make you feel wanted and it shows he appreciates the hard work you've just put in. He demands hard work, he demands 100 per cent."

At Dortmund, Klopp had this knack for getting more from less. He signed relative unknowns such as Subotic, Hummels, Kagawa, Lewandowski, Piszczek, Gundognan, Reus, Mkhitaryan, Aubameyang and Gotze, all for a collective £55 million and then polished them into diamonds worth at least four to five times that amount. His 'kindergarten' championship winning team was the youngest ever in German history with an average age of 24.2. Liverpool will be hoping that Klopp can replicate that ability to mine talent and polish young diamonds. The Liverpool squad inherited by Klopp is the second youngest in the Premier League, after Spurs, with an average age of 25.7 versus a division wide average of 27.4. Just like Klopp, Simeone talked about needing time and patience to build a footballing philosophy – "If you look away, you do not see the immediate step, and stumble. You have to go slowly." Patience is a rare commodity though, in today's 'three losses and you're out' environment.

Yet, developing and promoting youth of itself doesn't equal success. At some point along the curve it all has to come together in a winning formula. Young and old, youth and experience. Character. In the 2015/16 season the average age of the major League winning teams in Europe was as follows; Leicester 27.5, Barcelona 27, PSG 27, Bayern Munich 27 and Juventus 28. This suggests that winning teams tend to have more experience and are often teams that have grown and matured together. They also include the best of any age bracket, not the worst.

The best managers are never satisfied, and we can only assume that Klopp wants to add further silverware to his German haul. At Liverpool, when the winners' medals were handed around at the end of the season, nobody celebrated, instead the most important message was to note the date for the start of pre-season training and issue a warning to stay fit during the holiday period. Chapman would say at Arsenal, "There is one Golden Rule; it is never safe to be satisfied. No matter how good the team may be, there should always be an attempt to improve it. It is sometimes said that a winning team is got together by luck. This has not been my experience. One has to watch a team like a thermometer." Ferguson agreed, saying, "I believe that the cycle of a successful team lasts maybe four years, and then some change is needed."

Klopp, like some of the greats before him, believes in structure and shape. At Arsenal, Chapman the industrialist spoke of building a machine with his WM formation. He realised he was breaking the mould saying, "In my playing days no attempt was made to organise victory. The day of haphazard football has gone." Klopp talks of transforming his players into machines and of hugging them after the last drop of fuel had been expended. In these scenarios, the players lose some of their identity for the good of the whole, the power of the larger collective team-machine. Happel had a similar philosophy. "In football, specialists are only useful up to a point. That worries me. You can field a dilettante anywhere. That pleases me."

Klopp is all too aware of the expectations that weigh on his team and on him. Yet he wears it lightly. Stress seems alien to him. He is intelligent and thoughtful and always respectful. A manager for the people. Echoes of Shankly's socialist solidarity abound. "We are very much at the beginning of our journey." he reminds us. "I am the first to recognise that with this great commitment, comes a great responsibility. There is much to do and much to achieve and we look to do this by being the most completely together group anywhere in the world." Being together is a start, but more will be needed. Much more. Just like the Masters before him, Klopp seems to possess the DNA of a Goliath vanquishing 'David'.

ALLES DOOR OEFENING

'The Liverpool Way is the Hard Way' – Jurgen Klopp

Upon his appointment, FSG set one critical objective for Klopp. To implement a brand of football and instil within the club a footballing identity. By the end of the 2015/16 season this mission had been partially achieved. Klopp had always preached that he needed time to educate his charges fully, to shape them into prime physical specimens, to teach them over and over, what to do, and when to do it. "I'm really looking forward to the pre-season, it will make us stronger, make us fitter." Klopp would say, "If you train often enough, you can be a really strong side. It's all about change, it's all about development, it's all about training, and it's all about improvement." ADO, Alles Door Oefening and Happel spring to mind, everything through practice.

A Klopp team needs to be ultra-fit so that it can relentlessly hunt and press high up the pitch in their opponent's defensive third, where any loss of the ball or mistake can be pounced upon and punished to maximum effect. We saw this style in all its glory away to Man City in November 2015. That result and performance was achieved only one month into the German's stewardship. Klopp has always maintained, for those who wish to listen, that his success will come from the training ground, not from the transfer market. Fifty-two matches in 215 days has afforded scant opportunity to teach his manifesto on the green pastures of Melwood. He describes it as 'a short year', a period that has flown by.

July 2016 saw the beginning of pre-season training. The football world left the desert and renewed once more. Klopp explained what lay ahead. "It will be triple training sessions, of course. We have to do a lot to create a base for a full year. We have a special plan of what we want to do with the boys. Everything you do is based around physical potential and what you do in pre-season is key to that." Observers at the Melwood training sessions and on the pre-season tour of America spoke of players getting sick, others doubled over in agony, puffing for wind, many leaving the training pitches ashen faced from exhaustion, but no dissenters. Klopp had achieved buy-in. When he told them that more work now would pay dividends later in the season, they believed it, they went again, in spite of the pain. Pre-season training under Klopp was no summer camp, even if the crowd looked on in T-shirts and short skirts under the baking Californian sunshine.

Klopp's boys were not the first Liverpool team to be welcomed in America for pre-season boot camp. Upon resumption of football after the Second World War and with food rationing still very much an issue at home, Liverpool manager George Kay and his Chairman Bill McConnell had the inspired idea that a pre-season tour of the United States would benefit the players. From May to June 1946 the Reds toured the US, beating sides such as the New York All Stars and the Chicago Maroons on their travels. Kay commented, "The players are 25 per cent above par in football, due in my opinion to the quality, quantity and variety of food." The following campaign culminated in a trip to Molineux to meet Wolverhampton Wanderers with the League on the line. Wolves dominated the game, but Liverpool withstood the pressure, and two counter-attack goals from Balmer and big-money signing Stubbins, whose face would be one of many to grace the Beatles 'Sgt. Pepper's Lonely Hearts Club Band' album cover, sealed the win. Liverpool were crowned as champions for the fifth time. The American steaks had worked a treat.

Back to the future, and while Klopp's new signings were bedding in on the training pitches, other key recruitments were also settling down to work off the field. If Kay and McConnell thought diet was important, then so too did Jürgen Klopp. Countryman Andreas Kornmayer would be enticed from the arms of Bayern Munich to transform Liverpool's training and fitness programmes, and he would be joined by another colleague from Munich, nutritionist Mona Nemmer. Kornmayer had converted Munich into one of the fittest teams in Europe during his spell at the Bavarians and helped reduce the number of injuries suffered. Thomas Mueller, the superb Bayern and German international striker, albeit never one renowned for his pace, would say of Kornmayer, "He transformed me from a slow snail into a speedy snail." Now, Klopp has tasked him to work the same transformation at Liverpool. Emre Can summarises the simple goal set by Klopp, "To be the fittest team in the League." The engine is being built. If you are to beat Klopp's Liverpool, it will not be by running harder or longer.

A philosophy is also being taught, one that is all about the team, literally. Klopp's assistant Peter Krawietz explains, "We've tried to create an atmosphere among the squad which is always really competitive. As a team, we know that the only way we can reach anywhere is by working together. We try to 'live' this in our coaching team. Six, eight, or ten of us will always see more than just one or two. We can have more ideas if we all work together, discuss and find the best solutions. We try to show the players the same too. For them, it's really important. 'TEAM: Together Everyone Achieves More' – that's what we always stress to them." Shankly's socialist ideals are coming up through the roots.

Klopp expands. "Stability wins games and gets you points. The willingness of the players to work together as a team is crucial. We wanted to be part of a group and that is something we need to accept as a Golden Rule until the end of our lives. I'm only as strong as my team mates let me be. Then it works beautifully. Thanks to stability."

With Klopp, though, these are not just words, there is a reason that Liverpool under the German have become a team that never seems to know when it is beaten, staging last gasp comebacks or victories time and time again. The German has created a strong and unified bond between his men. They have become a band of brothers, a fighting troop. James Milner talks of the connection within the group. "This team has a lot of togetherness and team spirit. I think we play as a team probably better than any team I've been involved in. With and without the ball, people knowing their jobs, and getting around the ball and winning the ball back as a team as well. In the way we play, if one person doesn't do it, the whole system breaks down – both with and without the ball. Everyone has to be on the same page."

Milner's words tell the story of how Klopp wants his sides to play. Klopp describes it himself, "The best moment to win the ball is immediately after your team has lost it. The opponent is still looking for orientation, where to pass the ball. He will have taken his eyes off the game to make his tackle or interception and he will have expended energy. Both make him vulnerable. You have to train the impulse… to move into a ball-winning position immediately after losing the ball. You don't teach a situation, you teach the impulse until it becomes a natural action." Klopp describes 'geggenpressing' as the best playmaker he has. Liverpool's John Moores University agrees, with their study showing that the team who gave the ball away most won only 27 per cent of the time. In American Football the turnover has for a long time been seen as a key decider between winning and losing, to such an extent that the term itself 'Turnover' is part of the everyday lexicon of the game. A study by Minitab concluded that in the NFL, 44 per cent of the variation in a team's winning percentage can be explained by their turnover differential. As former Dallas Cowboys lineman, Dave Widell, once remarked: "Turnovers are like ex-wives. The more you have, the more they cost you."

For Klopp, discipline, hard work and a team-first ethos are absolute non-negotiables. His own work ethic sets the tone for all. There are clear echoes to Liverpool's gloried past. Paisley once remarked, "The secret is that our Liverpool team never know when to stop running and working. Effort is the magic that makes success. Talent and technique are one thing, but fans will always reward effort." Shankly proclaimed: "For a player to be good enough to play for Liverpool, he must be prepared to run through a brick wall for me, then come out fighting on the other side. No football club is successful without hard work." I speak to Roy Evans to gauge his views. "I'm starting to believe in Klopp. It's good, but early days. I don't think Jürgen is one of those guys who wants to spend ridiculous amounts of money. He's confident in what *he* sees in players. He's happy to get a bargain, but occasionally of course you do need to get a really top player, a game changer. We've had them before. Keegan, Dalglish, Suarez. Maybe Mane is a game changer because of his pace. It's not just about Jürgen though, it's about everybody joining in, fans too."

New signing, Sadio Mane, is not long in the door, but already he's singing from the hymn sheet. "It's a system where everybody knows their job. Roberto, Coutinho, Sturridge, Adam… we know each other's game. It's become easier for us thanks to working on it and we are enjoying playing this way. Whether I'm starting up front or out wide isn't really the most important thing, the manager says be free and get into dangerous areas where you can hurt the opposition."

Klopp expands further on his footballing philosophy – "It's very emotional, very fast, very strong, not boring, no chess. Of course tactical, but tactical with big heart. Tactical things are so important, you cannot win without tactics, but the emotion makes the difference. Life in our game, that is important." Interestingly, not all see this emotion as an absolute positive, when I spoke to respected journalist Guillem Balague he urged some caution commenting: "My fear for Liverpool is that it's an emotional team with an emotional coach and emotional fans. Sometimes that works against you, but if they can manage that expectation and emotion, then brilliant. It's fascinating times."

Liverpool finish their pre-season preparations with a resounding 4–0 victory against Barcelona at a packed Wembley stadium. The team look fit and already new signings Mane and Grujic are having an impact and scoring goals. The Reds appear prepared for the challenges that lie ahead. Klopp talks of the club's aspirations. "Why should I limit expectations? I am sure at this moment, as sure as I can be, that we will be successful – but what does it mean at the end? That is the question. We will fight for everything. We cannot say we don't have a chance for this, because right now we have all chances, but so do other clubs." Speaking of transfers he would say, "We did the business we thought we needed. The players will not be an excuse for me, the moment they sign, we share responsibility. They are responsible for their performance. I am responsible too. Its 50-50, let's just try and do the best." Klopp is under no illusions though, as to how hard his task will be. On the eve of the kick-off he reveals what he believes Liverpool will need to do to be successful – "Start perfect, be fantastic in the middle and have a world-class finish." Former Liverpool player Jamie Carragher agrees. "We only lost two league games during the 2008/09 season, but still we fell short. It's getting harder and harder. We're at a point in our history where only by doing everything 100 per cent right, especially making the right calls with transfers and selections, can we have any hope of finishing first."

My son is not convinced. "Discipline and hard work can't beat spending money and signing the best players," he tells me. He may be right, I'm not sure. Certainly in the past the work done by groundbreaking managers had a better chance to stand out from the pack as the financial disparities were not as wide. With the escalation in points collected by the top four teams over the last sixteen years, today it seems clear that the rich are pulling away. Yet I still want to believe that great men can do great things and make a great difference. It will take time though, and patience, and we won't know that we have arrived until we get there. However, if nothing else, with the effervescent Klopp driving, the ride should prove exciting.

PART VII

CONQUEST

LIFT OFF

'The beginning is always today.' —Mary Shelley

It's half-time at the Emirates – Liverpool's first game of the 2016/17 season. The scoreboard reads Arsenal 1–1 Liverpool. Jürgen Klopp's very first opening day in England. He has been preparing his team all summer to be the fittest in the land, but you wouldn't know it, the performance has been sluggish, fitful and error-prone. It lacks confidence and belief and but for a late wonder strike from Coutinho, the Reds would be trailing at the break. In the dressing room Klopp turns to his team in black and demands more.

"You are fitter than them, go and show it. If you show it, you win!"

Within twenty minutes of the restart Liverpool lead 1–4. Approaching full-time some trademark sloppy defending has allowed the Gunners back into the game but come the final whistle the Reds deservedly hold on to win 3–4. They have covered 117.6 km in the sunshine, the highest ever distance since league records began. In the first ninety minutes of the new season we have seen, in its very essence, the Jekyll and Hyde of Klopp's Liverpool. On one hand, turbo charged, dynamic and lethal going forward. On the other, timid and error prone at the back. Solid defences win leagues, but for an opening salvo, away to one of the big boys, this will do nicely.

Klopp's game plan resembled a high octane form of 'Total Football'. A Germanic version of Dutch fluidity. Rinus Michels' Ajax teams of the early seventies and his Dutch team of the 1974 World Cup never gave their opponents time to properly build from the rear, relentlessly applying pressure until they were forced into rushed errors and strewn passes. Similarly, Klopp favours this 4-3-3 formation of Michels and of Happel before him. It is not surprising either, that he is happy to play without an out and out centre-forward. Instead the attacking players interchange roles with fluidity and speed, defenders never quite sure where the next offensive or defensive attack might emanate from. Michels didn't like to call his style 'Total Football'. He would say, "I want to get people away from 'Total Football', as this is not my expression. For me, it would be better to call my game 'Pressing Football'. This is what I wanted to create with my Ajax and Dutch national team in 1974, a basic game where all ten outfield players push forward even when we don't have the ball. We're always pressing forward." Michels did have one caveat though, a large one. "To play the game to its full extent you need at least three or four of the world's best players. Lesser teams will be hit on the break and this could lead to disaster." Here is the lesson for Klopp and he won't need me or anybody else to highlight it. Going forward Liverpool resemble a pack of wolves. A demented, wild and chaotic pack of wolves. While this is very effective in wreaking maximum damage near the opposition's goalmouth, when possession is lost, the pack are less controlled. Huge gaps appear, co-ordination and structure implode. The pack spreads to the winds, exposed and allows itself to be picked off with relative ease. Images of the goals conceded in both of last season's cup finals spring to mind. The last minute goal at Villarreal may be the perfect example. Michels had it right, for who would know better than him. With more quality players in the pack, the fewer mistakes you make both in and out of possession. The pack of itself can win you games. Great players in pack formation can win you trophies.

Regardless, an away victory to Arsenal should always be celebrated and in addition to the result many other positives abound. New signings Wijnaldum and Mane excelled, both contributing to goals with Mane scoring the last himself, a superb solo effort that left three Arsenal players in his wake. In celebration he would run to Klopp on the sideline and leap onto his back. That these players want to play for their manager, there can be no doubt. It seems too that Klopp has mainainted his eye for talent. This is a priceless commodity. Klopp said he wanted players to push the train, hungry players. At fifteen, Mane left Sedhiou in Senegal, to make the 500 mile journey north to Dakar to attend trials. A man approached him and told him that he was in the wrong place. "He asked me 'are you here for the test? With those boots? Look at them, how can you play in them?' They were really bad – torn and old." Mane remembered, it was all he had, he just wanted to play. And when he did, everybody stopped to watch. After the football session the man approached him once more. His tune had changed. "I'm picking you straight away. You'll play in my team." That was the start for Mane. Years later, he is now big-time, yet his £34 million move to Liverpool has not quelled his desire. Mane looks every bit a Klopp player, brimful of daring, bravery and immense speed. And of course, crucially… hunger.

Even more important than the new players is the effect that Klopp was having on those that he inherited. Henderson had been converted into a defensive deep-lying midfielder and, at Arsenal, he controlled the game, nobody running or passing more. Lallana exudes confidence and it showed with his great finish and goal. Firmino now looks every bit a £29 million player and more. Coutinho continues to get better. It will be important for Klopp to keep him on the books when the elite of Spain come prowling.

Arsenal fans are already growing tired of the new season and throughout the second half manager Wenger is subjected to a torrent of abuse. 'Spend some fucking money' being the general refrain. This has been the familiar exhortation for the last ten years, a ten years that has brought no League success and only two FA Cup wins. Qualification for Europe and the Champions League had become a guarantee but it was not enough. Blood was boiling at the Emirates.

For two years running we have left the Emirates listening to the grumbling of the home supporters. This year it is considerably more venomous than before. At times today, it was men against boys. It was hard to know if Liverpool were that good or whether Arsenal had become that bad. It will be a pivotal year for the Gunners and their leader Wenger. Something will have to give.

Yet over the last ten years Arsenal have been more successful than Liverpool. One can only think that, under Klopp, things have to change, ambitions will need to be set higher. Maybe today, in the bright autumn sunshine, we are witnessing the start of a new era of expectation.

***

Gameweek two arrives and Liverpool's Achilles heels wreak havoc away at Burnley. The pack is all over the place. Despite achieving 80 per cent possession Liverpool lose 2–0. This time the statistics lie, the Reds deserve nothing from a poor performance. Punishing the so-called 'weaker' teams remains an enigma for Klopp. In his first season, Klopp's team always seemed to rise to the occasion against the big boys: Chelsea and City would be beaten away in the League. United and Dortmund would be vanquished in Europe. Yet on the flipside, Liverpool would lose at Newcastle, Watford, West Ham, Southampton and Swansea. This Achilles needed healing before a title assault could be waged, but, at the first time of asking Liverpool fail miserably. Two calamitous defensive errors see the home side through with relative ease. I could hear Springsteen singing in the background. '*Same sad story that's a fact, one step up, two steps back*'.

Next, at White Hart Lane, Liverpool did what they do against the big teams. They stood up and took charge. The Reds overpowered Spurs in a way that few sides have managed since Pochettino took charge in North London. A 1–1 result offered the scantest of reward for what was a fantastic team performance. In Klopp's very first game, away at Spurs the season before, his team ran and ran, but managed little else. This time, the story was different. The Reds would outrun the home team but allied to effort came intricate passing and swashbuckling skill. This performance signified a coming of age for the Reds under Klopp. Now, could they repeat it consistently?

The early season statistics show that Liverpool are running faster, stronger and harder than any other team in the League. They are also completing more sprints, which is defined as an action of movement over 25.2km/h. The number of sprints completed has long been held to hold a direct correlation to victory, with the most successful teams completing the most. Early on, Liverpool are also in the top two sides in the League in possession statistics along with Man City. Being tops in possession, running, pressing and sprints makes for a potent combination. Having possession determines that you can choose, more often than not, where you lose the ball, the plan being that this will be in the opponent's danger zone. Of course better still, don't lose it at all.

At Spurs, Liverpool's defence looked better. New centre-half Matip exhibits airs of the great Alan Hansen. Milner, the top class player that he is, makes the conversion to left-back with ease. Klopp, like Shankly and Paisley before him, has the knack of improving a player by changing his position. Polish great Lewandowski would say that spending time on the wing at Dortmund under Klopp, made him into the complete striker as he learned to understand what other players needed from a frontman by way of runs and movement. Not every manager can pull this trick off, players need to buy into the change, for they fear that they will become jack-of-all-positions and master of none.

Early performances see Milner hailed as one of the best left backs in the League. Klopp's credentials are again being validated. His signings have already impressed. His team forage and attack the opposition with a ferocity seldom witnessed in the English game. The team brims with confidence as it exudes from their manager's pores. Time to teach and an arduous pre-season are now yielding early rewards.

Now the stage is set for Klopp's Reds to return home, to play for the first time in a revamped and rebuilt Anfield against champions Leicester. A new stadium awaits a new team in the early days of a new epoch at Liverpool. Klopp is right to say that his team are not twenty-six years without a league title, they are only one and even that wasn't a full season.

With each passing game, Klopp takes the cut of an over-achiever, of a man keen on cementing his legacy, on winning again. He rallies his troops with a call to arms: "We want to go to the best teams in the world and give them hell in the moment we face them – in Manchester, in London, wherever, I don't care. It depends on our attitude. If always the people with the best circumstances would win, this world would be an ugly place. This is football. If there is one part of life where you can challenge the best in the world, then its football." The battle lines have been drawn.

FOR COUNTRY AND LIVERPOOL

'When I have a terrible need of – shall I say the word – religion. Then I go out and paint the stars.' —Vincent Van Gogh

The day before the new Anfield is to open, the great and the good of Liverpool's past are invited to attend an opening ceremony. I think of one man who won't be there, a man who helped shape the stadium itself and the club which calls it home – Bill Shankly. On Tuesday 29th September 1981, Liverpool and the footballing world mourned the passing of the legend. In 1982, the 'Shankly Gates' were erected in honour of the Scot's great service. With the revamp, the gates have been moved a few hundred yards along Anfield Road. A few days before the first game an unlocking ceremony is attended by the Shankly family, at which they are presented with the key.

Later that week I joined Bill's grandson, Christopher Shankly Carline, for a coffee to discuss the changes at Liverpool and what his grandad might have thought of them. Bill Shankly once commented, "Although I'm a Scot, I'd be proud to be called a Scouser," and in truth many felt he was, until he spoke that was. His descendants qualify by birth and have the accent to prove it. Shankly's grandson bears a resemblance to the great man that Bill's wife Nessie often noted. Christopher remarked, "One of the many things that makes me so proud is the fact my Nan, Nessie, and my mum, Jeanette, would often tell me how similar I am to my grandad. From the way I walk, my mannerisms, to the way I look and right through to how I would analyse things. I would constantly be told – 'it's just Bill'."

Christopher manages the family hotel, recently opened in the city centre. The common areas are a shrine to his grandad. The feature which stands out most for me and which says everything about the great man is his Olivetti Lettera 32 typewriter. On this portable aqua-blue machine, Shankly would painstakingly punch out, key by key, responses to every fan mail, letter, or query he received. No person was below him, everybody got a personal reply.

His grandson tells a story, which similarly shows Shankly's empathy with the common man. During Shankly's reign Anfield underwent many facelifts, most driven by the great man himself. A new cantilevered stand was built on the Kemlyn Road in 1963. The Anfield Road stand was rebuilt and given a roof in 1965 and the Main Stand underwent an extensive redesign in 1973. "My grandad would be very proud of the new stadium. I know even going back to when he was manager, he used to personally go in and visit a lot of the residents who lived around the ground to see what their perspectives would be on the expansion. Even back then the club were talking to adjacent property owners about buying properties and expanding, and always with my grandad he went the extra mile. He sat and had a cup of tea with them and had a chat and stuff. When he first came in, he transformed the ground pretty much immediately, there wasn't even any running water. To see the way it is now, it's absolutely fantastic. I'm sure he would be extremely proud."

The words of the grandson echo the memories of the great man himself – "When I arrived, the ground was not big enough for the public of Liverpool and the team was not good enough for the public of Liverpool." Today at 54,000 the ground is getting closer to the size it should be and as far as the team being good enough, we will have to put our faith in Mr Klopp to make it so.

"Will you make it to the game?" I ask Shankly Junior.

"I will yeah, definitely. I'm a season ticket holder in the Main Stand so I'll be sat in that new stand tomorrow. The tickets that I use are actually his season tickets, I took them over when I was seven years old. I sat in those seats for twenty-seven years and then at the end of last season we had to pick new seats in the new stand, so we will be in the new seats for the first time tomorrow. We kept the old seats, they'll go on display in the hotel." The seats like so many other items of treasure and memorabilia in the Shankly Hotel offer those too young to have been there a vision of the past. What Bill Shankly cherished most was his home, our home – "My greatest treasures are memories, and what means most to me is that

Anfield is my memorial. When I came to Liverpool, the ground was a shambles, now it is neat, with three new stands and good facilities. When I go to Anfield now, that is the reward. I can sit there and say to myself, I have had something to do with this." From grandfather to grandson, it seems that the soul of Liverpool lives on.

Our conversation drifts to other great managers of old with Christopher remembering some of his grandad's old pals. "Matt Busby, Jock Stein, they were both very, very close friends of my grandad. You know, he was always catching up with them, chatting with them, going and meeting with them when he was a manager and things like that. They were all cut from that same kind of cloth weren't they? With the really humble upbringing which shaped the characters that they became later on in life. Certainly your Jock Steins, your Matt Busbys are the kind of guys you'd put in that similar bracket." It did indeed seem that adversity moulded these men of character. They had to work relentlessly for whatever came their way. That spirit translated to the pitch and to the dugout. They knew only one way, the hard way. We have seen already the long list of great football men that emanated from the north eastern mining towns near Newcastle and Sunderland. From Shankly's small home town of Glenbuck, that rarely had a population in excess of one thousand, fifty men progressed to become professional footballers. Fifty men who played their way from the mines to the football pitches of Scotland and England. Five of them were Shanklys, Bill and his four brothers. These men worked hard and played hard, with honesty and fairness. Some even passed on next to the green turf. Shankly's Brother John died of a heart attack while attending the Real Madrid–Eintracht Frankfurt European Cup Final at Hampden Park in 1960. His great friend Jock Stein would die in the dugout when manager of Scotland many years later. True football men to the last.

We discuss the modern breed of manager and Shankly Junior seems to be in no doubt that all is different. "I think it has changed so much. I always say about my grandad, I don't think you'll ever see anybody else like him in the game. I firmly believe that. I think the game has changed too much to have personalities like the way he was. It's interesting, you see modern-day guys getting compared to him. Jürgen Klopp gets compared to him, and that's nice. I've met Jürgen, he's absolutely a top,

top guy and he's got a really great charisma and passion. You look at other managers and a lot of the time I think they quite fancy themselves as being a bit of a Shankly, but they fall short. If you want to play the game, and be the master of psychology, and be the witty charismatic guy in the press and all that, you've got to be able to do that when you win and lose. You can't throw the toys out of the pram when it's going wrong, you can't suddenly turn nasty. That's why I think many have tried to be that modern day Shankly, but I don't think you'll ever get somebody who actually achieves it."

"The game has changed so much, with all the money, with the billionaire owners, with player power," I suggest, "it's not the same anymore."

Shankly agrees, "I don't think the game is better at all you know. Is it strong enough to use the word 'worse'? Possibly. Football back then when my grandad was managing, it was about clubs building success form hard work, grit and determination. From the ground up, which might have taken five, six, seven, eight, nine, maybe ten years, before it came to fruition. Developing players from within, building a club from the roots. The problem you've got with football now is that it has moved into that kind of stratosphere, with the explosion of TV rights and everything else, and now it's literally about money and that's it. It's probably not an exaggeration to say that any billionaire company or organisation around the world could go and buy any football club, and within two or three years, or maybe less, have them competing at the highest level of the game, if they throw enough money at it. In some ways that's a shame I think, it completely takes out what went before that, the likes of what my grandad did, which was to take a club, and shape it and mould it. To take it to a new level. Success built on hard work and determination. It's a shame in a way. The problem you've got with football is, and with Liverpool too, is that is just the way it is now. And if Liverpool want to move to those levels and compete at the highest level, the fact of the matter is that they are going to have to fall in line with that, because that's just the order."

"If you look at the last transfer window with zero net-spend, do you feel Klopp is taking the long view, maybe a little like your grandad, trying to develop some values; we'll work for this together, we won't just throw a cheque at it, or is it more he can't get the players he wants?" I wonder aloud.

Shankly considers this and replies, "I think it's probably a combination of all of what you said. I think he's definitely trying to instil more traditional beliefs and build something for the long term with stability behind it. I think there's definitely an element of he couldn't get the players that he wanted to get too, and you know, it's quite refreshing. You know the pressure from fans now, they are almost forcing you to spend the money, they want you to win X, Y and Z, and maybe that sometimes pressurises managers into buying players that are not the right fit. So I like the fact that he has done it his way, waiting to see what he can get, get the right players in and go from there. Fingers crossed you know, he certainly looks like someone who's got the characteristics of my grandad, and if he can go on and achieve half of what my grandad has achieved we'll all be very happy! The hotel is full the whole weekend with people who have flown in from all over the world to watch the game. I know lads who I have grown up with going to the game week in week out, of all different ages. It means as much now to us as it did back then. I don't think that will ever change. It's a footballing city at the end of the day."

"This influx of foreign fans, it's part of your grandad's legacy, isn't it? Do you mind that?" I say, as I look around at the diverse variety of people that buzz around the hotel.

"It's a hard one. I'm not going to lie. Me, myself, to begin with, when I was a lot younger and kind of naïve, I viewed it as a bit of a bugbear because initially you feel like you're losing your local roots, you're losing your core . You feel like you are being priced out of the game by people who are willing to come in and buy the tickets at the more expensive price. But as I've grown up I've seen that's not the case, if you're a fan you're a fan at the end of the day, it doesn't really matter where you are from, and that's just the way football is, it's a global game. If you become successful and you have success the way Liverpool Football Club have, you are going to attract fans from all over the world. You'd have to speak to fans themselves, individually, as to why they support Liverpool Football Club and I'm sure there's a story behind it you know. I know some local fans still view it with some animosity and that but I don't think that's exclusive to Liverpool Football club, I think that you'll find that with Manchester United, I think that you'll find that with Chelsea, Manchester City and so on, it's the way of the world now, it's just the way it is. As you grow up you learn to embrace it, the different fans and the different cultures."

"The family motto from your ancestral crest is 'For Country and Religion'. Do you think Bill's religion was Liverpool?"

"Yes," his grandson replies. "He was not a religious person in the sheer sense of the word religion, but you've hit the nail on the head. His religion was football, from day one until the day he died."

THIS IS ANFIELD

'Home is the nicest word there is.' — Laura Ingalls Wilder

After twenty and more years of ponderous deliberation, Liverpool FC finally resolve the great stadium issue. Should they stay or should they go? For whatever reason, whether it be financial prudence or nostalgic heritage, the powers that be decided on staying put. Staying at Anfield, the place where it all began. Thank the heavens. Watching the mighty Reds at a shiny new soulless stadium might have been too much to take. This place is home. This is Liverpool. This is Anfield.

The book *Ordinary Landscapes, Special Places, Anfield, Breckfield and the Growth of Liverpool's Suburbs* describes how Anfield came to be. *'The origin of Anfield football ground can be traced to the 1870s, when the population of Anfield and Breckfield was growing at an unprecedented rate and football was just emerging as the nation's premier sport, providing simultaneously a healthy pursuit for young men and a male spectator sport, promising rich rewards to enterprising promotors. Football appealed especially to the clerks and skilled workers with which Anfield and Breckfield abounded, unlike their unskilled counterparts these groups enjoyed the crucial privilege of a half-day on Saturdays.'* Today, September 10th 2016, over 140 years later and after a mere 643 days of construction, FSG have delivered where before them many others failed. Some things remain the same, three sides of the old ground have stayed as they were, watching on in awe and maybe envy, as one enormous and imperious new stand took shape and towered over them.

Roy Evans tells me that he is glad to see the ground enter the modern era of sporting facilities. "With this new stand they're building a better environment around the stadium and in the Anfield area which is good." As we walk in the shadow of the old ground former Liverpool super-sub David Fairclough points to his left and remembers fondly, "I grew up not more than 100 yards over there and kicked a ball every day on those streets." I ask him for his favourite memory of the old stadium and in replying he doesn't miss a beat. "The goal against St Etienne of course, but any goal in front of the standing Kop was special, particularly at night, under the lights." He looks back at the new bright structure and remarks somewhat forlornly, "It can never replace that feeling, that intensity and magic." I look too and nod in agreement, but time moves on and so must we.

Terry McDermott scored two of Liverpool's most famous goals. On a balmy summer's evening in Rome in 1977, with the time approaching 7.42pm, Steve Heighway cut in from the right wing and passed the ball forward to McDermott who was advancing into the Borussia Monchengladbach penalty box. With a swish of his right boot McDermott sent the ball fizzing into the bottom left corner of the net and forever marked his name in the history books as Liverpool's first player to score in a European Cup Final. I asked McDermott how scoring that goal felt. "I was off," he replied laughing, "up the other end, I went on a run celebrating. I would have beaten Mo Farah." Liverpool went on to lift their first European Cup defeating the Germans 3-1.

On September 2nd 1978, McDermott scored another goal that would forever be remembered around the fields of Anfield Road. The Reds, now back-to-back European Champions, having retained the trophy with a 1-0 success against Bruges at Wembley in May 1978, were already 6-0 to the good versus a helpless Spurs at Anfield. It wasn't that Spurs were bad, more that Paisley's Liverpool were simply awesome. Michael Charters of the Liverpool Echo would write "*Have you ever heard 50,000 people purr with pleasure? Well, the Anfield spectators were doing that constantly as Liverpool stroked the ball around with one-touch moves of staggering accuracy. This display confirmed for me, particularly after the splendour of their wins at Ipswich and City the previous week, that the current Liverpool team is playing better, more exciting, attacking football than any side I've seen since the war*". From a Spurs corner the ball broke outside the Liverpool box and was passed forward to David Johnston. Liverpool legend Alan Kennedy takes up the story. "David Johnston found Steve Heighway. Steve Heighway one touch, the ball curled to the far post. Who was there? It was Terry Mc. He'd made the run. Which was a full eighty-five or ninety yards just to get this goal." With three exquisite passes of over thirty yards each, Liverpool had moved the ball the full length of the pitch. There to meet it rising high into the air was Terry McDermott and he powered his header into the net at the Anfield Road End. Today, Mc Dermott looks wistfully with pride and admiration around the revamped arena. I ask him was that goal his fondest memory of the old stadium. As a true Scouser and a true Red, he remembers the team achievements first. "Winning League championships was always first. It happened here two or three times when we won it in the last home game. They were always big memories." Then he remembers that goal. "From a personal point of view, the goal against Tottenham when we won by seven. Bob Paisley said it was the best goal he had ever seen at Anfield, so who was I to argue?" I muse aloud of how proud Paisley would be to see this new arena and McDermott agrees reflecting, "Bob, Bill Shankly, Joe Fagan. They would all have loved it". A look of sadness sits softly on this ebullient man's ever smiling face and he whispers, not to me, not to anyone in particular, "All great people". Hopefully, in time, this bright new vessel will provide as many glory days and nights as it did for Evans, Fairclough and McDermott and for those since departed.

***

The time for reminiscing is over. A match awaits. In his programme notes Jürgen welcomes us to our new home and acknowledges how important Anfield is to what the club stands for. He warns that the extra capacity, "only means something if we make it mean something," imploring the Reds fans to "make the 'new' Anfield something incredible." He, like us, knows how important home-form will be for any team that wants to challenge. Finally, he welcomes visiting champions, Leicester, and offers his congratulations.

The Liverpool crowd too, as always, is magnanimous and affords the title holders a warm welcome when they take to the field. To greet this fresh dawn an incredible rendition of our famous anthem rings through the new rafters for the first time. We are ready for the journey.

Our players are ready too and Klopp's men are at Leicester from the off. Coutinho is late back from international duty with Brazil, so

Sturridge takes his place. Immediately he strikes a lethal partnership with Mane and Leicester find themselves run ragged by the duo. On thirteen minutes, Milner plays an exquisite ball to Firmino and after some lovely trickery, the Brazilian coolly slots it past Schmeichel to become the first goal scorer in the revamped stadium. On thirty-one minutes, Sturridge and Mane combine again and Liverpool go 2–0 up after Mane slots the ball home. Before long defensive calamity strikes and Leicester are gifted a lifeline. Half-time and Liverpool lead 2–1 but it should be more. The second half eases all worries. Liverpool run riot. A cracker from Lallana and a late second goal from Firmino put seal to a comfortable 4–1 victory.

Eleven months ago, after Klopp's very first game at Anfield, a 1–1 draw against Rubin Kazan, he apologised for not bringing gifts. Today he made up and then some. His team performed wonderfully for all who were fortunate to be present at the launch. But Klopp need not gift us anymore, for now it is his home too. Together we must make it a fortress, a bastion. If we are all very, very lucky, then someday Klopp's new home may include a set of gates that bear his name, or a bronze statue showing him leaping in the air, punching the sky. If so, our long wait will have ended.

THE HOLY TRINITY

'Never do anything against conscience even if the state demands it.'
— Albert Einstein

The Leicester win emboldens Klopp's Reds. The champions were put to the sword and Anfield christened. The team are gelling nicely and getting rewarded for their efforts. The next League game takes the Reds to Chelsea. Under new manager Antonio Conte, the Blues are no match for their northern foes. Liverpool outrun and outfight the Londoners and win 1–2. Klopp has now amassed six points from his two visits to the Bridge. His ability to win the big games bodes well for the future. After Chelsea, Hull City are thrashed 5-1 at home and Swansea are beaten 1–2 away. A draw against Man Utd is followed by a wins against WBA and Crystal Palace. On November 6th we leave Anfield with smiles on our faces, dreaming just a little. Watford have been thumped 6–1 by a Liverpool masterclass and Liverpool sit atop the League table. Before the game Klopp spoke of outsiders 'singing nice songs' about Liverpool in a reference to their title hopes, but he plays it down and urges the focus to be game by game. But many Liverpool fans also sing happy songs in their own minds, thoughts drifting to the long awaited dream. Can one man really make such a difference? Was confidence and coaching all that was needed? Klopp made a profit in the transfer window, was it even possible to contest like this? Maybe the miracle maker had arrived.

After an unlucky draw away to Southampton, Liverpool slipped to second place before the visit of Sunderland on November 26th. New leaders were Chelsea by one point. Defences win titles and Conte had sorted his, reverting to a three centre-half formation flanked by two athletic wing-backs. It was working a treat as Chelsea rolled off six consecutive League wins. Where the Chelsea players had given up on Mourinho, they were now playing their hearts out for their new manager. Back at Anfield, Klopp was encouraging the Reds fans to 'take their support to the next level' for the visit of the Black Cats of Sunderland. Thirteen home points had already been collected from the fifteen available. Anfield was once more becoming a fortress, a feared place to visit. Another Achilles heel was being healed.

When teams want to shut up shop it is said that they 'park the bus' and put ten men behind the ball. Such tactics can prove nearly impossible to break down. Before the game David Moyes speaks of 'parking the double decker bus'. He hasn't lied. Late in the second-half the match sits mired at 0–0. Liverpool's display has been dogged but uninspiring. The crowd are silent, nervous, these are the games you have to win if you want to win the League. Klopp is having none of it. Leaping to his feet, he turns his back to the pitch and gesticulates wildly to the home fans. Not in encouragement, but in visceral anger. He wants more and he isn't hiding it. A manager has to have 100 per cent trust from his supporters to get away with a stunt like this. Klopp knows he has, if he didn't he wouldn't be there. Immediately, the atmosphere ratchets up a few levels and, inspired by their fans, Liverpool break the deadlock and two goals in the last fifteen minutes secure a valuable 2–0 win.

Shankly once remarked that, "At a football club, there's a holy trinity – the players, the manager and the supporters. Directors don't come into it. They are only there to sign the cheques." This is as true now as it ever was, more so even. In the week before the Sunderland game various news outlets revealed that Liverpool owner John Henry had just splashed out £80 million on a new luxury yacht. In the old days if David Moores, former Liverpool owner, had a spare £80 million sitting around, Liverpool fans would have been able to rest assured that some of it would find its way into the club for new signings to bolster the team. His heart was in it and so was his money. Sitting in Boston, FSG seem to show little heart for Liverpool, bar the value of their investment and that's okay in many ways, as that's the deal we signed up to, that is modern football. They have committed to allow the club to spend whatever it can earn itself. They won't withdraw, nor will they lodge, the maths are simple enough. With financial absentee owners like this, the bond, the holy trinity between managers, players and fans becomes even more important. The manager becomes the conscience of the club. It becomes his role to safeguard ambition for the fans. They must trust that he wants what they want and that he will hold his bosses accountable to provide the means and the structure to achieve it. With Klopp we believe this. We believe he wants to win as much as we do. Part of the reason we believe is because he is a winner and winners want to maintain their status. We also hear it in what he says, constantly reminding us that winning is the long plan. It is not guaranteed, nor easy, but it is the plan. And he shows us. In the modern game where trust and patience count for little, to have a manager show you week in and week out that it matters as much to him as it does to you, well that means something. So when he yells and roars and the veins look like popping in his neck, that's okay, we understand, we are doing that too. When he grins, laughs and radiates confidence it assures us that he knows what he is doing.

Klopp is one of the new breed of demonstrative managers. Conte at Chelsea is another. Simeone at Atletico, Guardiola at Man City, they are the elite of this new breed. All are under fifty years of age. The species continues to evolve. This specimen can be found prowling the sideline, living and breathing the game, often times encroaching onto the playing field as if a participant themselves. They shout, roar, jump, dart to and fro, waving their arms and effectively 'kick every ball' with the players. They bellow orders, gesticulate to players to take up positions. In sports parlance, the crowd has often been called the twelfth man, but these days that moniker should rest literally with the manager. I have heard professional footballers query – why all the shouting? We can't hear you when we are on the pitch anyhow. So why do they do it? There are good reasons.

The modern manager is not a club builder or rebuilder (Wenger may be the last of these dinosaurs). The stadiums are already modern, as are the training facilities, as are the administrative and communication structures. Today's managers are the purveyors of a philosophy. They stand for something. For Wenger, read symphonic pretty football. For Guardiola, read possession and control. For Klopp, read 'geggenpress', heavy metal and relentless motion. For Conte and Mourinho, read the compact, defence-first structure, laced with poison darts in attack. For Simeone, read an army at war. In each case the great manager is defined by his footballing philosophy. After twenty years at Arsenal do we now think of an Arsenal style or a Wenger style? The latter I believe would be most observers' answer. Funnily enough, the most successful team in the game do it differently, Madrid. At Real, managers come and go like ships in the night. World Cup winner Vincente Del Bosque lost his job after winning the League. For the Madridistas it is the players that are most important. Stack the team full of Galacticos and let loose the artists of football. Not surprisingly, most other clubs have to go the philosophy route, not being suitably resourced to shop in the same avenues that Madrid dominate.

So Klopp stands for something. This 'something' is what the minted professional signs up to. They don't automatically respect the 'Boss' as in the days of Shankly and Busby, now they need to believe in his philosophy. They need to buy in. One way a manager earns the 'buy in' is through demonstration. He hugs them, talks to them, explains what he needs from them. He wins them over. Being a former winner and having a track record helps. If the player believes that the manager can bring him success and fame, then that helps the 'buy in' big time. When a player sees a manager literally busting a gut on the sideline, it sends a signal, subliminally if nothing else – he's in this with us, he's living this philosophy with us. If he is giving it all, so then should we. Centre-half Dejan Lovren confirms this hypothesis. "We see he is so passionate on the side of the pitch – so you can't not be passionate on the pitch. He is always positive."

Klopp has achieved full buy in from the players, they drip blood for him. Captain Henderson is effusive; "We've got the best manager and staff in the world for players that want to improve and think of football in a different way. Since the manager has come in, everyone has bought into the way he wants to play football and we all know exactly what the manager expects and wants us to do."

Klopp helps the fans buy in too. In this era of the mega-rich player, the social distance between the team and the fans has widened, in fact the two seldom, if ever, converge. In the old days you might have met and even shared a pint with one of your team's players in the local pub. These days you might be run over by one of their seven Lamborghini cars as they speed away from the ground. In today's them-and-us environment, football crowds are quicker to turn their anger on any player perceived not to be pulling their weight on the pitch. The demonstrative manager now acts as the foil between players and fans. With all of the emotion and passion on display, the manager has effectively positioned himself as a fan, reacting just as we do. In this scenario, he is just like us. If the manager is effectively one of us, and is roaring at the players, well, then we can leave him to it, he's got it under control. In this way, we, the fan, can feel as if we are on the line ourselves, within touching distance of the combatants. We trust our vociferous boss to sort out any nonsense. He even acts as the conductor, instructing us to roar with him. In some ways the responsibilities become shared, we all have our jobs, with the focus more on togetherness and encouragement, than negativity.

So regardless of whether half the team can see or hear what Klopp shouts or gesticulates, his body language is important as a brand. It sends a message for all to see, whether that be the fans in the stadium, the watching public or even the other team. We stand for something, we believe in something, we are a collective. We trust each other. It's not just the players that you have to beat today, it is all of us. A holy trinity indeed.

DREAMERS

'I went further on less talent than anyone, but I was a damned good entertainer' — Jimmy Dean

Christmas arrives and it brings a mixed bag down Klopp's chimney. From five games, Liverpool collect ten points, but that sees them fall further behind Chelsea at the top as the Londoners collect a maximum fifteen. The bar is being set back to previous lofty heights.

December starts with an awful reversal at Bournemouth. After a superbly executed game plan, Liverpool lead 1–3 with fifteen minutes remaining. It's a masterful display, where power and skill punish every Bournemouth mistake. Origi, Mane and Can grab the goals. But then, after conceding a sloppy goal on seventy-six minutes, Liverpool panic and implode. Once again they cannot manage a game that they lead in, unable to shut up shop and wind down the clock. It's a combination of things. A lack of poise, experience and mental toughness. Most of all it is the lack of an innate winning know-how. Come the final whistle, on a sunny winter's afternoon, Bournemouth have performed a Houdini and have beaten the Reds 4–3.

Next up West Ham visit Anfield and once again they leave L4 with a result. A 2–2 draw does little to bolster Liverpool's title ambitions. Yet at least, if you can't win, don't lose. How costly taking no points from the trip to Bournemouth's seaside might prove in the final reckoning. For now, in the helter-skelter Christmas season, it's heads up and keep battling.

An away trip to the Riverside stadium to meet Middlesbrough sees the Reds hit form once more. Lallana grabs two to add to his goal against West Ham and Origi scores for the fifth game in succession. A clean sheet is very welcome too and the 3–0 win puts Liverpool in good stead for the fiery trip to Goodison Park that awaits five days later.

The derby proves to be a cagey, hard-fought, yet somewhat dour affair. Few chances are created at either end. It is the first Merseyside derby for home manager Ronald Koeman and it is Klopp's first time to visit Goodison Park. Nobody wants to lose and, deep into injury time, it seems nobody will. Then, on ninety-four minutes, Daniel Sturridge scuffs a speculative shot goal-bound from the edge of the box. Keeper Stekelenburg can't reach it, but the bobbling effort avoids the net and bounces back off the foot of the post. Mane reacts quickest, in mind and body, pouncing on the loose ball and blasts it home. Hear ye, hear ye, Christmas celebrations can now begin. Everton 0 Liverpool 1.

Man City arrive to Anfield on the last day of 2016. Twelve months earlier, Klopp was less than three months in the job and still finding his feet. He even joked (I think) that he still had to locate certain English towns. Back then, in his New Year's address he outlined both his and the club's ambitions for the year that lay ahead. "Last year was an intensive year for all LFC fans. The only thing I can really promise is that we will do everything to make sure that, when we are at this same day in 2017 and we look back, it's easier for all of us to have a smile on our face." The Reds had found goal scoring a bit of a dark art in 2015 and in his address Klopp assured all that he was determined to rectify the matter. "We want this. I know, usually, you want to see football because of the goals, but it's not about talking about this, it's about working, and that's what we are doing. We have the situations but we have to use them more often, that's the truth. We had our games with a lot of goals, they weren't often enough in the Premier League, but we had a few situations: the Southampton game, Manchester City, Chelsea. I see it, we are seventh place with a nil goal difference, the same number of goals scored and conceded and that's not perfect. But it's not the way to talk about it only, we have to work on it and that's what we try."

One full year later and it seems that Klopp is a man of his word. We smiled all the way to Wembley and Basel, not so much on the way home, yet the journeys were worth the eventual pain. And we saw goals, lots of goals. By the end of 2016, Liverpool had scored eighty-six League goals in the calendar year, the most in the Premier League, and the best total by Liverpool since 1985. In Season 2016/17 the Reds have scored an incredible forty-five goals from eighteen games, not just six better than the next best of Man City and Arsenal on thirty-nine, but also topping Real Madrid (40), Barcelona (41), Juventus (36), Bayern Munich (38) and Paris Saint-Germain (38). Problem solved it would seem.

So Liverpool are the Entertainers, that seems clear, yet the thrills come at both ends. If Klopp shares his 2017 resolutions with us, they will surely include a wish to tighten up at the back. In 2015/16 the Reds conceded fifty goals. With eighteen games of the new season gone, Liverpool have conceded twenty-one goals compared to table toppers Chelsea's eleven. Since the Premier League began in 1992, the League winners have conceded on average 32.7 goals. Liverpool will need to buy a few buses for the second half of the season if the dream is to be realised.

That said, Liverpool are in rude health as they look forward eagerly to 2017. They sit in second place, six points adrift of a Chelsea team that can't stop winning. Forty points from eighteen games, albeit not League winning form, if continued will guarantee Champions League qualification. That will very much be mission accomplished for Klopp's first full season, it will also see him enter the summer transfer window with European glamour to offer prospective train-pushers. His cheque book will hopefully be brimming with dollars too, given FSG's frugality to date. With a young, hungry squad (second youngest in the Premier League at 25.5yrs), things can only get better it would seem. Klopp confirms the belief saying, "We are on the right path and in a really good way. Together we can make the next year even better than this one. That should always be our aim. Appreciate what has gone before, enjoy the present and be excited about the future."

In his first truncated season, Klopp inherited a number of Achilles heels. First, the team couldn't score goals, now they score freely, more than any other Premiership team since the arrival of the German. Second, Anfield had started to intimidate the home team more than the visitors. That problem too has been cured, the Reds losing only one home League game in 2016, and that, a very unlucky loss to Man United all the way back in January, in a game dominated by Liverpool. What's more, the famous old cathedral has got its mojo back, with Klopp experiencing for the first time the true aura of the Kop when United, Dortmund and Villarreal were all vanquished on the road to Basel. League title wins are built on home form, so making Anfield a fortress again is mission-critical and it is why Klopp beseeches the home crowd to give more and more. The last two major Achilles are poor defending, particularly from set pieces and poor showings against the so-called lesser teams. In 2015/16 Liverpool dropped twenty-two points against the bottom nine sides, with champions Leicester losing only eight points to the same teams. Klopp is all too aware of the problems when he says, "When you build a team you start with the defence. To build up a stability in defence is a big target for next season."

2016 ends with an impressive 1–0 win against City. New signing Wijnaldum heads the winner and he, like each of Klopp's summer signings, has started his career brightly at Anfield. Mane in particular has added a special edge to the team, with his pace and flair. His form has been spectacular. Unfortunately for the Reds he will be missing for most of January and February while he plays in the African Cup of Nations for his country, Senegal. Klopp and FSG will be looking to the transfer window to bolster a thinning squad for the New Year title push. January may prove to be a season-defining month for the Reds, a month in which they will play Southampton in the League Cup semi-final, compete in the FA Cup and also try to close the gap on League leaders Chelsea. A year from now, when the earth completes another orbit of the sun, will we still be waiting or will our dreams have finally come true?

DIRTY TACTICS

'As a jumper, I try to defy gravity as long as I can. But no matter how far I jump, I'll always hit the earth eventually' — Greg Rutherford, Olympian

There it goes again, humming away in the background, that old Bruce Springsteen number *'One step up and two steps back'*. Over and over it goes around in my head. I can't escape it. Nor can Liverpool. With January comes a reality check. A big one. Nine games bring one solitary victory, away to fourth tier Plymouth Argyle. Liverpool exit the League Cup to Southampton, a team that the Reds have plundered for players continuously for the last number of years. The bitter irony. They also exit the FA Cup to Championship side Wolves. To cap it off, Swansea pick up their first ever league win at Anfield and put an end to Liverpool's year-long unbeaten home record in the Premier League. For the first time in five years the Reds lose three successive home games. The roll of shame looks like this;

Jan-02	PL	Sunderland	2	–	2	Liverpool
Jan-08	FA Cup	Liverpool	0	–	0	Plymouth
Jan-11	League Cup	Southampton	1	–	0	Liverpool
Jan-15	PL	Man United	1	–	1	Liverpool
Jan-18	FA Cup	Plymouth	0	–	1	Liverpool
Jan-21	PL	Liverpool	2	–	3	Swansea
Jan-25	League Cup	Liverpool	0	–	1	Southampton
Jan-28	FA Cup	Liverpool	1	–	2	Wolves
Jan-31	PL	Liverpool	1	–	1	Chelsea

By the end of the month, Liverpool have slipped out of the top four and their title hopes have evaporated. The bubble has burst and gravity takes over. Bang, the Reds crash to earth. Questions are now being asked, as yet another failed title attempt passes the team by. It's not that anybody expected Klopp to challenge so soon, but having been afforded the opportunity, many can't understand why the club didn't invest in some much-needed squad additions to bolster the assault. By the end of January the Reds looked both jaded and deflated. New blood would have helped, but none arrived. Oh for the profligacy of Man City. With their two existing strikers, Iheanacho and Aguero, already topping the Premier League's all-time best 'goals converted per minutes played' ratio at 102 and 109 minutes respectively, what else to do but add another top striker in young Brazilian import, Gabriel Jesus, for the princely sum of £30 million.

Few blame Klopp, instead FSG bear the brunt of the fans' ire. Where are they when needed? Off buying yachts instead of players seems to be the conclusion. Klopp defends his owners, stating that the money was there but that the players he wanted weren't. We have to trust our manager, for he is part of our holy trinity. If he says that's the case, then so be it. We must all bite our tongues and carry on. But the taste of defeat is there again, never far from the bite. More chances at silverware frittered away. A crack at a title gone. They may not come around too often.

If Klopp didn't know it before, now he does. Even his charisma won't work if Reds fans don't see ambition. And rightly so, that's our job. For the first time his mastery and ability is being questioned. Liverpool are back where the smart money says we should be. Fifth. Champions Leicester are in a relegation battle. You can't buck the system, not for long anyway. Liverpool spend to come fifth and fifth they are. It seems to many outside the club, and some within, that even Klopp can't change that.

Pain and anger is etched across the mostly effervescent German's face. His team have surprised him and not in a good way. He trusted his squad enough not to enter the January transfer window and they didn't pay him back. Maybe they weren't good enough. "Did I learn anything about them in the last few weeks? – Yes," he would say, answering his own question. "A lot of what I wanted to learn? – No," he continues, explaining that while his team have character, they lack a winning mentality. For many fans, that revelation is very old news, however Klopp must learn these things for himself. All the doubts start to rise again.

The press delight in the fact that after fifty-four Premier League games Klopp's record is no better, and is in fact identical to that of his predecessor Brendan Rodgers. It reads twenty-six wins, sixteen draws and twelve defeats. Others claim that Liverpool's high energy game has run out of steam and that Klopp lacks tactical nous. The first chinks have appeared in the German's armour. When teams sit deep in defence against the Reds and knock the ball long, Klopp's team seem to have no Plan B. Klopp doesn't like what he calls 'dirty tactics'. When manager of Dortmund, his team played Sevilla in the Europa League. Dortmund needed two goals to go through but Sevilla packed their defence. Klopp was furious, "Sevilla parked the bus for sixty minutes and ran the clock down to such an extent that my players were lost for words at their cowardice afterwards." One big reason that Klopp has no Plan B is that he doesn't believe in them. He is adamant that you stick to your own game plan and he remembers when this realisation came to him. "As a very new manager we played Rot Weiss Ahlen. We played 4-3-3 instead of our normal 4-4-2 and they brought on a third central-defender and started man-marking us. And then we thought, young and wild as we were 'Right, let's change the system', so we had only two strikers left on the pitch to escape the man-marking. That's all a load of rubbish. Always, always stick to doing your own thing." He may be right, but if Liverpool are being blocked from scoring and are unwilling to adapt to a Plan B, then at a minimum they need to defend better.

Klopp believes that his team need to adopt some of league-leaders Chelsea's 'clever tactics' to enable them to see off more games. Again, for us fans, this I'm afraid is old news. The away trip to Bournemouth in December must have been on his mind, where Liverpool led 1–3 late on, but still conspired to lose 4–3. That would not have happened to Conte's Chelsea. Sloppy goals from defensive errors were also conceded at Burnley, Sunderland and at home to Swansea. All, bar Sunderland, resulted in defeats. If you can't win a game, then don't lose it. It is clear that Klopp can build an exciting team going forward but when faced with 'dirty tactics' as he describes it, a big problem remains. It is one that will require solving and quickly. Liverpool's defence is nowhere near good enough and hasn't been for a long time. Can Klopp find the right men to solve the problem? Time will tell.

Former Red and European Cup winner, German Dietmar Hamann, questions FSG's haste to award Klopp with a six-year deal and remarks that the Reds 'need a wake-up call'. But for most, it is not FSG who should be questioning the six-year-tie up, instead it should be Klopp taking another long hard look at his bosses. What is the reach of their ambition? Does it match his own? Does it match that of the fans? Hamann is right on one thing though, a very loud wake-up call needs to bellow around the fields of Anfield and Fenway Park.

The best managers hate to lose, it's always been that way. They live to win and they breathe that same fire into their players. "If you are first you are first. If you are second, you are nothing," Shankly espoused. Paisley echoed the sentiment; "We never celebrate second place here." For now, we must believe that a similar fire is stoking inside Klopp. An angry fire. A fire to prove the doubters wrong.

SILVER LININGS

'When things go wrong, don't go with them.' — Elvis Presley

As bad as January was, and it was bad, at the end a chink of light appeared. Despite being second-best to Chelsea, Liverpool managed to scrape a 1–1 draw at Anfield on the very last day of the month. Chelsea looked every bit the Champions-in-waiting and, but for a late penalty save by Mignolet, Liverpool would have been counting four home losses in succession. With their red-hot form, few teams were earning even a point against the Pensioners, so all in all it was something to build on.

February's first fixture saw Liverpool lose abysmally 2–0 away to Hull. The wheels were coming off. Royally. Following the game, the statistics told us all we needed to know. Liverpool lead the league for possession, tackles, goals and sprints. However, for goals conceded they lie in tenth, clean sheets, twelfth, and defending from set pieces a miserable eighteenth. Dire, atrocious, soft, unworthy, these were but a taste of the words that venomously filled the internet forums following the game. Reds fans were losing patience and more crucially, trust in a stuttering team. The silent January transfer window was now looking like a grievous inexplicable error. Rarely against Hull did the 'great entertainers' look like scoring or even offering a move to cheer. If this was showbiz, we would be asking for our money back.

Yet as they keep doing on this rollercoaster ride, the Reds bounced back from the defeat to Hull with a resounding home win against second-place Spurs. The victory put a halt to the Reds' worst start to a calendar year since 1954. Mane bagged a brace in a comfortable 2–0 result.

Spurs should have finished 2015/16 in second place but somehow, they allowed Arsenal to nip ahead of them on the final day. This year they are once again developing a head of steam. In many ways, their project echoes that of Liverpool's. How to achieve more with less. Spurs will believe that they have moved ahead of Liverpool in the pecking order. Yet, on a head to head basis, the form guide has the Reds firmly ahead, Liverpool having not lost to Tottenham in nearly five years. Second place under Rodgers proved better than any Spurs finish since 1963. However, the Londoners have been more consistent, if less flamboyant, in their recent steady-as-she-goes progress, proving that without the highs, you don't get hammered as much for the lows. Spurs, as a club, have Liverpool in their sights. So, while keeping our eyes ahead, the rear mirror will need constant checking too. For this reason, the win had more significance than a mere three points. It also provided a much-needed injection of confidence after a miserable start to the year. By close of play the top of the table read as follows:

	Premier League 13/02/2017	**P**	**Pts**
1	Chelsea	25	60
2	Man City	25	52
3	Spurs	25	50
4	Arsenal	25	50
5	Liverpool	25	49
6	Man United	25	48
7	Everton	25	41

At the bottom, champions Leicester were sliding perilously close to the drop zone. Hull, thanks to their victory over Liverpool, were staging a late season rally while once again the sleeping north-eastern giants Sunderland were going to have to conjure another escapology trick.

	Premier League 13/02/2017	**P**	**Pts**
13	Bournemouth	25	26
14	Swansea	25	24
16	Middlesbrough	25	22
17	Leicester	25	21
18	Hull	25	20
19	Crystal Palace	25	19
20	Sunderland	25	19

After Spurs, Liverpool headed to La Manga in Spain for a warm weather training camp while others continued to campaign in the late stages of the various cup competitions that remained on offer, both at home and in Europe. For Liverpool, the league now fills their solitary focus. Klopp rallies the troops and calls for a winning finale to the season. Indeed, he asks for thirteen wins from thirteen games. Next up comes an away trip to struggling champions Leicester City.

If the Reds' fall from grace in January had been hard to swallow, a silver lining or two were still to be found. One signing had been made, well, more a re-signing. After enduring the sagas of Suarez and then Sterling itching to leave, Liverpool have successfully batted away any avaricious eyes that have been fixing their lusty gaze on Philippe Coutinho. Talk abounds of a move to Barcelona or Madrid. That talk dissipates when the welcome news is released that Coutinho has signed a new long-term deal, with no buy-out clause. He will be a key man alongside Mane in Klopp's rebuild and his presence will encourage others to stay and new faces to join. It is a great signing and a huge show of support from the young Brazilian for Klopp's project. Klopp is effusive in his praise of the deal, "The fact he wants to stay here and be part of what we are looking to build and develop shows his personal commitment to make himself better and be an integral part of something that is very special. We have total belief in our project, but when a player of Phil's calibre and status commits for this length of time it shows that our faith is shared throughout the game. He knows he can fulfil his dreams and ambitions here at Liverpool. This is a big statement. I look forward to seeing Phil create many more great memories and moments for this club."

Coutinho joins the love-in with praise for the boss; "Jürgen is a great manager. We all can see how much has changed here since he arrived, and how much he will change in future. He is a winner. It's not only me, but every other player feels honoured to play at this great club for this great manager. This feeling has a very positive influence on us as players." Even in the midst of the January Blues, this is great news. What Klopp has managed better than any Liverpool manager in recent times is to be able to mix it with the big boys and win. This convinces players like Coutinho that better days lie ahead.

Another silver lining is found in new-signing Mane's form. Rafa

Benitez believed that major signings made major impacts saying during his reign, "To progress as a club, we needed to make at least one headline signing, to capture a player that would make the rest of Europe sit up and take notice." Many parts of Rafa's sentence are interesting. 'At least' is one, for at no stage over the last twenty-five years has the signing of one star player been good enough. More were needed. Arsenal have seen this too with Ozil and Sanchez, two alone have not been good enough to turn the tide, not when the competitor's first eleven and substitute benches are weighed down with expensive stars. Dalglish brought in Barnes, Beardsley, Aldridge and Houghton within a very short period of time and they transformed the team. It feels that something akin to that will be needed again.

'To make Europe sit up and take notice' was the other noticeable comment from Rafa. This had resonance back then as Liverpool campaigned successfully through Europe. Rafa summed it up saying, "All of football's elite faced us then, and all of them were beaten". Unfortunately, these days Europe is neither watching nor fearing Liverpool, despite the great run to Basel. The first goal is to make the Premier League sit up. In Sadio Mane, Klopp may have found a new star to shine alongside Coutinho. Another piano player. When the £30 million attacker took his tally to eleven goals with his match-winning brace against Spurs, it was only his twenty-second appearance for the Reds. Just three Liverpool players have got there quicker in the last twenty-five years. This is only a sign of potential, but it is a good sign. For Klopp, it is the start of adding quality, improving the squad. But it is only that, a start. Rafa saw clearly that without real action, the gap was unbridgeable. In his post-match European Cup Final press conference in 2007 Rafa called his set of American owners out. "The owners tell me that they want to win the Premiership and the Champions League. They can, but they need to understand the business here. We need to do things quicker than Chelsea and Manchester United. If we don't spend money, change things, improve in a lot of areas, we could fight to finish fourth. If we don't change things, we will not be contenders." Rafa hadn't slept all night, having walked the streets of Athens in the rain after losing 2–1 to Milan, musing, strategizing how he could break the stranglehold. His lack of sleep and anger at defeat must have shaped his words. Every single Liverpool fan worldwide greeted them with euphoria. Not so his owners. Matching ambition with money wasn't their plan. Klopp will need to be sure that his own game plan is firmly in synch with that of his bosses, for, if not, then another wasted era awaits us all.

One further silver lining could be gleaned following the home win against Spurs. Klopp's Liverpool were unmistakably a big-game team. No fear existed when going toe to toe with the big boys. This had rarely been the case over the barren years. The mini-League below tells the story for 2016/17. Liverpool are the only team from the top six not to lose against their peers. Even with games to play, they can only be caught by Chelsea in this table.

	Premier League – Top Six Mini League 13/02/2017	P	W	D	L	Pts
1	Liverpool	8	4	4	0	16
2	Chelsea	8	4	1	3	13
3	Spurs	8	2	3	3	9
4	Man City	6	2	1	3	7
5	Man United	6	1	3	2	6
6	Arsenal	6	1	2	3	5

What we do know about Klopp is that when confronted with a problem, he invariably finds a way to solve it. Klopp's team have taken only thirty-three points from seventeen games against the bottom sides, compared to Chelsea's forty-six points from sixteen games. Beating the basement dwellers is something Arsene Wenger's Arsenal have perfected during his twenty-year tenure, earning the Gunners year-on-year Champions League qualification but also the moniker of flat track bullies. When faced with a fight against the big teams, in his last ten years, Wenger's boys have invariably squealed and run away. It would seem logical to assume that learning to beat your peers should be a harder task than beating up those beneath. If this is true, then the easier Achilles heel awaits the treatment of Dr Klopp. Yet Klopp takes no solace from the mini-league. "There is one major problem with this," he says, "there is no such thing as a mini-league, there is for us, only the Premier League. We will not be satisfied with being the best team with results against these five other teams only. Our ambitions are to be the best team involving ourselves and the nineteen other clubs. We do not have an attitude issue in this area, we are not complacent and we are not arrogant enough to think we can pick and choose where and when we perform. But of course, these are words, we need actions."

March brings games against Man City and Arsenal followed by the Merseyside derby on April 1st. After that Liverpool will play eight games in succession against teams outside the current top seven places. With no European or cup distractions, it is time for Klopp to show us that he and his team can be bullies too.

DILLY DING, DILLY DONG, THE GAME IS GONE

'Et tu, Brute?' – Julius Caesar, William Shakespeare

Sometimes it is the timeline that tell us all we need to know. What happened, how it happened, and when. It can speak a thousand words. For Leicester City and lovers of football at large, the below makes for grim reading;

1884 – Leicester Fosse are formed (to become Leicester City).
May 2nd, 2016 – Chelsea draw 2–2 at home to Spurs and Leicester become the 2015/2016 Premier League winners and champions of England for the first time, 132 years after their formation. The entire world of football celebrates maybe the greatest and most unlikely victory in the history of the game.
May 16th, 2016 – 250,000 attend a victory parade in Leicester to celebrate their team's success. Manager Claudio Ranieri wins League Manager of the Year to become only the second non-British manager to do so, after Arsene Wenger. He also wins the Premier League Manager of the Year.
January 9th, 2017 – Ranieri wins FIFA World Coach of the Year.
February 22nd, 2017 – Leicester fight to a credible 2–1 first-leg defeat away to Sevilla in the Champions League last sixteen.
February 23rd, 2017 – Claudio Ranieri is fired by Leicester City.
February 24/25th, 2017 – Icons from the world of football past and present pay homage to the miracle achieved by Ranieri as manager.
48 hours after firing – Goalkeeper Kasper Schmeichel is the first Leicester player to go public with his thanks for his former boss.

It is to this sorry mess that Liverpool arrive to play Leicester on Monday 27th February, 2017. After the weekend games, the Foxes have slid into the bottom three. Despite being in a relegation battle as champions, his peers and the pundits still believed that Ranieri was the man to drag the team clear of trouble. Klopp bemoans the end of "one of the nicest stories in world football of all-time," bracketing the 'strange decisions' of 'Brexit, Trump and Ranieri' with a quizzical shake of his head. Mourinho is dumbfounded. He, himself, was fired as a champion by Chelsea only one year previously. He remarks that at the time, his dismissal "was a giant negative thing" but when now compared to Ranieri, "it was peanuts". Leicester legend Gary Lineker agrees and is genuinely shocked at the sacking, tweeting, "Claudio Ranieri? Sacked? Really? Dilly Ding, Dilly Dong, Game's Gone", paraphrasing Ranieri's 'Dilly-ding, dilly-dong' catchphrase which the Italian would use to get his players to wake up or improve focus. It's not just in England that the footballing world looks on bemused. Back in Italy, Juventus manager Allegri bemoans the loss of the man who "made history for football". It seems something really is rotten in the state of football.

Most pundits are livid and call out the players, many labelled as snakes. The view at large is that they have betrayed their mentor, having grown too big for their footballing boots. Hubris has won the day. When Ranieri arrived as boss his name was bigger than that of any of his players. Now, as iconic celebrities it seems that their memories have erased any consciousness of who helped them up the ladder. Like a virus, a wish spreads outside of the city of Leicester, more a spell. Where last year the neutrals hoped for Leicester to break the big boy stranglehold, now the wires are filled by a unified prayer hoping that Leicester are relegated, as punishment for their wicked ways.

Fear and loathing can set in quickly these days when you start to drift towards the murky waters at the bottom of the Premier League. There is too much to lose. Up to £50 million a year in revenue if you go under. Brand value dives from the loss of prestige. As a Premier League team, the world knows who you are. Below that level, you can be quickly forgotten. Managers bear most of the brunt and their stock can turn from revered to reviled in no time at all. Everything takes on a short-term hue. The next game becomes more important than the next five years.

Arriving in Leicester the reverse is true for Liverpool. They are planning for the long term. In the same week that Ranieri gets stabbed in the back, Liverpool announce that they will be moving from training ground Melwood, the base that Shankly rejuvenated, to join forces with the nearby youth Academy at Kirkby five miles away, where their 170 youngsters dream of making the grade one day. Brendan Rodgers had hoped to combine the two, and now it seems that Klopp agrees and has convinced his American bosses to push ahead with the project. It's mooted as a £50 million development and it smells of long term planning and stability, two words that sit very uncomfortably in modern football. Klopp calls it a 'big step forward'. He continues, "I really love Melwood but football changes. It's fantastic, but we have no space for anything. We cannot avoid this. We can't stay like we always were and hope we can cope with the other clubs. We need to develop the club. Sometimes you have to set standards. Bringing the Academy and the first team together is one point but it's also about improving a lot of things that we can't improve here. It will be good for the future of the club. I really believe that infrastructure keeps responsibility up. Things like this, it's much longer-term than my contract. It's important that we do the right things so this wonderful club can be successful both in my six years but later on too."

Klopp has only known the long term, serving seven years at both Mainz and Dortmund. He has never been fired, not yet. The average tenure of a manager in England is a meagre 1.23 years. Maybe today with football, as with dogs, one year really equals seven. "I'm not experienced in other situations where you don't get time," remarks Klopp, "I've always had this. I've always been on a long contract, as long as I wanted, and I have no idea why exactly it happened to me. Liverpool, as a club, wants to have a long-term relationship with its manager but as always it all depends on success. If we cannot win anything or even come close to big things over the next few years then it will be difficult to go for it. But in this moment, everyone is absolutely convinced about going for it with this manager, this team and these coaches. With a few changes we believe we can reach the highest level and that is what we are all working for, we think that it will happen. But we have to fill the period between now and then with as many wonderful performances as possible. That will make it easier for the people to wait."

In a further act of future planning, Lallana signs a contract extension to follow Coutinho. He is delighted with himself and also professes his belief in the club's progress. "Signing for a club like Liverpool is a big thing, but to re-sign shows you've obviously contributed. This is a really good place to be at the moment for a player who wants to be part of something special. I heard Coutinho's comments after he signed, and what he said about the manager echoed what we all think, he's world class, he's a winner and we trust him completely. The manager is a special talent and we are lucky to have him here and great he's committed for the long term as well. The most important word with our manager is 'trust'. We trust him and in turn he places a lot of trust in us – and hopefully we reward that on the pitch for him."

Trust indeed. It seems the well of trust ran dry around the green fields of Leicester. Ranieri would say to friends after his departure that he felt most of the players supported him. In time, as the true stories emerge, as they always do, we will know just who sat where and when. More and more we see player-power, businessmen-owners ignorant of the game and a wolf-like media continue to make a mockery of a once proud sport. For sixty-five-year-old Ranieri, a man universally described as a gentleman of the game, there must seem echoes of a former leader of his own race, one Julius Caesar. Looking behind to see who perpetrated the fatal stabbing blows, Caesar saw an old friend, one he trusted. "You too Brutus, you too?" he would sadly say.

***

Yet amidst all the clandestine and tragic skulduggery, a football match is to be played. One of crucial importance to both sides. Leicester hope to lift themselves from the bottom three and Klopp hopes to notch up Win One from a final thirteen and to prove that his team can doeth unto others as it does unto the big boys. Coutinho hopes for no more Hull-shaped pitfalls. "We can learn that we have to be focused from the first minute. We were not 100 per cent focused in the Hull game. I do not know why, it sometimes happens. What we have to try to do is the same as we did in the game with Tottenham. That game should serve as an example, we have to play well from the first minute." He thinks about achieving aims by the end of the year. "From the start, the aim was to qualify for the Champions League. It is important for Liverpool to play in these competitions, fighting with the other great teams. We expect to give great performances and to accomplish our goals."

As I've said before, I become worried any time a Liverpool player predicts a positive team performance prior to a game. It never comes. It doesn't this time either. Leicester's players are steaming from all the traitor and snake vilification and they come out seeking revenge on someone, anyone. That someone is Liverpool. Liverpool need to fight hard to match the Foxes intensity, but they don't; inexplicably they lie down, roll over and whimper. The Foxes maul the quivering Reds and the game is over by half-time with Leicester leading 2–0. It's not that a 2–0 lead can't be pegged back in this league, that happens regularly. More, it's the demeanour of this Liverpool side, it's clear to see that they have not turned up, they have no stomach for the fight. By full-time Leicester have won 3–1 and for some, Ranieri's sacking has been justified. They are wrong, it can never be justified. Nor can Liverpool's performance tonight.

Leaving the stadium, I hear grumbles from fellow Reds that we are right back to square one, and it's hard to argue with the thought. Defensively the team is inept and is no better than any Reds team that went before it. They concede 1.3 goals a game, or an average of fifty goals per season. The same average for the last three seasons. The same average that Rodgers was vilified for. Good teams concede fewer than one a game, fewer than thirty-five a year. Klopp said at his very first press conference that he would build a team from the back. He needs to start again. He too is at a loss for words. When he does find them, he tells us what we already know. "It was not good enough in the beginning, not good enough in the middle, and not good enough in the end. We can't blame anyone else for this performance, we don't want to look for excuses. We have to react. It's happened too often." Klopp, for the first time, alludes to the dangers if Liverpool continue to slide. "It's getting more serious now, we all play for our future, myself included. We get judged every day, especially on match days. Of course, performances have influences on things." Asked about the quality of his team, he replies, "I don't think they aren't as good as I thought," said Klopp. "But I think they need my help more to show it every week. Bad performances don't help anybody, that's clear."

Trudging back into Leicester town centre, tails between our legs again, one moment of brightness illuminates the gloom. Some Leicester fans are collecting money to raise £10,000 to build a statue in honour of Ranieri. They obviously have no faith in the club's owners getting around to it anytime soon. I throw a token offering, he deserves it. They do too. Some respect still exists in football, just.

THE CIRCUS

'Who sees the human face correctly: the photographer, the mirror, or the painter?' — Pablo Picasso

Klopp sits at his desk at Melwood preparing his notes for the match day programme. Arsenal are up next. A chance to right the many wrongs of the Leicester debacle. Everyone was now on trial after such an inept display, a display that he and the team had two weeks to prepare for. They were bullied plain and simple, no excuses existed.

The boys had been angry all week in training, but would it transfer to the pitch? He hoped so. Arsenal sat one place ahead of Liverpool, in fourth. One point ahead and with one game in hand. This had the feel of a must-win game if a top four place was not to evaporate completely despite all their early season endeavour. Mind you, the visitors were under fire too, as was their manager Arsene Wenger. Two weeks previously they had been demolished 5–1 away to Bayern Munich in the Champions League and for the seventh season in succession, it seemed certain that they would not progress beyond the last sixteen. They were still on course for their twenty-first consecutive top-four finish, but that wasn't the threshold anymore at the Emirates, not for the fans anyway. A glorious first ten years had now withered into an inglorious second. No League title since 2004. No Champions League crown ever. 'No more' was the prevailing cry.

Management is a tough game. Last week Ranieri, this week Wenger. A life on the edge. They were making out that Wenger was a fool, that he didn't understand the game. That he kept making the same mistakes. Klopp remembered the crowd behind him at the Emirates on the opening day, raging and roaring at his counterpart, beseeching him angrily to go, to leave. Enough was enough they claimed. What should happen at Arsenal wasn't for him to judge, but the life of a critic is always easier than that of the performer, this he knew. His own patience had evaporated in the face of the poisonous Leicester aftermath. "I am not a clown – even though a few people think I am," he told them. "It is not about laughing the whole week and ignoring the problems you have. We cannot ignore the things that happen around us, I am 100 per cent optimistic again when I think about the Arsenal game, but I cannot say I am in exactly the same mood as at the start of the season." He wasn't, he had much to consider, but that would be for another day.

His mind drifted back to Arsenal, to Wenger and he put pen to paper.

'Arsene Wenger is rightly regarded as one of the greatest managers of all time because of what he has achieved. His record and legacy will be more than just a collection of trophies. He is a pioneer. He is someone who has translated a vision into success and built a club for long-term sustainable success. And he continues to put a team on the field that competes at the very top of one of the most competitive leagues in the world, playing attacking, exciting football.'

Wenger had indeed been a pioneer. Klopp remembered how he found stars where no one else could see them. How he analysed data and statistics before the words had found their way into the English footballing lexicon. There was the story of Flamini, a young kid at Marseille. Wenger spotted his stats before anybody else – an incredible 14km covered per game. He could play too. Flamini didn't even have a contract. Wenger signed him and he became a star alongside other previously unheralded players such as Viera, Petit and Anelka. Yet over time everybody woke up to the idea and joined the revolution. If you can't beat them.... Wenger lost his competitive edge, the secrets were out. However, in the process, he changed the game.

His own bosses, FSG, held the Frenchman in very high regard. The Arsenal model was one to be admired. FSG loved 'Moneyball' and its greatest exponent, Billy Beane had said of Wenger that, "he was the sports executive whom I admire the most." Clever respects clever. Yet clever wasn't working anymore it seemed, not at the Emirates.

After Leicester, he declared there could be "no excuses" and that it was "on us to make it better". Yet he knew he needed to say more. Trust levels were ebbing. Since the New Year the mood had changed, faith had been lost with one inept performance following the other. Not in-house, but certainly in the stands, on the streets. The big picture needed to be clarified again.

"I have said during the many good moments this season and during the few not so good, that we are on a journey, that this is a long-term project. Of course we want to be as successful as possible in the quickest time possible, this is our collective goal. But we must remain focused that we are looking to build something for the long term and maybe sometimes that means experiencing bumps on the way." Earlier in the week he also spoke of new signings arriving in the summer, improvements. The flock needed reassurance, a gentle reminder that he knew there was work to be done and improvements to be made. He did.

He looked again at the words he had written for Wenger. His honest views. He had said once before that Wenger's football "was like an orchestra, but it's a silent song" when compared to Dortmund's "heavy metal", but it was in jest, a play on words. Arsenal's play was controlled, his Dortmund team ran more on passion. Yet now, words like these stuck to Wenger. Was this how one of the greatest gets treated when the wheels come off? Had they even come off? His Liverpool team were still some way from even qualifying for the Champions League, never mind getting to the last eight or better. If ever he knew it, he knew it now. He had his work cut out. This is what awaits when the honeymoon ends, and since the turn of the year it had certainly ended. He hoped that the Red faithful read his words, digested them, and remembered them. Good things can come to those who wait.

By Saturday evening, 4th March, Liverpool had climbed back above the Gunners and sat in third place in the League. A comprehensive 3–1 victory had sealed a dominant performance, with Firmino, Mane and Wijnaldum bagging the goals. Arsenal's star player Sanchez had started on the bench, punishment for an alleged training-ground bust up. It was said that he wanted out of the club and was tired of Wenger's rule. He had lost his allegiance. If it was true then it was kicking a man when he was down. Arsenal's fans were in caustic form, cheering ironically when they managed a rare shot on goal, so poor was their performance. Yet, based on recent history they are still more likely to grab a top four place than Liverpool. It may not be good enough to save Wenger's job though. One must wonder at what point the same words will be uttered at

Anfield? For now, the Reds need to climb the hill again before engaging in a debate about who halts any descent down the opposite side.

When penning his pre-match notes, I wonder did Klopp cast a thought to his own legacy? If he were to lift one of the league crowns that Wenger had, then he'd leave Liverpool as a legend, assured of his place in its gloried history. In football, in life, perspective is everything.

BACK ON TRACK

"Of course I accepted, but becoming manager was not something I'd ever envisaged, but then again, neither had Bob nor Joe before me."
— Ronnie Moran

With just seven minutes gone, following some woeful Reds defending, it is visitors Burnley who take the lead through an Ashley Barnes goal. The Anfield crowd groans and settles in for another long afternoon. This wouldn't happen against Arsenal. Only eight days after pummelling the Gunners, Liverpool are struggling once more against a no-nonsense bottom-half outfit. This time, however, the determined Reds dig deep and with a display of steel and grit they prove the doubters wrong. Two goals from the central midfield pairing of Wijnaldum and Can seal a hard-fought, but crucial, 2-1 victory and help solidify Liverpool's place in the top four.

Next up comes an away trip to Man City, who sit one place above the Reds in fourth. City are licking their wounds following an unexpected and agonising Champions League exit at the hands of a young Monaco side. With no hope of winning the League title, it's been a tough first year for City's much-lauded manager Guardiola. The Spaniard is now all too aware of how hard the task is, to become champions of England. "If anyone thinks I have to win all the time, they are wrong because other teams are good, other managers are clever, you are bound to lose sometimes," he insists. Following a phenomenal summer 2016 spending spree, more was predicted for both this disciple of Cruyff and his team. Guardiola doesn't believe that the anticipation stifled results though, remarking, "I know I am here with big expectation because I won a lot in Barcelona and Bayern Munich but, if the expectation were less, maybe I wouldn't win anyhow. I never said I was going to win a title or a double or a treble." He may not have said it, but when you spend the fortunes that City have spent, you have to win, it's plain and simple, there can be no excuses. How long Guardiola gets to justify the investment and the faith shown in him remains to be seen. For today, he must deal with Klopp's Liverpool, a team that knows how to play against the big boys. And play Liverpool do.

City versus Liverpool, Sunday March 19th throws up a classic and for me, the stand-out game of the season. With neither team blessed in defence, both do what they do best and attack, relentlessly. It's back and forth in a ding-dong battle for the entire 90 minutes and more. Liverpool lead through a Milner penalty only to be pegged back by a late Aguero equaliser. Both sides go close to grabbing a winner in injury time and when the whistle finally blows, it brings an end to the most entertaining 1-1 draw you are ever likely to see. The Reds will feel unlucky not to have collected all three points, but any result at the Etihad, at such a pivotal stage of the season, cannot be lamented for too long.

Chelsea continue to dominate the division and their lead over Spurs looks unassailable. Spurs seem sure of a lofty second place position but must rue their luck in coming up against opponents in such red-hot form. Any other season they would be serious title contenders, if not Champions. Next best are City and Liverpool, but their hard-fought draw opens the door for Manchester United and Arsenal to apply pressure in the race for the top four. If United win their games in hand they jump ahead of the Reds. Having mostly occupied a place in the top four since September, that would be a bitter pill for Klopp and his troops to swallow. There will be no room for slip-ups as the run-in approaches. Next comes a home derby versus the Toffees.

Off the pitch, life too moves on. Saturday April 1st sees an emotional outpouring of grief, respect and thanks from all corners of Anfield, as Kopites mourn the passing of one of their own, club legend Ronnie 'Bugsy' Moran. Moran was recruited as an amateur by Manager George Kay and after a Liverpool playing career consisting of 379 appearances, including 47 as Captain, Shankly promoted him to the coaching staff. Over a period of 49 years Moran fulfilled nearly every role at Liverpool including player, coach, physio and assistant manager. The 'sergeant major' as he was known kept the club and its players in check, never allowing anyone to get above their station. As the Reds dominated at home and abroad, Moran instilled a philosophy that guaranteed any success would not be rested upon. "'It's all about what you are going to do next, son', was the sergeant major's constant challenge," recalled Graeme Souness. The matchday programme cover shows a picture of Moran in his Liverpool playing shirt with the caption 'Mr Liverpool'. It is a fitting testimonial. The Kop pays its own tribute with a mosaic that covers the entire stand, spelling out his nickname in red on a white backdrop – 'Bugsy'. Another Boot Room icon had departed but the myth and the legend live on.

In his programme notes, Klopp talks about 'doing his memory proud' and after 90 minutes of battle in the 228th Merseyside derby, that is exactly what he and his team do. A resounding 3-1 win barely does justice to a superb performance, with Mane, Coutinho and Origi bagging the goals. A young Everton side hardly showed up and despite a spate of injuries and a very youthful bench, Klopp can be delighted with the result. The German has now accumulated a maximum haul of nine points from this local encounter since his arrival in October 2015.

After a jittery start to the New Year, Klopp and his troops are back on track and a place in the top four seems achievable. However, the Everton triumph comes with a heavy price, as Mane, Liverpool's most effective player so far this season, is ruled out for the remaining games. With Henderson and Lallana also injured, the ranks are starting to look thin again, at just the wrong time. Eight games remain against teams all below the top seven places. It is time for those Liverpool troops still standing to prove that they can bring their 'A' game to these less glamorous 'B' ties. Crucially, it is also time for Liverpool to prove that they can achieve something and not fall short, even if that task is simply to finish in the top four.

Manchester United legend Roy Keane reveals that he "cringes" when he hears Liverpool or Man United celebrating a top-four finish. "Do you think Real Madrid and Barcelona would be celebrating getting fourth? Come on, get a grip," he implores, emphatically answering his own question. I see his point and on the whole, agree. With the money that United have spent, his argument is bang on. With Klopp and Liverpool, he is a little off the mark. For the Reds, the top four this season is only a pathway to future ambitions. I can still vividly remember watching Barcelona celebrating wildly when a last game, last gasp overhead kick from Rivaldo secured fourth place and Champions League qualification in 2001. It may seem hard to believe, in this era of a Messi-led Barcelona, but the Catalonians haven't always been great. By the time Barcelona won their first ever European Cup in 1992, Liverpool had already lifted the trophy four times. Empires rise and fall. The hope for Liverpool must be that a fourth place finish this year provides the platform for a new era of Reds glory. If achieved, thereafter, silverware will have to be the measure. Only then will I concur with the fiery and straight-talking Mr Keane.

THE HOME STRETCH

"When you see a finish line, you should sprint" — Jürgen Klopp

Liverpool's last eight games would whet the appetites of Chelsea, Spurs, City, Arsenal or United. These are the games that Liverpool's peers seem to win with the minimum of fuss. However, few Liverpool fans see the Reds run-in as easy. Experience tells us that for Liverpool, these fixtures are perilous and littered with danger. First up is a Wednesday night match versus Bournemouth under the floodlights at Anfield. After consecutive home wins against Arsenal, Burnley and Everton, maximum points seem certain against a Bournemouth side that have secured Premier League safety again and who sit in eleventh place. The matchday programme includes two interesting snippets that speak of undeniable progress under Klopp. He ties Paisley and Fagan as the third fastest Liverpool manager to reach one hundred League points, having taken fifty-seven matches to reach the milestone. Kenny Dalglish got there quickest after only forty-eight matches with David Ashworth taking fifty-six. Liverpool have also amassed thirty-three League points at Anfield this campaign, one more than in the whole of the previous season, with four home games still to play.

Leading 2-1 after 86 minutes, following goals from Coutinho and Origi, Liverpool suddenly step on a mine. With Bournemouth hardly posing any threat at all, Liverpool's defence press the panic button and gift a late goal to Joshua King. He accepts gleefully and the night ends horribly. All the doubts start to surface again. Can this team complete any job? Does the sight of a finishing line fill them with dread, leaving them frozen to the spot? Once more the upper hand has been ceded and Liverpool offer their foes a way back in. Instead of sprinting, Klopp's troops are stumbling and limping towards the finishing line.

The quantum of injuries suffered provides a mitigating factor, but one must ask why the squad is so bare in the first place? Week in week out, the bench is filled with teenagers. Injury has robbed the Reds of both Mane's and Coutinho's services for long chunks of the season, arguably the Reds best two players. Henderson too, the midfield driving force, has not played since February, and will not play again till next season. Add Lallana and the 'always-missing-due-to-injury' Sturridge to that list and it's easy to see the reason for the inconsistency. Yet, all of these players suffered spells on the line in 2015/16. It should have been expected that some would again. When the best players are available, the Reds are very hard to beat. When the back-ups are introduced, Liverpool stutter.

Saturday, April 8th, away to Stoke, Liverpool are forced to field teenagers Alexander-Arnold and Woodburn. Coutinho and Firmino are both sick and can only be included on the bench. Few would choose an away trip to The Potters as a suitable time, or place, to blood youth, but only three days after the home draw with Bournmouth, needs must. The Reds are awful and at half-time they trail 1-0. Injured, sick, no matter, it is all hands to the pumps. Coutinho and Firmino are brought on for the teenagers and the introduction of real quality sparks the Reds into life. Two cracking goals from the poorly duo, one each on 70 and 72 minutes, swings the game in Liverpool's favour. With the help of some miraculous goalkeeping from Mignolet, Liverpool hang on for an invaluable three points and at last they have proven the ability to dig in and win ugly. It is a fortunate win, but a win nonetheless.

April 16th and again Liverpool win away from home to another team that they normally find hard to beat – West Bromwich Albion. It's a scrappy, dour affair but no one is complaining as the Reds collect another three points, through a header from Firmino. Liverpool are starting to dispel the belief that they can't compete against the smaller teams.

Next to wage battle is Crystal Palace at Anfield. Bogey team or not, this is Anfield and on the whole, we've been very good here. Today, April 23rd, 2017, I also have a secret lucky charm with me. My eleven-year-old daughter attends her very first game. Till now, she has been quite apathetic towards football but, when out of the blue she declared that the time had come, I couldn't say no.

As the teams warm up on the pitch in the bright spring sunshine, the first player named in a Liverpool matchday squad to be born in the new millennium, seventeen-year-old Rhian Brewster, proudly takes his place on the bench. His presence there brings the teenager quotient to three. I tell my daughter that Brewster is only six years her senior and at this news all she can do is stare back in disbelief. I'm all for the kids, however, this late in the season, we need experienced heads too. I hope we're not chasing a result late on and need to look to the rookies for rescue. Liverpool dominate possession but create few clear-cut chances with Palace defending in numbers. Midway through the first half the breakthrough arrives. Liverpool take the lead through an expertly taken curling free kick from who else but Philippe Coutinho. The Reds press for a second but only half chances come and go. Then, out of the blue, Liverpool are caught napping and are pegged back just before the break by a goal from returning ex-Red Christian Benteke. It was bound to happen.

The Reds huff and puff in the second half but can't blow the Palace blockade down. Instead, it is Palace who nick a second from a rare attack. A poor cross from a corner-kick somehow manages to evade a plethora of Reds defenders and all Benteke has to do is bend down to head home his second. Teenager Alexander-Arnold enters the fray and injects some zealous endeavour, but it's a goal we need and a goal scorer. Many Liverpool fans leave early, it seems full trust has yet to be earned. Anfield is starting to stifle the Reds once more. Away teams bring as many buses as they can, park them and then break upfield in Ferraris. It's a tried and tested plan that works and with the creative door-opening talents of Lallana and Sturridge missing, Liverpool are unable to alter the inevitable outcome. Palace leave Anfield with full points once again. On a positive note, Liverpool have found one new fan. My daughter proclaims that she loved her day out – the colour, the singing, the flags and that she wants to go again. Just as she is finding her inner footballing spirit I feel my own enthusiasm waning. I welcome her aboard, all the while wondering what future suffering have I bestowed upon her.

Liverpool's destiny is now out of their own control. If United or Arsenal win out, then the Reds will most likely miss the top four. A tough away trip at Watford comes next. I'm not really up for this game, but I've made the long trek regardless. As I approach the ground on a Monday May Day evening, it is hard not to think of the Christmas 2015 3-0 drubbing. Any repeat of that showing will find the Reds in big trouble. Thankfully, this time around, Liverpool are much better and Watford rarely threaten. The Reds dominate possession but don't create much. Chances are few and far between. Then a moment of sheer class arrives. One that will have me someday saying "I was there when he did that". Just before half-time, from a lofted Lucas pass, Emre Can leaps salmon like on the edge of the Watford penalty area and upside down, he connects sweetly with the floated ball propelling an unstoppable eighteen-yard overhead kick into the top right-hand corner of Watford's goal-net. It might be the best goal that Vicarage Road has ever witnessed and come full-time it's good enough to seal all three points and keep Liverpool's push for Europe alive with three games to go. The season's clock continues to tick down.

A week later, Liverpool once again falter at Anfield and draw 0-0 with Southampton. Thankfully, Man United are stuttering too, following defeats at Arsenal and Spurs and now, only City, Liverpool and Arsenal vie for the last two Euro spots. Arsenal as they do, start to find some late season form and seem determined to push the matter all the way to the wire. To be sure of fourth place, Liverpool will need to win both of their remaining games, away to West Ham and at home against already relegated Middlesbrough on the final day.

A first ever trip to West Ham's fantastic new Olympian arena, the 'London Stadium' sees Lallana and Sturridge make a welcome return to the fray. Although resolute in the run-in, Liverpool have not been at their free-flowing best. Klopp, like any top manager devises a change of plan and tweaks the system. With Lallana fit again, Klopp drops Coutinho deeper in the park, into the heart of midfield, where he can see more of the ball and better conduct the play. Brendan Rodgers believed that one day Coutinho would become the "beating heart of Liverpool" and now it seems that this time has come. Klopp explains the tactical change, noting "He is not a winger, he is always a playmaker. He needs to be in the decisive area." On 35 minutes, I am reminded why we the fans are sat in the stands and Klopp is the one managing from the line. Coutinho demands the ball in the middle of his own half. He pushes it out of his feet and sends a fifty-yard ball through the heart of the West Ham defence. It's the kind of ball that a predator like Daniel Sturridge lives for but rarely gets, as all too often his snooping on the shoulder of the last defender goes unnoticed by less gifted compatriots. Not this time. Coutinho's ball has sent him racing clear. Ice-cool he rounds goalkeeper Adrian and slots the ball home. Deadlock broken and the Reds lead 1-0. Klopp's tactical change yields immediate dividends. The score stays that way till half-time, but only after an incredible double miss from West Ham's Andre Ayew, who sends two shots onto the same Liverpool post, both from one yard distance. Liverpool gleefully accept their lucky breaks and run riot in the second half. One man does all the damage, virtually single-handedly – Coutinho. When the Reds need him most, he rises to the occasion. El Magico bags two goals for himself and Origi finishes off a comprehensive 4-0 rout. All the while, Klopp looks on, a Cheshire cat smile fixed firmly upon his face.

Now, only one round of fixtures remains and most of the important issues have been resolved. A win for Man City in their final game at Watford will see them secure third spot. A home win for Liverpool against Middlesbrough sees them grab, at worst, fourth. Anything less and an Arsenal win over Everton at the Emirates will see the Gunners and a much beleaguered Arsene Wenger, prevail.

Jürgen Klopp is sanguine about the task ahead: "Have a look at my career, my seasons were always on the last match, I would like to change it but obviously, it is part of my life. I am completely used to working until the last minute, being concentrated until the last minute. Most decisions are made in the last moment. The more you try, the bigger your desire is, the more likely you will have these kinds of finals. For me, it is kind of a normal situation. I know how people will feel when they go the stadium but we have to be smart as well as emotional. We have to be well organised but fluid also. Only if you let it be more difficult, it is more difficult. It's all about us and this team has showed me so often that they are really ready for situations like this. We have to show it again. It will be fine."

The *Liverpool Echo* runs a piece which shows that, unfortunately for Klopp, 'fine' was not the word used to describe the outcomes of many of his previous last day encounters with Mainz, Dortmund and of course most recently with the Reds. Heartbreak seemed a better description. The always-upbeat German has grown accustomed to late sucker punches, yet, he always comes back for more, ever confident he can mould success from failure. In the past, he did. Can he do it again? Can he be the pathfinder to guide Liverpool forward from the barren crossroads to that glory paved road once more?

JUDGEMENT DAY

"The best thing that ever happened to me was losing last year in the Finals. I had to change." — LeBron James

Sunday May 21st 2017, 3pm. The final day of the season. Sunshine bathes the green turf as flags and scarves are held aloft for the singing of our glorious anthem. Liverpool FC have arrived at that familiar crossroads, one from which they have U-turned many times. Now, yet another Reds manager will attempt to lead his team forward on the right path, a path that might finally bring them back home. Today, Klopp and his Reds need to push through and make progress. A top four finish is in their own hands. Not to win at home against relegated Middlesbrough, to fall at this final hurdle, as the team did in Basel a year previously, would be unbearable. So much goodwill follows Klopp and his team, yet what fans want to see this time, is evidence of progress. This season has seen a marked improvement in League form but now, for the first time in a long time, the team need to achieve and deliver a stated objective. Klopp concurs asserting in his programme notes that the Reds need to "finish the job". Not to do so, will be seen as one thing, and one thing only, failure.

That the season would come down to effectively another cup final offers the Reds some semblance of redemption for previous disappointments. Klopp isn't afraid to outline its significance stressing "it's everything, it's the end of the season, it's in the middle of development, it's the start of the new season".

Before kick-off Steven Gerrard takes to the Anfield pitch once more, this time to present an award to Liverpool's 'Player of The Year' Sadio Mane for having been selected in the Premier League 'Team of The Season', despite missing so many games. My son agrees with the decision. My pick would've been Lallana followed by Coutinho and then Mane but that's the beauty of football, everybody has an opinion. Milner, Firmino and the later season form of Mignolet also deserve special mention. Today's team sees Coutinho start once more in his new deeper lying conductor's role. Ahead of him in attack are Firmino, Lallana and Sturridge with Origi dropping to the bench. That foursome should be good enough to crack what will be a stubborn Middlesbrough defence.

The Reds take to the pitch for the first time, in their 125th anniversary retro kit featuring a new commemorative crest, with an embroidered Liver bird flanked by '1892' and '2017'. This version sees a return to a richer, darker red, framed by a V-neck white collar. Drawing inspiration from the past, hopefully the kit may inspire too, a return to the days of lifting trophies. Liverpool start brightly and an early chance falls to Clyne at the Kop end, but he snatches at the loose ball and his attempt flashes past the right post. Word filters through that both Man City and Arsenal have taken quick leads in their respective matches and now the task is stark and clear, only a win will do for the Reds. Yet, Liverpool fail to make the hoped for speedy breakthrough and soon the match settles into a worrying pattern, one that has become all too familiar. Middlesbrough park a ten-man bus behind the ball, just as Palace and Southampton did to great effect before them, and manage to stifle any Red advances into their danger zone. Clear attempts on goal are rare specimens. From a long ball counter-attack, Bamford runs free and clear into the Liverpool box. Lovren chases him and seems to bring him down. It looks for all the world a penalty but thankfully the referee waves play on. We breathe a collective sigh of relief. To come back from 1-0 down against a ten-man defence would be a tall order. At the Kop end, a Can effort from outside the box goes close. Soon after, Sturridge conjures a half chance with some clever footwork but his right-footed effort is wide of the post.

Half-time approaches as the game runs into injury time. News arrives that Man City lead 4-0 at Watford and Arsenal lead Everton 2-0. As things stand, the Reds sit in fifth place and another year without Champions League football looms. It is now or never. On 46 minutes Wijnaldum collects a ball midway inside the Middlesbrough half and feeds it to Clyne. Clyne plays it forward to Firmino who immediately flicks the ball into the path of the on-rushing Wijnaldum. Beautiful triangles. The Dutchman takes the ball in his stride and advances unchecked into the Middlesbrough penalty box. The angle is narrow and goalkeeper Guzan has his near post well covered. Yet somehow, with a thunderbolt drive Wijnaldum manages to power an unstoppable rocket past the flailing keeper and into the back of the net. The breakthrough arrives with virtually the last kick of the first half and Anfield erupts in a mix of delirium and relief. That's the goal we've been praying for.

With the shackles off, Liverpool play with more freedom in the second half and the floodgates open. Come full-time, the Reds have triumphed three-nil after further goals from Coutinho and Lallana. It could have been six or seven but it doesn't matter. Mission accomplished. City beat Watford 5-0 to finish the season in third place and Arsenal beat Everton 3-1 to secure fifth. Liverpool finish fourth and in truth, it is the least they deserve from a very positive campaign. A warm blanket of satisfaction descends over Anfield as the players and their families embark upon their lap of mutual appreciation. This team deserve every clap for hanging tough in the final stretch. Many, including plenty of Liverpool fans, expected them to falter. They didn't. In the final twelve games, twenty-seven points were collected from the thirty-six on offer. That is title-challenging form and it should earn a large reserve of trust in the hearts of Reds fans. The team are generously applauded, as too is crowd favourite and model professional Lucas. Kenny Dalglish presents the Brazilian and honorary Scouser with an award for ten years of steadfast service. For the modern-day professional, that's a lifetime. Elsewhere on the pitch, Klopp can be seen in a huddle, talking to our American owners, and we, the fans, must hope and pray that a large summer transfer kitty is being handed over to a manager who now needs to be backed to win.

Strolling back to town in the late afternoon sunshine I reflect upon the season just finished, and my mind wanders too, to what might lie ahead. Klopp summed it up perfectly saying that qualification would prove the "icing on the cake" of what had already been a positive campaign. Not to have won would have been a major setback. The German has booked our place at the top table of European footballing elite for only the second time in eight years. By any standard that is progress. All the statistics show improvement. Seventy-six points collected versus a paltry sixty the previous season, that proving to be the fifth highest points total for the Reds in a quarter of a century. Seventy-eight goals scored versus sixty-three. Forty-two conceded versus fifty. Only six games lost. Whilst it is good, it is still nowhere near good enough. Chelsea proved Leicester's title win was a freak, with the Pensioners' winning total coming in at a whopping ninety-three points, a full seventeen ahead of Liverpool. Klopp claims that if injuries had been as kind to the Reds as they were to Chelsea, that the gap would have been closer. He believes that the divide between the two sides "is not that big". Regretfully, I can't agree with him. Chelsea have a depth of talent that Liverpool can only dream of. Firstly, Liverpool must catch Spurs. No team has collected more points than the Hotspurs over the last two seasons combined, yet the title still eludes them. Fifty-six years and waiting.

Many Liverpool fans believe that we are back. Of course, the majority know we are not, but you have to start somewhere and this is as good a place as any. We can't say for sure that we have left the crossroads behind and that we are now firmly on the right road. It is too early to judge. Stand-in captain Milner hits the nail on the head when he declares that now the aim is "to stick a few trophies in the cabinet". Yet, when Klopp commented previously, that achieving a top four finish this season would be akin to "winning a trophy", he was wrong. It isn't and never will be, not for me anyhow, and not for legions of Liverpool fans. "Liverpool FC exists to win trophies", that's the old Shankly adage. I still believe it's true. When silverware is collected, the euphoria lingers. Memories are formed and can be recollected months and years later. Today, I've already moved on, fourth is forgotten, it's all about the next transfer window and building a team that can compete both at home and abroad. I understand what Klopp means, fourth is an accomplishment, but it is not enough, he knows that. Rafa Benitez's teams qualified for the Champions League four years in a row. He lifted that trophy and lost another final to boot. That is the level to which we aspire. Yet even Rafa's time was not a complete success with no League crown to be paraded. From here forward Klopp and FSG will be judged to these standards. We must challenge repeatedly for the title, and we must be competitive in Europe.

For me, the season gone, whilst constituting a solid step in the right direction, still reeks of a missed opportunity. With no European football to distract and having led the table in December, the Reds had a shot at glory, yet spurned the opportunity to strengthen a weak squad in January and subsequently lost their way. Many of us remember the impact of previous January signings such as Souness, Sturridge and Suarez and even one Ronny Rosenthal who arrived in March 1990 and sparked a late season run to the title in Liverpool's last League winning season, scoring seven goals in the final eight matches. Could new blood have turned fourth to first? We will never know. The clock ticks on. Twenty-seven years and counting.

THE END

"This is not the end. It is not even the beginning of the end. But it is, perhaps, the end of the beginning." — Winston Churchill

And so, another season had come to pass. It flashed by so quickly. When I was younger, days and months seemed to last forever. Not anymore. Maybe it was just that Liverpool were so entertaining, so often. When you are having fun, time flies. It hadn't all been rosy however, opportunities had again been missed. Defeat came in a semi-final and a golden chance to challenge for the title was squandered. Still, large steps in Klopp's development project had been taken. Fourth place and European qualification were secured. And incredibly, at long last, Liverpool won something. Well, to be more precise, one of their players did. Emre Can was awarded both the Premier League and *Match of the Day*, 'Goal of the Year' trophies for 2016/17, his wonder strike against Watford having topped the polls.

With Liverpool failing to maintain a title challenge in the New Year, Spurs confirmed what Reds fans had been denying till now. It was Pochettino's men who sat higher in the pecking order, as once more they snapped at the heels of the League leaders all the way to the wire. Having narrowly lost out in 2016, again they would come up short, this time to a resurgent Chelsea, even after accumulating five more points than League winners Leicester did, the year before. For consolation, at least this season there would be no St Totteringham's Day.

At United, Mourinho succeeded in turning the season around after a faltering start. Like every Mourinho team, United proved a tough side to beat, conceding only 29 goals. Winners win, and if nothing else, the Portuguese tactician has proven that he is a winner. In February, Mourinho would secure his first trophy with United after only nine months in charge, lifting the League Cup at Wembley. A final day home win against Palace saw United claim a sixth-place League position. Next season we can expect the Red Devils to mount a more concerted challenge for the crown.

One day later, on May 22nd, the city of Manchester could only look on in shock and horror as terrorism once again left its ugly stain. An Islamic terrorist suicide bomber detonated an explosion in the foyer of a packed pop concert at the Manchester Arena where parents had gathered to bring their kids home. Some never made it. Twenty-two lives would be lost with the youngest victim only eight years old. Two nights later Manchester United beat Ajax in Stockholm to lift the Europa League trophy, succeeding where Liverpool had failed in Basel. The victory secured United a Champions League berth. Mourinho and his sombre, respectful team dedicated their win to the bomb victims, and to all the people of Manchester. Life went on, even as hearts filled with sadness and despair. The win brought United a 42nd major trophy (20 Leagues, 12 FA Cups, 5 League Cups, 3 European Cups, 1 European Cup Winners Cup and 1 Europa League) and saw them become England's most decorated club, surpassing Liverpool's tally of forty-one (18 Leagues, 7 FA Cups, 8 League Cups, 5 European Cups and 3 UEFA Cups/Europa Leagues). This sorry fact would at any other time have left me feeling queasy, but that week and in those circumstances, I could only wish United, their fans and most importantly the people of Manchester the very best. We all shared their pain and stood beside them in their grief. One hopes that some found the tiniest grain of solace amid the heartbreak.

Wenger would continue to struggle at Arsenal and come the season end his position looked precarious. The famous old clock at the Emirates seemed to tick faster and faster, as the career of one of the game's best managers wound down. Arsenal fans waited impatiently to see whether the Frenchman would stay or go. Saturday, May 27th brought FA Cup Final day and Arsenal beat Chelsea 2-1 at Wembley, putting an end to the Blue's Double ambitions, with the much maligned Arsene Wenger becoming the first manager ever to lift seven FA Cup trophies. The victory proved timely as, after all the speculation, Wenger kept his job and agreed a new two-year contract, this to take his tenure to twenty-three years.

With the announcement that Wenger would be staying, news of board turmoil at the Emirates also surfaced. Alisher Burkhanovich Usmanov, a 30 per cent owner of the club and a Russian Billionaire even richer than Chelsea's Roman Abramovich, had his £1.5 billion takeover bid rejected by majority owner, American Stan Kroenke. Usmanov stated that he will be waiting in the wings if Kroenke fails to offer the "full support" required to protect Wenger's Arsenal legacy. A statement read "I am pleased Arsene Wenger will continue to manage Arsenal for the next two years – he is one of the best coaches in Europe. What is now of paramount importance is that he receives the full support of the board and the majority shareholder. He has a great opportunity to deliver the success that the fans deserve and the legacy his long contribution merits. However, without the right support, there remains a real risk his legacy will be tarnished. If the support is not forthcoming we stand ready to step in and do everything we can to deliver success on and off the field." Kroenke, who was the target of abuse from supporters on the final day of the Premier League season, retorted "Our ambition is to win the Premier League and other major trophies in Europe". With two mega-billionaires squabbling to outspend each other in the pursuit of Gunners glory, it seemed that Liverpool had yet another behemoth to deal with. The Arsenal of the next twenty years may come to resemble today's bloated giants of City and Chelsea.

At Man City, Guardiola's first season in England could only be described as a disappointment. An early European exit combined with a third-place League finish and an absence of silverware only added fuel to the theory that maybe it had been his superstar players who excelled in the past, more so than the emotional Catalan himself. Even before the full season had ended, Man City put down a marker for the year ahead, signing Monaco midfielder Bernardo Silva for £43m, this taking manager Guardiola's spend to £209 million since joining the club a mere 12 months previously. The press pack speculated that a further £300 million was still available to splash. As if to prove the point, within days City agreed a deal to sign Benfica goalkeeper Ederson Moraes for £35m. In Spain, Madrid agreed a £38 million deal for a sixteen-year-old Brazilian named Vinicius Junior, a kid who had played only one senior professional game. Again, I wondered how large 'the gap' between the haves and the have nots in football must become before we all start to switch off.

In 2016/17 the top four teams in the Premier League collected an average of 83.25 points. Southampton, in eighth place, collected a mere 46 points. The ever-widening gulf in class between the top and the rest can't be good for the game. When we look back in years to come, Leicester's miracle might sadly be seen as a final salvo, the dying of the light. Today, we face into an era wherein only a handful of teams will realistically have the resources to win. To join that elite group, one will need to find a willing multi-billionaire investor. Is that what the game of football aspires to be? Has the die been irreversibly cast, the murky Rubicon crossed?

Leicester showed that anything was possible, but also demonstrated that not everything was repeatable. They, too, confirmed that the game's heart and soul may have been replaced by an iron piggy bank that counted only Premiership survival as being of any worth. Yet romantic stories still existed. Bournemouth continued to live the dream, two consecutive years of avoiding the drop achieved. Burnley, too, could look forward to another year in the big time. Southampton battled to a Wembley final, to Liverpool's chagrin, but unluckily lost to Man United.

In the North East, the grim reaper made his annual visit and this season it would be Sunderland and Middlesbrough who were called. Hull City completed the relegated trio. Former Liverpool legend Rafa Benitez led Newcastle back up from the Championship at the first time of asking, once more franking his CV with the stamp of proven quality and adding a Championship crown for good measure. Brighton and Huddersfield would also be promoted.

After all the hype and all the drama, Antonio Conte had comfortably won the battle of the big managers and Chelsea were the titleholders. Deservedly so. From the turn of the New Year, the Pensioners' form had been unstoppable. Chelsea were relentless and earned their right to be called Champions, but they did lose five matches, just one less than the Reds. It still feels that Liverpool missed an opportunity, another one. This wasn't a great League full of great teams. It hadn't been a great League for a while. In Europe, not one English team had reached the Champions League Final in the last five years. This season, only Leicester got as far as the last eight. Second place Spurs were eliminated at the group stage and Man City were dispatched, tails between their legs, by youthful Monaco. Despite all the money and all the excess, English football was falling further behind on the continent. And all the while, at home, Liverpool F.C. still waited.

Off the pitch, change was afoot, England and the rest of the United Kingdom decided to turn their backs on Europe. Well, at least fifty-two percent of the voters did in an incredibly tight and divisive referendum. The 'Liverpool Stays' campaign proclaimed "regardless of the EU Referendum result, we stand alongside the people of Europe to show we are inclusive, open and patient". When the counting was over, fifty-eight percent of the city's voters agreed and opted to remain. Was it the fact that Liverpool had already seen enormous immigrant influxes since the early centuries, many of Irish, Chinese and Afro-Caribbean descent? Maybe it was because this port city once led the globe in industry, music and of course football and had developed a broader, less parochial view of the world? Or was it because so many of its citizens had travelled all over the continent supporting the mighty Reds, long before European travel became a common occurrence? Who knows, but as ever, the city of Liverpool had its own mind and its own unique view of the world.

Across the Atlantic, despite a vulgar and vile campaign, Donald Trump was elected the forty-fifth president of the United States. It seemed that regardless of whether or not their chosen candidate was suitable, or even sane enough, to preside as president, the one thing the masses wanted above all else, was a change to the status quo. Trump promised to break the Washington cartel and angry, white, rust-belt America bought in, hook, line and sinker.

With the world at large experiencing political and social unrest, slowly it was starting to seep into the football cocoon too. In the lower Leagues, a revolution of sorts was taking place with fans rebelling against what they saw as unworthy owners. A Leyton Orient game was abandoned due to a fan sit-in, only to be played later behind closed doors. Sunday, May 28th at Wembley, saw Blackpool play Exeter in the League Two play-off final. The clash pitted a well-run supporter-owned club, Exeter, against Blackpool, a club with derided owners and disenfranchised fans. Most of the unhappy Blackpool fans boycotted the game in protest at the unacceptable manner in which they believed their club was being run. Only six thousand from an expected thirty thousand would attend the Tangerines' biggest match of the season. Regardless, Blackpool triumphed and claimed promotion, but the bigger battle off the pitch was far from over. When the victorious team arrived back home, there was no open-top bus parade, and few fans came out to greet them. Blackpool had become a zombie club, devoid of its very heart and soul, detached from its own town and people.

Up north, old friends were in rude health. Celtic defeated Aberdeen 2-1 in the Cup Final, following a last-minute winner from Tom Rogic. Aberdeen's 27-year wait to lift the Cup would stretch to another season. The victors Celtic and manager Brendan Rodgers had completed the season to top all seasons, becoming the first Scottish team ever to go unbeaten in all competitions, 47 games in total, and in doing so, becoming only the fourth Celtic side to complete the treble. In the League, they amassed a record 106 points from a possible 114, winning a record 34 games and drawing only 4 of their 38 fixtures. Rodgers proudly took his place alongside Jock Stein in the gloried pantheon of the club he supported as a boy. Liverpool fans looked on fondly and applauded their former leader and their Celtic brethren.

Further afield, in Holland a former giant was awakening and achieving success without bags of gold. A one club structure from Academy to first team, excellent coaching standards and youthful endeavour, would propel Ajax all the way to the Europa League Final. In the League, Feyenoord were calling time on their long hiatus and were departing the waiting room, with those left behind praying that it might be their number called next. Feyenoord would beat Heracles 3-1 at home on the final day of the season, inspired by a hat-trick from former Liverpool favourite, the indefatigable thirty-six-year-old Dirk Kuyt, wearing the lucky number seven on his back. Later, in the centre of Rotterdam, Kuyt would lead one hundred and fifty thousand fans in a rendition of YNWA. Feyenoord had ended an eighteen year wait to lift the Eredivisie title. Once more hope had found a way.

In Germany, Klopp's successor Thomas Tuchel led his Dortmund team to German Cup success with a thrilling 2-1 win over Eintracht Frankfurt. Later, he would announce his departure from the Black and

Yellows after two years at the helm, with rumours circulating that he had fallen out with the top-brass. Despite being hailed by many as an upgrade on Klopp, Tuchel couldn't replicate Kloppo's mastery in the Bundesliga, with Dortmund struggling to finish only third with a squad that should have achieved more. The grass isn't always greener.

And in France, Monaco were upsetting the big boys, as incredibly they beat the oil money riches of PSG to lift the Ligue 1 title, while also reaching the semi-final of the European Cup, where they would fall to Juventus. In the French Cup, lowly Angers played in their first cup final since 1957. Only a 91st minute own goal would see them undone against PSG. Unless they find one of those elusive billionaires, they may have to wait another 60 years to get as close again. All across the continent it seemed that great things could still be achieved, or nearly achieved, from meagre means. David could beat Goliath, or put up a fight anyhow. But could David repeat the feat consistently? There lay the rub.

On June 3rd, at the Champion's League Final in Cardiff the last prize of season 2016/17 was claimed. The biggest one of all. Real Madrid faced off against Juventus at the Millennium Stadium, and for the twelfth time it would be mighty Madrid who lifted the crown after a comprehensive 4-1 victory, leaving poor Juventus to suffer a seventh final loss from nine attempts.

And so, down came the final curtain on the 2016/17 football season, the actors receeding into the background. Some bathing in the glow of glory, others still waiting for their day to arrive. For us the spectators, the heart and soul of this theatre, we looked forward, awaiting the new season, dreaming of the spectacle and drama ahead when August comes around once more.

Premier League 2016/17 – Final Table

	Team	Pl	W	D	L	F	A	GD	Pts
1	Chelsea	38	30	3	5	85	33	52	93
2	Tottenham Hotspur	38	26	8	4	86	26	60	86
3	Manchester City	38	23	9	6	80	39	41	78
4	**Liverpool**	**38**	**22**	**10**	**6**	**78**	**42**	**36**	**76**
5	Arsenal	38	23	6	9	77	44	33	75
6	Manchester United	38	18	15	5	54	29	25	69
7	Everton	38	17	10	11	62	44	18	61
8	Southampton	38	12	10	16	41	48	-7	46
9	Bournemouth	38	12	10	16	55	67	-12	46
10	West Bromwich Albion	38	12	9	17	43	51	-8	45
11	West Ham United	38	12	9	17	47	64	-17	45
12	Leicester City	38	12	8	18	48	63	-15	44
13	Stoke City	38	11	11	16	41	56	-15	44
14	Crystal Palace	38	12	5	21	50	63	-13	41
15	Swansea City	38	12	5	21	45	70	-25	41
16	Burnley	38	11	7	20	39	55	-16	40
17	Watford	38	11	7	20	40	68	-28	40
18	Hull City	38	9	7	22	37	80	-43	34
19	Middlesbrough	38	5	13	20	27	53	-26	28
20	Sunderland	38	6	6	26	29	69	-40	24

PART VIII

THE GOLDEN SKY

HAPPY BIRTHDAY

"Every birthday is a gift. Every day is a gift" — Aretha Franklin

On June 3rd, 1892, the new company name 'The Liverpool Football Club and Athletic Grounds Limited' was officially recognised after the split from Everton, and effectively Liverpool FC came into being. In June 2017, the club commenced their year-long 125th anniversary celebrations. Owners FSG and new CEO Peter Moore gushed in their praise for our proud institution. However, when club Chairman Tim Werner proclaimed that "The best is yet to come", I was far from convinced. Given our illustrious past, the boast seemed slightly far-fetched. From the lips of Sinatra, one might get swept away, but alas from a football chairman, the words left me a little less spellbound.

In the same month, KPMG released their annual 'Rich List' of the wealthiest clubs in Europe. Manchester United led with a valuation of €3.1 billion, followed by Real Madrid, Barcelona and Bayern Munich. Next came Man City, Arsenal, Chelsea and then Liverpool, the Reds ranking eighth with an estimated valuation of €1.3 billion. That translates to roughly $1.5 billion, a valuation uplift of roughly $1.0 billion for FSG on their investment. At least the financial plan was working a treat for the boys from Boston. Juventus ranked next in ninth, with Spurs concluding the top ten. Liverpool and Spurs, the two teams from that ten who attempt to achieve success 'cleverly' and on the cheap, relatively speaking, are also the only two not to have lifted a trophy in the last five years.

Not long after the report's release, Liverpool's newly appointed CEO Peter Moore confirmed that the Reds planned to continue their 'box clever' strategy, arguing that, in doing so, LFC could still compete with the richest clubs. "This is not about if Chelsea spend a pound then we have to spend a pound regardless of the quality of the player we're looking at," he told reporters at Anfield in his first meeting with the media in his new role. "This is less about an arms race for spending as much money as we can, it's more about spending smartly. It's not, 'They've spent £100 million, so we will spend £100 million'. It's about we have strengthened our squad in these positions and it has cost us this. I may be naive but I'm not looking at my competitor," To me, this did sound a little naive, as everybody else was, most of all the fans. Moore continued to talk the talk – "Jurgen made a point that it was taxing on him to be the face of the club. My job is to let him focus on what's on the pitch and then let me take responsibility for what's off the pitch. We've got to continue this improvement on the pitch, improvement off the pitch. We're a world-class football club, we act like it, we're a tremendous family – both here in Merseyside, as well as anywhere in the world". As fans, we were left to dissect and mull over the fine detail, the unspoken sentences behind the words, the nuances, the naivety. Was this another propaganda issuance to dampen expectations? Was it a realistic view of footballing life? It was hard to know.

Again, John Henry's proclamation came to me, the claim he made when FSG bought Liverpool FC in October 2010. "We are committed first and foremost to winning." The real test of FSG's mettle comes now, we have waited long enough for the winning days to materialise. Discontent was growing amongst a large group of Reds fans that FSG were not doing enough to back their proclamations with actions and, even more importantly, money. Klopp saw things differently. On a number of occasions, he declared that he was very happy with his bosses and the resources that were available to him. Somehow, I feared that he would say that regardless, for he loved difficult challenges. Would he whistle-blow if FSG weren't up to scratch? If they lacked his or our ambition? Even the ever-upbeat Klopp must have been shaking his head when his first foray into the summer transfer market, an attempt to sign defender Virgil van Dijk from Southampton had to be aborted, with the club being forced to issue an unprecedented and grovelling apology to the Saints, for having 'tapped-up' the player illegally. The *Liverpool Echo* would describe the affair as a '*complete and utter shambles*'. Once more, with no surprise to Reds fans, FSG's Transfer Committee were making an unholy mess of conducting what, for 118 years before they arrived, seemed relatively easy business. Hopefully it would be the first and last of the summer debacles.

Klopp kept reminding us that this was a "long project", that he didn't want a pot of gold to spend, even if many thought he might need it. There would be "ups and downs" while we waited for the masterplan to take shape. This would be a "rollercoaster ride". Longevity had brought success for Shankly, Paisley and down the motorway, for Ferguson too. If we were going to dig in for the long run once more, then to be honest, there were few more likeable people than our manager, to do it with. It seemed hard to believe that Jürgen Klopp had now presided over the Reds for twenty months. If we stood back and took stock, those twenty months had proved an unequivocal success. The team sat in eighth place when he arrived. Today, a tinge of disappointment dulls our delight at finishing fourth. The squad has improved with some excellent new additions and the players that Klopp inherited have grown in confidence and ability. He has also balanced the books on transfers, leaving the club as financially well positioned as ever. Great days and nights have arrived which will hopefully in the future be remembered as the first steps towards ultimate success. The Wembley Final. Vanquishing United. The Dortmund miracle. Taking over Basel. Christening the new Anfield versus the Champions. Beating Middlesbrough to qualify for the Champions League.

After less than two years most football observers could point to and recognise Liverpool FC's Kloppian style and philosophy. The German had glued back together the holy trinity of players, manager and fans. The team and club had found their identity once more. An impressive list of positives, however, Klopp knew better than anyone, that the biggest challenges still lay ahead. Fourth wasn't going to cut it in the long run. It hadn't for his predecessors, why would it for him? The only guarantee of a lengthy managerial tenure was silverware of the League crown or European Cup variety.

For much of the last twenty-five years of our 125-year history the club has drifted directionless. We can't afford to slip further away, lest we never right our course nor sail again to glory.

SHIP OF THESEUS

'Change is the law of life. And those who look only to the past or present are certain to miss the future.' —John F. Kennedy

From ancient Greek mythology, many of us know of Theseus and the Minotaur. The Minotaur, a monster with the body of a human and the head of a bull, was the son of Queen Pasiphae, born from a bestial coupling with a bull, after the Queen was cast under a lust-spell by Poseidon. This spell was the sea god's revenge for her husband, King Minos's wrongdoings. The couple's natural son, Androgeus, died in Athens while participating in the Panathenaic Games and, in his rage Minos demanded that, as punishment for his son's death, seven young boys and seven young girls would be sent annually from Athens to Crete to be sacrificed to the labyrinth-imprisoned Minotaur. King Aegeus of Athens agreed to the punishment despite his son Theseus' protests. In the third year of the penance, Theseus decided to end this barbarity once and for all. He would sail to Crete, masquerading as one of the youths, on a mission to slay the monster. Theseus promised his father that he would hoist white sails upon his return to Athens, allowing the King to know in advance that his son was still alive. The boat would return with black sails aloft if Theseus perished. Theseus's escapade proved successful and the beast was slain, but tragically on the return journey, he forgot to change the sails. King Aegeus awaited at Cape Sounion praying to see his son's white sails billowing, but instead saw only black. Presuming Theseus dead, in blind grief he leaped into the waters below and was seen no more, these same waters now bearing his name, the Aegean Sea.

Plutarch, a Greek historian, writer and philosopher, recounts this tale in his book, *Parallel Lives*, penned nearly two thousand years ago. "The ship wherein Theseus and the youth of Athens returned had thirty oars, and was preserved by the Athenians, down even to the time of Demetrius Phalereus, for they took away the old planks as they decayed, putting in new and stronger timber in their place." Plutarch noted how the ship had become a source of much intriguing debate. "The ship became a standing example among the philosophers, for the logical question of things that grow; one side holding that the ship remained the same, and the other contending that it was not the same." Plutarch and the Greek philosophers had set upon the thorny issue of identity. Every year, a piece of the ship would be replaced, until after many, many years, every single plank and oar had been substituted. The vessel looked the same, identical even, but Theseus and the youth of Athens had never set foot on the ship that stood in harbour a thousand years later. So, was it still his ship? Was it still the 'Ship of Theseus'?

Today, under the stewardship of American owners, with a German hipster manager and with players from all over the world, we too must ask the thorny philosophical questions. Is this still Liverpool FC? What even is Liverpool FC? In the old days, if one thing stood for what the club was, it was the legendary Boot Room, instigated by Shankly and manned by his loyal staff, the heirs to his throne. Dalglish hailed the Boot Room as, 'fundamental to the success of Liverpool Football Club, past, present and future' continuing, "It was just a cramped area, ten foot by ten foot off a corridor near the dressing rooms. The Boot Room made an unlikely nerve centre for Liverpool operations. Match boots hung from pegs and a carpenter's bench provided space for working on studs. A calendar reminded everyone what year it was. It was the heart and soul of Liverpool's footballing operation, a centre for research and strategy. Shanks set it up and it proved to be a breeding ground for future managers – Bob, Joe and Roy Evans."

There in that little boot room, that beating heart of Liverpool FC, Shankly's men plotted, planned, studied and schemed their way to thirty major trophies. Paisley, with his eye for a player or a tactic. Fagan, a fountain of honesty and pragmatism. Moran, ready to tear strips off any player who got too big for his boots or whose hunger to win waned. Evans, painstakingly taking notes, filling journals with tactics, training programmes, technical details. Bennett, the toughest trainer in the business. Each listening to the other, learning from the other, the collective greater than the individuals, just as Shankly had taught them. In his diaries, Fagan spoke of the room's simplicity: "In time it would become furnished with luxuries like a rickety old table and a couple of plastic chairs, a tatty piece of carpet on the floor and a calendar on a wall that would later be adorned with photographs, ripped from newspapers, of topless models… there was little evidence to suggest this room was even part of a football club." A simple room for men to talk football. Great football men.

Their influence would span nearly half a century from the 1950s until the winter of 1998 when the last of these greats, Roy Evans, would honourably step down after managing the Reds for four seasons. Evans didn't get his team over the line and lift the title but he did leave Liverpool as the Premier League's most successful English manager with the Reds never falling below fourth under his watch. After the sad passing of Ronnie Moran few men living understood better the heartbeat of Liverpool FC than Evans. When I met him, we talked about many things including our current American owners. Evans is mostly positive about their tenure but urges caution too: "I don't think they are very knowledgeable about football but they are not stupid enough to start trying to make decisions that they can't make. I think that is an important part. If you don't know how the game goes, you have to have people who do." Evans could never have envisioned where Liverpool are today, all these years without the title. "No, not in a million years. I thought we would win it in my time. It was always about trying to win games. We scored a lot of goals, we made defensive mistakes too, but that was part and parcel of how we played, with the players that we had. One year we got very close but we didn't get over the line, but from there on you would have expected to go forward. Brendan made a good challenge, but between those times it's never really been that close. The biggest thing is winning. I'm a Liverpool lad. I stood on the Kop and understand the football expectations of all our supporters. It's like Jürgen at the minute, he's saying some great things but eventually you'll always be judged on what you achieve and what you win." Evans had the battle scars to prove that he knew what he was talking about.

On that horrible day when Stoke stomped on the liver bird and won 6–1, Stevie Gerrard played his last game in Red. Gerrard connected us to our heritage. He came through the youth-ranks when Roy Evans was still the manager and Ronnie Moran still growled at anyone and anything that moved. That linked Gerrard to Fagan, to Paisley and of course back to Shankly himself. It linked him to the Boot Room. Gerrard, like Evans, was a Scouser, he knew what the Boot Room stood for, what the Liverpool Way was. If cut, he bled Red, Liverpool Red. He knew too what the Kop was, for he was one of them. He understood Hillsborough, as much as anybody could. The disaster had taken one of his own. As long as Gerrard played in red, captaining our team, we knew that the spirit of Liverpool was safe. Carragher was another totem and he understood how important his DNA was, saying "we were the link between past and future, the last of the Boot Room boys." With these links now gone, was Liverpool at risk of losing its identity? Again, the question gnawed, 'What exactly is Liverpool FC?'

There are many still around that protect the heritage actively and whom we know bleed Red. Phil Thompson, Jimmy Case, David Fairclough, Terry Mc Dermott, Sammy Lee, John Aldridge, Steve McManaman and Robbie Fowler to name a few. All were hometown men playing for their hometown Reds and all now still love their club. This condition, or state of 'being Liverpool', is not confined to locals. It has been instilled in others too by osmosis. Bill Shankly, Bob Paisley and Kenny Dalglish all Red to the core. When I think of these men, I need to be reminded that none were born within 100 miles of the banks of the Mersey. Other blow-ins such as Hansen, Hughes, St John, Barnes, Molby, Alonso, Garcia and Benitez have all shown the stigmatic trait of bleeding Liverpool Red.

Yet it's not only players and managers who have lived and breathed the cause. In the old days owners did too. Founder, John Houlding, lived and worked in the city, acted as its Mayor. Similarly, David Moores and his family had been involved with owning and running the club for over fifty years, back to the days of Shankly. Only when they sold ownership to Gillett and Hicks in 2007, did the new era of foreign ownership begin. In this burgeoning financial age of English Football, anybody with money, or purporting to have money, could own a club, regardless of their true bona-fides. Did they love football, or was it only about financial gain? Had the game lost its soul? Had Liverpool?

So, when Steve Gerrard set sail for the Californian sunshine, many took a look around and wondered who was left standing? Who else had felt the original planks of the good ship Liverpool beneath their feet? Was there one person left at the club, on or off the pitch, who got it, who understood what this club was all about? Rodgers had always shown a sense of respect for our history and tradition and he wore dignity as a badge. Yet he's not a Red. FSG are baseball men, originally currency traders. They are private equity investors, they buy low and sell high. They are in the profit business. If they can have fun with trophy assets like Liverpool FC and the Boston Red Sox along the way, then why not? What they are not, is Red. Not real Red. They talk of winning, however, so far, the builders haven't been called in to extend the trophy room. As Plutarch pondered over the ship in the harbour, I and many fellow Reds ponder too. In the rapidly changing world of moneyed football, what now is Liverpool FC?

Have all the originals departed leaving behind only facsimiles? Was Steven Gerrard the last true king, the last blood line? If so, FSG yet again proved that they had smarts, enticing Gerrard back to Liverpool to assume the role of Under-18s manager. Maybe, one day, he would prove Klopp's successor and the bloodline would continue. Another FSG announcement followed. The Centenary Stand was to be renamed 'The Kenny Dalglish Stand'. With the possible exception of Bill Shankly, no man had done more for Liverpool FC and its fans than our most famous number seven, King Kenny. FSG proved that they understood and respected the importance of our heritage.

To their credit, albeit maybe for the wrong reasons, FSG also made the decision to maintain another undeniable and critical link to the Reds' past, the stadium itself. Anfield fulfils many roles; a home, a shrine, a gladiatorial stage, a bastion. Thankfully, with the decision to expand, instead of move, this crucial connection to our heritage remains. It will continue to need repair, further expansion and modification, but unlike Theseus' Greek ship of old, you couldn't build it anywhere else. There is only one Anfield Road.

Another special bind remains, the most important one of all. The fans. For if one really wants to find the true essence of the Ship of Liverpool, it is the supporters. Unlike the club itself, we can never be bought or sold. Our allegiance must be earned. It is we who have steered this great club from its earliest days. It is we who made the Kop what it is, the most revered stand in world football. It is we who first sang that famous song and made it our own. When philosophers pondered the human equivalent of the Ship of Theseus paradox they asked the same question. If, over time, all of our limbs and organs are replaced one by one, are we the same person as before or a new altered version? The deciding factor seems to be that one's 'soul' is what makes you who you are. In religious belief it is our soul which passes on. It does not die. For the non-religious, the 'soul' is but a name attached to that which we don't yet fully understand, the complex interaction between the brain, the nervous system and the body's organs and muscles. Either way, the brain is what holds the things that define us, our cognitive faculties of awareness, of knowing self. It stores the memories and experiences that inform and shape us and which become an integral part of our being.

In this new era where the motives of those who own our football clubs are at best unknown, or at worst known to be solely about profit extraction or ego inflation, then those of us who are part of this game for the sake of the game itself, need to be on guard. We are the Watchmen. Liverpool fans are the keepers of its memories, its folklore. It is we, the fans, who pass the stories down through time to our children and their children and their children's children. Shankly's grandson now sits in the seat where once the great man watched his former charges play. Just one of a million love stories. Every time two or more of us are gathered, the spirit of Liverpool resides. We are a family, a nation. We share this lineage, this culture. Although we did not gather on Houlding's stands 125 years ago, our forefathers did. Over and over, on and on, life renews, Liverpool FC renews. We are the beating heart, we are the soul.

Just as Klopp spoke of 'great responsibility' in acting as Liverpool FC's manager, we too must show great responsibility. For this reason, when on February 6th, 2016, 10,000 fans left Anfield early, long before a match had finished, it marked a very important moment in Liverpool's storied history. Sunderland were the visitors but they were not greeted by the usual sea of colourful flags on the Kop, instead only black flags hung, just as they had mistakenly upon Theseus's ill-fated return voyage. After seventy-seven minutes of football, a mass walk-out was staged in protest at the proposed escalation of ticket prices for the soon to be reopened

Main Stand. In protest against being called customers, not fans. In protest at absentee landlordism. Owners, FSG, were sitting on a small fortune with their Liverpool investment, its value estimated at upwards of £1.2 billion. Having spent £300 million to buy the club and an estimated £115 million to revamp the Main Stand, the Americans were looking at a very tidy profit. Many fans wanted to see some of this uplift invested back into the club to improve the chances of sporting success. Was the plan to compete or not? The new TV deal was pumping money into the club making any need for increases in match-day revenue unnecessary and irrelevant. Still our Landlords thought it wise to stick the fans with inflated ticket prices. Enough was enough. Before the exodus, Liverpool led 2–0. Come full-time, in front of a half-empty Kop, Sunderland had clawed their way back to 2–2. It was as if our team understood the anger streaming from the stands and downed tools in sympathy. Klopp could only watch on from his hospital bed following an appendix removal. All around the world, ordinary decent fans applauded the Liverpool militants. The club's soul was alive and well. This was a game-changer. FSG's card had been marked. They were being watched. Liverpool FC needed to be treated as more than just an investment or a business.

Throughout Europe, clubs remain owned within the communities in which they play. Fans are shareholders and stakeholders. They have a say. They vote in elections to appoint club officials. There is accountability. Somehow this ability for fans to be represented in a true and meaningful way needs to be reintroduced to English football, otherwise the revolution will spread and the ensuing war will either kill or cure the game. Until then, we must be vigilant. If Reds fans can't control the motivation or identity of those who own our great club, of those who manage our players, of those who wear our red shirts, well at least we can hold them to account if they are not up to the honour. This is our role. This is our obligation. In this age of ownership for profit and ego, our voices are more important than ever before.

With the arrival of our 125th Anniversary, so too begins a new era for a new generation. We remember Klopp's words beseeching us to believe. We should, to a point, yet we need not believe solely in Klopp or our American owners, nor in the generations of future managers or owners. To believe is to take something on faith, without fact or substantiation.

Liverpool is too precious for that sort of risk. Those men are not our messiahs, they do not walk on water. That said, we should support, always support. We must believe in our past, our ancestors, our heritage. We must take pride in our flags, our songs, our colour. This is Anfield. We are Liverpool. We must unite as one, set the standard and hold all who act in our name accountable. Fairly. Honourably. With dignity.

Klopp asks us to put the weight of our history to one side, not to burden his team with it and he is right. We must give each new player, manager and owner a chance, a fair crack of the whip. Yet in every other way we must carry that history with us at all times. We must cherish our heritage carefully until others have proven that they are ready to share the load with us. We must remind our current owners, our future owners and those after them, of what is expected. This is Liverpool FC, these are the high standards to which you must hold yourself.

These standards include our ambition. We cannot go meekly into that dark night of also-rans. Current and future owners need to match the ambition of the great Red men that went before them. Liverpool Football Club exists to win trophies. We've been lost in the wilderness too long. It is time to raise our voices, to be heard. Time to ask, where to from here? Where to from these barren crossroads?

THE GOLDEN SKY

'Out of the North parts, a great company and a mighty army'
– Liverpool War Cenotaph at St. George's Hall

My mind drifts back to that bright sunny day in early September. The day when our new odyssey began. We were about to set sail with a new crew, on an old vessel, now revamped, and readied for voyage. We hoped to chart old waters, familiar straits, yet we were unsure. The storm had not passed, not yet. However, the words of our forefathers inspired us to be brave, to throw off the bow lines, raise the sails and catch the wind.

***

If you turn your back to Goodison Park, home of Everton Football Club, and walk across Walton Lane, towards Priory Road, a grand clock-towered entrance greets you and beckons you into Anfield Cemetery. On an early September day like today, sunny and mild, a walk amongst the tombstones and cenotaphs is a serene and pleasurable experience, just as it was more than a century ago. In 1889, three years before Liverpool FC was founded, the *Liverpool Mercury* described just such a visit. *"A walk to Anfield Cemetery on a fine Sunday is a treat. About seventy acres of fertile land is laid out as a garden and a burial place. Here, grow the privet, the willow, the thorn, the holly, the sycamore, the rhododendron and myriads of beautiful flowers. Cenotaphs to men who died in far lands, costly tombs to tell of the virtues of quiet sleepers. On finely carved tombs sit young men and bonnie English lassies and the old, old story is told over again amid the flower decked graves of the peaceful dead."*

The *Friends of Anfield Cemetery* work to protect this beautiful old cemetery, telling us, "It is not just a cemetery but also a huge story book. There isn't a more complete physical narrative for Merseyside's links with world events than our 142 acres. Visiting the past helps us understand the present and connect with the future."

Six hundred thousand souls have found their way to these beautiful green acres, surrounded by old sandstone walls, since they opened the gates and the ground in 1863. Some of Liverpool's fighting dead from two World Wars lie here, as do many of the thousands who died in the fifteen-month-long German blitz of the city from 1940 to 1942, Liverpool suffering the largest aerial assault outside of London.

Less heroic souls also reside. James Maybrick, an international cotton trader, died of arsenic poisoning in 1889, with his estranged wife Florence being found guilty of his murder. She would later be acquitted and move to the United States. In 1993, a long-lost diary alleged to be that of Maybrick came to public attention with its contents claiming that Maybrick was the infamous 'Jack the Ripper', who had slain and mutilated five prostitutes in the Whitechapel district of London in 1888. Many learned historians view the diary to be a fake, however, it divides opinion to this day.

Another unfortunate dweller is one William Huskisson, the first person ever to be killed by a train. At the inaugural launch of the Liverpool-to-Manchester railway line in 1830, Huskisson would be run over by Stephenson's Rocket.

Here, too, lie a collection of men who found footballing fame and legend only a few hundred yards away at Anfield Road. Tom Watson arrived at Liverpool FC from Sunderland in 1896 and led the Reds to their first two title triumphs. He would also be the first Liverpool manager to reach the FA Cup final. For a long period of time the markings of where Watson, Liverpool's longest ever serving manager, lay had gone missing and it was not until 2015, the 100 year anniversary of his death, that a new gravestone would mark his resting place. 'Ned' Doig, Watson's goalkeeper from 1904 to 1908, and a pallbearer at his funeral in 1915, would eventually find his own eternal rest but a few yards away from his manager, having been struck down by the Spanish Flu epidemic of 1919.

These two are not the only men from Liverpool FC's historic past to call these acres their final home. Another would be Dubliner

W.E. Barclay, the first secretary and manager of Liverpool FC. It was Barclay who suggested to owner John Houlding to simply use the name 'Liverpool' after the split with Everton.

At Anfield Crematorium, managers Shankly and Fagan bade their last farewells. Shankly's ashes would be taken and dispersed over the Kop. My son and I pass another memorial to a former Red, one William Henry McConnell, Chairman from 1944–1947. McConnell was the man who decided to take the Reds on a pre-season tour of the US in 1946, to improve their diet and nutrition. The Reds returned fit and strong and pipped Man United to the first post war title. Unfortunately, McConnell would fall ill and pass away shortly after. I am not sure how many Reds in total rest here, whether they be managers, players or fans, but a feeling comes over me that today their spirits must be rising up to take a peek over the wall, out over Stanley Park, towards the historic old stadium, where they once gathered, where today stands a new edifice, one that rises into the evening sky, one that they could never have imagined possible.

Leaving the cemetery, we walk for a few short, reflective minutes and arrive at the new Anfield. We show our tickets and are welcomed aboard. Gazing around, we smile, our ship is ready, prepared for the voyage ahead. It's been bleak around this place since our favourite son slipped and fell at the feet of reviled foes. Truth be known, it's been bleak for longer. There have been fewer and fewer bright days in the last ten years. The scars we earned will hold us in good stead for the future. We have acquired character. Quite possibly we may need to sink again, maybe more than once, yet each time the waters will be shallower, until finally someday we arrive at that hallowed port. We must believe. We must hope.

Many here today were not even born when Liverpool last won the League. So, it is time to create new tales of wonder. Our new stadium glistens in the early evening sun. It is our first home game of the season, the first chance to welcome back our Red men since defeat in Basel. As the new Anfield hosts its inaugural match, fittingly the opponents are champions Leicester. There is a carnival atmosphere amongst the fifty-four thousand fans who have congregated. Everyone is smiling, the air fizzes with excitement. It is a happy day. A day of celebration. A whole new world of possibility awaits.

Family is not forgotten and never should be. On the sacred green pitch below, legends of yore parade and are cheered warmly. These men must be cherished. They are flag-bearers. We are too. From the cemetery wall the ghosts look on, their eyes squinting in the dazzling sunlight, eager to catch a glimpse of this bright future. From our seats in the new stand we gaze too in awe and wonder. And with love.

Our boys perform their roles impeccably, roared on by Klopp, who gesticulates for us to do likewise. We do. Liverpool win 4–1. It is a fitting result for a maiden voyage. Are these the men to walk in the shoes of the icons who have now taken their seats above them? Maybe, yet one swallow does not banish the storm clouds of twenty-seven years.

As we leave, the dipping sun's honey rays settle over the red bricks, the shiny metal and the sparkling windows of the new Main Stand. The warmth of the last hazy beams rests softly on our skin. The horizon glows in a hue of colours from yellow to red. A siren beckons us forward, the sweet silver song of the lark. Onwards towards the golden sky. We heed its call and stride together in unison. Family, brethren, descendants. Not alone.

Never alone.

EPILOGUE

The phone startled him. He let it ring out, he'd get back to them. Reclining in his chair at Melwood, his mind had been whirring, eyes closed, football dreams. Questions, answers, possible solutions. The season was over. Right here, right now, the new season began. Planning, calling, culling, adding. Things had to change. Not everything. There was a good base, yet there was a lot to improve on too. In a way, he was happy about that. It meant things could get better. Progress, always progress.

He'd been asked could he see himself here for ten years, the fans wanted it. He had smiled, knowing of course, such an outcome depended on success. The Champions Wall both here and at the stadium proudly displayed that success. All the trophies. Big trophies. Big managers had won these. He had only started, yet to one day be spoken of in the same breath as these names would require a monumental effort. He was living the dream. Loving the challenge.

At times this season, they had been great. At times, awful. He had warned the fans to expect this. Development was a rollercoaster. January had killed their hopes, for now. He understood the anguish, for he himself was a really, really bad loser. In the silence of defeat, the voices of the sceptics were loudest. Should they have signed players? Yes. Were they available? Maybe? But mistakes make you better, stronger. They had to take all the criticism. Him. The team. They had not responded well to adversity. Even if some of the comments were undeserved, there was little point in moaning, action was everything. If he lost to the big teams they would complain. If he lost to the smaller teams, they would complain. It was clear that he would have to beat them all.

It was mentality they said. Sixteen corners in the Hull game. One to Hull, fifteen for Liverpool. Hull scored from theirs. Mentality. He never believed in cheap words. They must show the response. That's what he told the players. He trusted them, keep working, it would come. It did. The team showed resolve and in the run-in they stood up and were counted. They had achieved a stated target and that was good, but now expectation would be huge. The honeymoon was well and truly over.

Still, could more have been achieved? He'd get more chances to win the League, wouldn't he? He'd always come back before. He could do it again. Just as he knew the silence of defeat, so too did he know the sound of victory, of celebration and joy. He'd only started this project. It was early days. Patience, they needed patience. The long steady path had always worked. But he would need to win, he knew that. He knew how to beat the smaller teams in Germany, he could learn to do it here. But could he keep beating the big spenders if he couldn't match their firepower? Would he have to do things differently this time? Could he? How far could the club stretch to succeed? He wasn't fully sure. Had Rodgers been right, was par it? Could they beat par? Brendan did for a while but they let him go. He was convinced that he was on the right path though. He believed he could leave this great club in a good way, better than he found it. Yet did anyone understand 'long term' in football anymore? At Liverpool it seemed they did, the fans here seemed to have, dare he say it…patience. He was only the twentieth man to have the job. This was the 125th anniversary. They'd taken to him so quickly, made him feel at home. This club was family and that's how he liked it. He'd brought all the staff and their kids to training camp in Spain with the team. One hundred and forty people. It was wonderful. There was a bond here, a unity.

Still, he needed time. He had told them he couldn't walk on water, to stop chanting his name all the time. It must be the team, always the team. They were 100% behind him, for now anyhow. Like fans of any great club, they expected, maybe some even felt entitled to, great things. Forget the history he'd instructed, it was too heavy. It seemed impossible though. Wembley and Basel had disappointed, as if confirming a new chapter in that history. The 'so near, yet so far' chapter. Soon, he would have to win.

This was a long-term project, no quick fixes. He'd always done it this way, the hard way. Would it work here though, in a League where League winners are fired the year after? He himself had never been sacked. They'd always believed in him. Mainz, Dortmund. Yet here, it would be so much harder. So many teams wanted it and had the resources to go and get it. So much ambition. So much money. So much history. To do it here, with Liverpool, would be worth ten times that of a Bayern or a Chelsea. Nobody knew or would know who was part of the teams that won their 8th, 9th, 10th Leagues in a row. Everybody still knew his Dortmund team. That had been different. This would be too. To win here would mean more.

To achieve something special, you have to arrive in a particular moment. When he arrived the club was stuck, trying to move forward but always with an eye to the past. The moment was now. His moment was now.

His first twelve, thirteen players were really good. But, he needed more at that level. He hadn't spent any real money yet but now it was time, there would be no badges awarded for transfer surpluses. There must be new recruits this summer. Good enough to appease? Good enough to win? Time would tell. Would his war chest be big enough? Someone said that Shankly had argued to his bosses that they couldn't afford not to back him. Would FSG see it that way? If they stood still, they ran the risk of going backwards. He also needed to keep his stars, particularly Coutinho. He could not be sold at any cost. FSG said he had the last word on this, he hoped so. They were good owners, interested in development, long-term success. They wouldn't throw money away though. They weren't going to stomach the 'eat shit' prices that Man United paid. Or the others. PSG had just spent £198m buying Brazilian Neymar from Barca, more than doubling the world record transfer fee. He'd heard Wenger saying, "Once a country owns a club, everything is possible." He was right. On the BBC, a poll claimed 61% believed football had 'lost the plot'. They might be right too. This wasn't financial fair play. The rules neeeded changing. He hoped this deal was an exception. For him, success would have to come the hard way, always the hard way. Ronnie Moran had died this year, a Red legend. He had met the man, heard the stories. "It's all about what you are going to do next, son," he once said. So it was. What lay next for him? For Liverpool?

His mentor Wolfgang Frank had said of him that his strengths were instilling motivation, confidence and belief. It was true, but they'd been so long without the win here, that belief seemed to be the most fragile commodity of all. He had said it, day one – Believe! Did they? Did he still? Yes, he was sure. Great things lay ahead. They would walk together, a band of brothers. Liverpool could rise. This he knew. They would make it better. They deserved that in these parts. Football meant too much. It's about more than just a game. Hard work could do it. His father had taught him that.

BIBLIOGRAPHY

Adam Menuge, *Ordinary Landscapes, Special Places; Anfield, Breckfield and the Growth of Liverpool's Suburbs,* English Heritage 2008

Alex Ferguson, *Managing My Life, My Autobography*, Coronet Books 2000

Andrea Pirlo, *I Think Therefore I Play*, BackPage Press 2013

Andrew Fagan and Mark Platt, *Joe Fagan: Reluctant Champion,* Aurum Press

Bill Shankly, *Shankly, My Story; The Autobiography*, SportMedia 2011

Bill Shankly, *Shankly; The Lost Diary*, SportMedia 2013

Bob Paisley, *Bob Paisley; An Autobiography*, Arthur Barker 1983

David Fairclough. *Supersub; The Story Of Football's Most Famous Number 12*, DeCoubertin 2015

Derek Dohren, *Ghost On The Wall; The Authorised Biography Of Roy Evans*, Mainstream 2004

Elmar Neveling, *Jurgen Klopp; The Biography*, Ebury Press 2016

Hunter Davies, *The Glory Game,* Contemporary Books 1972

Jamie Carragher, *Carra; My Autobiography*, Corgi 2009

Jim White, *A Matter Of Life And Death; A History Of Football In 100 Quotations*, Head Of Zeus 2014

John Barnes, *John Barnes; The Autobiography*, Headline 1999

John Keith, *The Essenial Shankly*, Robson Books 2001

Joseph Heller, *Catch 22*, Vintage 1994

Kenny Dalglish, *Dalglish; My Biograpy,* Hodder and Stoughton 1996

Kenny Dalglish, *Kenny Dalglish; My Liverpool Home,* Hodder and Stoughton 2010

Leo Moynihan, *The Liverpool Miscellany,* Vision Sports 2012

Luis Suarez, *Crossing the Line; My Story*, Headline 2014

Maarten Meijer, *Louis Van Gaal; The Biography*, Ebury Press 2014

Michael Lewis, *Moneyball,* WW Norton 2003
Michael Walker, *Up There; The North-East, Football, Boom and Bust,* DeCoubertin 2014
Miguel Angel Violan, *Pep Guardiola; The Philosophy That Changed The Game*, Meyer &Meyer Sport 2010
Mike Carson, *The Manager*, Bloomsbury 2013
Rafa Benitez, *Champions League Dreams*, Headline 2012
Richard Giulianotti, *Football; A Sociology Of The Global Game*, Polity Press 2004
Robbie Fowler, *Fowler; My Autobiography*, Macmillan 2005
Simon Kuper and Stefan Szymanski, *Soccernomics,* Harper Sports 2009
Simon Kuper, *The Football Men; Up Close With The Giants Of The Modern Game*, Simon & Schuster 2011
Stephen F.Kelly, *Dalglish,* Headline 1992
Steven Gerrard, *Steven Gerrard; My Story,* Penguin 2015
Terry Venables, *Terry Venables, Born To Manage; The Autobography*, Simon & Schuster 2014
Walter Tevis, *The Hustler,* Penguin 1959

Newspapers and Magazines

Four Four Two
The Liverpool Echo
The Times
The Sunday Times
The Telegraph
The Mirror
The Independent
The Guardian
The Sunday Observer
When Saturday Comes
World Soccer

Internet and TV

The BBC Sport Website, www.bbcsport.com
The Boston Globe Website, www.bostonglobe.com
The Liverpool Football Club Official Website, www.liverpoolfc.com

The LFC History Website, www.lfchistory.net
The Sky Sports Webiste, www.skysports.com
The UEFA Website, www.uefa.com
LFCTV
BT SPORT
BSKYB SPORTS TV